Making Connections
in Elementary *and* Middle School
Social Studies

*Dedication: This book is dedicated to the memory
of my father, Glen D. Johnson. He was a good man.*

Making Connections
in Elementary *and* Middle School
Social Studies

Andrew P. Johnson
University of Minneapolis, Mankato

SAGE Publications
Thousand Oaks ■ London ■ New Delhi

For information:

Sage Publications, Inc.
2455 Teller Road
Thousand Oaks, California 91320
E-mail: order@sagepub.com

Sage Publications Ltd
1 Oliver's Yard
55 City Road
London EC1Y 1SP
United Kingdom

Sage Publications India Pvt. Ltd.
B-42, Panchsheel Enclave
Post Box 4109
New Delhi 110 017 India

Printed in the United States of America

Library of Congress Cataloging-in-Publication Data

Johnson, Andrew P. (Andrew Paul)
Making connections in elementary and middle school social studies / Andrew P. Johnson.
   p. cm.
Includes bibliographical references and index.
ISBN 1-4129-2664-5 (pbk.)
  1. Social sciences—Study and teaching (Elementary)—United States.
2. Social sciences—Study and teaching (Middle school)—United States.
3. Active learning—United States. I. Title.
LB1584.J57 2006
372.83—dc22

                 2005021209

This book is printed on acid-free paper.

06 07 08 09 10 9 8 7 6 5 4 3 2 1

Acquisitions Editor:	Diane McDaniel
Associate Editor:	Margo Crouppen
Editorial Assistant:	Erica Carroll
Production Editor:	Denise Santoyo
Typesetter:	C&M Digitals (P) Ltd.
Indexer:	Pam Van Huss
Cover Designer:	Michelle Kenny

BRIEF CONTENTS

CONTENTS

INTRODUCTION

The function of education, the goal of education—the human goal, the humanistic goal, the goal so far as human beings are concerned—is ultimately the "self-actualization" of a person, the becoming fully human, the development of the fullest height that the human species can stand up to or that the particular individual can come to. In a less technical way, it is helping the person to become the best that he (or she) is able to become.

—Maslow, 1971, page 169

PURPOSE OF THIS TEXT

In comparison with reading, math, and science, social studies is often met with a certain amount of indifference. Why is that? It may be because people do not understand the true nature of social studies education. Social studies is not simply a body of knowledge and a set of skills. Instead, social studies is a dynamic process that uses knowledge and skills to enable greater understanding of self, others, societies, institutions, nations, and environments. In this way, it has the potential to become a vehicle for improved community, national, and global citizenship. The purpose of this book is to describe this view of social studies education and to demonstrate strategies, activities, and pedagogical skills that will enable you to implement it.

Making Connections

This textbook is based on the idea that in social studies education, making personal connections with the material to be learned is integral. Each chapter in this book describes a variety of ways for teachers to help students make these connections. Also, connecting activities are included at the end of each chapter so that you might make these same kinds of personal connections with the material you are reading. If you are reading this book as part of a college class or a teacher professional development group, these connecting activities can be used as discussion questions. They can also be used as homework, class activities, journal prompts, learning log entries, pre-reading activities used to activate prior knowledge, or simply as reflection points while you are reading. You will note also that some of the connecting activities in this book involve questions that may seem somewhat personal. The whole point of personal connections is this: Learning is enhanced whenever students (or readers) are able to connect their own emotions, experiences, and observations with the concepts to be learned (or read).

VIEW OF TEACHING IN THIS TEXT

As you know, teaching is not simply opening up the teacher's manual, doing the activities described there, and then assigning homework. Rather, teaching is a complex, multidimensional endeavor requiring you to break down complex concepts and present them in ways that students can comprehend. You then must design learning experiences to meet the needs of students of varying abilities and learning styles. And at the same time, effective teachers strive to help all students discover their special talents and learn the skills they need to reach their highest potential.

Three Views of Teaching

There are three common views of what constitutes teaching: teaching as transmission, teaching as transaction, and teaching as transformation (see Table 1).

Table 1   Three Views of Teaching

	Transmission	*Transaction*	*Transformation*
Guiding Philosophy	positivism	constructivism	holism
Psychological Basis	behaviorism	cognitive psychology	transpersonal psychology
Role of Teacher	supply students with designated body of knowledge	help students transact with knowledge to create personal meaning	create transforming conditions and experiences, enable students to perceive connections, and encourage inner exploration
Role of Student	passively receive information	interact with information	use information and experiences for self-transformation; reflection and search for meaning; discover and develop talents

1. Teaching as transmission. This view perceives teaching to be the act of transmitting knowledge from Point A (teacher's head) to Point B (students' heads). This is a teacher-centered approach in which the teacher is the dispenser of knowledge, the arbitrator of truth, and the final evaluator of learning. A teacher's job from this perspective is to supply students with a designated body of knowledge in a predetermined order. Academic achievement is seen as students' ability to demonstrate, replicate, or retransmit this designated body of knowledge back to the teacher or to some other measuring agency or entity. From this perspective standardized tests are considered to be an apt measure of students' learning. While there are instances when this approach is useful, this text does not support it as a general teaching philosophy.

2. Teaching as transaction. This view perceives teaching as creating situations whereby students are able to interact with the material to be learned in order to construct knowledge. Constructivism is an educational philosophy consistent with this view. Here, knowledge is not passively received, rather, it is actively built up or constructed by students as they connect their past knowledge and experiences with new information (Santrock, 2004). And just as each student's past knowledge and experiences are different, so too is the interpretation, understanding, and meaning of the new information that each ultimately constructs.

As a teacher you are not expected to pour knowledge into the heads of learners; rather, you assist learners in their construction of knowledge by creating experiences where students' old information can transact with new information to create meaningful knowledge. Academic achievement from a constructivist perspective is seen as students' ability to use this knowledge to solve real-world problems or to create products or performances that are valued in one or more cultural settings. This also reflects Howard Gardner's (1983) definition of intelligence.

A common constructivist learning strategy is to help students generate what they know about a topic before a lesson. This helps them to strengthen the connection between known and new. Generating prior knowledge can be done through the use of advanced organizers, anticipatory sets, or prequestioning. To be consistent with this approach, this text generates prior knowledge through the *Thinking Ahead* sections at the beginning of each chapter.

3. Teaching as transformation. This view perceives teaching as creating conditions that have the potential to transform the learner on many different levels. Transformational teaching and learning invite both students and teachers to discover their full potential as learners, as members of society, and as human beings. The ultimate transformational goal is to become more nurturing human beings who are better able to perceive the interconnectedness of all human, plant, and animal life (Narve, 2001). Holistic education is an educational philosophy consistent with the transformative view. It centers on the principle of interconnectedness and seeks to integrate multiple levels of meaning and experience (Miller, 1996). Learning is said to have occurred when these experiences elicit a transformation of consciousness that leads to a greater understanding of and care for self, others, and the environment. Academic achievement from this perspective is seen as discovering and developing your unique talents and capabilities to the fullest extent possible. Academic achievement also involves becoming aware of the multiple dimensions of self and expanding one's consciousness.

Learning can take place using all three views or approaches. This textbook, however, emphasizes the idea that the most powerful and sustaining learning experiences are created when transactional and transformational approaches are used.

THE PHILOSOPHIC FOUNDATION OF THIS BOOK

One's philosophy, whether stated or not, is the basis for all thought and action. This is true of one's life philosophy or one's educational philosophy, although at the deepest level these two are the same. Below, some of the ideas that comprise the philosophical orientation of this text are briefly described.

The Most Important Variable

In the act of teaching and learning, it is not a particular methodology, technique, computer program, textbook, or standardized test that determines how much students learn. Rather, the teacher is the most significant variable in affecting the quality of education students receive. Thus, as teachers or future teachers, it is a good use of your personal resources to invest some time and energy in understanding this most significant variable: you. Who are you? What is your motivation? What brings you to this place? Why did you decide to become a teacher? These are not mundane questions to ask. Maria Montessori said that the best preparation for becoming a teacher is a study of oneself (Wolf, 1995). This means that if you want to help children find their strengths and accept who they are, you must first do so yourself.

Teaching and preparing to teach then is as much an inward journey as an outward journey. The same could be said of learning in social studies and other classes. While we need to learn concepts and skills, it is also helpful to learn who we are, what we value, what philosophies seem to guide our lives, and what strengths, limitations, and passions we have. These are the essence of authentic human learning experiences. They also describe the highest form of social studies education. So who are you? What do you think about first thing in the morning? What are you afraid of? What issues or events seem to always appear in your life? What gets in the way? What are your dreams? What things make you happy? What things move you? What life lessons do you need to learn?

A Holistic Approach to Social Studies Education

This text sets social studies education, teaching, and learning in the context of holistic education. Holistic education is a philosophy or worldview that seeks to address the problem of fragmentation and compartmentalization in education. The focus here is on helping students see things in terms of the whole instead of discrete parts. An equal emphasis is put on helping teachers see students in terms of the whole human being instead of just test scores and academic performance. Jack Miller offers an apt definition of holistic education:

> Holistic education . . . involves exploring and making connections. It attempts to move away from fragmentation to connectedness. . . . The focus of holistic education is on relationships: The relationship between linear thinking and intuition, the relationship between mind and body, the relationship among the various domains of knowledge, the relationship between the individual and community, the relationship to the earth, and the relationship between self and Self. (Miller, 1996, p. 8)

The holistic education framework includes a wide range of ideas and approaches; however, all are based on the principle of interconnectedness.

As we have shown, the main principle of holistic education is the principle of wholeness, which holds that everything in the universe is interconnected to everything else. Everything that exists is related in a context of interconnectedness and meaning, and any change or event affects everything else. The whole is more than the sum of its parts. This means that the whole is comprised of relational patterns that are not contained in the parts. Therefore, a phenomenon can never be understood in isolation. (Narve, p. 29)

One important holistic learning principle is the idea that you cannot separate the teaching and learning experience from the human experience. We are human beings first, who happen to be teaching and learning. We are not teachers and learners who happen to be human. This very aptly reinforces the definition of social studies used in this text as the study of humans. And what is it that makes us human? Among other things, it is our capacity to think reflectively, imagine, dream, create, intuit, emote, and create. It makes sense then that these dimensions be included in education in general, and in social studies education in particular.

THREE HOLISTIC LEARNING IDEAS

Throughout this text you will see holistic learning ideas related to making three kinds of connections:

1. Intrapersonal connections. Social studies and other curriculum areas should be used to understand oneself.

- nurture and give to self.
- develop intrapersonal intelligence
- self-actualize
- align actions with values/philosophies
- understand emotions, pursue interests, develop strengths
- imagine and create

2. Interpersonal connections. Social studies and other curriculum areas should be used to understand others.

- nurture and give to others
- empathize and understand others
- understand humans and humanity
- develop interpersonal intelligence and social skills
- perceive interpersonal connections

3. Interconnectedness. Social studies and other curriculum areas should be used to understand the whole, to see the world in terms of interrelated and interconnected experiences.

- nurture and to give to all—environment, humans, other
- develop transpersonal intelligence—use logic, knowledge, intuition, and emotion to solve problems
- understand interconnectedness
- perceive multidimensionality of all things

- see systems not parts
- embrace seemingly paradoxical ways of thinking—things are not either/or; rather they are

BRIEF OVERVIEW OF THIS TEXT

Finally, this text perceives social studies education to be a powerful vehicle for citizenship education. However, in the interdependent world in which we now live, we can no longer afford to think of citizenship education simply in terms of developing "good" American citizens or Canadian citizens, or citizens related to any specific community, religion, country, or region. Rather, we must strive to develop conscientious global citizens who are able to live responsibly within a global community. And hopefully, these citizens of tomorrow will be able to cooperate and work together for the greater good of all humans and other life forms who share this planet.

Chapters 1 through 8 describe the field of social studies and strategies for meeting the needs of a diverse population. **Chapter 1** defines social studies education as a study of humans interacting, and sets it in the context of the various standards described by the National Council of Social Studies (NCSS). **Chapter 2** explores seven kinds of diversity: social economic status, ethnicity, culture, religion, gender, sexual preference, and ability, exceptionalities, and language. It offers strategies for how these might be acknowledged within a classroom and a social studies context. **Chapter 3** describes the NCSS teacher expectations for teaching history and geography and provides a variety of strategies for meeting these expectations. **Chapter 4** describes the NCSS teacher expectations for teaching civics and government and economics and provides a variety of strategies for meeting these expectations. **Chapter 5** is devoted to planning. You will see how to develop social studies lessons and units as well as integrated studies that incorporate all curriculum areas, expanded views of intelligence, and multiple levels of thinking. **Chapter 6** focuses on assessment and offers a variety of authentic assessment alternatives for use in social studies and other curriculum areas. **Chapter 7** contains a variety of inclusive classroom strategies for meeting the special learning needs of students with learning disabilities, emotional or behavioral disorders, attention deficit/hyperactivity disorder, students who are creative or intellectually gifted learners, and students who are bilingual or have limited English proficiency. **Chapter 8** provides strategies and other tips for helping students of all ability levels comprehend their social studies textbooks.

Chapters 9 through 15 describe specific strategies that can be used in each social studies disciplinary area. **Chapter 9** demonstrates how to use cooperative learning, creative dramatics, communication skills, and leadership skills within a social studies curriculum. **Chapter 10** shows how to use a variety of problem-solving activities within a social studies curriculum, including service learning and conflict resolution. **Chapter 11** is devoted to inquiry. Inquiry is using methods of science within a teaching and learning context. This is an advanced teaching strategy. **Chapter 12** defines creative and critical thinking skills and shows how they might be used to enhance learning in social studies. **Chapter 13** is about using current events in social studies and how to create effective classroom discussions. **Chapter 14** describes various aspects of Internet literacy and contains several Internet strategies that can be used to enhance learning in social studies. **Chapter 15** demonstrates strategies for incorporating children's books and a variety of writing activities in a social studies curriculum.

Chapter 16 is devoted to character education. Here character and character education are defined. Virtues and ethical codes from a variety of world religions and other sources are described. Finally, a variety of strategies are provided for addressing values education and morality issues within a social studies context.

FEATURES OF THIS TEXT

Making Connections in Elementary and Middle School Social Studies contains the knowledge and skills necessary to help you design interesting and effective learning experiences for elementary and middle school social studies. This text also addresses some of the major concerns of preservice and inservice teachers of social studies: What are some interesting activities that I can use to enhance my social studies lessons? How do I motivate and get my students fully engaged in social studies? How can I help my students make personal connections and see the relevance of social studies education? To answer these questions and to enhance comprehension, this text contains a variety of unique features.

Strategies, Techniques, and Activities

Each chapter contains a wealth of classroom strategies, pedagogical techniques, activities, and lesson plan ideas that can be used to enhance learning and make lessons more interesting, active, and student-centered.

Overview

The beginning of each chapter contains an advanced organizer in the form of an outline of the content found in that chapter. This advanced organizer provides a sense of structure for the material that follows, thus aiding comprehension. It also provides a sense of context for easy reference and review.

Thinking Ahead

This feature contains questions and thinking points that invite you to link your own experiences with the chapter context before reading. These can be used as discussion points for class or small group or simply as pre-reading prompts to enhance comprehension.

How Do I?

This feature provides explicit step-by-step instruction for strategies, techniques, or activities described in the chapter. This will show you exactly how to implement and apply them.

Example

This feature demonstrates exactly how a concept, strategy, or technique is applied in a primary, intermediate, or middle school setting.

Teachers in Action

This feature contains the real-life narratives of teachers as they discuss issues or concerns relative to teaching and learning. These cases are designed to expand upon key issues presented in each chapter. Every case is accompanied by the author's personal reflection on the case. These reflections are not intended to tell readers what to think about the case, but rather to give them an opinion against which they can measure their own reactions. After each case, readers are prompted to think about the narrative presented and the way that their reactions compare with those presented by the author.

Go There

This feature links you to websites that provide a wealth of online resources, lesson plans, and other activities to enhance your social studies teaching and learning.

NCSS Standards

Each chapter ends with a list of NCSS thematic standards, pedagogical standards, disciplinary standards and/or the essential skills of social studies that are germane to that chapter. This feature allows you to easily reference the standards related to a particular topic, as well as see how the chapter content fits into a broader social studies context. Using these end-of-chapter sections in conjunction with the appendices will enable you to most effectively digest the standards and easily refer back to particular ones as you need them.

Appendices

The appendices contain a complete listing of the NCSS disciplinary standards for history, geography, civics and government, and economics; as well as the complete NCSS thematic subject matter standards for elementary and middle school students; and the NCSS essential skills for social studies. These are resources that can be used to guide and inform lesson planning as well as unit design.

RESOURCES FOR INSTRUCTORS

A full suite of resources to aid instructors in making full use of this rich text is available and may be ordered through the publisher. Developed by the author, this package is specifically tailored to the text and includes the following elements.

Sample Syllabi

These are designed to suggest how instructors might structure their courses using the book.

PowerPoint® Presentations

The presentations can double as lecture outlines. Each one includes the overviews that appear at the beginning of each chapter, as well as relevant graphics from the text.

Ready-Made Lesson Plans

These are intended to be shared with students. They could be used as examples to help facilitate the creation of one's own plans. They can also be incorporated into one or more class projects.

Video Clips

Video footage related to particular sections of the text is provided for use during lectures. Each clip is accompanied by a brief synopsis, as well as discussion points and questions. The discussion points and questions can be used to help students to connect what they see in the videos with what they have learned from the material presented in the text.

Test Banks

A diverse inventory of assessment items is provided for each chapter.

Study Guides

These guides could be used to direct study sessions or to help students prepare for exams.

Project Ideas

This offering consists of group and individual assignments that could be used as an alternative assessment method.

Web Resources

This list of links includes, but is not be limited to, the links in the text. Other Web addresses include links to teacher certification agencies, practice certification tests, and state standards.

Teaching Resources

Additional real-world cases, journal articles, and a list of trade books to use in teaching with the text.

ACKNOWLEDGMENTS

I am greatly indebted to all of those who helped bring this book to fruition. Thanks to all the SAGE staff, most especially editors Diane McDaniel, Margo Beth Crouppen, and Marta Peimer for their insight and patience in working with a very impatient author. Thanks also to Mary Ellen Lepionka, the developmental editor for this project, and to Cate Huisman, the copy editor. Last, I wish to thank the following reviewers, as well as other anonymous readers for their contributions to this book.

Scott Waters, Emporia State University

Andrew Hunt, University of Arkansas, Little Rock

Cathy R. Seymour, Northwestern State University of Louisiana

Sandy Kaser, The University of Arizona

James Lane, Columbia College

Reese Todd, Texas Tech University

Sally R. Beisser, Drake University

Donna K. Pearson, University of North Dakota

Elizabeth R. Hinde, Arizona State University

Chapter 1

DEFINING SOCIAL STUDIES

Thinking Ahead

1. What do you associate with or think of when you hear the words *social studies*?

2. What do you remember about your own social studies education in K–12 schools? What was most interesting? What would you have liked to learn more about? What was the least interesting?

3. In what ways are performance standards effective? In what ways might they detract from learning experiences?

WHAT IS SOCIAL STUDIES?

The National Council for the Social Studies (NCSS) defines social studies as follows:

> Social studies is the integrated study of the social sciences and humanities to promote civic competence. Within the school program, social studies provides coordinated, systematic study drawing upon such disciplines as anthropology, archaeology, economics, geography, history, law, philosophy, political science, psychology, religion, and sociology, as well as appropriate content from the humanities, mathematics, and natural sciences. The primary purpose of social studies is to help young people develop the ability to make informed and reasoned decisions for the public good as citizens of a diverse, democratic society in an interdependent world. (1994, p. 3)

One meaning of the word *social* refers to humans interacting. By definition then, social studies can be thought of as a study of humans interacting. As noted in the Introduction, social

Social studies is the study of human beings interacting.

studies is not simply a body of knowledge or a set of skills. Instead, social studies is the process of using knowledge and skills to study humans as they interact in local, national, and world communities. Within this context, the NCSS describes two distinct features of social studies: it is designed to promote civic competence, and it integrates or incorporates many academic areas (NCSS, 1994).

Civic Competence

Civic competence means that you are willing and able to contribute to, and participate in, a democratic society and the global community in ways that serve the common good. To this end, your students need to know about the basics of government, democracies, and democratic processes. They also need to have knowledge related to history, geography, economics, and other areas of the social sciences as a context for understanding the various forces affecting the many dimensions of human interaction. Civic competence also requires certain skills such as critical thinking, problem solving, analysis, inquiry, evaluating sources, listening, conflict resolution, collaborating, moral reasoning, and the ability to distinguish the personal good from the common good. Citizenship education or educating for democracy is designed to promote civic competence and is described in Chapter 4.

Integration

Social studies integrates knowledge and skills across academic areas. Science, mathematics, the arts and humanities, as well as the social sciences can all be used to study concepts in our social world (see the section on curriculum structures). This integration makes it possible to see things from multiple perspectives and to perceive the interconnections and relationships among a wide variety of peoples, cultures, and phenomena. Integrative approaches also help students to learn more deeply, to think more broadly, and to develop more meaningful understandings (Roberts & Kellough, 2000). Global education is another important form of integration. Here you seek to integrate local and national issues with global concerns.

GO THERE

- National Council for the Social Studies: http://www.ncss.org/
- 1994 NCSS Curriculum Standards for Social Studies: http://www.socialstudies.org/standards/

WHAT IS INVOLVED IN SOCIAL STUDIES TEACHING AND LEARNING?

Given the defining features, how do you go about designing effective social studies instruction in your classroom? How do you create learning experiences that matter or have a positive impact on students? What elements need to be present to make your social studies classes interesting and engaging? This section answers these questions.

Creating Powerful Teaching and Learning Experiences

According to the National Council for the Social Studies (1994), powerful teaching and learning experiences are created when social studies is meaningful, integrative, value-based, challenging, and active (NCSS, 1994). These five features are explained below:

Social studies teaching and learning should be meaningful. Instead of presenting students with disconnected bits of information, create learning experiences in which students are able to see how social studies concepts affect their lives or relate to their experiences. Invite them to make personal connections as well as conceptual connections with the subject matter.

EXAMPLE: Making Learning Meaningful

When studying the United Nations' *Universal Declaration of Human Rights,* Ms. Eller asked her 6th grade students to select the three articles from the Declaration they thought were most important and then to support their choices. This served to link their opinions and values with the areas to be studied. She also asked students to identify instances in the news or in their community that reflected a particular principle described in one of the articles of the *Declaration*. This helped them link the concepts to their personal experience. (Visit the UN web site at http://www.un.org/rights/)

In a meaningful social studies curriculum, activities and assignments are not created to keep students busy or to get a wide dispersion of scores. Rather, they are designed to reinforce learning or to increase understanding. These activities make connections with students' own lives.

EXAMPLE: Making Connections With Students' Lives

After reading a biography about Andrew Jackson, Mr. Page creates a personal connection by asking his 4th grade students to describe similar feelings, events, characters, or situations from their own lives. Also, instead of having students do worksheets as a postreading activity for their social studies text, he sometimes makes social studies more meaningful by asking them to select three interesting or important ideas from the reading. Students then depict these ideas using words or pictures. In small groups they brainstorm to find ideas as to how each might touch or connect with their lives.

Social studies teaching and learning should be integrative. As suggested above, social studies can be integrated across the curriculum (see the section on integrative curriculum). In reading class, find trade books, Internet sites, magazine articles, or other material about social studies concepts for students to read. Language arts, math, art, music, and science classes can also be used to explain, explore, or reinforce ideas from social studies class. Specific ideas for creating integrative studies are presented in Chapter 5.

You can also integrate social studies across time. This means that you revisit and reinforce social studies concepts throughout the year and in ensuing years. We do not learn by being exposed to a concept once. Rather, we learn by being exposed to concepts a number of times in different ways at successively more challenging levels.

Social studies teaching and learning should be values-based. Invite your students to explore the ethical dimensions of social studies concepts. This is different from telling them what to value or pointing out right and wrong on the issues of the day. Instead, encourage your students to develop their own opinions and come to their own conclusions based on a set of principles (see Chapter 16). This sort of values-based instruction can occur through the use of cooperative learning, conflict resolution, role-playing, problem solving, critical thinking, discussions, debates, moral reasoning, value clarification, and other strategies where students are not expected to come to a predetermined conclusion or create a standardized product.

Social studies teaching and learning should be challenging. There are four ways to make social studies challenging:

- Design your lessons to address specific curricular goals and lesson plan objectives. This will help you create purposeful learning experiences.
- Use open-ended activities and assignments that allow students to thoroughly explore ideas and concepts. In these activities students are invited to share and support their opinions and employ creativity, imagination, and inferential thinking.
- Create tiered activities and assignments at two or more levels in order to meet the varying ability levels of students in your class. Chapter 6 offers examples of how to do this.
- Incorporate varying levels and types of thinking in your instruction and in the activities and assignments given to students. Use multiple intelligence theory, Bloom's taxonomy of thinking, and critical and creative thinking skills to design these.

GO THERE

- Bloom's taxonomy: http://www.coun.uvic.ca/learn/program/hndouts/bloom.html
- Gardner's multiple intelligence theory: http://www.thomasarmstrong.com/multiple_intelligences.htm
- Critical and creative thinking skills: http://curry.edschool.virginia.edu/it/projects/Museums/Teacher_Guide/Time_Line/creativethinking.html
- List of best practices in social studies: http://www.talpiot.macam.ac.il/hishtalmut/principles.htm

---

Do not confuse challenging learning experiences with quantity or complexity. Assigning more homework does not challenge students or enhance their learning; it simply gives them more to do. Less homework that is thoughtfully designed is preferable to more homework given simply to measure progress. You create challenging learning experiences by having your students think deeply about a few things, not by having them think superficially about many things. Also, complexity that is at or above students' frustration level is not the same as challenge. Your activities and assignments should be designed to reinforce learning and extend students' thinking. Just giving them hard problems without instruction or support will frustrate most students and become a detriment to learning.

Finally, challenging students also refers to challenging their preconceived beliefs and assumptions. In your classroom, look to present ideas that are new to your students. Challenge traditional ways of seeing things through questions, discussions, and classroom activities. Use dialectical thinking activities in which students must support both sides of an issue. Invite them to look at issues from the perspective of people living in other parts of the world.

HOW DO I? Challenging Students' Thinking

You can help students think at higher or more complex levels by designing questions or activities that utilize operations from the top of Bloom's taxonomy: analysis, synthesis, and evaluation (see Chapter 5). These are all examples of thinking that goes beyond basic facts and challenge students' thinking.

Analysis level operations: identify parts, distinguish, diagram, relate or associate, break down, discriminate, subdivide, analyze, separate, order, explain, connect, classify, arrange, divide, explain, infer, analyze, appraise, calculate, categorize, compare, contrast, differentiate, distinguish, examine, experiment, question, or test.

Synthesis level operations: combine, compose, create, design, rearrange, integrate, modify, substitute, plan, invent, formulate, prepare, generalize, or rewrite.

Evaluation level operations: appraise, criticize, compare and contrast, support, conclude, find main points, deduce, assess, decide, rank, grade, test, measure, recommend, convince, select, judge, discriminate, support, argue, choose, defend, estimate, judge, predict, rate, select, value, or evaluate.

Social studies teaching and learning should be active. Students learn best when they are actively engaged in interesting activities that allow them to manipulate ideas and practice skills (Chapman, 2003). When you present new information in your social studies class, create interesting classroom activities that enable students to manipulate that information. Students learn more by doing and less by passively listening. Do not be afraid to go beyond the teacher's manual. Take field trips, use creative dramatics or role-playing, create small group discussions, or use any of the many activities described in this textbook to get students to actively participate in their learning experiences.

Best Practice in Social Studies

In their book, *Best Practice: New Standards for Teaching and Learning in America's Schools*, Zemelman, Daniels, & Hyde (1998) examine educational research related to best practice in all subject areas. They describe the following research-based recommendations for best practice in teaching social studies:

Students of social studies should have regular opportunities to investigate topics in depth, and to participate in the choosing of these topics. Optimal learning does not occur in the 40- to 60-minute blocks we usually ascribe to teaching and learning in each of the subject areas. Most adults would have difficulties learning with these limited time restraints. Instead, you can enhance learning by creating instruction where your students are immersed in an idea over longer blocks of time. For example, use integrated instruction to blur the line between subject areas.

Choice is also a powerful element in learning of any kind. As adults, we are motivated when we are able to choose the topics we want to study. Students also need to be able to make these kinds of choices. This however does not mean total choice all the time. There are three kinds of topic choices that can be given to your students at various times:

- Give them total choice of learning topics. Ask your students what they would like to study. What are they curious about? What have they always wondered about? What interests them? Then design units around their topics or use inquiry learning to enable them to investigate their topics. Chapter 11 offers examples of inquiry learning.
- Give students choices within a topic or theme. For example, if you are studying science, technology, and society, you might invite students to choose an area of technology for study. Both whole-class and inquiry learning could be used here as well.
- The third type of choice is to allow students to select from a series of options that you offer. For example, in studying science, technology, and society at the turn of the century, you would allow students to choose one of the following areas to study: (a) the effect of the telegraph on American society, (b) the effect of factories on American society, (c) the effect of radio on American society, (d) the effect of the automobile on American society, or (e) the effect of electricity on American society. Small learning groups would be then created around students' choices, and inquiry learning would be used to investigate their topics.

Social studies teaching should involve exploration of open questions that challenge students' thinking. You can enhance learning in your classroom by creating lessons and learning situations where students are not always led to a predetermined conclusion. This means that you ask questions or create inquiries for which you do not have the answers. A typical less-challenging activity would be to assign students to read a chapter or an article on some issue, and then give a homework assignment with comprehension-type questions that ask students to reiterate the ideas found in that article. This assignment would not challenge students' thinking, as it simply asks them to comprehend and restate the author's ideas so that you can evaluate their learning. Chapter 5 describes how to use Bloom's taxonomy, Howard Gardner's theory of multiple intelligences, and Robert Sternberg's triarchic theory of intelligence to create challenging activities. As stated above, challenging students' thinking also refers to challenging stereotypes or preconceived beliefs and assumptions.

Social studies should involve students in active participation in the classroom and the wider community. Learning is enhanced when it is active and also when it extends beyond the classroom and connects to the community. You can create this community connection by inviting students to use problem-solving skills to address real-life community problems (Starko, 1995). Active involvement can be created through the use of service learning. Chapter 9 explores service learning in more detail. In service learning students learn by participating in service experiences designed to meet community needs (Bussler, 2002).

Social studies should involve students both in independent inquiry and cooperative learning. In inquiry learning students are taught how to ask their own questions, collect data, and use the data to answer their questions or come to their own conclusions. In cooperative learning students are taught how to work cooperatively in groups to accomplish tasks. Inquiry learning and cooperative learning are taken up in Chapters 11 and 9 respectively. Both should be included in your social studies curriculum to enhance learning and develop important life skills.

Social studies should involve students in reading, writing, observing, discussing, and debating to ensure their active participation in learning. Teaching is far different from telling things to students. Instead, teaching is creating the conditions whereby students can learn, and students learn best when they are actively involved in the construction of knowledge. This can occur by using the best practices listed here as well as all the strategies and activities described in this book. These will also serve to enhance learning as well as to create interesting, multimodal learning experiences.

Evaluation in the social studies should be designed to value students' thinking and their preparation to become responsible citizens, rather than rewarding memorization of decontextualized facts. Evaluating students' learning only on the basis of scores on objective exams and homework assignments recognizes only a limited view of intelligence and learning and does little to prepare students for active participation in a democratic society. Instead, effective evaluation of learning recognizes and rewards many kinds of thinking and provides a variety of ways for students to demonstrate what they have learned. In your social studies classes, use authentic forms of assessment as well as more traditional forms to describe your students as learners. Authentic and alternative forms of assessment are subjects of Chapter 6.

Social studies should involve students in reading, writing, observing, discussing, and debating.

HOW IS THE SOCIAL STUDIES CURRICULUM STRUCTURED?

Traditionally, social studies has used a "widening horizons" approach to curriculum, which starts with the child and expands outwards in concentric circles as it moves up in grades (see Figure 1.1). This approach has been the dominant structure in social studies curriculum over the past 50 years. However, while it is appropriate that students first study things in their local environments before moving conceptually outward, there is no research to support the effectiveness of the widening horizons approach as an organizing curricular structure (Ellis, 2002). As a matter of fact, this approach runs contrary to what we know about how humans learn and could actually hamper learning, as it creates artificial borders around students' natural inquiry tendencies. Also, in the interconnected and interdependent world of the twenty-first century, it is appropriate and necessary for children in the early grades to examine world and national events in developmentally appropriate ways. In the same way, it is also appropriate and necessary for students in the middle and high school grades to continue to reflect upon and examine themselves in the context of their family, school, and community.

Another approach to curriculum is the spiral curriculum (see Figure 1.2). This approach is designed to introduce key concepts or themes in the early grades, and reinforce or expand them at successively higher levels as students move through the grades. The National Council for the Social Studies takes this approach in describing the ten thematic strands that form the basis of their social studies standards (see below). These are to be implemented across early grades, middle school, and high school. This invites students to address various themes at successively higher levels.

Figure 1.1   Typical Widening Horizons Curriculum

Kindergarten—self and others

Grade 1: home and family

Grade 2: school and community

Grade 3: regions and cities

Grade 4: the state

Grade 5: the nation

Grade 6: the western hemisphere

Grade 7: the world

Grade 8: ancient civilization

Grades 9–12: history, geography, economics, psychology, anthropology, sociology, political science

Figure 1.2   Spiral Curriculum

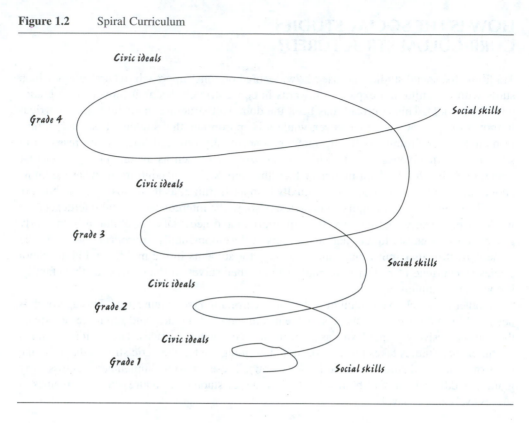

Similar to the spiral curriculum is the issues-centered curriculum (Wraga, 1999). Here social studies curricula are centered around social issues. This approach has students using knowledge and skills from a variety of subject areas and incorporating many modes of thinking in coming to understand an issue. This also provides students with a more accurate picture of reality, as most real-world issues transcend specific subject matter boundaries. Issues here may include things such as world hunger, AIDS, population growth, taxation, health care, defense spending, the war in Iraq, global warming, energy, transportation, or environmental issues.

There are three forms an issues-centered curriculum might take (Wraga, 1998). First is the correlated curriculum. This uses two or more subjects to examine a specific topic, issue, or problem. The goal is to look for connections among subject areas and to develop a broader understanding. The second is the fused curriculum. This approach combines content from two or more traditional subject areas to examine a variety of issues. For example, a science-ethics-society course would look at a variety of issues and examine the implications relative to these three areas. Finally, there is the core curriculum. Here students investigate personal and social issues that are meaningful to them. With this approach, students choose the issues to study. The teacher then introduces knowledge and skills from a variety of subject areas to help students understand each issue. The ideas in Chapter 5 related to integrated studies can be applied here.

TEACHERS IN ACTION: Getting It All In by Integrating Subjects

The only way to get it all in is to integrate. When I got behind in social studies, I put away the regular fiction stuff in reading class and had the children get out their social studies books. We worked in the skills of main idea, cause/effect, paraphrasing, and summarizing. These are important skills for all grade levels, and our state test requires children to read nonfiction and be able to perform these skills.

This week, I plan to bring the social studies textbook into my writing block so that I can return to fiction in my reading class block. I plan to have the students read the textbook on Alaska and Hawaii (our next lesson). Then, they will research and write reports on one of them. They will use the writing process to write their reports from an outline.

Also, don't feel afraid to spend an hour on writing one day at the expense of not getting in spelling. You can always do the spelling the next day. Math can also be integrated into social studies and science. We do measurement in science, for example, and we do graphing in both science and social studies.

These are just a couple of ways I'm dealing with getting it all in, because our students are tested in social studies at the end of the year and we are expected to teach the content.

—Carolyn

Author Reflection: I wonder sometimes if we serve our students well by rushing to try to cover a lot of separate things. We know that students learn best by having extended contact with an idea or concept and looking at it from a variety of perspectives, yet our teaching doesn't always reflect this. We herd students from one subject area to another every 50 minutes like cows. We give them a bit of reading to chew on, a bit of math, a bit of social studies, and a bunch of other things with the idea that they can put these splintered bits together and some make sense of it. In trying to cover the curriculum like this we often make it more confusing and instead, cover it up. (I'd rather uncover the curriculum.) Carolyn has used her teacher intelligence (Robert Sternberg would call it pragmatic intelligence) to solve the problem of splintering, and at the same time, to meet curriculum demands. She has chosen to erase the imaginary curriculum boundaries and integrate her curriculum. In this way students learn more deeply and they have a meaningful context in which to practice skills associated with reading, writing, spelling, and even math. Social studies lends itself nicely to integration. Chapter 5 of this text describes ideas for integrating social studies across the curriculum and integrating the rest of the curriculum across social studies.

What is your response to the case? How do your reactions compare with the author's reflection?

THE NCSS STANDARDS

Educational standards help to define what you are teaching and what you expect students to know and be able to do as a result of your instruction. Educational standards generally include defined bodies of knowledge and sets of skills that are used as criteria for advancement or evaluation. But standards are not the same as standardization. Standardization implies uniformity. However, teachers and students are not uniform products. You cannot expect to create standardized learning experiences with standardized outcomes. Thus, educational standards should describe the expectations but should not prescribe the experience.

The NCSS has two types of standards. The first are subject matter standards, which include both disciplinary standards and thematic standards. (The complete NCSS disciplinary standards for history, geography, civics and government, and economics are found in Appendix A.) The second are pedagogical standards, which focus on the pedagogical knowledge, competence, and dispositions that teachers should possess for effective social studies instruction.

Disciplinary Standards

Disciplinary standards describe what students should know and be able to do in each of four subject areas related to elementary and middle school social studies: history, geography, civics and government, and economics. The NCSS describes specific learner and teacher expectations along with school applications for each of the four discipline areas. These can be found at http://www.socialstudies.org/standards/teachers/v011/disciplinary/.

Below are Internet links to the national educational organizations in history, geography, civics and government, and economics. The disciplinary standards designed by these national organizations areas are also included in Appendix A. These standards provide a sense of the content that should be taught in each of these areas. Also included below are the NCSS teacher expectations in each of these subject areas.

History. The national standards for history were developed by the National Center for History in the Schools. They list important historical thinking skills as well as topics related to U.S. and world history in a variety of eras for grades K–4 and 5–12. Substandards, student expectations, and grade level designation can be found at. www.sscnet.ucla.edu/nchs/standards. Lesson plans, units, and other teacher resources can be found at www.sscnet.ucla.edu/nchs.

NCSS Learner Expectations for History

The study of history allows learners to understand their location and place in time. The knowledge base of historical content drawn from U.S. and world history provides the basis from which learners develop historical understanding and competence in ways of historical thinking. Historical thinking skills enable learners to evaluate evidence, develop comparative and causal analyses, interpret the historical record, and construct sound historical arguments and perspectives on which informed decisions in contemporary life can be based. Historical understandings define what learners should know about the history of their nation and of the world. These understandings are drawn from the record of human aspirations, strivings, accomplishments, and failures in at least five spheres of human activity: the social, political, scientific/technological, economic, and cultural (philosophical/religious/aesthetic). They also provide learners the historical perspectives necessary to analyze contemporary issues and problems confronting citizens today.

—http://www.socialstudies
.org/standards/teachers/vol1/disciplinary/

Geography. The national geography standards were developed by the National Council for Geographic Education. Specific geographic skills related to these standards, as well as assessments, internet resources, and activities related to geography can be found at www.ncge.org.

NCSS Learner Expectations for Geography

The study of geography allows learners to develop an understanding of the spatial contexts of people, places, and environments. It provides knowledge of Earth's physical and human systems and the interdependency of living things and physical environments. Studying geography stimulates curiosity about the world and the world's diverse inhabitants and places, as well as about local, regional, and global issues. Geography allows learners to understand and make decisions about issues at the global as well as the local level.

—http://www.socialstudies
.org/standards/teachers/vol1/disciplinary/

Civics and Government. The national standards for civics and government were developed by The Center for Civic Education. Curriculum, programs, teacher resources, and contact information can be found at. www.civiced.org. The national standards can be found at. www.civiced.org/stds.html.

Learner Expectations for Civics and Government

The goal of education in civics and government is informed, responsible participation in political life by competent citizens committed to the fundamental values and principles of American constitutional democracy. This effective and responsible participation requires the acquisition of a body of knowledge and of intellectual and participatory skills. Effective and responsible participation also is furthered by the development of certain dispositions or traits of character that enhance the individual's capacity to participate in the political process and contribute to the healthy functioning of the political system and improvement of society.

—http://www.socialstudies
.org/standards/teachers/vol1/disciplinary/

Economics. The voluntary national content standards in economics were developed by the Foundation for Teaching Economics. Specific information related to each standard, plus skills and grade level benchmarks can be found at www.fte.org/teachers/standards. Lesson plans, hot topics, and a teachers' forum can be found at www.fte.org.

NCSS Learner Expectations for Economics

The study of economics provides learners with basic information about how people attempt to satisfy their wants and helps them employ logical reasoning in thinking about economic issues. It enables them to understand the economic issues that affect them every day, the roles they play as consumers and producers, and the costs and benefits associated with their personal decisions as well as governmental practice.

—http://www.socialstudies
.org/standards/teachers/vol1/disciplinary/

HOW DO I? Use the Disciplinary Standards

The NCSS disciplinary standards as well as the disciplinary standards described by each national educational organization can be used in three ways: to design units and lessons, to design curriculum, or to align curriculum with standards.

• To design units and lessons, use the standards as an organizing structure. The structure will provide a general sense of the concepts and skills to teach. Select those standards that seem to be interesting and that reflect or are relevant to your teaching goals. You will then need to do additional research to get background information related to each standard. Organize this information into units or lessons (see Chapter 5). Design activities to manipulate the information presented in each lesson. Finally, look for ways to make personal connections in order to create a deeper, more meaningful learning experience.

• To design a curriculum, assign standards to various grade levels. This is usually done at the level of the district or school. Look for a meaningful progression and an alignment with other curricular goals. Then develop units and lessons around the standards assigned to that grade level. Note that most of the disciplinary standards do not tell you exactly what to teach; rather, they provide a guide as to the content and skills to be taught.

• To align a curriculum with the standards, check the current curriculum to make sure all the described standards and skills are being addressed. Add and assign standards and skills where there are gaps.

Thematic Standards

The NCSS thematic standards describe what students should be able to do as a result of social studies instruction. They do not prescribe a specific curriculum or a body of knowledge that students should study; rather, they describe important themes arising from the disciplinary standards. In so doing, they integrate knowledge and skills from a variety of academic disciplines and can be met across the curriculum. Figure 1.3 contains the ten NCSS thematic standards. The specific performance expectations for each thematic standard for early and middle grades are found in the Appendix B. Teacher expectations along with school applications for each thematic standard can be found at: www.socialstudies.org/standards/strands/

EXAMPLE: Applying Thematic Standards Across the Curriculum

You could address NCSS thematic standard IIc for early grades in a variety of curriculum areas and in a variety of ways. This standard states that the learner should be able to "Acompare and contrast different stories or accounts about past events, people, places, or situations, identifying how they contribute to our understanding of the past." Important concepts related to this standard could be taught as part of any unit or set of lessons that examines past events from more than one perspective. You could use newspaper articles, stories, art, music, poetry, song lyrics, mythology, historical accounts, biographies, interviews, surveys, personal stories, or scientific explanations all to help illustrate and teach this concept. Students would then demonstrate their knowledge and skill here using the critical thinking skill, *Comparing and Contrasting* (see Chapter 12), to define similarities and differences between two or more of these perspectives.

Figure 1.3   NCSS Thematic Standards

1. **Culture**—Social studies programs should include experiences that provide for the study of culture and cultural diversity.

2. **Time, Continuity, and Change**—Social studies programs should include experiences that provide for the study of the ways human beings view themselves in and over time.

3. **People, Places, and Environments**—Social studies programs should include experiences that provide for the study of people, places, and environments.

4. **Individual Development and Identity**—Social studies programs should include experiences that provide for the study of individual development and identity.

5. **Individuals, Groups, and Institutions**—Social studies programs should include experiences that provide for the study of interactions among individuals, groups, and institutions.

6. **Power, Authority, and Governance**—Social studies programs should include experiences that provide for the study of how people create and change structures of power, authority, and governance.

7. **Production, Distribution, and Consumption**—Social studies programs should include experiences that provide for the study of how people organize for the production, distribution, and consumption of goods and services.

8. **Science, Technology, and Society**—Social studies programs should include experiences that provide for the study of relationships among science, technology, and society.

9. **Global Connections**—Social studies programs should include experiences that provide for the study of global connections and interdependence.

10. **Civic Ideals and Practices**—Social studies programs should include experiences that provide for the study of the ideals, principles, and practices of citizenship in a democratic republic.

HOW DO I? Teach to NCSS Thematic Standards

Because the NCSS thematic standards do not prescribe curriculum content, you can apply them to the social studies curriculum as well as other curriculums that are currently in place. You can use the NCSS thematic standards in four ways.

1. Formally adapt and incorporate them into a social studies curriculum. This is usually a decision made on a school or district wide basis. Here teachers or curriculum directors assign thematic standards to specific grade levels based on a curriculum already in place. They make sure that all standards are covered throughout the grade levels. Teachers then insert and teach to the assigned standards in their social studies and other classes. Performance based measures are used to document the performance expectations for each standard.

2. Use them to build a social studies curriculum. Here the standards are first assigned to specific grade levels. Then a curriculum is designed around the thematic standards. Performance- based measures are also used here to document the performance expectations for each standard.

3. Use them to guide your instruction. Here the thematic standards are used in a less formal manner to provide ideas related to content, skills, and activities to use as part of social studies instruction. For example, Mr. Elway's 3rd grade class was studying family histories. He used thematic standard IIc for early grades to help him create an activity where students interviewed a grandparent or an older adult to get their version of a historic event. His students then wrote up a summery of the interview and compared that description to a newspaper article of the time or an internet article describing the event. He also used the performance expectations III, People, Places, and Environments to guide his instruction and performance expectations IV, Individual Development and Identity to create mapping activities related to the historic event.

4. Use them to design integrated instruction. Here the thematic standards provide structure to use in creating thematic units or integrated instruction described in Chapter 5. For example, Ms. Plumber's 8th grade class was studying colonial America before the Revolutionary war. She used performance expectations for each of the thematic standards to help her design the unit and create lessons and activities for her integrated unit.

NCSS Standards and This Text

Included at the end of each chapter in this book (except for this chapter) will be a section listing the NCSS thematic and pedagogical standards as well as the NCSS essential skills that are addressed in the chapter. The standards in social studies have been developed and defined by those national organizations with particular expertise in their respective disciplines. These standards ensure that we are covering the main ideas and teaching important skills and concepts in each area. Standards serve to enrich and enhance education, however, only if they are used intelligently. A thoughtful application of standards informs the educational experience but does not define it. This means that standards should not be seen as replacing your ability to make the important decisions that affect students. Standards should also not interfere with your ability to design educational experiences that (a) are best suited to your students' interests, learning styles, and abilities; (b) are appropriate for your own teaching situation; and (c) enable you to utilize your own strengths, teaching style, and interests in the teaching of social studies and other subjects.

NCSS PEDAGOGICAL STANDARDS

The NCSS pedagogical standards focus on what teachers should know and be able to do in social studies instruction. There are nine standards, and each is described below along with the chapter in this textbook in which it is addressed in more detail. More detailed information can be found at: http://www.socialstudies.org/standards/teachers/vol1/pedagogical.

Standard *Social Studies teachers should possess the knowledge, capabilities,* *and dispositions to*	*Chapters That* *Address This* *Standard*
I. Learning and Development Provide learning opportunities at the appropriate school levels that support learners' intellectual, social, and personal development.	1, 2, 3, 6.
II. Differences in Learning Style Create at the appropriate school levels learning experiences that fit the different approaches to learning of diverse learners.	2, 3, 6, 8.
III. Critical Thinking, Problem Solving, and Performance Skills Use at the appropriate school levels a variety of instructional strategies to encourage social interaction, active engagement in learning, and self-motivation.	2, 3, 4, 6, 8, 9, 11, 12, 13, 14, 15.
IV. Active Learning and Motivation Create at the appropriate school levels learning environments that encourage social interaction, active engagement in learning, and self-motivation.	2, 3, 4, 6, 8, 9, 11, 12, 14.
V. Inquiry, Collaboration, and Supportive Classroom Interaction Use at the appropriate school levels verbal, nonverbal, and media communication techniques that foster active inquiry, collaboration, and supportive interaction in the classroom.	3, 4, 5, 6, 7, 8, 9, 10, 11, 12, 13, 14.
VI. Planning Instruction Plan instruction for the appropriate school levels based on understanding of subject matter, students, the community, and curriculum goals.	1, 2, 3, 4, 5, 6, 7, 8.
VII. Assessment Use formal and informal assessment strategies at the appropriate school levels to evaluate and ensure the continuous intellectual, social, and physical development of learners. They should be able to assess student learning using various assessment formats, including performance assessment, fixed response, open-ended questioning, and portfolio strategies.	4, 5.
VIII. Reflection and Professional Growth Develop as reflective practitioners and continuous learners.	Introduction, 15, Epilogue.
IX. Professional Leadership Foster cross-subject matter collaboration and other positive relationships with school colleagues and positive associations with parents and others in the larger community to support student learning and well-being.	Introduction, 1, Epilogue.

NCSS ESSENTIAL SKILLS FOR SOCIAL STUDIES

The NCSS Essential Skills for Social Studies list and describe those skills that students should know and be able to do as part of social studies education. Below are listed the three skill areas and the major skills in each area. More detailed information related to these skills and a full list of the subskills and microskills in each of these areas can be found in Appendix C.

I. Acquiring Information
    A. Reading Skills
      1. comprehension
      2. vocabulary
      3. rate of reading
    B. Study Skills
      1. find information
      2. arrange information in usable forms
    C. Reference and Information—Search Skills
      1. the library
      2. special references
      3. maps, globes, and graphics
      4. community resources
    D. Technical Skills Unique to Electronic Devices
      1. computer
      2. telephone and television information networks
	II. Organizing and Using Information
	    A. Thinking Skills
	      1. classify information
	      2. interpret information
	      3. analyze information
	      4. summarize information
	      5. synthesize information
	      6. evaluate information
	    B. Decision-Making Skills
	    C. Metacognitive Skills
	
	III. Relationships and Social Participation
	    A. Personal Skills
	    B. Group Interaction Skills
	    C. Social and Political Participation Skills

NO CHILD LEFT BEHIND

Since NCLB is changing the educational landscape, it makes sense to include a short analysis of it here. NCLB has four main principles: (a) an emphasis on research-based methods that have been demonstrated to work, (b) stronger accountability, (c) greater flexibility for states, and (d) more choices for parents. Two of these are addressed here.

Research-Based Methods

NCLB requires schools to use "scientifically based research evidence" to support programs. As a teacher, you should always look for research studies to support what you are doing. The U.S. Department of Education has set up an excellent website where you can get literally thousands of research articles on almost any subject as well as lesson plans and other teacher sources: http://www.eric.ed.gov.

When looking for research however, do not come to a conclusion based on one study alone. Instead, look for general trends by reading several studies or descriptions of studies. Also, the words "scientifically based" denote that the results have to be publicly verifiable (Stanovich, 2003). This means that the results need to be presented to a jury of one's peers for evaluation. This is why peer-reviewed academic journals are so important to our field. Doing a report or study where data are collected to support preconceived conclusions hardly qualifies as scientific. There are many of these on the web that disguise themselves as "scientifically based research."

Accountability

Most would agree that teachers should be accountable for what goes on in their classrooms. But this is not the case with NCLB. Here teachers are held accountable only for standardized test scores. These scores have little to do with what teachers actually do in their classrooms or how much learning takes place. Yet, they are viewed in this bill as a form of quality control in an educational assembly line, used to assess the effectiveness of schools and teachers. What is never reported or discussed is the fact that the most significant variables affecting students' performance on these tests are not curriculum approaches, methodology, or teachers' pedagogical strategies; rather, parents' level of education and social/economic status (Popham, 2001). Yet, these test scores are made public and used to justify important educational decisions, under the guise of teacher accountability.

Like doctors and lawyers, teachers should not be held accountable for particular outcomes; instead, they should be held accountable only for engaging in the best professional practice (Cunningham, 1999). Best practices are those validated strategies and research-based approaches that have been shown to be effective in enhancing learning. These strategies and approaches can be flexibly applied in a variety of situations (Marzano, Pickering, & Pollock, 2001; Zemelman, Daniels, & Hyde, 1998). They include such things as cooperative learning (Johnson & Johnson, 1999; Marzano, Pickering, & Pollock, 2001) providing both choice and time for pleasure reading (Allington, 2001; Campbell & Donahue, 1997), embedding thinking skills within content areas (Johnson, 2000b), allowing teachers to make decisions related to teaching and learning (Marks, & Louis, 1997; Sweetland & Hoy, 2002), using homework as practice and not as a measuring device (Good & Brophy, 1995), teaching the processes of writing instead of only the mechanics (Allington, 1994; Goldstein & Carr, 1996), and using silence in the classroom (Jensen, 2000).

NCLB asks for report cards to be issued for each school for stronger accountability; however, NCLB report cards would only contain test scores. If stronger accountability and more accurate dissemination of information related to the effectiveness of a school are indeed goals, a report card for a school should include the following: (a) number of students per classroom, (b) number of books per student in the classroom, (c) number of books per student in the school library, (d) square feet of space per student, (e) the number and type of professional development opportunities given to teachers, (f) daily preparation time given to teachers, (g) teacher empowerment in regard to educational decisions, (h) the number and type of validated research-based strategies utilized by the school, (i) the number and type of validated research-based strategies used by teachers, and (j) the number and type of student products and performances unrelated to test scores or grades used to describe learning.

For a more thorough analysis of NCLB, visit www.nochildleft.com.

Chapter Review: Key Points

1. Social studies is the process of using knowledge and skill to study humans interacting.

2. Social studies should be designed to promote civic competence and to integrate a variety of academic areas.

3. Civic competence means that you are willing and able to participate in a democratic society in ways that serve the common good.

4. Powerful teaching and learning experiences are created when social studies is meaningful, integrative, value-based, challenging, and active.

5. Effective social studies instruction should allow for in-depth investigation of topics and should involve choice, open questions, independent inquiry, cooperative learning, and active participation.

6. Evaluation of learning in social studies should recognize students' thinking and their preparation for becoming responsible citizens.

7. Standards define what we are teaching and what we expect students to know and be able to do as a result of instruction.

8. Standards are much different than standardization, thus, they should describe the expectations but not the experience.

9. The NCSS has two sets of standards: subject matter standards and disciplinary standards.

10. Subject matter standards contain both thematic standards and disciplinary standards.

11. Thematic standards describe what students should know about and be able to do; they go across subject areas.

12. Thematic standards can be
    - formally adapted and incorporated into a social studies curriculum,
    - used to build a social studies curriculum,
    - used to guide your instruction,
    - used to design integrated instruction.

13. Disciplinary standards describe what experts believe learners should know in each of the social studies subject areas.

14. Pedagogical standards describe what teachers of social studies should know and be able to do.

15. NCSS essential skills describe what students should know and be able to do as part of social studies education.

16. NCLB has changed public education and has four basic components:
    - an emphasis on research-based methods,
    - stronger accountability,
    - greater flexibility for states,
    - more choices for parents.

Making Connections

1. List three interesting or important ideas from this chapter. Put them in order from most important to least important.

2. Describe one idea from this chapter that you would like to try in your classroom. What will it look like?

3. What is your definition of a good citizen? Compare your definition with three others and look for common elements.

4. Think of a place that is interesting or important to you. Use two or more of the following to describe this place: art, music, geography, history, creative writing, sociology, and science.

5. What would the perfect social studies class look like? Compare your vision with somebody else's. What are the common elements?

6. Find an interesting picture book related to a topic you might introduce in a primary classroom. Use the thematic standards to create three to five interesting lessons or activities related to the picture book.

7. Find a social studies teachers manual. Choose one lesson and use the thematic standards to augment the lesson, create activities, or design related lessons.

8. Visit the NCSS websites described above. Describe five interesting or important things you find there that you might use in your future classroom.

9. Rank order the NCSS pedagogical standards from what you feel are your strongest areas to your weakest.

10. In a small group, brainstorm possible teaching ideas for each pedagogical standard.

11. Choose a thematic standard and list ideas for how you might apply that standard in other areas of the curriculum besides social studies.

12. In what ways do you see the three holistic learning ideas related to intrapersonal connections, interpersonal connections, and interconnectedness reflected here?

Chapter 2

CELEBRATING DIVERSITY
IN SOCIAL STUDIES EDUCATION

1. What do you think of when you hear the word *diversity?*

2. What areas of diversity do you think are the most underrepresented in education?

We hold these truths to be self-evident, that all men (and women) are created equal, that they are endowed by their Creator with certain unalienable rights; that among these are life, liberty, and the pursuit of happiness.

—from the American Declaration of Independence, 1776

All human beings are born free and equal in dignity and rights. They are endowed with reason and conscience and should act toward one another in a spirit of brotherhood (and sisterhood) . . .
Everyone is entitled to all the rights and freedoms set forth in this Declaration, without distinction of any kind, such as race, color, sex, language, religion, political or other opinion, national or social origin, property, birth or other status.

—From the UN *Universal Declaration of Human Rights*

This chapter celebrates the diversity of the human experience in all its richly varied forms. As social studies educators we must recognize that respect for every human being, regardless of situation or circumstance, and reverence for human dignity is the ideal of any democratic society (Snauwaert, 2001). This is an ideal that transcends cultural and national boundaries. And yet, in spite of these variations on the human theme, there is a commonality, a shared humanness that binds us. Our differences, such as religion, race, culture, or sexual preference, are mere surface-level things. At the deepest level we are the same. At the deepest level all humans strive for love, acceptance, and friendship. All parents want to be able to care for and raise their families in peace. All humans want to pursue their dreams, be joyful, and find meaningful endeavors. These similarities are the things that connect and bind us. Thus, a celebration of diversity in our classrooms recognizes both the variations and the similarities of the human theme.

Embracing these seemingly paradoxical ideas of commonality and diversity reflects the principle of interconnectedness, one of the holistic themes guiding this text. All humans are interconnected at many levels: social, economic, political, environmental, and religious. We are also interconnected at the deeper level of the human psyche, what Carl Jung (1933) described as the universal conscious and unconscious mind. Thus, while this chapter recognizes and honors the diversity of the human experience, it does so in the context of our shared humanity.

The following areas of diversity are examined next: social economic status, race and ethnicity, culture and religion, gender, sexual preference, ability, and language. The information and ideas presented here are not meant to be used to predict behavior in any way; rather, they are put forth to further your understanding of the people you will encounter in your classrooms.

SOCIAL ECONOMIC STATUS (SES)

Poverty is the great equalizer that cuts across and affects all other areas. The gap between rich and poor in America continues to increase (Salend, 2004). According to the U.S. Census Bureau (2003), the United States' official poverty rate rose from 12.1% of the population in 2002 to 12.5% or about 35.9 million people in 2003. The number and rate of families living in poverty also increased, going from 9.6% to 10% or about 7.6 million. During this same time, the number of people without health insurance rose from 15.2% in 2002 to 15.6% or about 45 million in 2003. The number of uninsured children in 2003 was 11.4% or about 8.4 million.

Poverty has a tremendous impact on the education of children, affecting both their cognitive development and school performance (Park, Turnbull, & Turnbull, 2002; Salend, 2004). Children living in poverty are more apt to have experienced undernutrition while in utero and to suffer hunger or malnutrition during the preschool and school years (Bowe, 2005; Park, Turnbull, & Turnbull, 2002). The effects of an insufficient diet on children in school are fatigue, irritability, inability to concentrate, and frequent colds (Park, Turnbull, & Turnbull, 2002). Children living in poverty have more health problems but are less likely to receive medical care (Borich, 2004; Bowe, 2005; Park, Turnbull, & Turnbull, 2002; Salend, 2004). Also, children living in poverty often live in substandard housing, and are more likely to be victims of child abuse and neglect (Salend, 2004). All of this means that these children will be less likely to come to school each day ready or able to learn.

Academic Skills

In lower SES areas, children have less access to books and social networks, and are less apt to have computers (Borich, 2004). They are also less likely to have acquired knowledge of the world outside their home or neighborhood. As a result of these and other factors, children from poverty enter kindergarten and first grade with lower verbal, reading, and math skills than their peers (Park, Turnbull, & Turnbull, 2002; Salend, 2004). By the end of 3rd grade they have made smaller gains than other children (NCES, 2004). These students are more apt to be absent or move, fail in school, or be recommended for placement in remedial or special education programs (Salend, 2004). Students coming from low-income families are also five times more apt to drop out of high school than their peers from high-income families (Bowe, 2005; NCES, 2004; Salend, 2004).

SES affects achievement test scores (Borich, 2004; Woolfolk, 2005). The number of free and reduced-price lunches served daily is one indicator of poverty in a school. Table 2.1 compares the reading test scores of 4th and 8th grade students who were eligible and not eligible for free and reduced-price lunches.

Educational Response

Sadly, there is little a school or classroom teacher can do to negate the effects of poverty; however, the four strategies below can be used to reduce these effects.

Institute early intervention programs. Early intervention such as Head Start and Early Head Start provide nutrition and early education to preschool-age children. These programs negate some of the effects of poverty (Bowe, 2005).

Table 2.1   SES and Reading Test Scores

Year	Grade 4 Not Eligible	Grade 4 Eligible	Grade 8 Not Eligible	Grade 8 Eligible
1998	227	198	269	245
2000	227	193	—	—
2002	230	203	272	249
2003	229	201	271	247

Note: Average reading scale score (out of a possible 500), correlated with the number eligible for free or reduced-price lunch from 1998 through 2003 (NCES, 2004).

Create full-service schools. A school can address the needs of a low SES community by offering a range of integrated services such as child and after-school care, health care, tutoring, transportation, job training for adults, and assistance with social services and employment (Salend, 2004). Access to proper nutrition and day care outside of school, and quality instruction and remediation programs in school, will make it more likely that students are ready and able to learn (Bowe, 2005). On the societal level these programs may seem fairly expensive to implement; however, spending a little money up front to ensure that all citizens in our society are healthy and well-educated will save a great deal of money and resources down the line in the form of expensive social services, law enforcement, crime, and other costs associated with poverty.

Present learning material in smaller, self-contained segments. Many students living in poverty tend to move more often from school to school. As such, their learning experiences can be fragmented. This fragmentation can be reduced by presenting material in small pieces and providing opportunities to practice what has been learned after each small piece (Borich, 2004).

Find ways for students to experience success. Provide higher levels of engagement with higher rates of success (Borich, 2004). This will keep students actively involved in their learning experience, address self-esteem issues, and prevent a sense of learned helplessness. Also, find ways of teaching that match students' ways of thinking (see Chapters 5 and 7). Finally, instead of only using tests, written reports, and worksheets, allow students to demonstrate their learning in a variety of ways.

HOW DO I? Plan for Students Who Frequently Move

For a variety of reasons, students living in poverty often move frequently. They may be in your classroom for only a few weeks or months. Imagine how difficult learning must be for these students who have to drop in and out of various classrooms. Their curriculum becomes more fragmented and piecemeal.

To help counteract this fragmentation, reexamine your current social studies and other curricular units. Look for logical dividing points to create smaller subunits. Make sure each subunit makes sense when encountered in isolation. Create a graphic organizer or outline so that students can see how the subunits relate to the whole. When teaching a subunit, always describe new information in terms of how it relates to the larger unit and beyond. Also, look for ways for students to demonstrate their knowing that utilize authentic forms of assessment (see Chapter 6). Describe their learning in terms of what students know and are able to do to avoid a sense of learned helplessness.

GO THERE

- National Center for Education Statistics: http://nces.ed.gov/
- NAEP: The Nation's Report Card: http://nces.ed.gov/nationsreportcard/
- U.S. Department of Education: http://www.ed.gov/index.jhtml
- U.S. Education Statistics: A Research Guide: http://docs.lib.duke.edu/federal/guides/ed_stats.html
- U.S. Census Bureau: http://www.census.gov/
- National Head Start Association: http://www.nhsa.org/
- National Center for Children in Poverty: www.nccp.org
- Center for Research on Education, Diversity, and Excellence: http://www.crede.ucsc.edu

At the deepest level, all humans strive for love, acceptance, and friendship.

ETHNICITY

Race refers to the classification of people according to specific physiological features or characteristics such as hair or skin color; however, the word ethnicity is more often used in education. Ethnicity refers to a shared sense of identity or a pattern of characteristics based on nationality, race, religion, or language (Woolfolk, 2005). Table 2.2 contains the U.S. population data related to race/ethnicity from the 2000 census (U.S. Census Bureau, 2001).

Academic Skills

Table 2.3 shows the average reading scores for U.S. students broken down by ethnicity. You can see that there are significant differences in the performance of varying ethnic groups on these measures of academic achievement. Why do you think this might be so? When looking at these data remember that correlation does not imply causation. It would be incorrect to conclude that students' ethnicity caused them to score higher or lower on these measures as there are far too many variables that affect these scores including the possible cultural biases of the standardized testing instruments (Borich, 2004). What these data do tell us is that there are factors that make school easier for some and more difficult for others. Our job as educators is to find out what these difficulty factors might be and to try to eliminate or reduce their effects as much as possible.

Table 2.2   U.S. Population Data From 2000 Census

Race/Ethnicity	Total Number	% of Total Population
White	211,460,626	75.1%
Hispanic or Latino	35,305,818	12.5%
Black or African American	34,658,190	12.3%
Asian	10,242,998	3.6%
American Indian or Alaska Native	2,475,956	0.9%
Native Hawaiian and Other Pacific Islander	398,835	0.1%
TOTAL	**281,421,906**	**100%**

Table 2.3   Ethnicity and Reading Test Scores

Race/Ethnicity	Grade 4	Grade 8
American Indian	202	246
Asian/Pacific Islander	226	270
Black	198	244
Hispanic	200	245
White	229	272

Note: Average reading scores (out of a possible 500), for 4th and 8th graders by race/ethnicity (NCES, 2004).

CULTURES

Ethnicity and culture are not necessarily the same things. As stated above, ethnicity is based on nationality, race, religion, or language. Culture is a set of attitudes, beliefs, values, and behaviors of a particular social group or organization that defines their general behavior, worldview, or way of life. There are a variety of cultures within schools, communities, or society that are based on ethnicity. There are also cultures based on interest, belief systems, and circumstance. For example, there is an academic culture found at universities, a jock culture found in high schools and colleges, a gay culture, a computer culture, a biker culture, a religious culture, a drug culture, and a Goth culture. These cultures all provide group members with a shared sense of identity, knowledge, values, or attitudes that helps to shape their customs and behaviors. While the study of cultures and subcultures that arise in schools is fascinating, the focus in this section is on culture as it relates to ethnicity and social economic status. This is what most people refer to when they think of cultural diversity and multicultural education.

Ways With Words

Cultures can influence the way individuals perceive, interpret, and organize information, which in turn affects learning (Salend, 2004). Schools tend to be based on academic and social expectations for mainstream, middle-class culture. This often results in a cultural mismatch with minority cultures between school and home. As a result, minority students often achieve below their potential. This was demonstrated in Shirley Brice Heath's groundbreaking ethnography, *Ways with Words* (1983). She spent ten years interacting with three different communities in the Piedmont region of the Carolinas from 1969 to 1978. The students she studied were the first to move from their isolated community schools into a common integrated school in the early days of desegregation. In this classic study, she came to understand how language learning at home and in a community can affect school success and achievement.

The three communities examined were Trackton, Roadville, and Gateway. Trackton was a working class black community. The language structures, social interaction customs, and literary traditions here did not match those found in school. As a result, children developed ways of thinking and communicating that were much different from those used by teachers, texts, and standardized tests. These differences negatively impacted the way children performed in school.

Roadville was a working class white community. Although it was not as distinct as at Trackton, there was still a mismatch between school and community in the use of language, social interactions, and literary tradition. This difference also negatively affected children's school performance. Children here performed better in school than those from Trackton, but not as well as those from Gateway.

Gateway was a mainstream, middle-class community that contained both blacks and whites. These children were the most successful in school because the language structures, the use of language, and the types of questions found in textbooks and used by teachers most closely matched those used in their homes and community.

This study is significant today, not in describing the differences that currently exist, rather in illustrating how language acquisition, tradition, and culture affect students' learning and academic performance.

Multicultural Education

There are two philosophical perspectives in regard to educating culturally diverse populations: assimilation and cultural pluralism. Assimilation would have students leave their own cultures behind and assimilate into the dominant culture. This would not be sound educational practice as it would diminish learning for this population. This in turn would affect the general functioning, economic growth, and intellectual vitality of our democratic society. We are strengthened by a well-educated population and also by the influx of talent and perspectives that come from the many cultures in our society. This diversity enhances the possibilities of new insights and innovations. To insist on a mythical homogeneous perspective would be to lessen the possibilities for our society.

Cultural pluralism celebrates cultural diversity within our society and encourages students to embrace their own cultures while succeeding in school. This philosophical perspective manifests in our schools in the form of multicultural education. Multicultural education uses the diverse backgrounds of students to enhance or expand their learning (Salend, 2004). This approach embraces and celebrates the variety of cultures within a school setting (Mastropieri & Scruggs, 2004). Paul Gorski (2000) offers the following working definition of multicultural education:

> Multicultural education is a progressive approach for transforming education that holistically critiques and addresses current shortcomings, failings, and discriminatory practices in education. It is grounded in ideals of social justice, education equity, and a dedication to facilitating educational experiences in which all students reach their full potential as learners and as socially aware and active beings, locally, nationally, and globally. Multicultural education acknowledges that schools are essential to laying the foundation for the transformation of society and the elimination of oppression and injustice. (http://www.edchange.org/multicultural/initial.html)

James Banks (1997) describes multicultural education as a process consisting of five dimensions: (a) content integration, (b) knowledge construction process, (c) prejudice reduction, (d) an equity pedagogy, and (e) an empowering school culture and social structure. To implement multicultural education effectively, a school must attend to all five of these dimensions.

Content integration. Use examples from a variety of cultures and groups to illustrate concepts or ideas across the current curriculum. In social studies in particular, look for examples and viewpoints that represent a variety of perspectives including various cultural and gender perspectives (see Figure 2.1). For example, when teaching about civics and government include both historical and contemporary perspectives of Native Americans in regard to government and tribal leadership. And to get a sense of how other cultures might perceive government and civic responsibilities, teach about the forms of government and some of the societal values found in other countries. Finally, explore how women were kept out of government and leadership positions for much of our country's history, and examine their new emerging role here.

Equity pedagogy. Match your teaching style to students' learning style. The goal is to facilitate achievement by teaching in a way that matches that of students from diverse

Figure 2.1   Perspectives

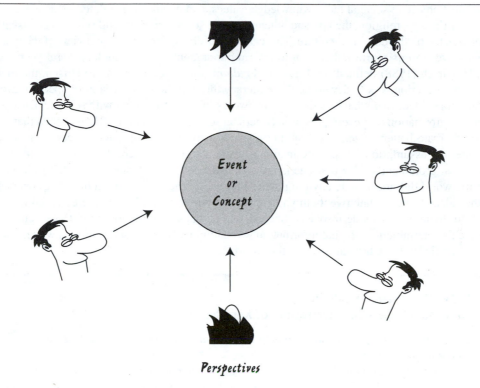

Perspectives

cultures. Vaughn, Bos, and Schumm (2003), suggest that you begin to learn about your students' culturally specific learning styles through observation. Specifically, look to see how students may have different concepts, practices, or values related to the following: time, personal space, gender roles, leisure activities, social status, teaching and learning, household chores and family responsibilities, communication styles (verbal and nonverbal), and life goals.

Empowerment of school cultural and social structure. Create a school culture that values and empowers all cultures. At a schoolwide level as well as in your classroom, examine the differing ethnic and racial groups. Look at the labeling practices that may occur, as well as recess and play activities, and social interaction, and examine the participation in extracurricular activities. Make sure that one group is not overrepresented at the exclusion of others and that all students are able to comfortably participate in all activities.

Prejudice reduction. Identify students' racial, ethnic, and religious attitudes and look for instances of prejudice. This can be done formally through surveys or informally through observation and class discussion. Then, look for ways that these attitudes might be modified through teaching, school events, and class discussions.

Understanding of the construction of knowledge. Realize the subjective nature of even the most objective societal facts. Knowledge, values, and perspectives related to all aspects of society (history, religion, the arts and humanities, the social sciences, and science) are usually constructed by the dominant culture. This can lead to a biased and parochial view of the world that serves to misinform rather than to inform our students. For example, several years ago E. D. Hirsch (1988) defined what he called *cultural literacy*. According to Hirsch, the main goal of education was to develop culture literacy through the transmission of specific information. He identified what he called "great" works of literature along with specific dates and bits of information that every person in American society should know. He reasoned that this would create better citizens by enabling a shared national dialogue with a common set of values and assumptions. There are many mistaken assumptions here, but two seem to stand out most prominently: The first one is the idea that knowledge is static. Hirsch's 1988 view of the world did not include anything about Internet literacy, or about technologies or many other ideas from the late twentieth and early twenty-first centuries that are essential to successful living in our modern society. Second, and perhaps more important to this discussion, Hirsch's determination of what information was culturally biased, representing a white, male, Eurocentric, Judeo-Christian view of the world.

HOW DO I? Help Students
Understand the Subjective Nature of Knowledge

There are three things you can do to help your students begin to understand the subjective nature of knowledge:

Recognize the culturally biased nature of our knowledge and view of the world. Our view of the world is shaped, to a large extent, by our belief systems and values. People from different cultures and with differing cultural, religious, and metaphysical paradigms view events differently. Use the Internet to get news accounts of the same event from differing perspectives around the world. Present these to students, always looking to see what is believed and valued by each. Use a Venn diagram or a comparison web to compare and contrast differing accounts.

Make sure your social studies curriculum does not center on mainstream and dominant groups; rather explore events, issues, and concepts from a variety of perspectives and points of view. Look to include descriptions of history and current events from the point of view of a minority culture or from a women's perspective. Also include literature, art, and music in your social studies units from a variety of multicultural perspectives.

Help students to see that people's views of the world and events are based on their own experiences and understanding. An interesting activity is to have students separately describe the same event and what they believe to be true and then compare descriptions. This can happen on the personal level, as students separately write a description of an event they experienced on the playground or in their neighborhoods. Also, have students look for oral accounts of the same historic events described by people in their families or neighborhoods. Compare descriptions to identify the difference in perspectives. Finally, look for examples of how scientific discoveries have lead to differing explanations of physical phenomena.

GO THERE

- Multicultural education in history and social studies: http://www.edchange.org/multicultural/sites/history.html
- National Association for Multicultural Education: http://www.nameorg.org/
- Multicultural Pavilion: http://www.edchange.org/multicultural/
- Electronic Magazine of Multicultural Education: http://www.eastern.edu/publications/emme/
- Center for Multicultural Education: http://depts.washington.edu/centerme/home.htm

RELIGION

Religion is an integral part of many people's lives that shapes their worldview and also affects the way in which they interact with others and their environment. Both religion and religious expression are aspects of diversity that can be appropriately addressed within a social studies curriculum. What about the separation of church and state? Article I of the Bill of Rights states that "Congress shall make no law respecting an establishment of religion, or prohibiting the free exercises thereof; . . ." This means that government, or by extension, a public school, cannot promote a particular religious view. However, this does not mean that schools should be religious vacuums (see Figures 2.2 and 2.3). We do not serve our students' interests by ignoring this important part of human society. Instead, our social studies curriculum can be used to prepare them to interact respectfully with the diverse religious traditions and perspectives that they will encounter in life outside of school. Also, by addressing religion within our social studies curriculum in a fair and impartial way, we are able to model one of the trademarks of our democratic society, which is civility and respect for religious differences. From this perspective, people look to find common values within the differing religious practices.

Figure 2.2   U.S. Department of Education Guidelines

Religious Expression In Public Schools

"Public schools may not provide religious instruction, but they may teach about religion, including the Bible or other scripture: the history of religion, comparative religion, the Bible (or other scripture)-as-literature, and the role of religion in the history of the United States and other countries all are permissible public school subjects. Similarly, it is permissible to consider religious influences on art, music, literature, and social studies. Although public schools may teach about religious holidays, including their religious aspects, and may celebrate the secular aspects of holidays, schools may not observe holidays as religious events or promote such observance by students."

—http://www.ed.gov/Speeches/08-1995/religion.html

Figure 2.3   ACLU Guidelines

ACLU Guidelines for Teaching About Religion

Students may be taught about religion, but public schools may not teach religion. As the U.S. Supreme Court has repeatedly said, '[i]t might well be said that one's education is not complete without a study of comparative religion, or the history of religion and its relationship to the advancement of civilization.' It would be difficult to teach art, music, literature and most social studies without considering religious influences.

"The history of religion, comparative religion, the Bible (or other scripture)-as-literature (either as a separate course or within some other existing course), are all permissible public school subjects. It is both permissible and desirable to teach objectively about the role of religion in the history of the United States and other countries. One can teach that the Pilgrims came to this country with a particular religious vision, that Catholics and others have been subject to persecution or that many of those participating in the abolitionist, women's suffrage and civil rights movements had religious motivations."

—http://www.aclu.org/ReligiousLiberty/ReligiousLibertyMain.cfm

---

Belief Systems and Worldview

Religious beliefs and our metaphysical assumptions are instrumental in structuring our belief systems, shaping our view of the world, and defining our conceptions related to the nature of reality. Each of us has a vast network of belief systems that act as a scaffold to help interpret and organize information and experiences. These belief systems can also act as filters to eliminate data that do not correlate with our constructs. In this sense, our belief systems can limit our perceptions and keep us from learning or developing other ways of thinking.

Willis Harman (1998), describes three different levels of belief systems, each successively harder to access and more resistant to change (Table 2.4). As we move higher in the levels of belief systems, our beliefs become increasingly data-resistant. They are relied on more heavily to define which data are relevant and how these data should be processed. At the highest levels our belief systems are more important in determining what we believe to be true than data are. Knowing this helps us to understand why students and parents perceive and process different types of data as they do. This also helps to explain why issues that reflect people's religious perspectives, both locally and in the world, can become so contentious.

Addressing Religions Within a Social Studies Curriculum

So what are some tips for addressing religion within a social studies curriculum? The usual method is to provide a thumbnail sketch of each world religion. The danger of this is that it can result in a distorted or cartoonish view that creates more stereotyping than understanding. Douglass (2002) instead suggests the following guidelines in teaching about religion in public schools. First, the approach to studying religions should be academic, not devotional. Look for the moral and ethical principles that have informed the lives and choices of people in different places and in different times (see Chapter 16). Engage students in the study of religion while

Table 2.4   Levels of Belief Systems

Level One– Knowledge	• Assimilated facts: Basic knowledge about physical reality and the way things work. New knowledge fits within existing knowledge structures. • Accommodated structures: Knowledge structures based on general tendencies. New knowledge that does not fit is used to revise existing structures or create new ones.
Level Two– Personal and Cultural Paradigms	• Personal values and related organizing structures: Beliefs based on a set of personal values. • Cultural values and related organizing structures: Beliefs based on culture-based values. • Psychological structures and sense of self: Beliefs about ourselves and how we define ourselves. • Values-based intellectual paradigms: Primary mode of thinking and organizing knowledge based on our values and perspectives. • Personal religious/philosophical values and organizing structures: Religious or philosophical beliefs based on a set of personal world view. • Cultural or institutional religious/philosophical values and organizing structures: Religious or philosophical beliefs based on a set of cultural or institutional world view.
Level Three– Metaphysical Paradigms	• Basic religious/philosophical assumptions: Beliefs about humanity's purpose and place in the cosmos, and the meaning of our existence. • Nature of reality: What is real and possible?

avoiding the practice of it. Second, be as objective as possible in your presentation. The goal is to develop an awareness and appreciation of each religious perspective. Do not press students to accept or reject any one perspective in particular. Educate about all religions without promoting or denigrating any particular religion. And third, look to embed the study of religion into current curriculums. For example, instead of creating a separate unit on world religions, embed the study of religions within the context of current curriculum. This will serve to enhance understanding of people and societies existing in differing places throughout history.

GO THERE

- U.S. secretary of education's guidelines on religion and religious expression in public schools: http://www.ed.gov/Speeches/08–1995/religion.html
- Teaching About Religion: www.teachingaboutreligion.org/
- Anti-Defamation League: http://www.adl.org/religion_ps/religion.asp
- Council on Islamic Education: http://www.cie.org

GENDER

Whereas sex refers strictly to the biological dimensions of being male or female, gender includes the sociocultural and psychological dimensions as well (Santrock, 2004). In other

There are gender differences in communication styles, personality, and classroom behaviors.

words, one's gender identity refers to sexual differences which include the general parameters for acceptable behavior as established by society, peers, and one's family, and the sociocultural context that describes what it means to be male or female.

There are many reported gender differences related to personality, classroom behaviors, communication styles, and attitudes and expectations, as well as differences in how teachers respond to boys and girls (Good & Brophy, 1995). It is beyond the scope of this text to delineate each of these. However, described below are some gender differences reported on achievement tests scores and some strategies for creating a gender-fair environment in schools and classrooms.

Educational Response

Gender stereotyping occurs when people develop broad categories of behavior that describe what is typical or appropriate for males and females. Stereotypes can be limiting in defining possibilities and potential. Sexism is prejudice or discrimination against somebody based on his or her sex. Both of these are often products of students' social and cultural conditioning. Below are nine strategies that can be used to help create a gender-fair environment.

Use instructional materials that are gender-fair. If you have to use curriculum material that is outdated or contains sexist language, point out the stereotypes as part of the teaching experience. Also, allow students to make the necessary corrections in the textbooks (but get permission from your building principal before doing this).

Model and use gender-neutral language at all times. Be aware of your own language, especially the use of gender-neutral pronouns in every situation. For example, "As a president begins his new term he generally selects some new cabinet members." Instead, "As presidents begin their new terms they generally select new cabinet members." Or, "As a president begins a new term, he or she generally selects new cabinet members." The use of language sends subtle but powerful messages about the limits and possibilities of one's gender.

Physically organize the room so that students are not separated by gender. If students have permanent desks, make sure that boys and girls are seated next to each other. In middle school classrooms where students may be in a room for only one period, it may be appropriate to have assigned seating.

Use gender-mixed cooperative learning groups. As will be described in a later chapter, sometimes you will want to select students for cooperative groups so that each group is heterogeneous in terms of gender, as well as ability, culture, and ethnicity. At other times, it is best to use some method of random selection such as drawing names. This creates groups that can be fairly mixed, as well as single-gender groups, and groups where a male or female may be the minority. All are good in coming to understand gender differences.

Select trade books with an equal number of male and female lead characters. A trade book generally refers to narrative texts in chapter form written for students in grades two to twelve (see Chapter 15). In selecting trade books for use in a social studies, reading, or other classes, look to achieve a gender balance in terms of the hero or lead character. Also, in choosing books, make sure you have an equal number written from the female as well as male perspective.

Introduce and include female role models. Female role models have traditionally been under-represented in social studies and other curriculums. Look for accomplished females in math, science, the society, the arts, athletics, and other areas to highlight. Create bulletin boards, units, and lessons, and design other types of studies around these accomplished women.

Introduce and include feminine perspectives. Traditionally, history has been written from a fairly exclusive male point of view. Look to include women's perspectives on historical events as well as on current events.

Encourage students to cross outdated gender lines. Encourage girls to use equipment or become involved in activities that have traditionally been reserved for boys. Likewise, encourage boys to become involved in activities that have traditionally been reserved for girls.

Establish a zero tolerance policy on sexual harassment. Social studies is a good place to begin teaching about sexism, sexual discrimination, and, when developmentally appropriate, sexual harassment. Most definitions of sexual harassment include unwanted touching, physical contact, or sexual advances; suggestive remarks or derogatory comments related to sex; or some sort of social or physical coercion for sexual favors. Again, when developmentally appropriate, teach your students what these are and what they look like, along with the appropriate responses. The goal is to create a safe and respectful environment. Teaching your students to respect the rights, feelings, and personhood of other students is the first step to eliminating sexual harassment as well as other types of discrimination and harassment.

TEACHERS IN ACTION: Recognizing Modern Families

I teach grade one and for six months we cover families and traditions and then other Canadian families for our social studies units. Every year, it just seems to get more interesting.

Many of my kids come from homes where out of five or six kids there could be five or six dads. We have a lot of foster kids as well. When we talk about families I have the kids guide the conversations and topics. I think it is important that they realize there are different types of families and that we should respect all families no matter how they look. We talk about single-parent families, families where there are more than one dad or mom in the picture, families where grandma and grandpa are the parents. I have one girl this year who is being raised by her older teenage sister, as their mom passed away two years ago from drug and alcohol abuse.

For days like Mother's Day and Father's Day, we talk about how it is a holiday to celebrate the people who take care of us. I mention that while many families may have a mom or dad, there are families that may not, so each person in the class can choose to give his or her gift and card to someone else who takes care of each of them. Mother's Day is always easier, as it seems that most kids have a mom in their lives. For Father's Day, we talk about how they can choose to give something to their dad even if they don't live with their dad. Or if they have a step-dad, uncle, grandpa, or even a family friend they can give something to those people. I've had a few of my kids want to give to two people and I've let them do this as well.

I find that kids are much more open to differences and accepting them than the adults in their lives. In my community I have kids come to school who wear the same clothes for a week or who are going to court for paternity testing, etc.; the problems are there just not quite the same as what you are witnessing. And I think as far as gender goes, children should be read stories with moms, dads, single parents, etc. Same-sex families, as far as I'm concerned, should only be introduced if it is something that happens in your community.

—Cathy-Dee, First Grade

Author Reflection: Families are the people who love and care for us. To me, loving and caring are the important issues. These are what children need. I don't think gender or sexual preference have much to do with these issues. However, I understand they are controversial to some, and that people have differing views here.

I agree with Cathy-Dee that children are much more accepting of each other and far less concerned with differences than adults are. What happens to them? Where do they learn that everyone should be exactly like them? The question for you as a future teacher is: How can you educate students about differences in a way that encourages them to maintain their less fragmented view of the world?

What is your response to the case? How do your reactions compare with the author's reflection?

SEXUAL PREFERENCE

In a democratic society that practices the values of social justice, every person deserves to be treated with dignity and respect; to be protected from violations of their human rights; and to be free from discrimination, harassment, and violence. To educate our students for democracy, these values should be clearly elucidated and modeled.

In our schools, all students deserve an education in a safe environment that allows them to reach their full potential (Scheider & Owens, 2000). All students also deserve to be allowed and encouraged to learn and to grow intellectually and emotionally without having to deny an essential part of their identity (Human Rights Watch, 2001). However, this is not the case for many students who are gay, lesbian, bisexual, or transgender (GLBT) (Evans, 2000). A conservative estimate is that there are over 3 million students who are GLBT in our schools (Scheider & Owens, 2000). Like all adolescents, these students struggle with identity issues, usually starting in 5th grade and continuing through early adulthood. They have the extra burden of trying to grapple with their sexual identity in an atmosphere that is often intolerant and even hostile toward anything other than the heterosexual norm (MacGillivray, 2000). They fear being rejected or ostracized by their families and peer groups or encountering harassment and discrimination because of who they are. This may account for the fact that these students report higher levels of alcohol and other substance abuse than their heterosexual peers and are more likely to display depressive symptoms and attempt suicide (Scheider & Owens, 2000).

Educational Response

For many reasons, sexual preference is an area of diversity that does not get as much attention as other areas. However, to prepare students to live and work in a democratic society, they need to learn about all the people and groups who make up our diverse, pluralistic society, including those who are GLBT. Below are four strategies that can be used toward this end:

Introduce the principle of respect and tolerance at an early age (Human Rights Watch, 2001). Students should be taught, not simply to tolerate differences, but to celebrate them. Starting in kindergarten, this principle can be introduced in a general way, and then be applied to all people and groups as developmentally appropriate.

Integrate age-appropriate discussion about gay issues into curriculums (Human Rights Watch, 2001). Usually gay issues are only addressed in a health or sexual education class, and usually only in terms of possible health risks. Students are rarely invited to address stereotypes or come to know GLBT people in a less than cartoonish fashion. It is this lack of knowledge and personal experience that serves to create fear and discrimination. Social studies is the most relevant curriculum area in which to address this; however, it can also be addressed in literature, the arts and humanities, and current affairs. Middle school is when it is developmentally appropriate to begin introducing GLBT issues into the curriculum.

Introduce a zero tolerance to all forms of physical and verbal harassment (Lamme & Lamme, 2002; MacGillivray, 2000; Scheider & Owens, 2000). Terms such as "dyke," "faggot," and "queer" should not be tolerated. Teachers must be aware of this and be willing to address these issues immediately. Schools need to establish the same level of intolerance for harassment and discrimination for GLBT issues as they do for racial and ethnic issues.

Communicate your commitment to creating a safe, nurturing environment (Scheider & Owens, 2000). All students need to hear you as a teacher make a commitment to creating a classroom that promotes social justice and is free of intolerance to any group including students who are GLBT. Likewise, principals and other school leaders should communicate to teachers, parents, students, and the community that harassment or discrimination against any group, including students who are GLBT, will not be tolerated. This is also the first step in educating for democracy. Children learn what they experience.

EXAMPLE: Responding to Harassment and Intolerance

Mr. Hovan teaches in a 2nd grade classroom. In the hallway, he overhears one student calling another a "fag." Even though younger students may not understand the word exactly, they often use words they hear older people using. Instead of letting is pass, he makes this a teaching experience by stopping the students and using a gentle but very serious teaching mode to tell them that this is a very hating word used to hurt people who are different. It cannot be used. If these children continue to use the word, he should get the principal and parents involved.

It is obvious to Ms. Sapp that several 6th grade boys have been teasing Edmond, a boy who displays overt feminine mannerisms. Ms. Sapp calls the boys in after school for a confidential conference with her and the principal. A teaching mode is also used with these students to help them understand that this sort of hateful language has been used to make those who are different appear less than human and thus, easier targets for discrimination, harassment, and other forms of abuse. They are informed that these types of comments are not tolerated in any school or any future workplace. To help them understand what it might feel like to be picked on for being different, she assigns them to read *The Goat* by Brock Cole (1990) as part of their reading class. This book describes the experience of a boy and a girl who are considered social outcasts (goats), at a summer camp and the harassment they encounter. While this book is not specifically about students who are GLBT, it does capture the feeling and experience of being singled out and picked on. It allows you to get inside the head of each and can be a marvelous teaching tool in developing empathy.

GO THERE

- Creating safe schools for gay and lesbian students: http://members.tripod.com/~twood/guide.html
- Gay, Lesbian and Straight Education Network (GLSEN): www.glsen.org
- Human Rights Campaign: www.hrc.org
- Children of Lesbians and Gays Everywhere (COLAGE): www.colage.org
- Parents, Families and Friends of Lesbians and Gays (PFLAG): www.pflag.org
- Students and gay-straight alliances: www.glsen.org/templates/student

ABILITY, EXCEPTIONALITIES, AND LANGUAGE

Ability, exceptionalities, and language are other areas of diversity that need to be considered in conversation related to diversity. *Ability,* in an educational setting, refers to those students with learning disabilities, those who may be less able learners, as well as high ability, highly creative, or gifted learners. *Exceptionalities* refers to physical limitations and also to students with emotional or behavioral disorders (EBD), or attention deficit/hyperactivity disorder. *Language* refers to students who are bilingual or have limited English proficiency (LEP). These are all addressed in Chapters 5 and 7.

NCSS STANDARDS

Thematic Standards

The following NCSS thematic standards are addressed in this chapter. See Appendix A for a full description of the relevant thematic standards.

Early Grades

   I. Culture: a., b., c., e.

  II. Individuals, Groups, and Institutions: a., b., e.

 III. Individual Development and Identity: b., d., e., f.

 IV. Individuals, Groups, and Institutions: a., b., d.

  V. Global Connections: a.

 VI. Civic Ideals and Practices: a.

Middle Grades

   I. Culture: a., b., c., d., e.

  II. Individuals, Groups, and Institutions: a., b., e.

 III. Individual Development and Identity: b., c., d., e., g.

 IV. Individuals, Groups, and Institutions: a., b., d.

  V. Global Connections: a.

 VI. Civic Ideals and Practices: a.

Pedagogical Standards

The following NCSS pedagogical standards are addressed in this chapter:

I. Learning and Development.

II. Differences in Learning Style.

III. Critical Thinking, Problem Solving, and Performance Skills.

IV. Active Learning and Motivation.

V. Planning Instruction.

Essential Skills for Social Studies

The following NCSS essential skills for social studies are addressed in this chapter:

I. Relationships and Social Participation.
   A. Personal Skills.
   B. Group Interaction Skills.
   C. Social and Political Participation.

Chapter Review: Key Points

1. In social studies we can celebrate our unique differences while at the same time recognizing the elements of our shared humanity.

2. Poverty is an area of diversity that affects children's cognitive development and academic achievement.

3. Four ways to negate the effects of poverty are to institute early intervention programs, create full service schools, present learning material in smaller, self-contained segments, and find ways for students to experience success.

4. Ethnicity refers to a shared sense of identify based on one's nationality, race, religion, or language.

5. A culture is a group with a shared set of attitudes, beliefs, values, and behaviors that defines their general behavior, worldview, or way of life.

6. Culture influences the way in which we perceive, interpret, and organize information.

7. A mismatch between home or environmental culture and school culture can negatively affect school performance.

8. Two approaches to multicultural education are assimilation, where students are expected to leave their old cultures, and cultural pluralism, which encourages students to embrace their own culture in their learning experiences.

9. Religion and religious diversity can be addressed within a public school setting as long as one religious view is not promoted and other views are not denigrated or disparaged.

10. Our current belief systems and metaphysical assumptions affect how we perceive and integrate data and perceive the world.

11. Gender refers to the biological differences as well as the sociocultural and psychological dimensions of being male and female.

12. In a democratic society every person deserves to be treated with dignity and respect and have access to an education that is free from harassment, discrimination, and violence.

13. Teachers need to be aware of the special difficulties faced by students who are gay, lesbian, bisexual, or transgender and take proactive measures in addressing harassment, discrimination, and violence.

Making Connections

1. Describe three or four Level II beliefs and three or four Level III beliefs that you have.

2. At the deepest level, what are some traits or desires you think all humans share?

3. What is one culture that you might be a member of? How has your culture shaped the way you see the world? What are some values or beliefs that are shared by your culture?

4. In a small group, brainstorm to generate some ideas for reducing poverty. Also, brainstorm to generate ideas for reducing the effects of poverty on young children.

5. Interview a person from one of the areas of diversity above (adult, student, parent, or other). Ask the person to describe their experience in school, what they like/liked about school, to describe a person who made a difference, and to describe how school could have/can be made different to meet their educational needs.

6. What are some ways of studying history or historical items that might provide a different view of history?

7. What are your personal feelings related to talking about religion in a public school setting? Of what things might you be afraid or confident? What things do you feel are important to include and exclude?

8. In talking about religion, one of your students suddenly becomes very dogmatic, insisting all who do not share his or her particular views are wrong. How might you handle this?

9. Describe an instance of prejudice related to one of the areas of diversity that you have discovered in yourself.

10. In what ways do you see the three holistic learning ideas related to intrapersonal connections, interpersonal connections, and interconnectedness reflected here?

Chapter 3

TEACHING HISTORY AND GEOGRAPHY

Thinking Ahead

1. How do history and geography relate to social studies as the study of humans interacting?

2. As an adult, what maps skills do you use? What maps skills are important for humans existing in our society? How would you go about teaching these skills to primary, intermediate, and middle school age students?

3. Why is the study of history important?

4. How might you help a first-grade student understand that we live on a giant spherical object that travels through space?

Chapters 3 and 4 examine four disciplines usually associated with elementary and middle school social studies: history, geography, civics and government, and economics. Chapter 1 listed the NCSS learner expectations for each of theses discipline areas and contained links to their respective national educational organizations. Appendix A contains the standards for each discipline area. Both Chapter 1 and Appendix A will provide you with a sense of the content and skills that should be taught in each of these discipline areas. These two chapters contain the NCSS teacher expectation in each of these content areas as well as ideas for teaching. Keep in mind as you read these two chapters that social studies is not a particular body of knowledge or set of skills. Rather, social studies is a process that uses content knowledge and skills to study humans as they interact in local, national, and world communities. In this sense, the four discipline areas examined here are simply four dimensions of human interaction.

TEACHING HISTORY AND CHRONOLOGY SKILLS

Teaching history allows students to touch the lives of people who have lived before. History is the story of humans. We study it in order to get a sense of who we are and to better understand ourselves. We also study history so that we can learn from the past. Traditionally it was thought that students should study only local and state history in the primary grades, state and national history in the intermediate grades, and world history in the middle and high school grades; however, this approach takes an atomistic, linear approach to learning not consistent with a holistic philosophy. It also keeps younger children away from some of the wonderful stories from people living in past times and distant lands.

NCSS Teacher Expectations for Teachers of History

Teachers of history at all school levels should provide developmentally appropriate experiences as they guide learners in their study. They should

• assist learners in utilizing chronological thinking so that they can distinguish between past, present, and future time; can place historical narratives in the proper chronological framework; can interpret data presented in time lines; and can compare alternative models for periodization;

• enable learners to develop historical comprehension in order that they might reconstruct the literal meaning of a historical passage, identify the central question(s) addressed in historical narrative, draw upon data in historical maps, charts, and other graphic organizers; and draw upon visual, literary, or musical sources;

• guide learners in practicing skills of historical analysis and interpretation, such as compare and contrast, differentiate between historical facts and interpretations, consider multiple perspectives, analyze cause and effect relationships, compare competing historical narratives, recognize the tentative nature of historical interpretations, and hypothesize the influence of the past;

• assist learners in developing historical research capabilities that enable them to formulate historical questions, obtain historical data, question historical data, identify the gaps in available records, place records in context, and construct sound historical interpretations;

- help learners to identify issues and problems in the past, recognize factors contributing to such problems, identify and analyze alternative courses of action, formulate a position or course of action, and evaluate the implementation of that decision;

- assist learners in acquiring knowledge of historical content in United States history in order to ask large and searching questions that compare patterns of continuity and change in the history and values of the many peoples who have contributed to the development of the continent of North America;

- guide learners in acquiring knowledge of the history and values of diverse civilizations throughout the world, including those of the West, and in comparing patterns of continuity and change in different parts of the world;

- enable learners to develop historical understanding through the avenues of social, political, economic, and cultural history and the history of science and technology.

History and Historical Skills

Literature: trade books and picture books. Good books are the best way to tell the stories of the humans who have come before us. Both historical fiction and nonfiction books are marvelous tools for understanding the stories of people. Chapter 14 describes techniques for using literature in social studies education. You can go to the NCSS web site at www.ncss.org

Chronology skills help children develop a sense of time on both a personal and historical level.

for a list of recommended books to use in social studies. In reading these stories, it may be helpful to ask some of the following questions: What does this story tell you about people living in this time and place? What did they value? What motivated their behavior or what did they want or aspire to? What is interesting or important here? How are these people like you? How are they different? What would you do in this same situation?

Historical inquiries. Chapter 11 describes inquiry as a technique that uses processes of science for teaching and learning. Simply put, a question is asked and students gather data to answer that question.

EXAMPLE: Historical Inquiry

In her second grade classroom, Ms. Udeze asked her students to conduct a simple historical inquiry. They were to find out what kind of things parents, grandparents, or other adults did for fun when they were in second grade. Children used the data retrieval chart (DRC) below to help gather and organize information. They asked adults to figure out what year they were in second grade and then recorded their responses. Students then created simple books and drew pictures to illustrate their findings. Ms. Udeze also used a large sheet of butcher paper to create a timeline on which each student listed the types of activities at the appropriate years.

Year	Things you did for fun in 2nd grade

Oral histories. Collecting direct stories or oral histories from adults can provide unique historical insight. This is also something that real historians and ethnographers do. Students can collect oral histories from a grandparent or other elderly people about a specific event or time period. They might ask what life was like growing up in his or her generation.

GO THERE: Lesson Plans and Activities for Oral History

- Library of Congress, lesson plans and other learning material related to American Life Histories from 1936 to 1940: http://rs6.loc.gov/ammem/ndlpedu/lessons/oralhist/ohhome.html
- National Endowment for the Humanities: http://edsitement.neh.gov/view_lesson_plan.asp?id=406

Cause and effect. This activity invites students to use deductive and inductive reasoning to infer the possible cause or causes of an event or the possible effects of an event. The graphic organizers in Figure 3.1 below can be used to guide students' thinking here. It is important that students list all clues or important information before inferring a cause or an effect as guessing is much different than inferring and deducing. Also, to avoid the notion of simplistic conclusions remind students that events rarely have one cause or one effect. There are usually a great many circumstances that lead to certain events. Likewise, actions and events often have a myriad of effects, both long-term and short-term.

Figure 3.1   Graphic Organizers for Cause and Effect

Deducing the Possible Cause

Event—Effect	*Clues or Important Information*

Possible cause:

Inferring the Possible Effect

Event—Cause	*Clues or Important Information*

Possible effect:

Cause and effect can be done on both a personal level and a public/historical level. That is, you can look at the cause of an effect to examine historical and current events. You can also use it to help students examine the forces in their lives. For example, what might be the possible effect of a certain choice or course of action? These sorts of interpersonal examples invite students to make personal connections with the curriculum. They should, however, be used with discretion and only after you get to know your students.

Chronology Skills: Activities for Teaching About Time

Chronology skills help children develop a sense of time on both a personal and public or historical level. Primary age students should also know how time is related to the rotation of the earth around the sun and the spinning of the earth on its axis. In regard to time increments, primary students should also develop a sense of time denoted in seconds, minutes, hours, days, weeks, and months. Intermediate-grade students should expand this knowledge to include years, decades, centennials, and millenniums. Middle-grade students should begin thinking about geographic and cosmic time denoted in millions and billions of earth years.

The activities below can be used in elementary and middle school classrooms to develop chronology skills. These can be applied to students' personal lives as well as to history.

Time lines. Time lines enables students to see events in the context of time. This can be done on the personal level first by asking students to list interesting or important events in their lives. (Primary students should identify five to ten events, middle-grade students should identify ten or more.) Once a list is created, numbers are used to order the list from past to present. Finally, these events are placed on a personal time line. Personal time lines can be created for the week, month, or year, or for their lives. To extend this, personal time lines can be made multidimensional by including important national and world events. Old newspapers and magazines are a good source here.

For public time lines, students work in small groups to create time lines related to current events happening at school or in the community, state, nation, or world over the period of a week, month, or year. Time lines can also be used to show events as they occurred in history. A good source of incidental learning is to paint or construct a time line around a classroom or down a hallway. Interesting or important events encountered in students' reading, in various subject areas, or in current events can also be placed on the time line. For example, the trade book, *The True Confessions of Charlotte Doyle* (Avi, 1992) takes place in 1832. A time line could be created showing events occurring around that time.

Future time lines. Students are asked to list events that they would like to take place in the future in their lives. These events are put on a time line in chronological order with a possible date given to each. For each event, students describe those things they need to do in the present to bring about the desired future. Future time lines can also be created to infer or predict future inventions, technologies, and events.

Future impact. Students examine current scientific, technological, or other types of innovations (*Popular Science* magazine is a very good place to find pictures and short descriptions of these). Using the form in Figure 3.2, students brainstorm, individually or in small group, to find both the positive and negative future consequences. Finally, they describe how their

Figure 3.2   Future Impact Chart

Event, Activity, Decision, or Choice:	
Future Positive Consequences	*Future Negative Consequences*

How your life will be different as a result of the event, activity, decision, or choice:

lives might be different as a result of the innovation. Future impact can also be applied to students' lives. Here, instead of an innovation, they might list either a future event or a decision that they have to make.

GO THERE

- Lesson plans, units, and other teacher resources related to history: www.sscnet .ucla.edu/nchs/
- National Council for Geographic Education, Internet resources and activities related to geography: www.ncge.org/

TEACHING GEOGRAPHY AND MAP AND GLOBE SKILLS

The purpose of geography education is to help students learn about the people and places existing on the planet on which they live. The Association of American Geographers and the National Council for Geographic Education has identified five themes that should be explored as part of geography education: location, place, human interactions with environments, movement, and regions (Backler & Stoltman, 1986).

Location. Location refers to one's location or position on the earth's surface. Here students are able to use the coordinates of latitude and longitude to depict exact or absolute locations.

History is the story of humans.

Maps and globes are used to determine relative location or where something is in relationship to something else (towns, rivers, mountains, roads, etc.). There are many activities described below for map and globe skills that can be used to teach location.

Place. Place refers to the differences in natural and cultural characteristics on the earth's surface. These differences are related to the physical environmental as well as cultural features and may include things such as religion, language, society, social customs, economies, government, and political organization.

EXAMPLE: Geography Activities

Mr. Gbaja-Biamila has his 3rd grade students interact with students from different parts of the world using the Internet (see Chapter 13). Each week, students are asked to find out about specific things in the various regions, as well as to find out about interesting or important things going on in the lives of these students living in different parts of the world.

Ms. Rivera has her 1st grade students describe the unique features of the place that they live using words and pictures. This includes what the neighborhood looks like (physical features), as well as their neighbors and people living in their families and any interesting games, customs, or traditions. Their pictures and descriptions are put together to create a class book.

Mr. Driver has his 5th grade students create a travel brochure for a particular place or create video commercials that might encourage people to visit there. Students are encouraged to write to the local chamber of commerce for specific information.

Ms. Farve has a map of the United States in her 2nd grade classroom. Each week she selects five featured cities or towns in the United States and assigns them to students. With her help, students use the Internet to find the weather report in each of these places. As part of their morning meeting, students give the weather report and record the temperature and conditions on a chart in front of the room.

Mr. Green selects five featured cities or towns in the United States or around the world. He has his 4th grade students use the Internet to find two interesting or important items from local daily newspapers to report each day. These headlines are recorded on a chart in front of the room.

Ms. White plays a clue game with her 6th grade class. She selects a place someplace in the world. Each day a different clue is put up on the bulletin board until a student can guess the place.

When students read a trade book in Mr. Sharper's 3rd grade class, the location in which the story takes place is recorded on a map using a tack, yarn or string, and card. If the location is not indicated, students record clues as they read to make an informed guess.

Human interactions with environments. People's natural environments influence a wide range of human activities. You can teach this theme by looking at how the lifestyles and technologies of people vary across time and place in response to their physical environments. In the same way, humans have interacted with their natural environments to change them and some of these changes have not been positive. They include the loss of forest land, the pollution of air and water, the thinning of the ozone layer protecting our earth, and the loss of plant and animal life. This geographic theme is one of the areas where science and social studies converge. You can teach this theme by having students look at how their neighbor, town, or city has changed physically over varying increments of time from two years to one hundred years. Pictures and satellite images can also be used to show the effects of human habitation on the environment.

Movement. Movement refers to the interaction, travel, and communication between people in various regions. There are physical features, transportation systems, and political boundaries that prevent or enhance the movement of people from one place to another. With the advent of the Internet, satellites, and cell phones, people are now able, for the first time in human history, to communication with each other from virtually any place on the earth. You can teach this theme by examining how goods and products move from one place to another, how the global economy has made us interdependent, how humans get to school or to work, and the many ways we use to communicate with each other. As part of oral history, students might locate the different places that parents, grandparents, and even great-grandparents have lived.

Regions. A region is a basic unit of geographic study. It can be defined as an area of any shape or size that has a common characteristic or set of characteristics. Regions can be determined by physical characteristics as well as other common characteristics such as culture, government, politics, language, heritage, religion, or metaphysical beliefs (see Chapter 2).

NCSS Teacher Expectations for Teachers of Geography

Teachers of geography at all school levels should provide developmentally appropriate experiences as they guide learners in their study. They should

• guide learners in the use of maps and other geographic representations, tools, and technologies to acquire, process, and report information from a spatial perspective;

• enable learners to use mental maps to organize information about people, places, and environments in a spatial context;

• assist learners to analyze the spatial information about people, places, and environments on Earth's surface;

• help learners to understand the physical and human characteristics of places;

• assist learners in developing the concept of regions as a means to interpret Earth's complexity;

• enable learners to understand how culture and experience influence people's perceptions of places and regions;

• provide learners opportunities to understand and analyze the physical processes that shape Earth's surface;

• challenge learners to consider the characteristics and spatial distribution of ecosystems on Earth's surface;

• guide learners in exploring the characteristics, distribution, and migration of human populations on Earth's surface;

• help learners to understand and analyze the characteristics, distribution, and complexity of Earth's cultural mosaics;

• have learners explore the patterns and networks of economic interdependence on Earth's surface;

• enable learners to describe the processes, patterns, and functions of human settlement;

• challenge learners to examine how the forces of cooperation and conflict among people influence the division and control of Earth's surface;

• help learners see how human actions modify the physical environment;

• enable learners to analyze how physical systems affect human systems;

• challenge learners to examine the changes that occur in the meaning, use, distribution, and importance of resources;

• help learners to apply geography to interpret the past and present and to plan for the future;

• enhance learners' abilities to ask questions and to acquire, organize, and analyze geographic information so they can answer geographic questions as they engage in the study of substantive geographic content.

HOW DO I? Teach Map Reading

The idea that a piece of paper and the symbols found on it represent things and places in physical space is a fairly large jump in thinking for young children in kindergarten through 2nd grade. In these early grades, always move from the known to the new in your teaching. Start by using maps to represent space in students' physical experience such as the classroom and school, and then branch out to the community, region, state or province, and beyond. While explicit instruction should be used to learn some of the basic map-reading skills, much learning occurs through incidental learning. This occurs when maps are used in all subject areas to point out locations related to lessons, stories, or events. Also, like all skills, map reading is learned over time through repeated exposure, instruction, practice, and review.

For young children, reinforce the idea that maps are a view from above. With classroom or school maps, students can be told that it is the view of a bug on the ceiling. For larger maps, it is the view from a cloud or airplane. Satellite images can be used to help make this transition from the concrete to the abstract map.

The initial map-reading skills of older students should replicate those used in real life as much as possible. Think about the ways in which you use maps to find locations and directions to a city or street address. By the end of the middle grades, students should (a) have a general sense of where things are, (b) know how to locate places on a map, (c) know how to get to those places from their current location (d) have a sense of time as it relates to distance, and (e) know how to use maps to get a variety of other information related to location including relief features, social data, economic data, scientific information, topographical information, and political boundaries.

Six Map-Reading Skills

There are six essential map-reading skills for elementary- and middle-school students:

Directional orientation. Students need to understand cardinal directions and how they manifest in reality and on the map. In the early grades, identify these in the classroom by putting signs on each side of the room to indicate north, south, east, and west. Reinforce this by also putting signs in the halls with arrows to indicate cardinal directions.

Since north is always at the top of the page, it is sometimes useful to have them turn their desks or chairs to face the north side of the room when teaching cardinal directions to younger students (see Figure 3.3). In this way the maps they are looking at correspond with physical reality. This also helps them make the transition from concrete reality to the abstract map.

Locate places on a map and globe. Students should be able to find towns, cities, states, provinces, territories, and countries on a map or globe. Along with explicit instruction, students will get better at this through practice and repeated exposure to maps. A large globe and wall map of the country should be available in primary classrooms. These should be fairly basic allowing students to identify bodies of water and basic land formations. As students move into the middle grades more complete globes and world maps should be available. As

Figure 3.3   Compass-Classroom

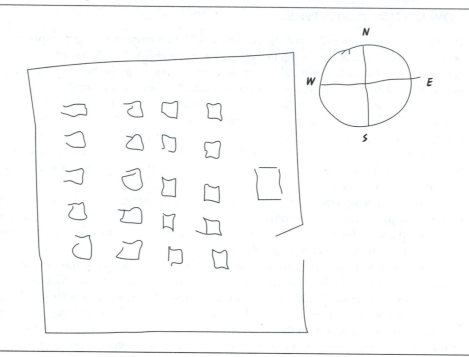

stated above, always put lessons, stories, and events in a geographical context whenever possible by locating them on the map.

Getting maps and globes into students' hands and asking them to locate places is essential in helping them learn how to find places and in developing their own mental maps (a general sense of where things are). Traditionally, the primary grades were concerned with the community and region, intermediate grades studied the state or province and country, and middle school grades focused on the world. However, while this may be a general focus, all of these areas should be touched on at all levels. Locating specific places on maps and globes is done using longitude and latitude or with a grid. Most state and local maps use the grid system with numbers on the vertical axis and letters on the horizontal axis.

Express relative location. Students should be able to describe the location of one place in relationship to another in terms of direction. For example, Canada is north of the United States, Minneapolis, Minnesota is northwest of Madison, Wisconsin, and the St. Croix River is west of Grantsburg, Wisconsin and runs north and south.

Use scale and compute distances. Scale is the process of reducing space by comparative amounts so that distances can be computed. A scale is also the symbol on a map that describes the proportional relationship (see Figure 3.4). In order for students to be able to use this scale they must first understand the concept of proportional relationship. Creating maps to scale helps younger students understand this concept. A simple activity is to create a proportional map of the

Figure 3.4   Map Scales

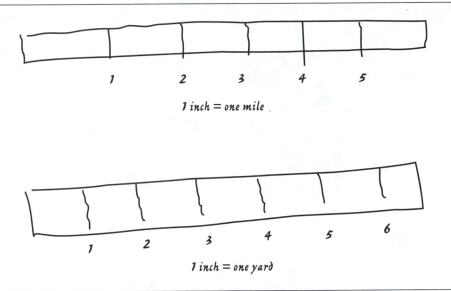

1 inch = one mile

1 inch = one yard

classroom. First measure the classroom in feet, yards, or meters. Then, convert this to inches, centimeters, or some smaller unit. Students are then ready to create a map of the classroom that is proportional to the actual classroom. A scale should always be included on this map. Graphing paper can also be used with each square on the page representing a larger unit in physical space.

Students in kindergarten and first grade should generally not be asked to create maps to scale as it is not developmentally appropriate (see Figure 3.5). Simply having them create maps, regardless of the accuracy, is an important step in helping them learn the space-to-paper relationship. Creating simple maps to scale should begin in 2nd or 3rd grade (see Figure 3.6). Start by working with inches and feet or with centimeters, decimeters, and meters before moving to larger units of miles and kilometers. In the middle grades students can begin to create more elaborate maps. Computing distance using scale is a matter of measuring the distance on a map with a ruler and placing it next to the scale. In the middle grades, students should also be able to use a scale to find or compute distance on state, country, and world maps.

Use scale to estimate traveling time. Scale can also be used to determine approximate traveling time. This is figured by measuring the distance between two points, and dividing the distance by speed (see Figure 3.7). In this computation, distance and speed must be measured using similar units (miles, hours, and miles per hour). For example, the distance between Mankato, Minnesota and Grantsburg, Wisconsin is 157 miles. If I am traveling by car with an average speed of 55 miles per hour, the equation would be: 157 divided by 55 = 2.85. Thus, it would take about two hours and 50 minutes to make this trip. Hint: To help children understand 85 percent of an hour, use a clock that is broken into percentiles like a pie chart (see Figure 3.8). If I increased my average speed to 60 miles per hour, 157 divided by 65 = 2.42. At this speed it would take me about 2 hours and 25 minutes to make the trip.

Figure 3.5   Map Drawn by a 1st-Grade Student

Source: Miguel Santoyo, age 6. Used with permission.

Interpret map symbols and visualize what they mean. A symbol is a figure or picture that stands for something. Start teaching this using classroom and school maps. Create symbols to represent water fountains, bathrooms, doors, and other familiar places or objects. For primary children, reinforce this initial instruction by putting a large copy of the map symbol on or near the actual object or place. For example, put the map symbol for a water fountain above the actual water fountain. Once students grasp the concept of symbols related to school and classroom, they can be introduced to more traditional map symbols found on community, state, country, and world maps.

When symbols are used on a map, a key is always present to tell what each symbol means (see Figure 3.9). Most maps include symbols for roads, railroads, rivers, capitals, and borders; however, geological maps contain symbols for common geographic terms (see Figure 3.10). The symbols for these often vary, thus the map key is important in using any kind of map. Also, the geological map is another instance of where science and social studies converge.

Figure 3.6   Map Drawn by a 3rd-Grade Student

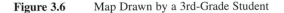

Source: Marissa Santoyo, age 9. Used with permission.

Figure 3.7   Trip Time

---

distance / speed = traveling time

Working With Globes

In teaching globe skills, invite students to see the earth as a spherical planet moving through space. Reinforce the idea that we are all members of the human community, all living on the same planet sharing space and resources. The Internet contains some fascinating satellite images for use with both map and globe study (see Figure 3.11). Some show the curvature of the earth as well as clouds and the shadow line created by the earth turning away from the sun.

Figure 3.8   Clock Divided Into Percentiles

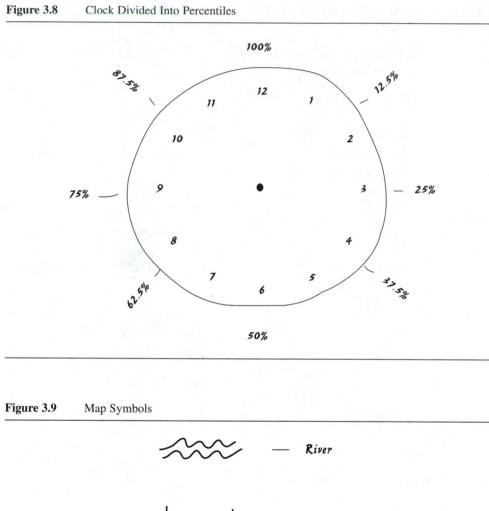

Figure 3.9   Map Symbols

— River

— Bridge

— Mountains

— Road

Figure 3.10   Common Geographic Terms

Aquifer. An underground body of porous sand, gravel, or fractured rock filled with water, capable of supplying useful quantities of water.

Basin. A low place in surface of land; often occupied by a body of water at the lowest point.

Bay. A body of water that is partly enclosed by land (and is usually smaller than a gulf).

Bedrock. The solid rock that underlies any unconsolidated sediment or soil.

Butte. A flat-topped rock or hill formation with steep sides.

Canal. An artificial waterway used for navigation.

Canyon. A deep valley with very steep sides—often carved from the Earth by a river.

Cape. A pointed piece of land that sticks out into a sea, ocean, lake, or river.

Cave. A large hole in the ground or in the side of a hill or mountain.

Channel. A narrow body of water that connects two larger bodies of water (like the English Channel). A channel is also a part of a river or harbor that is deep enough to let ships sail through.

Delta. A low, watery land formed at the mouth of a river. It is formed from the silt, sand, and small rocks that flow downstream in the river and are deposited in the delta.

Desert. A very dry area

Gulf. A part of the ocean (or sea) that is partly surrounded by land (and usually larger than a bay).

Hill. A raised area or mound of land.

Island. A piece of land that is surrounded by water.

Isthmus. A narrow strip of land connecting two larger land masses. An isthmus has water on two sides.

Lagoon. A shallow body of water that is located alongside a coast and separated from the ocean by a strip of land or a sandbank.

Lake. A large body of water surrounded by land on all sides. Really huge lakes are often called seas.

Marsh. A type of freshwater, brackish water, or saltwater wetland that is found along rivers, pond, lakes, and coasts. Marsh plants grow up out of the water.

Mesa. A land formation that has a flat area on the top and steep walls—mesas usually occur in dry areas.

Mountain. A very tall, natural place on Earth—higher than a hill. The tallest mountain on Earth is Mt. Everest.

Ocean. A large body of saltwater that surrounds a continent. Oceans cover more than two-thirds of the Earth's surface.

Peninsula. A body of land that is surrounded by water on three sides.

Plain. Flat lands that have only small changes in elevation.

(Continued)

Figure 3.10 (Continued)

Plateau. A large, flat area of land that is higher than the surrounding land.

Prairie. A wide, relatively flat area of land that has grasses and only a few trees.

Range. A chain of mountains and/or high elevations.

Reservoir. A human-made lake that stores water for future use.

River. A large, flowing body of water that usually empties into a sea or ocean.

Sea. A large body of salty water that is often connected to an ocean. A sea may be partly or completely surrounded by land.

Sound. A wide inlet of the sea or ocean that is parallel or at an angle to the coastline; it often separates a coastline from a nearby island.

Strait. A narrow body of water that connects two larger bodies of water.

Swamp. A type of freshwater wetland that has spongy, muddy land and a lot of water. Many trees and shrubs grow in swamps.

Valley. A low place between mountains.

Volcano. A mountainous vent in the Earth's crust. When a volcano erupts, it spews out lava, ashes, and hot gases from deep inside the Earth.

Wetland. An area of land that is often wet; the soils in wetlands are often low in oxygen.

Figure 3.11   Satellite Image of the Earth

> **GO THERE: Websites Containing Satellite Images**
>
> The following web sites contain satellite images that can be used for classroom purposes:
>
> www.goes.noaa.gov/
>
> www.terraserver.microsoft.com/
>
> www.ssec.wisc.edu/data/
>
> http://www.usgs.gov/Earthshots/
>
> www.ghcc.msfc.nasa.gov/GOES/
>
> www.fourmilab.ch/earthview/vplanet.html

Besides the six essential map-reading skills just described, elementary- and middle-school students using globes should be familiar with the terms and concepts in Figure 3.12.

Figure 3.12   Important Terms and Concepts for Using Globes

Longitude lines are the imaginary lines running from the North Pole to the South Pole. They are also called *meridians*. Looking at the Earth from above the North Pole, it is divided by 24 meridians. They run from 0° to 180° west and 0° to 180° east. The line through zero degrees longitude is called the *prime meridian*. Each meridian represents a separate time zone.

Latitude lines are the imaginary lines or parallels running horizontally around the globe from 0° to 90° north and 0° to 90° south with 0° being the *equator*. They are also called *parallels*.

Geographic coordinates are the meridians and parallels that form a grid system. These are used to find specific places.

The axis is an imaginary vertical line that goes from the North Pole straight through the center of the Earth to the South Pole. Our planet turns on this imaginary line.

The equator is the imaginary horizontal line found at 0° latitude that divides the planet in half.

A hemisphere is half the earth's surface. There are both Northern and Southern hemispheres, as well as Eastern and Western hemispheres.

The prime meridian is 0° longitude, the line that runs through the Royal Greenwich Observatory in Greenwich, England. This divides the earth into the Western and Eastern hemispheres.

The international date line is located at 180° longitude. Regions to the east of the International Date Line are one calendar day earlier than regions to the west.

The Arctic Circle is the line of latitude located at 66° north that delineates the Northern Frigid Zone of the earth.

The Antarctic Circle is the line of latitude located at 66° south that delineates the Southern Frigid Zone of the earth.

Activities for Teaching Map and Globe Skills

Below are a variety of activities that can be used to teach or reinforce concepts and skills related to maps and globes. There are some fairly simple ones for primary students as well as more complex ones for middle grade students. In each case, the activities should be adapted for a particular class and grade level.

Sponge activities. Sponge activities are short, fun activities designed to soak up a few extra minutes before lunch, recess, or another activity. These are good opportunities to reinforce concepts. A sponge activity to reinforce cardinal directions is an I'm-thinking-of riddle. "I'm thinking of something round on the east side of the room." "I'm thinking of a rectangle with words on the north side of the room."

Simon Says. For younger students, Simon Says can be used with directions. "Simon says, turn to the south. Simon says, take one step west."

Hide-the-thimble with directions. In the classroom, one student is sent out of the room and a thimble or some small object is hidden. Next, the student enters the room and is directed to the thimble using steps and cardinal directions until the thimble is found. For example, the direction giver would say, "Enter the room and walk south five steps. Walk three steps to the south," etc. At first, the teacher should give directions. Later, students are selected to give directions.

Map directions. Give each student a map of a region or state that has a fairly small grid or squares on it. Starting at a given place, try to get students to find out where the imaginary thimble is hidden by guiding them to another place. Directions are given to help them move about the grid. For example, "Move three squares south, two squares west, and three squares north." Older students can use a road map and be asked to find a specific location. "Go to Highway 7, turn north and travel for about 20 miles. At Flying Cloud Drive, turn east and drive for 10 miles. Turn north on Anderson Lake Parkway. Where are you?"

Map grid bingo. Create bingo cards in the form of a city map with grids and coordinates. The city map can be real or imaginary. Six letters are listed along the horizontal axis and six numbers are listed on the vertical axis. Use two dice or create two spinners, one with numbers and one with the letters A through F on it. Students play in teams of two, two pair to a game. One person throws the dice while the other places a marker on the correct grid. To place a marker on the map, the player must identify a city, road, or something with the grid on the map. The pair that gets six in a row first wins the game.

Body maps. This is an activity for kindergarten and first grade that allows students to see that the map stands for something. Using a large sheet of butcher paper, students have a partner trace an outline of their body. They then create a map of their body by putting in organs, joints, or specific muscles.

Maps from stories. In the inside cover of the book *Winnie the Pooh* (Milne, 1926), there is a map of the Hundred Acre Forest that shows where events of the story occurred. This makes a good starting place for students to begin to see physical spaces in relation to other physical spaces. For older students, use the maps of Middle Earth from Tolkien's *Lord of the Rings*

(1954). Also, as students read any story, imagination and inference can be used to create a map based on things and events found in a story.

Make a map/make a village. Create a community using milk boxes, paper, tongue depressors, and other items. Strips of paper can be used to indicate roads, railroad tracks, rivers, and lakes. Depending on the size, small cars, airplanes, and people can be included. As a learning center, ask students to make a map of the village. Students can also be given a map and then asked to create a village.

City planning. Students can develop their own imaginary kingdoms, cities, or towns and use maps to show the layout. Encourage them to be creative, but at the same time, talk about city planning and the resources necessary to maintain a population within a community.

Community map. Put up a map of the community and use a pin, yarn, and a picture to indicate where each student in the class lives

Radar and minerals deposits. This game is similar to the old *Battleship* game and can be used to reinforce the concept of longitude and latitude and to practice finding locations using coordinates. This is a game played in pairs. First, two identical maps are created or used that have longitude and latitude coordinates. As children sit at a table facing each other, a box, book, or some other barrier is created so that students cannot see each other's maps. Next, both students are given three to five identical small shapes of paper. These are valuable mineral deposits. Each student places them on their map so that the other can't see them. The goal is to use coordinates to guess where the other person's mineral deposits are hidden before that person finds yours. The first person to find all the mineral deposits is the winner.

Map board games. Create simple board games that are in the form of maps with cardinal directions on them (see Figure 3.13). Eventually, students will want to create their own board games.

Mapquest. Students can visit Mapquest at *www.mapquest.com*. This can be used to find or check the distance and travel time between two or more locations.

Time, distance, and speed. Time is often used to convey distance. It is common to hear somebody say, "I'm about 20 minutes away." Use mathematics to calculate distance, speed, and time. For example, if I drive 60 miles an hour, how long will it take me to get from Mankato to Minneapolis? For advanced students, substitute different forms of travel. Most airline airplanes travel at about 550 miles per hour. The speed of sound is about 761 miles per hour at sea level. (Here's where science, math, and geography converge. The speed of sound is faster at different elevations as the density of the atmosphere it has to travel through affects the speed.) How long does it take a jet traveling at the speed of sound to get from Minneapolis to New York? The speed of light is 186,000 miles per second. If it were possible to travel at the speed of light, how long would it take to get from New York to Los Angeles? Students studying history might be interested in calculating walking speed. Take the class out to a running track to find an average walking speed for one tour around the track. Four times around a 440 yard track is a mile. Multiple their time by four to find the average speed per mile. Then have students figure how long it will take to walk certain distances. For example, how long would it take Napoleon's army to travel from Paris to Moscow on foot?

Figure 3.13   Board Game for Learning Cardinal Directions

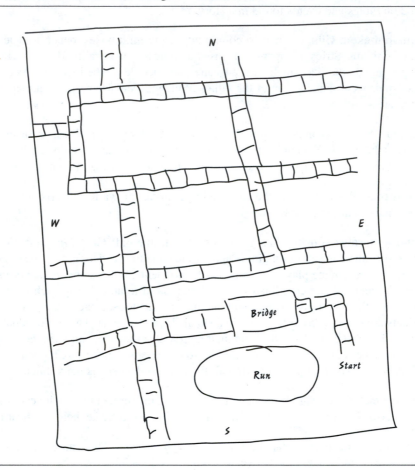

A travel map. Given a simple community map, students can use a colored pencil or marker to trace and record the places they went during the week or over the weekend.

Map the gerbil. In a box or on a table top, create a village with artifacts. Blocks could be used or you could actually create a replicate village. Students would then create a map of this village. Next, put a gerbil in this village and have students record its path as it moves about the village, using a line on the map to indicate its movement. To extend this into science, put a gerbil in the imitation village with some food at one part. Have students time it to see how long it takes it to find the food, and chart the time with a colored pencil. Then, select a different gerbil and record its path using a different colored pencil. This allows students to make comparisons.

Classroom travel map. This is a version of hide the thimble. Here, two students leave the room. A thimble or some object is hidden in the room. Each student in the classroom has a map of the classroom at their desks. The hallway students enter the classroom individually and classroom students record on their maps the path that each student takes in looking for the object. This is a fun way to begin to develop the space-to-paper relationship. Students might also look for similarities in searching patterns.

Sand table maps/environments. Commercially developed sand table maps can be purchased for use in a classroom. Some teachers instead use a small inflatable swimming pool with a small layer of sand. You can also create a sand table map using a sheet of plywood nailed to a rectangular frame of two-by-six-inch boards. The bottom should be lined with a heavy plastic drop cloth. Sand maps can be used in a variety of ways. Younger students can create villages using artificial houses. Older students can begin to explore city planning and topography. The sand allows you to easily rearrange. However, you might also experiment with a denser soil to enable students to create hills and valleys.

Global positioning satellites. There are a variety of websites that describe how global positioning satellites (GPS) or geographic information systems (GIS) software and websites might be included as part of map and globe activities. Websites for activities and lesson plans are in the GO THERE box on the next page.

TEACHERS IN ACTION: Using Oranges to Examine Globes and Maps

One fun activity is to peel an orange. Have students discuss the shape of the earth. Show a globe and discuss how it is a model of the earth. But could explorers carry around a globe? Have kids discuss this idea. What would be the problems with it? Too big, not detailed enough, etc. Someone will say something about maps. You can lead the discussion to how a map isn't a true model of the earth. The next part you can do as a whole group activity or you can work in small groups. Peel an orange and try to lay the peel out as one smooth sheet. I like to try out the oranges ahead of time and find one where the peel separates from the orange easily. A tangerine sometimes works better. Anyway, the point is for the kids to see that the curved skin just can't be made to lie in a flat sheet like a map. How did map makers solve this problem? Now you can discuss that and the kids can come up with their own ideas while you fill in the real ways maps are distorted to show land masses.

—Julianne

Author Refection: Teaching is an intellectual activity. That's what keeps it fresh and exciting. I have taught students in kindergarten through graduate school. By far, the most demanding is teaching kindergarten and 1st grade. Here you have to break things down so that a five- or six-year-old person with very little life experiences can understand. Then you have to find a meaningful activity to manipulate or reinforce concepts and skills. All of this has to be done knowing that young children have very short attention spans, they need a lot of movement in their learning, and their ability to imagine is much greater than their ability to reason. From a pedagogical point of view (pedagogy refers to teaching skills), it is a lot easier to teach college students. College students have a wealth of background knowledge and experience that can be applied to new information.

Using her teaching intelligence, Julianne made the relatively abstract concept of a map more concrete with her orange peel analogy. I like also how she introduced problem solving into this lesson (see Chapter 10) by asking her students to solve the problem of the map makers.

Every day, teachers like Julianne are coming up with unique and creative ways to help their students learn. This is why it is so important that teachers be able to experiment, try new ideas and creative solutions, and make decisions about how their students learn best and how they can best teach them.

What is your response to the case? How do your reactions compare with the author's reflection?

GO THERE

- Global positioning system overview: www.colorado.edu/geography/gcraft/notes/gps/gps_f.html
- Lesson plans using GPS: www.remc11.k12.mi.us/bcisd/classres/gis.htm#lessons
- A variety of teaching resources related to GPS: www.dcet.k12.de.us/instructional/teachingaids/allthingsGPS.html#device
- NASA's Earth Observing System: www.eospso.gsfc.nasa.gov/
- Digital Library for Earth System Education (DLESE): www.dlese.org
- Satellites & Education Conference: www.SatED.org
- ESRI for GIS software: www.esri.com
- The GLOBE Program: www.globe.gov
- Geographic information systems (GIS) website for teachers: www.gis.com/whatisgis/
- GIS in the classroom: www.tlc.umsl.edu/gis/
- GIS used in a middle school: www.mapcity.terc.edu
- Ideas for teaching geography: www.teachingideas.co.uk/geography/contents.htm
- National Council for Geographic Education: www.ncge.org/
- Education website for *National Geographic:* www.nationalgeographic.com/education/
- *National Geographic for Kids:* http://www.nationalgeographic.com/geobee/

NCSS STANDARDS

Thematic Standards

The following NCSS thematic standards are addressed in this chapter. See Appendix A for a full description of the relevant thematic standards.

Early Grades

I. Time, Continuity, and Change: a., b., c., d., e., f.

II. People, Places, and Environments: a., b., c., d., e., f., g.

   III. Individual Development and Identity: a., g.

   IV. Power, Authority, and Governance: a., b., c., d., e., f., h.

Middle Grades

    I. Time, Continuity, and Change: a., b., c., d., e., f.

   II. People, Places, and Environments: a., b., c., d., e., f., g.

   III. Individual Development and Identity: a., b.

   IV. Power, Authority, and Governance: a., b., c., e., f.

Pedagogical Standards

The following NCSS pedagogical standards are addressed in this chapter:

    I. Learning and Development.

   II. Differences in Learning Style.

   III. Critical Thinking, Problem Solving, and Performance Skills.

   IV. Active Learning and Motivation.

    V. Inquiry, Collaboration, and Supportive Classroom Interaction.

   VI. Planning Instruction.

Essential Skills for Social Studies

The following NCSS essential skills for social studies are addressed in this chapter:

    I. Acquiring Information.
      A. Reference and Information-search Skills.
         1. maps, globes, and graphics

   II. Organizing & Using Information.
      A. Thinking Skills.
         1. classify information
         2. interpret information
         3. analyze information
         4. summarize information
         5. synthesize information
         6. evaluate information

Chapter Review: Key Points

1. History is the study of humans and should be studied at all grades and levels.

2. Chronology skills are used to help students understand and describe time.

3. There are five themes that should be explored as part of geography education:
   - location,
   - place,
   - human interactions with environments,
   - movement, and
   - regions.

4. The purpose of geography education is to help students learn about the people and places on our planet.

5. Spatial skills involve teaching students how to use maps and globes.

6. Essential map reading skills include
   - directional orientation,
   - locating places on a map and globe,
   - expressing relative location,
   - using scale and computing distances,
   - using scale to estimate traveling time, and
   - interpreting map symbols.

7. You can help students learn about the globe by helping them conceptualize the earth as a round planet traveling through space, and through the use of satellite images found on the internet.

Making Connections

1. Describe the instances when you use a map.

2. Use scale to estimate the traveling time between two places. Use *Mapquest* on the Internet to check your accuracy.

3. Do one or more of the activities related to time.

4. In what ways do you see the three holistic learning ideas related to intrapersonal connections, interpersonal connections, and interconnectedness reflected here?

Chapter 4

TEACHING CIVICS AND GOVERNMENT, AND ECONOMICS

Thinking Ahead

1. What are three important rights and three important responsibilities of citizens living in our society?

2. What do you consider to be the main function of government?

3. What are three important concepts that primary students should know about economics? What are three important concepts that middle school students should know?

This chapter examines the teaching of civics and government, and of economics. Below are listed the NCSS teacher expectations in each of these content areas as well as ideas for teaching. This chapter ends with a description of global education, a newer area of social studies that incorporates a variety of disciplines and their global impact.

CITIZENSHIP EDUCATION: CIVICS AND GOVERNMENT

Citizenship education prepares students to be full participants in a democratic society and is usually broken into three parts: The first part is the process of government. Here students examine American democracy and how our form of government works. The second part is civic ideals and practices. Here students examine the rights and responsibilities involved in being a citizen within a democratic society. They also explore values, traits, and dispositions that will enable them to live in relationship with others and to live harmoniously within a community. The third part is world or global citizenship where students examine what it takes for individuals and governments to live peacefully and respectfully in a world community.

NCSS Teacher Expectations for Teachers of Civics and Government

Teachers of civics and government at all school levels should provide developmentally appropriate experiences as they guide learners in their study. They should

• assist learners in developing an understanding of civic life, politics, and government, so that the learners can explore the origins of governmental authority and recognize the need for government; identify the crucial functions of government, including laws and rules; evaluate rules and laws; differentiate between limited and unlimited government; and appreciate the importance of limitations on government power;

• guide learners as they explore American democracy, including the American idea of constitutional government, the impact of the distinctive characteristics of American society on our government, the nature of the American political culture, and the values and principles that are basic to American life and government;

• help learners understand how the government of the United States operates under the Constitution and the purposes, values, and principles of American democracy, including the ideas of distributed, shared, and limited powers of government; how the national, state, and local governments are organized; and the place of law in the system;

• enable learners to understand the relationship of the United States to other nations and to world affairs;

• assist learners in developing an understanding of citizenship and its rights and responsibilities, and in developing their abilities and dispositions to participate effectively in civic life;

• ensure that learners are made aware of the full range of opportunities to participate as citizens in the American democracy and of their responsibilities for doing so.

Citizenship education prepares students to be full participants in a democratic society and to be global citizens.

The Government Process

What is government? How does it work? How is it used to organize our lives? Why do you need government? How do citizens participate in government? What role does the government play in the allocation of resources? These are some organizing questions that can be used for the study of the process of government. The process of government looks at how our government functions. The U.S. Constitution is a good place to start here. Summarize it and put it in terms that are appropriate to the grade and developmental level of the students you teach. Studying this will lead naturally to the development of a school or classroom constitution. And just like the U.S. Constitution, school and class constitutions should be living, dynamic documents that change over time just as amendments change the U.S. Constitution over time.

> **GO THERE**
>
> U.S. Constitution online: http://www.usconstitution.net/const.html#Am1

The process of government can be studied informally and experienced in the early primary grades by providing students the opportunity to vote on various choices within the class such as preferred activities, treats, books, or games. In the intermediate grades a classroom council might be elected to make various decisions or organize functions within the classroom such as holiday parties or room decorations. In middle school students can experience a representative form of government by electing members to a student council. However, classroom or student councils must have some power to make changes, choices, or decisions if this is to be an effective learning experience. If classroom or student councils do not have the power to do anything, they become nothing more than a popularity contest. In classroom and student councils it is most effective if elections are held once a quarter or twice a semester.

Many of the NCSS student performance expectations for *Thematic Standards VI. Power, Authority, and Governance* described in Appendix A can be used as guides in organizing lessons, units, and activities related to the process of government.

Civic Ideals

What rights do all individuals have within our democracy? What principles do individuals within a democracy share and value? What responsibilities or obligations do individuals have within our democracy? What responsibilities or obligations do our society have to the individuals living within it? What practices are important in maintaining a well-functioning democracy? These are some of the organizing questions that can be used for the study of civic ideals and practices. Civic ideals and practices are the shared values, principles, and actions necessary to maintain a democratic society. The first ten amendments to the Constitution or the Bill of Rights can be the foundation of this part of citizenship education. This document describes the basic freedoms that are accorded all U.S. citizens, and just like the U.S. Constitution above, it should be put in terms that are appropriate to the grade and developmental level of your students.

> **EXAMPLE: Creating a Classroom Bill of Rights and Responsibilities**
>
> In order to make the Bill of Rights more salient, Ms. Dillon at Grantsburg Elementary School decided to have her 4th grade students develop a Bill of Rights and Responsibilities for their classroom. She first asked students to define what rights they thought they should have within their school and classroom. She listed their responses on the board. She then asked students what responsibilities they have as citizens and participants in the classroom community. These were also listed on the board.
>
> To simulate the operation of Congress, students elected six students to work in committee to put together a draft for a classroom Bill of Rights and Responsibilities based on

the ideas generated in class. After a week, the committee presented their draft version to the class. Students were able to discuss the parts of the Bill of Rights they liked and to suggest changes or additions. Eventually a vote was taken and the Bill of Rights was approved. Throughout the year, Ms. Dillon would revisit the Bill of Rights to see if there were any amendments that needed to be added. If there were, a committee was again elected and a similar process was used; however, to simulate the amendment process used with the U.S. Constitution, Ms. Dillon told her class that amendments needed a two-thirds vote in order to pass. (Like any classroom simulation, this was not meant to replicate the exact process used to amend the U.S. Constitution; rather, it was meant to give students a sense of the concepts and procedures used.)

Bill of Rights and Responsibilities for Room 112

Rights

1. Each person has the right to be treated with kindness in the classroom and on the playground.
2. Each person has the right to be heard and to share his or her ideas and opinions.
3. Each person has the right to feel safe in the classroom and on the playground.
4. Each person has the right to learn in the way that he or she learns best.

Responsibilities

1. Each person will do his or her best in school.
2. Each person will respect the rules and the rights of others.
3. Each person will treat others with courtesy and respect.
4. Each person will play fairly in gym class and on the playground.

GO THERE

Lesson plans, examples, ideas, and activities for a classroom constitution and a student bill of rights:

http://voyager.snc.edu/education/s2000middle/wq-projects/FF/Bill%200f%20Rights

http://www2.umatilla.k12.or.us/CBMS/WickstromD/page3.html

http://exchanges.state.gov/EDUCATION/ENGTEACHING/CIVIC/billrights.htm

http://ted.coe.wayne.edu/sse/lesson/clcnst.htm

Societal Ideals

Encompassed in the study of civic ideals are both societal ideals and individual ideals (see Figure 4.1). Societal ideals are the principles held by a society that enable it to protect and nurture the individuals within it. The laws, regulations, educational systems, and functioning of government within the society should reflect these principles. Some societal ideals that could be identified and discussed as part of citizenship education include the following:

Life, liberty, and the pursuit of happiness. In writing the Declaration of Independence, Thomas Jefferson is attributed with writing the following: "We hold these truths to be self evident: that all men [sic] are created equal; that they are endowed by their Creator with certain unalienable Rights; that among these are Life, Liberty, and the pursuit of Happiness." All human life is of value, and all humans have the right to do what they want to do within the limitations of the law.

Activities or discussions here would have students identify the things that make them or other people happy, and then describe the opportunities they have to do those things. Also, within a school or classroom these concepts can be subtly reinforced by providing students with opportunities to make choices. In early primary grades students can be reminded of their right to play whatever they want to play on the playground (within a set of rules). Nobody tells them what they have to play. This is reinforced also by allowing choices within the classroom such as reading materials, books, topics of study, independent programs, and activities in learning centers. In intermediate and middle school grades this can be reinforced by allowing the most choice possible within a given structure. Remember that choice does not mean total choice all the time; rather, it most often means having a set of choices in given instances. In these grades choice might consist of classes to take, activities to demonstrate their learning, study hall times, learning activities, and seating arrangements, as well as those described already.

Justice. Justice is different from revenge. Justice says that there are logical consequences for breaking the law or denying others their rights. These consequences apply to all, regardless of their race, cultural, religion, level of education, or social economic status. In schools and classrooms this concept is reinforced by developing a set of rules and identifying some of the

Figure 4.1   Civic Ideals

Societal Ideals	Individual Ideals
1. life, liberty, and the pursuit of happiness	1. individual responsibility
2. justice	2. civility
3. the common good	3. following the law
4. equality	4. participation
5. celebration of diversity	

logical consequences for breaking the rules. The comparison can then be made to the laws and logical consequences that occur in society.

The common good. Our laws, government, business transactions, actions, allocation of resources, and educational systems should be based on what is the most good for the most people, instead of what benefits a few rich, powerful, or influential entities. Here students can identify the rules, structure, and allocation of resources in a school or classroom that help all do their best and are of most benefit for the most students. The comparisons can then be made to society and the world. Other organizing questions include: What laws or action can be identified in which only a few seem to benefit? What laws or structures are in place to address the needs and interests of the less powerful? What are instances that can be found where only a few seem to benefit at the expense of the many?

Equality. All humans are of equal value and worth regardless of their age, social economic status, religion, race, culture, political views, gender, or sexual orientation (see Chapter 2). All should have equal opportunities within a democratic society. Each human is a valued entity. In schools and society, some people such as presidents and principals may have more influence than others, however none of them is of greater worth than another. Every human being, by virtue of being a human being, is accorded certain dignity. The preamble to the *Universal Declaration of Human Rights* put forth by the United Nations opens with the following statement: "Whereas recognition of the inherent dignity and the equal and inalienable rights of all members of the human family is the foundation of freedom, justice, and peace in the world . . . "Each of these words should be unpacked for students. For example: What does *inherent* mean? What is *dignity?* What does *inalienable* mean? In what way are you all members of the human family?

The study of history is ripe with examples of certain groups declaring other groups to be inferior. These examples include religious conflicts, the destruction of indigenous cultures, slavery, economic oppression, gender inequity, the exploitation of labor, and others. In looking at the amendments to the Constitution, it was only in 1920 that the 14th amendment was passed giving women the right to vote, and it was only in 1964 that the Civil Rights Act was passed. Sadly, studying current events will also provide many examples of conflicts based on perceived inequality that occur today.

Celebration of diversity. We do not simply tolerate those who differ from us. We celebrate these differences. These differences lead to multiple perspectives, which in turn, strengthen our society. This celebration can be manifest in schools or classrooms by studying other cultures, religions, political systems, and histories. When studying these new areas look to identify the universal truths, common components, and positive elements of each.

Freedom of expression. All humans have a right to their opinions, regardless of whether you agree or disagree. All should be allowed to express their views and engage in our societal conversations. In looking at the issue of freedom of speech, students need practice in having and sharing opinions. In class, teachers should often stop and ask, "What do you think?" And then listen quietly without qualifying or commenting on student responses. The activity *Support a Statement* works well here. Here students describe their opinions related to something occurring

Figure 4.2   Support-a-Statement

Statement	Supporting Information
"We should recycle the unused food at lunch."	1. Responsible use of resources. 2. Could be fed to pigs and other animals. 3. Could be used as compost. 4. Won't cost the school any money. 5. Helps develop environmental awareness. 6. Student helpers could be used.

nationally, locally, or within the school or class. They then list ideas to support their opinions (see Figure 4.2). This is also good practice for writing paragraphs (topic sentence and supporting ideas), and can be used to write opinion pieces to be shared orally or in written form.

In the primary grades the *support-a-statement* visual organizer in Figure 4.2 can be used with the whole class. Here the teacher would elicit supporting statements from the class and record them on the board or on a large sheet of butcher paper. It can also be used at intermediate and middle school levels to analyze opinion pieces or newspaper editorials. Students identify the writer's essential view or opinion (statement); then, they look for facts within the editorial that support that view (supporting information).

Freedom of expression can be reinforced informally by having discussions in which students may have differing points of view. However, make sure these interactions are much different from what often passes for a discussion on television news programs. These discussions often become debates in which people cut each other off, talk over other people, or try to monopolize the conversation by not letting others in. They are not respectful and serve only to polarize and entrench participants and listeners.

Rule of law. Laws are of value in organizing and maintaining our society. Without laws there would be chaos and the vulnerable in our society would not be protected. This societal ideal can be reinforced by identifying and examining the rules within a school and classroom. What would life be like if there were not certain rules or without any rules? These ideas can then be expanded to the societal level as well. What would happen if people could do whatever they wanted without any consequence? How would our school or community be different? Which laws or rules do you think are important? Which laws or rules do you think should be changed? What laws or rules should be added? These kinds of questions will naturally lead to a study of laws and legislation and how each are made.

Individual Ideas

Individual ideals are the principles held by those living within a democracy that enable them to give to society and live harmoniously with others. Some individual ideals that could be identified and discussed as part of citizenship education include the following:

Individual responsibility. Each person takes responsibility for working or contributing to society to the best of his or her ability. This may be by taking care of and raising a family or by working to support themselves and those for whom they are responsible. Individual responsibility asks you to be responsible for your own actions and, to the best of your ability, for your own welfare.

Civility. You treat others respectfully and respond courteously. You realize that people of good will often have differing opinions on important issues. While you may not always agree with others' opinions, lifestyles, or choices, you respect their right to live, think, and express themselves as they see fit.

Following the law. While you may not agree with all laws, you realize there would be chaos without them. Citizens are thus obligated to do their best to follow the letter and the spirit of our laws. Also, as our representatives used to help enforce these laws, police officers are respected.

Participation. A democratic society is based on the concept of participation. Citizens participate by voting, jury duty, and staying informed on local, national, and world events. Participation also asks individuals to take action when they do not agree with a policy. This can be done through writing letters or editorials or through public protests. A good citizen is not necessarily one who passively agrees with all aspects of government; rather, it is one who actively engages in the formation of new laws and in the constant evolution of society.

Many of the NCSS student performance expectations for *Thematic Standards X. Ideals, Principles, and Practices of Citizenship* described in Appendix A can be used as guides in organizing lessons, units, and activities related to civic ideals and practices.

HOW DO I? Explain Political Perspectives

There seems to be an increase in partisanship and acrimony in politics recently. Negative attacks, name-calling, labels, and mischaracterization seem to have taken the place of political discourse. Instead of on facts, positions, and ideas, political choices are made based on how bad the other side can be made to look. If one has a differing view, often the first response is to attack his or her patriotism, credibility, or motives. A strong case can be made that this leads to a weakening of our democratic system as it creates a misinformed and under-informed public.

So what are the basic political perspectives in American politics and how do you explain these perspectives to your students in a way that leads to understanding? And how do you do this in an objective way? Below is an admittedly simplistic explanation of two basic political perspectives. However, this information will help middle school students understand current events and ultimately become better decision makers about the policies that will affect their lives.

(Continued)

(Continued)

Common Goals

There are two major political parties and perspectives: Democrats, who tend to have what is called a liberal perspective, and Republicans, who tend to have a more conservative perspective. Even though they have differing perspectives, it helps to find similarities or common goals with which most people from both perspectives and parties could agree. For example, most people from both perspectives would say that we all want

- safety and security,
- the ability to feed and provide for ourselves and our families,
- the ability to raise our children according to the values we feel are important,
- employment opportunities for all,
- the ability to pursue our dreams,
- to be rewarded for our hard work and effort,
- good health care,
- good public education,
- freedom to pursue our religious ideas,
- justice for all,
- equality and egalitarianism,
- the ability to make informed decisions,
- support and care for the aged and less able.

The differences in political perspectives lie in how we reach these common goals. These differences tend to be on three major dimensions: (a) economic issues, (b) issues related to government regulation and interference, and (c) social issues. But none of these is an either/or proposition; rather, the differences are a matter of degree and vary with individual issues in each of these areas. There are extremist positions at both ends of the spectrum; however, for all labeling, most people are usually on varying places in the middle of these continuums. If a scale were created with an extreme liberal perspective of 0 and an extreme conservative perspective of 100, most people would most likely find themselves in the 40th to the 60th percentile on most issues.

Economic Issues

In general, a liberal economic perspective would say that our government, energies, and resources should be invested in people as a way of reaching our common goals and building a strong, worker-centered economy. Various forms of welfare and assistance should be given on the personal level as a means of helping people to better themselves and thereby contribute to a strong economy. It is thought that the economic gains of working class people will trickle outward and upward for continued economic growth. A controlled form of capitalism where you are rewarded for your hard work, creativity, and ingenuity is seen as the ideal. Government regulations are put in place so that the wealthy and more powerful do not take advantage of the poor or less powerful.

In general, a conservative economic perspective would say that our government, energies and resources should be invested in business as a way of reaching our common goals and building a stronger business-centered economy. Various forms of welfare and assistance should be given on the corporate level as a means of helping corporations better themselves and thereby contribute to a strong economy. It is thought that the economic gains of business will trickle down to all people. Unfettered capitalism where you are rewarded economically for your hard work, creativity, and ingenuity is seen as the ideal. The free market system is seen as providing an adequate system of checks and balances; thus, little or no government regulation is needed.

Government Regulation and Interference

A liberal perspective would support the need to have government intervention in regard to regulating businesses, corporations, and some other aspects of our society so that the strong do not dominate or exploit the weak. Government regulation would also be necessary to protect health, safety, fair labor practices, civil rights, and the environment. Also, taxes are seen as a means of contributing to the greater good and fairly distributing resources. The view here is that people are basically good and the government has a responsibility to take care of all its citizens. The preference here is for a larger federal government with oversight at the state and local level.

A conservative perspective would say that there should be little or no government intervention or regulation of businesses, corporations, and other aspects of society. This would favor economic prosperity as a means to contribute to the greater good. The view here is that the government should stay out of people's affairs and not force the more productive citizens to subsidize the less productive citizens. The preference here is for a smaller federal government and more control at the state and local level.

Social Issues

A liberal perspective generally supports a secular view in which the separation between church and state is clearly delineated and maintained. More liberals than conservatives are pro choice and against the death penalty, prayer in schools, and a flag burning amendment. Also, more liberals than conservatives support gay marriage, family leave, stronger environmental regulations, affirmative action, and the regulation of handguns.

In the United States, people with a conservative perspective tend to give priority to tradition and religion. More conservatives than liberals are pro life and against gay marriage, affirmative action, and the regulation of handguns. Also, more conservatives than liberals support a flag burning amendment, prayer in schools, and the death penalty.

The Danger of Labels

As you can see, there is danger in relying on labels for easy categorizing as they tend to keep people from true understanding of issues and of other people. There are no such things as liberals and conservatives operating in a monolithic block; rather there are people with liberal and conservative perspectives who use these perspectives to make decisions about the society in which they live. And regardless of your overall political perspective, people tend to have varying views on each of these issues in each of the three dimensions above.

Global Education: World Citizenship

With increasing technological advances and the ever increasing interconnectedness of world economies, you can no longer think of yourself only as citizens existing within a particular country. Rather, you are a citizen of the world with certain rights and responsibilities as nations and citizens within those nations. "A world citizen is an individual who accepts global responsibilities or expands his or her social consciousness to include the people of other countries" (Strain, 1999).

Teaching for world citizenship, sometimes called *global education,* involves helping students develop a sense of themselves as human beings living in community and sharing the planet with others. On the most basic level, bring current events, issues, and concerns from around the world into your classroom. You can also help your students connect social studies and other curriculum areas with people and events from around the world. On the more complex level, teach for world citizenship by creating activities that invite your students to act and interact with others from around the world or to become a part of organizations and activities that are working on global issues. You can also build an integrated unit based specifically around current issues and events from around the world. Some of the current global issues for citizenship education are the following:

- AIDS crisis in Africa and other parts of the world
- Diseases and other health issues
- Hunger and starvation
- Wars, violence, and terrorism
- Labor migration
- Land mines
- Economic and cultural exploitation
- Diminishing oil, gas, and other nonrenewable energy resources
- Workers' rights and wages
- Women's rights
- Global warming
- Pollution and global warming
- Human rights
- Rain forest and exploitation of natural resources
- The diminishing ozone layer

Global education is a discipline in which all discipline areas merge into a larger worldview. From here the world is perceived as a whole entity or a complete system, not as a series of separate and competing parts. And just like in any system, damage to one part affects all. This reflects the holistic education principle of interconnectedness.

GO THERE

Information, activities, and lesson plans for world citizenship or global education:

http://www.education-world.com/a_curr/curr008.shtml

http://www.citizenship-global.org.uk/primary.html

http://www.peacecorps.gov/wws/educators/lessons.html

http://www.globaled.org/

http://www.gsn.org/

http://www.globaleduc.org/index.shtml

http://www.gng.org/home.html

On December 10, 1948, the General Assembly of the United Nations adopted and proclaimed the *Universal Declaration of Human Rights.* This document can be referred to in the early grades, however, because of developmental levels; formal study should begin in intermediate and middle school grades.

GO THERE

- Universal Declaration of Human Rights: www.udhr.org/
- UN Universal Declaration of Human Rights: www.hrw.org/universal.html
- Association of World Citizenship: www.worldcitizens.org/
- Intercultural E-mail Classroom Connections: www.iecc.org/
- Middle Educators Global Activities: www.ncsu.edu/mega/

Global education helps students develop a sense of themselves as human beings living in a global community and sharing the planet with others.

TEACHING ECONOMICS

Economics is a study of the way in which goods and services are produced, distributed, and consumed. Studying economics should help us understand how things such as supply and demand, materials, resources, and free market competition affect our lives. Economics also serves to illustrate the principle of interconnectedness in that goods and services are not created in a vacuum. That is, other people and systems are needed to provide the material resources, distribution, and the markets for these goods and services.

The NCSS teacher expectations and the important economic terms and concepts in Figure 4.3 provide a good context for beginning to think how economics could be taught in the primary, intermediate, and middle school grades. In the primary grades, students should learn about money, work and compensation, factories and the production of goods, services, profit, wants, needs, and supply and demand. These concepts should all be expanded in the intermediate and middle school grades and should include an examination of the three major economic ideas: capitalism, socialism, and communism.

NCSS Teacher Expectations for Teachers of Economics

Teachers of economics at all school levels should provide developmentally appropriate experiences as they guide learners in their study. They should assist learners in acquiring an understanding of the following principles:

- Productive resources are limited. Therefore, people cannot have all the goods and services that they want; as a result, they must choose some things and give up others.

- Effective decision making requires comparing the additional costs of alternatives with the additional benefits. Most choices involve doing a little more or a little less of something; few choices are all-or-nothing decisions.

- Different methods can be used to allocate goods and services. People, acting individually or collectively through government, must choose which methods to use to allocate different kinds of goods and services.

- People respond predictably to positive and negative incentives.

- Voluntary exchange occurs only when all parties expect to gain. This is true for trade among individuals or organizations within a nation, or among individuals or organizations in different nations.

- When individuals, regions, and nations specialize in what they can produce at the lowest cost and then trade with others, both production and consumption increase.

- Markets exist when buyers and sellers interact. This interaction determines market prices and thereby allocates scarce goods and services.

- Prices send signals and provide incentives to buyers and sellers. When supply and demand change, market prices adjust, affecting incentives.

- Competition among sellers lowers costs and prices, encouraging producers to produce more of what consumers are willing and able to buy. Competition among buyers

---

increases prices and allocates goods and services to those people who are willing and able to pay the most for them.

• Institutions evolve in market economies to help individuals and groups accomplish their goals. Banks, labor unions, corporations, legal systems, and not-for-profit organizations are examples of important institutions. A different kind of institution, clearly defined and enforced property rights, is essential to a market economy.

• Money makes it easier to trade, borrow, save, invest, and compare the value of goods and services.

• Interest rates, adjusted for inflation, rise and fall to balance the amount saved with the amount borrowed, thus affecting the allocation of scarce resources between present and future users.

• Income for most people is determined by the market value of the productive resources they sell. What workers earn depends, primarily, on the market value of what they produce and how productive they are.

• Entrepreneurs are people who take the risks of organizing productive resources to make goods and services. Profit is an important incentive that leads entrepreneurs to accept the risks of business failure.

• Investment in factories, machinery, and new technology, and in the health, education, and training of people can raise future standards of living.

• There is an economic role for government to play in a market economy whenever the benefits of a government policy outweigh its costs. Governments often provide for national defense, address environmental concerns, define and protect property rights, and attempt to make markets more competitive. Most government policies also redistribute income.

• Costs of government policies sometimes exceed benefits. This may occur because of incentives facing voters, government officials, and government employees; because of actions by special interest groups that can impose costs on the general public; or because social goals other than economic efficiency are being pursued.

• A nation's overall levels of income, employment, and prices are determined by the interaction of spending and production decisions made by all households, firms, government agencies, and others in the economy.

• Unemployment imposes costs on individuals and nations. Unexpected inflation imposes costs on many people and benefits some others because it arbitrarily redistributes purchasing power. Inflation can reduce the rate of growth of national living standards because individuals and organizations use resources to protect themselves against the uncertainty of future prices.

• Federal government budgetary policy and the Federal Reserve System's monetary policy influence the overall levels of employment, output, and prices in the United States.

Activities for Economics

There are a wealth of lesson plans and teaching ideas to be found on the Internet. Visit the websites in the next GO THERE box, or do an Internet search using the terms *economics,*

Figure 4.3   Important Terms and Concepts for Studying Economics

Capital. Materials and equipment used to make and distribute goods and services; and the money used to buy equipment and materials.

Capital formation. Gather or combing economic resources in order to build up industrial capacity.

Capitalism. The economic system where the means of producing goods and services are privately owned.

Communism. A form of socialism where the government determines what will be produced, how much, and where people will work.

Consumer. The person who buys goods and services.

Demand. The amount of a good or service that people are willing to buy.

Depression. A serious recession.

Economics. A study of how the economic system works.

Economic resources. The materials and work that go into producing things of value.

Economics systems. The way in which goods and services are produced, distributed, and consumed.

Entrepreneurs. People who risk their time and money to start and run a new business.

Expense. The cost of producing a good or services.

Free enterprise. A form of capitalism in which people are free to set prices. Supply and demand usually determine prices here.

Free market. A market in which buyers and sellers are free to exchange goods and services when they want to for the price that they determine.

Human resources. The labor of people.

Labor. The work that people do in organizing and shaping material resources into goods and services.

Market. The supply and demand for goods and services.

Material resources. All the material things used to create goods and services.

Monopoly. A market in which one seller controls the supply of a good or service.

Productivity. The measure of output of goods and services that workers or factories produce.

Profit. New money or wealth. The money left over when the cost of producing goods or services has been paid.

Recession. A fall in the demand in many markets with an accompanying fall in prices, products, and employment.

Socialism. An economic system in which the means of producing some or many of goods and services are owned or controlled by the government.

Supply. The amount of goods or services that businesses have for sale.

lessons, and *plans.* Below are described some of the types of economics lessons and activities you might use:

Simulated economy. Create a simulated token economy within a classroom or at your grade level. Use tokens to represent money. Create products and services which students are paid for or can purchase. This activity can be done on a very basic level in 1st or 2nd grade or be made very complex for use in the middle grades.

Birth of a product. Study the birth and life of a product, from materials, to production, to the shelf in the grocery store. For example, take a product like catsup. Find a company that produces it. Use a map to show where the factory is that produces it. Find out where the tomatoes and other ingredients come from and how they are delivered to the factory.

Economics in literature. Look for economic terms and concepts within stories or picture books. For example, find examples of a potential market, a demand for a particular product, investors, advertising, and materials for a product.

Economics in history and current events. As you study current events or history, look for economic terms and concepts.

Exploring jobs. Examine different occupations. Look to see how each contributes to the economy. Look also for goods and services that have a need for that occupation, thus exploring the concept of economic interdependence.

Personal finances. Give students a simulated monthly budget. Individually or in small groups, have them allocate how they would spend that money. Use advertisements or the Internet to get the exact costs of things such as rent, products, and services.

Simulated banking. Create a simulated economy where groups have to borrow money for start-up costs in order to create a factory or a business. Explore the concepts of borrowing, interest, investment costs, capital, resources (human, material, and capital), profits, supply, demand, market, and advertising.

Simulated spending. As part of a creative writing activity, have students list what they would buy if they had $10, $100, $1,000, $10,000, $100,000, or $1,000,000. As a follow-up, have students find the price of the items and make sure they do not go over their spending limit. For primary age students, do not go over $100.

Imaginary business. Have students identify a business that they would like to run. As part of an inquiry project, put them in small groups and ask them to identify start-up costs, materials necessary, human resources needed, and advertising budget.

Inquiry surveys. Have students create and conduct surveys to find out the demand for certain products or service. Use this information to design a product or service. Create imaginary advertising campaigns based on this information.

Analyze advertisements. Look for ads on TV and in magazines and newspapers. Identify who the target market audience might be and what persuasive arguments the advertisers are using to sell the product or service.

Advertising campaign. Given a product or a service, have students identify a particular market audience that might be most likely to use it, and then design an advertising campaign to sell that product.

CASE STUDY: Teaching Economics by Creating Mini-Societies

I did mini-society with my fourth graders last year, and Thunderville was the name of our society. I have my students again this year for fifth grade, and we are going to do it again this year. In fourth grade, we started a unit on economics—scarcity, opportunity cost, resources (natural, human, capital), bartering, money, etc. After that we worked on other mini-society components as they seemed to fit in throughout the year. For example when we were studying National and State symbols we designed and selected our Flag. We had to develop our currency and choose civil service employees. We did a market survey in Math and graphed the results to help decide which products would sell at what price—supply and demand. We created a product and wrote advertisements in language arts, when studying persuasive writing. We developed the idea of production, specialization, and education by doing an activity called "Cup Companies." We built up slowly to actual business sessions. It was a wonderful experience, and we only had three business sessions before the end of our school year. During the last session we joined with two other classes in our school cafeteria for an "International Day of Trade" among three societies. We had decided that our three units of currency were on par after we had a special speaker, who was just back from Australia, Europe, etc. and who showed us some examples of money from foreign countries.

Now, I am looking forward to delving deeper into the concepts, decision making techniques, and problem solving strategies. My students voted to keep the same name—Thunderville—the same flag, and the same currency for 5th grade which will be a huge time saver. I am anticipating a business session once every month. Students will create their products and/or prepare their services at home and bring them in the day of our business sessions. Good luck in your work!

—Anonymous, Fourth Grade

Author Reflection: John Dewey said that learning is most powerful when the line between the school world and the real world becomes blurred. That is, if we can make the things that happen in the classroom like things that occur in students' world, learning is more meaningful and more powerful. Students learn and remember more and are better able to transfer knowledge and skills to real-life situations. Simulations such as the one above serve this purpose and also get students actively involved in their learning. Think how much more powerful this is than simply reading a chapter in a textbook or doing a worksheet. Look also how this teacher was able to integrate a variety of subject areas into this study of economics.

As teachers, we are limited only by our ability to imagine and create.

What is your response to the case? How do your reactions compare with the author's reflection?

GO THERE

- Curriculum, programs, teacher resources, and contact information related to civics and government: www.civiced.org
- Lesson plans, hot topics, and a teachers' forum related to economics:
  - www.fte.org
  - www.proteacher.com/090041.shtml
  - www.mcrel.org/lesson-plans/economics/index.asp
  - www.fte.org/teachers/lessons/lessons.htm
  - www.econedlink.org/lessons
  - www.teach-nology.com/teachers/lesson_plans/economics
  - www.cob.jmu.edu/econed/Elementary.htm

NCSS STANDARDS

Thematic Standards

The following NCSS thematic standards are addressed in this chapter. See Appendix A for a full description of the relevant thematic standards.

Early Grades

I. Power, Authority, and Governance: a., b., c., d., e., f., h.

II. Production, Distribution, and Consumption: a., b., c., d., e., f., g., h., i., j.

III. Global Connections: a., b., d., e., f.

IV. Civic Ideals and Practices: a., b., c., d., e., h., j.

Middle Grades

I. Power, Authority, and Governance: a., b., c., e., f.

II Production, Distribution, and Consumption: a., b., c., d., e., f., g., h., i., j.

III. Civic Ideals and Practices: a., b., c., d., e., h., j.

IV. Global Connections: a., b., d., e., f., g., e.

Pedagogical Standards

The following NCSS pedagogical standards are addressed in this chapter:

I. Learning and Development.

II. Differences in Learning Style.

III. Critical Thinking, Problem Solving, and Performance Skills.

IV. Active Learning and Motivation.

V. Inquiry, Collaboration, and Supportive Classroom Interaction.

VI. Planning Instruction.

Essential Skills for Social Studies

The following NCSS essential skills for social studies are addressed in this chapter:

I. Acquiring Information.
   A. Reference & Information-Search Skills.
      1. maps, globes, and graphics

II. Organizing and Using Information.
   A. Thinking Skills.
      1. classify information
      2. interpret information
      3. analyze information
      4. summarize information
      5. synthesize information
      6. evaluate information

III. Relationships & Social Participation
   A. Personal Skills.
   B. Group Interaction Skills.
   C. Social and Political Participation.

Chapter Review: Key Points

1. Citizenship education helps students participate in a democratic society, and is composed of three parts: the process of government, civic ideals and practice, and world citizenship or global education.

2. Studying the process of government invites students to examine how our government operates.

3. Both societal ideals and individual ideas are involved in the study of civic ideals.

4. Global education examines the global connections and interconnection of our individual lives in all areas.

5. Economics is a study of the way in which goods and services are produced, distributed, and consumed.

Making Connections

1. Rank the societal ideals in what you consider to be the order of importance. Make a case for why you placed the top and bottom ideals in their relative positions.

2. In your lives, what values and personal traits do you see as important in enabling you to get along with others?

3. List eight things you would include in a bill of rights for humans living in our society. List eight things you would include in a bill of responsibilities for humans living in our society.

4. How would you explain capitalism, socialism, and communism so that a 6th grade student might understand and be able to make personal connections?

5. Do an Internet search using the terms: *civics, lesson,* and *plans.* Find interesting or important lesson plans that can be used with primary, intermediate, and middle school students.

6. Do an Internet search using the terms: *economic, lesson,* and *plans.* Find interesting or important lesson plans that can be used with primary, intermediate, and middle school students.

7. In what ways do you see the three holistic learning ideas related to intrapersonal connections, interpersonal connections, and interconnectedness reflected here?

Chapter 5

PLANNING

1. What do you associate with lesson planning?

2. What do you see as the need for lesson plans?

3. Some teachers insist on behavioral lesson plan objectives while others prefer objectives that contain a general description of what will be learned or covered in the lesson. Which would you prefer and why?

4. What do you know about multiple intelligence theory and how do you envision using it in a social studies context?

PLANNING A LEARNING EXPERIENCE

Good lessons and effective learning experiences do not magically appear. They must be planned. This chapter describes how to design and plan effective learning experiences. Included are suggestions for (a) planning individual lessons, (b) planning units, and (c) designing an integrated study.

Lesson planning is important for three reasons:

Thoughtful planning creates more purposeful instruction. Lesson planning is what links the curriculum to the particulars of instruction (Clark & Dunn, 1991). Thoughtful planning also helps you understand the content of the lesson, creates a logical sequence of instructional events (Freiberg & Driscoll, 1992), and links activities to instructional objectives.

Thoughtful planning enhances learning. Well-designed lessons increase time on-task (Stringfield & Teddlie, 1991), and help students perceive the structure of new information so they can more easily assimilate it (Walberg, 1991). Lesson design also affects classroom management by reducing chaos, guiding the flow of events, and keeping students interested and engaged (Freiberg & Driscoll, 1992).

Thoughtful planning enhances teachers' effectiveness. Planning enables you to incorporate new instructional strategies and use more complex learning activities (Freiberg & Driscoll, 1992), and helps you to feel more confident during instruction (Clark & Peterson, 1986).

Lesson Plans

Lesson planning is a complex endeavor in which you solve a myriad of problems: What is the goal? What are the specific objectives? Why is this worth teaching? What exactly should students know or be able to do? How can information be organized so that students can understand? What questions should be asked for discussion? How much information should be covered? What kind of activity would help students learn? How can I get students to be actively involved? How will we know if learning took place?

The purpose of the lesson plan is to organize your thinking as you put the lesson together, and to guide your thinking during implementation. Lesson plans should be descriptive and sequential with all questions listed and activities clearly explained. The rule of thumb is that a substitute teacher should be able to pick up the lesson plan and know exactly what to do. While there are a variety of styles and formats for individual lesson plans (state and local mandates may differ), most lesson plans contain some or all of the following elements: goal, objectives, input or background information, procedures, activity, closure/review, and assessment. However, not all these elements are found in every lesson, and sometimes elements are combined.

Goal. In planning a lesson, the goal is a statement that describes the general purpose of the lesson or lessons. This is where the planning process begins. Everything that follows should support the goal. One goal may serve as the basis for several lessons. Goals are often developed by the school district or the particular curriculum. A goal for one or more lessons might also be an NCSS thematic or disciplinary standard. Some examples of lesson plan goals are listed in Figure 5.1. Each of these is taken from the NCSS thematic standards and can serve as the basis for one or more lessons.

Figure 5.1   Lesson Plan Goals

- Students will explore and describe similarities and differences in the ways groups, societies, and cultures address similar human needs and concerns.
- Students will estimate distance and calculate scale.
- Students will explain the purpose of governance.

Objectives. Objectives are specific descriptions of what students will learn or be able to do as a result of their exposure to instruction. While goals are global descriptions of what is to be learned, objectives are specific descriptions that support the goal. Some prefer to use behavioral lesson plan objectives (Figure 5.2). From the perspective of behavioral psychology, learning is a change in behavior that occurs as a result of instruction. By describing lesson plan objectives in terms of a particular behavior that you want students to demonstrate, you are able to focus your planning and instruction to make that behavior appear.

Figure 5.2   Behavioral Lesson Plan Objectives

- Students will create a Venn diagram to illustrate similarities and differences between Hmong cultures and their own culture.
- Students will use a map and scale of Blue Earth County to calculate distances between towns.
- Students will demonstrate their knowledge of local government by successfully completing the government worksheet.

Some prefer to describe lesson plan objectives in terms of what they want students to learn (Figure 5.3). From a cognitive-constructivist perspective, learning takes place within each learner's head and cannot be standardized or observed directly. Describing your objectives in terms of general content or skills allows you to create a general focus for the lesson; however, learning is cyclical and students need to be exposed to topics and skills many times at successively higher levels. By not specifically defining exactly what the learning experience *must* be, you allow for what *might* be. That is, you allow for more open-ended learning opportunities. The type of objective you ultimately use is a matter of preference and philosophical orientation. Both types of lesson plan objectives can be used effectively.

Figure 5.3   Cognitive-Constructivist Lesson Plan Objectives

- Students will learn about Hmong cultures.
- Students will learn how to use a map and scale to calculate distances between towns.
- Student will learn about the local government: mayor, village board, city officials, and elections.

Input or background information. In this part of the lesson plan, you organize and describe the specific information that students need in order to meet lesson objectives and to support the goal of the lesson. Some teachers like to use list or outline form to organize this information; others prefer narrative or paragraph form. This also is a matter of personal preference. The questions you want to include for classroom discussion should be recorded here. (See Chapter 13 for specific information on creating questions for classroom discussion.)

Activities. Activities are used to manipulate ideas or information found in the input section of the lesson plan and to get students actively involved in their learning. Older students may be able to use more abstract activities, but younger students need to physically manipulate or interact with the input in some fashion. Examples of possible activities include: creative writing, drawing, simulation, discussion, problem solving, drama, songs, graphing, worksheets, dance or creative movement, games, experiments, inquiry, homework assignments, or thinking skills.

Procedures. The procedures list the exact sequence of events that will occur in the lesson. This lesson plan element sometimes merges with the activities.

Closure/review. The ending of a lesson varies depending on the type of lesson. Many end with a short review of the main ideas covered in the lesson and sometimes a preview of the next day's lesson. Examples of closure/review activities include group processing, journal entries, "I learned" statements, or orally sharing one or two interesting ideas with a classmate.

Assessment. Through assessment you determine whether or not you and your students have met lesson objectives. Assessment can range from formal tests, worksheets, or homework assignments (see Chapter 6), to informal questions, discussions, classroom activities, or observations.

HOW DO I? Use Standards to Develop Lesson Plans

Individual standards (NCSS or disciplinary) are usually found within larger themes or units at particular grade levels. To use a standard to create a lesson plan, first examine it to see exactly what it calls for and how it fits in with the interests and abilities of your students and with your larger curriculum. Next, research to get the necessary background information in order to fully understand and teach the standard. For example, *Thematic Standard VI. Power, Authority, and Governance* for early grades has the following performance expectation: "Students will explain the purpose of government." You would need to get background information related to the purpose of government: local, state, and federal. Next, create an outline that identifies the major ideas, concepts, and skills you want students to learn. Then, organize the outline into individual lessons and find activities to enhance, extend, or expand upon lesson content. Finally, when you are ready to plan individual lessons, determine the lesson objective and select the appropriate activities to manipulate the lesson input and enhance content.

Effective lessons require planning and careful preparation.

EXAMPLE: Using Thematic Standards Across the Curriculum

The disciplinary standards described in Chapter 2 are fairly specific and generally apply only to a defined social studies discipline. The NCSS thematic standards describe themes or big ideas that are an integral part of social studies education and can be addressed across the curriculum.

Thematic Standard IV. Individual Development & Identity has the following performance expectation for the middle grades: "Students will analyze a particular event to identify reasons individuals might respond to it in different ways."

This standard could be addressed within a reading or literature class by first identifying an interesting or important event in a story. You would then teach students how to use an *infer-o-gram* (see Figure 5.5 later in this chapter), to determine possible responses or interpretations of this event by two or more characters.

This same standard could be reinforced in studying current events. Here you would have students examine America's invasion of Iraq and again use an infer-o-gram to determine the possible response or interpretation of this from the perspective of any or all of the following: a Iraqi citizen living in Baghdad, an American army general, an Iraqi army general, a Shia religious leader, an American soldier.

This standard could be addressed in studying history by examining an event such as Columbus's landing on North America from the perspective of Columbus, his sailors, the Native Americans, and Queen Isabella of Spain. You could have students write short plays or use creative dramatics (Chapter 7) to bring each perspective to life.

Finally, this standard could be used in character education studies. Here you would ask students to examine an event from their lives from the perspective of each person involved. You could also use some of the conflict resolution strategies described in Chapter 9 that invite students to look at a conflict from the perspective of the other.

Sample Lesson Plans

Following are some examples of lesson plans. They provide a quick illustration of the various lesson plan parts.

GO THERE

Many excellent lesson plans in all content areas are available online. The following websites contain hundreds of sample lesson plans in every subject area:

Lesson Plans Page: http://www.lessonplanspage.com

School Discovery: http://school.discovery.com/lessonplans/

Ed Helper: http://www.edhelper.com/

Teachers Net: http://teachers.net/lessons/

Lesson Planz: http://lessonplanz.com/

Teach Net: http://www.teachnet.com/

Educators Reference Desk (formerly *Ask ERIC*): www.eduref.org

EXAMPLE: Sample Lesson Plan—The Common Good

Grade: 4

Subject: Social Studies—Democratic Ideals

Materials: (a) one sheet of paper for each group that contains a list of 20 rules, laws, and activities, and (b) scratch paper for students to record their initial ideas.

Goal: Students will understand the concept of the common good.

Objectives: The students will

1. be able to define the common good,
2. be able to determine which rules, laws, and activities are for the common good.

Input/Background Information*:*

1. We've been studying societal ideals in a democratic society. For the last couple days we've been looking at the concept of justice within a democratic society. Today we are going to starting looking at the concept of the common good.

2. The common good is that which is good for all people, not just one person or a group of people.

3. In a democratic society, rules, laws, and ordinances are designed to provide order.

4. These should be designed for the common good.

5. For example, we have laws to protect our lakes and rivers from pollution.
   A. Clean water is good for all of us.
   B. We can all swim, go fishing, canoeing, and do other activities in clean water.
   C. We can all drink clean water and be healthy.
   D. These laws are designed for the common good.

6. If a factory were to dump its wastes into a nearby river, this might be good for the factory.
   A. An inexpensive way to get rid of wastes
   B. More profits for the owners
   C. This would NOT be the common good, since it benefits only a small number of people.
   D. Question: Can you think of an activity in our society that seems to benefit just a few people?
   E. Question: Can you think of an activity in our school or community that seems to benefit just a few people?

7. In a democratic society people pay taxes to support our schools.
   A. A society is better if its citizens are well educated.
   B. We are able to make informed choices and decisions.
   C. We become more productive citizens.
   D. Everybody has a chance to get an education and a chance to be successful.
   E. Our schools are for the common good. Paying taxes is for the common good.
   F. Question: What do you think life might be like if there were no schools?

(Continued)

(Continued)

8. The common good can also apply to civility and how we conduct ourselves in a society.
   A. There aren't always rules or laws here.
   B. We must use courtesy, consideration, and good sense when we interact with people in public.
   C. An example is not butting in lines at the movie theater.
   D. Question: Does anyone have an example of when another person forgot to act with courtesy or consideration?

9. In our classroom and school we have rules that are for the common good.
   A. Question: Ask students to identify some rules in school and society that are designed for the good of all.
   B. Question: Ask students to identify some behaviors or activities that might be good for only one or a few people.

Procedures/Activities:

1. Lecture: Provide the information above to students while they are at their desks.

2. Move students into three-person cooperative learning groups with the following roles: president, scribe, and encourager.
   A. The president will appoint the other roles and make the final decision.
   B. The scribe will record important information.
   C. The encourager will make sure everyone shares and will identify interesting or important ideas.

3. Give each group a sheet that contains a list of 20 rules, laws, and activities.

4. In their small groups, they must decide which items are for the common good and which are for the good of only a few. If an item is for the good of only a few, students should identify who benefits.

5. On the back of the sheet, each group will use their own words to define and describe the common good.

6. Groups will be given 15 minutes to complete this task.

Extension:

1. If time permits, have students in small groups begin listing some rules that they could adopt in their classroom that would be for the common good.

2. Tomorrow, have students create a list of rules for their classroom.

Plan for Assessment:

1. In small groups, students will be able to provide a written definition and description of the common good. I will look to see if their definition and descriptions on the back of their sheets seem to be in their own words and capture the concept of the common good.

2. In small groups, students will be able to determine which rules, laws, and activities were for the common good and which ones seemed to benefit only a particular group or individuals. Of the 20 that were listed, 12 were for the common good. If groups can correctly identify at least 10 of these, I will assume that they have grasped the concept.

EXAMPLE: Sample Lesson Plan—The Changing Role of the Iron Range

Grade Level: 7

Subject: Social Studies—Geography

Materials: (a) pieces of real ore and taconite, (b) articles about taconite and ore, (c) pictures of the Iron Range, (d) text that describes economies, (e) overhead tally charts, (f) thinking paper for small groups, (g) Iron Range worksheets, (h) access to websites and a printer.

Goal: Students will understand the role that natural resources play in an area's economy.

Objectives: Students will be able to

1. list three different eras the Iron Range has gone through since the late 1800s,
2. define what economy means,
3. list at least three reasons why the Iron Range's economy has changed since the late 1800s,
4. describe the destruction to the land that mining causes.

Background Information:

The Iron Range is located in the northern part of Minnesota. It is composed of many little towns that were once thriving, but many are now becoming ghost towns. The area was developed in the late 1800s and many immigrants came to the area to work in the mines. The iron ore has been depleted since then and the land is barren. Today many people are hoping that development of taconite will revive the area. Tourism is also playing a part in the revival of the economies in the little towns around the Iron Range.

Procedures:

1. Hang pictures of the Iron Range up around the room, create an Iron Range bulletin board display; set pieces of real ore and taconite out. Let students explore these things on their own; this will hopefully raise questions.
2. Hand out articles about ore. Read as a class.
3. Discuss natural resources; ask critical questions.
   A. Question: Who can tell me what a natural resource is?
   B. Question: What natural resources do we have around our area for recreation?
   C. Use the overhead to make a quick tally chart to see what natural resources were used for recreation in the last month (lakes, forests, rivers, hiking trails, etc.).
   D. Question: What are some natural resources that are used for fuel?
   E. Make a tally chart to see what natural resources were used for fuel in the last month, and how they were used.
   F. Question: What are some of the other natural resources that we use every day?
4. Show pictures of the mines in the late 1800s.
5. Explain the process of extracting ore from the land.
   A. Question: What happens when the ore runs out?
   B. Discuss this further using the Iron Range as an example of what happens when the ore runs out.
6. Hand out taconite information and read as a class.
7. Tell what taconite is and how this has replaced mining.

(Continued)

(Continued)

8. Explain what taconite is doing for the Iron Range area.
9. Do cooperative learning activity.

Activity:

1. Students will move into small cooperative learning groups of four students. The following roles will be assigned: president, scribe, speaker, computer technician, artist.
   A. The president will appoint the other roles and make final decisions.
   B. The scribe will record important information.
   C. The speaker will share ideas with the class.
   D. The computer technician will do an Internet search to find and print an appropriate article or information.
   E. Some groups will need an artist. This person will create a picture or diagram as part of the task.

2. Each group will be given one of the following questions or tasks:
   A. Task 1: Think of and describe three to five ways this area might revive itself. Don't be afraid to be innovative, interesting, or unique. Do an Internet search to get some ideas. Try using the following search words: *community economic renewal, community economic development, community planning and development.*
   B. Task 2: Explain why areas sometimes change economically. Describe the eras of change that have occurred on the Iron Range since the 1800s. Create a picture or diagram that illustrates this process. Do an Internet search to get more ideas.
   C. Task 3: Describe what happens when natural resources such as forests, lakes, rivers, or wildlife are used up or destroyed. Describe the destruction to the land that mining causes. Create a picture or diagram that illustrates this process.
   D. Task 4: Explain what *economy* means using your own words. Find five interesting or important words related to the concept of economy.
   E. Task 5: List what gives people jobs in our area. Describe any natural resources that are found near our town. What attracts tourists? What factories or manufacturers are found in our area? Do an Internet search to find interesting or important information related to natural resources and tourism around our area.

3. Groups will be given 15 minutes to complete the task. Each group will have the following resources to use: articles, a textbook with a chapter related to economies, and taconite brochures.

4. Groups will share their findings and responses with the class.

5. When presentations are completed, students will work with an assigned buddy to complete an Iron Range worksheet. Both buddies will sign off before handing it in.

Plan for Assessment:

1. I will assess each group's product and presentation will be assessed to see if they are able to successfully complete their given task. An analysis here will also show how students are processing the main concepts.

2. Students will successfully complete the Iron Range worksheet. There are 20 questions here. If students can correctly answer at least 18 of these, I will assume that they have grasped the major concept.

Note: Lesson plan used with permission of Dr. Don Descy, Minnesota State University, Mankato, Minnesota.

EXAMPLE: Sample Lesson Plan—Wants and Needs

Grade Level: K/1

Subject: Social Studies—Civics/Economics

Materials: Pictures cut out of magazines that show various items that illustrate wants and needs.

Goal: The purpose of this lesson is to help children develop a sense of the difference between wants and needs.

Objectives:

1. Students will be able to differentiate wants and needs by putting various pictures of physical objects in the correct category
2. Students will be able to draw and write about a need and a want.

Background Information:

Adults have jobs to earn money so that they can buy the things that we want and need. The things we need are those things we need to stay safe and alive. They include food, clothes, and housing or rent. The things we want are those things we can live without but they make our life more enjoyable. They include entertainment, movies, books, and games or toys.

Procedures:

1. The teacher has many pictures of different objects cut out of magazines. Some of them illustrate needs, such as food, clothing, and shelter. Others include wants such as toys, games, and golf clubs.
2. After the difference between a want and a need is explained, each student will be given a picture. The teacher will create a bulletin board with a T-chart that has "Needs" written on one side and "Wants" written on the other side.
3. One at a time, students will be asked to come up and pin their pictures on the correct side of the T-chart.

Activity:

1. Students will be given a large sheet of writing paper with a space to draw a picture on top. The paper will be divided down the middle. One side will have the following written on it: "_____ is a need. It is important because _____."
2. Students will draw and write (dictate) to tell about one important need and why it is important.
3. The other side will have the following written on it: "_____ is a want. I like it because _____."
4. Students will draw and write (dictate) to tell about one want and why they like it.

Plan for Assessment:

1. Students' bulletin board performance will be observed to see if they can successfully determine between wants and needs.
2. Students' drawing and writing will be observed to see if they can successfully describe a need and a want.

PLANNING A UNIT

You do not have to rely on a textbook or teacher's manual to guide your teaching; rather, you can create your own social studies units. Units created by teachers are often more creative and interesting than commercially prepared material. An easy and interesting unit to put together is one on heroes or famous people. Simply choose a hero or a famous person from history or current news and use the steps described below to create a short two- or three-day unit. You can create a number of these short hero units, which then link up to become a larger unit on heroes. Such a unit has many potential spin-offs, leading you into mythology, heroic qualities, leadership, character education, and so on.

The Process of Developing a Unit

The following section describes a simple step-by-step process for creating units of any kind.

Decide on a topic. Some teachers like to think in terms of themes, such as friendship, honor, or heroism. Remember, however, that themes like these can be too abstract for elementary students. Thus, it may be easier to think in terms of more concrete topics, such as farming, sewage treatment, law enforcement, the civil rights movement, the Gulf War, or Title IX. By using the NCSS thematic and discipline standards as a guide (see Chapter 1), almost any topic can be designed for use in a social studies class.

Gather material, information, or data. Go to the library and look for books and magazine articles related to your topic. At any grade level, picture books are a good place to start because they provide basic information quickly. The pictures can be used as visual aids in lessons. The Internet, while not always accurate, can also be used as a source to find basic information and images.

Start organizing your data. Get the specific information you need in note form, then begin to organize this information into an outline. A good unit is based on an adequate knowledge base and is presented to students in an organized, coherent fashion. At this step you will need to create a logical structure and sequence for the lessons that appear your unit.

Break up the unit into specific lessons. You will need to decide on the information or skills to be covered in each lesson. Again, this initial plan should be flexible and not very detailed. In this case you are not creating individual lessons; rather, you are providing a road map or some sort of structure for your unit.

Look for specific activities or projects for each lesson. The goal of the activity is to manipulate the information provided (input), to apply a concept, or to practice a skill. It is helpful to list two to five possible activities for each lesson. Your unit plan should be a flexible, dynamic, ever-changing entity.

Look for trade books and picture books for the unit topic or theme. Stories in the form of trade books and picture books make topics come alive and put new information in a meaningful context (see Chapter 14). You can use books with a unit in one or all of the following situations: (a) have the whole class read a single book; (b) have four or five copies of several books and assign students to book clubs; (c) have many books available for students to read; or (d) create a unit around a text.

Integrate across the curriculum. Infuse vocabulary and concepts from your social studies unit across the curriculum. Weekly spelling lists, writing activities, math problems, science concepts and activities, art, and music can all be designed around your social studies unit.

Review, get feedback, tweak, and refine. Before implementing a unit, run it by a colleague to get ideas for other sources or activities. You will spend much of your teaching career tweaking, enhancing, and refining your units. Also, most of the units that you create can be transported from one grade to another by modifying and adapting the content and activities.

Skills in a Social Studies Unit

Along with the activities described in this text, the following kinds of skills can also be taught and used to manipulate content in a social studies unit:

Observing. Students categorize, record, describe, measure, compare and contrast, test, gather data, survey, research, classify, or create categories.

Thinking. Students predict, test, ask a question, organize data, generate ideas, solve problems, find related ideas, experiment, create an inquiry project, predict, hypothesize, deduce, infer, or generalize.

Communicating. Students describe, write, speak, draw, diagram, explain, graph, make a rule, report, create and perform a drama, create art, demonstrate, or interpret.

GO THERE

NCSS essential skills for social studies can be found at the following sites:

http://www.misd.net/Socialstudies/Essentialskills.pdf

http://www.educ.state.ak.us/tls/frameworks/sstudies/part3a3.htm

Planning Lessons That Engage

My idea this year was to model a project for the middle school teachers that would integrate several disciplines and encourage independent research for the students. I teach the Facing History and Ourselves program to eighth graders and each year try to add several hands on projects to the units in the book.

While in the airport, I found a small book called, Postcards from WW.II which contained both pictures and writings from American soldiers. I adapted this idea and worked with the art and English teachers. Each section (3) had a topic—rescuers, resistance, and world response. Pairs of students in each section chose a subtopic to research and then created a postcard from one person. They also created an illustration (which we tea dyed to age). For example, one pair of students studied Raoul Wallenberg; their postcard was from him to his government and the illustration was a picture of him issuing false passports.

This project took about three weeks to complete—with weekly checkups using a rubric. The students in each section presented their postcards and research as a walking display through the hallway. What I learned was that the students were totally involved because they chose their topics and were given the responsibility of setting up the display.

—Myrna, Eighth Grade

Author Reflection: Good teaching ideas come from all around us. One of the things I loved about teaching 1st and 2nd grade in the 1980s was designing new science and social studies units. These would always be based on things that I was interested in or on what I thought my students would be interested in. I knew my students far better than a curriculum developer so, of course, I was much better at designing meaningful units and active learning experiences that engaged my students' intellect and imagination.

Today, it seems like schools are becoming more like educational factories and less like places of learning. In this factory paradigm teachers become assembly line workers who are asked to simply implement a standard curriculum at a prescribed time and in the manner in which it is described in the textbook or curriculum guide. Standards then become synonymous with standardization. Education is seen as something you do to students instead of something students do. All learning is externally derived and evaluated. Teachers become measurers instead of educators. Standardized tests become a form of quality control to hold schools and teachers "accountable."

Let's get back to our teaching roots. Teaching is the most important function in our society. We are helping to prepare the next generation of human beings. Therefore, we want the best and brightest to go into education and become teachers in order to help shape our society.

As I write this, I am hoping you, the reader, will become an agent of change. I urge you to find a way to meet the requirements of today's schools while using your creativity and intelligence in designing learning experiences and making decisions about what and how your students learn.

What is your response to the case? How do your reactions compare with the author's reflection?

The arts can be used in social studies to enhance learning. They offer a more complete picture of humans interacting with their world.

INTEGRATED STUDIES

Quantum physics describes a universe in which all is connected at the quantum level (Al-Khalili, 1999; Talbot, 1991). Physicist David Bohm said that the universe cannot be understood in terms of particles and fields alone; rather, it can be understood only if the unbroken wholeness is perceived in a way that does not reduce things to a series of individual entities (Nichol, 2003). The word *unit* implies that a thing can be understood apart from its context. When looking at things from a greater perspective, however, there are no such things as units, only parts that are interconnected with greater systems and greater wholes.

An integrated approach to teaching social studies reflects this expanded view of reality by focusing on an area of study and then interconnecting it with as many other areas and ways of thinking as possible. An integrated approach to social studies creates a curriculum where everything is connected to everything else. Students learn more deeply by approaching an area of study from a multitude of perspectives. Also, an integrated curriculum employs a variety of forms of representation of ideas, and thus honors students' multiple forms of intelligence and the variety of cognitive strengths (Eisner, 1991). Taken to its furthest end, you could create a middle school or elementary classroom without any curriculum borders. In this sense, the ultimate compliment students might give a teacher is to ask what class they currently are in.

Elliot Eisner (1991) advocates that the arts also be included in a social studies curriculum. Far from a fluffy extra, the arts are able to capture ideas that are beyond the grasp of literal language and thus offer a much more accurate and complete picture of humans interacting with their world. Also, the arts are a powerful form of representation beyond the written text and should be employed to enhance the learning of all students, some of whom may process the world more efficiently through visual or artistic modes. The arts represent the human experience. Most humans come to know their social world, not through text, but through experience. Thus, it makes good pedagogical sense to include the arts in an integrated social studies curriculum.

HOW DO I? Develop an Integrated Unit

Start by finding a topic or an area of interest to study. The topic or theme could come from (a) the curriculum guide given by the school district, (b) a special interest that you or your students might have, (c) interesting or important school events, or (d) interesting or important local, national, and world events. Next, begin researching to collect a body of knowledge related to this area of study. Having an organized body of knowledge that is fairly deep makes planning and teaching easier. Also, this initial body of knowledge becomes the skeleton that holds the integrated study together. This organizing structure also helps students grasp major concepts. Next, begin looking for interconnected or related areas. Finally, create activities and assignments that manipulate the concepts found in the area of study. Strategies and activities that can be used with integrated studies can come from literature and trade books, music, visual arts, creative dramatics, language arts, mathematics, science and problem solving, and students' personal connections. Specific activities in each of these areas follow.

Literature and Trade Books

One way to start an integrated study is to use literature or trade books (see Chapter 15). A trade book is a piece of literature for children or young adults, usually a paper back with chapters, appropriate for readers from 3rd to 12th grade. Using literature in a social studies class adds depth and dimension to concepts learned and can enhance the study of geographical areas, time periods, cultures, social problems, or other social studies concepts. Literature can be used in parallel study or as text.

Parallel study. The parallel study is a minimal approach to an integrated study where the literature or trade books related to a unit are used as part of reading class. Thus, the trade book is not referred to specifically in the integrated study but is incorporated into a reading or English class.

Literature as text. Using literature as text, the trade book becomes the text for the integrated studies. The social studies text, if there is one, is used only as a reference text to get specific information. Social studies concepts found in the book become the basis for the integrated study. For example, in *The True Confessions of Charlotte Doyle* by Avi (1992), a 15-year-old girl travels alone from England to America in 1863 on a sailing ship. During the voyage, she finds herself involved in a mutiny. Charlotte sides with the sailors over a cruel captain. Eventually, she cuts her hair and works as one of the sailors for the duration of the voyage.

Social studies concepts that could be incorporated in this integrated study include, for example, maps, geography, forms of government, travel, the movement of goods and services, comparisons between then and today, global connections, technology and science of the day, societies and social expectations, gender expectations, health and diet aboard a ship, and the historical events happening around the world in 1863. These concepts also could be included with the other areas of integration described below.

Reading workshop. Literature can be used to enhance a social studies text or an integrated study by using a reading workshop approach (Atwell, 1987). In this approach you find a variety of trade books related to the integrated study unit. These books might tell stories about a time period, culture, subject, or problem that connects with the integrated study. In the reading workshop students spend one week simply reading the trade books. This can be done either after or before the integrated study. They can choose the books they want to read and read at their own pace.

Music

Analysis of related music. Look for music of a time period, place, or culture. What does the music say about the people or events? What messages can be inferred from the lyrics?

Find song lyrics. Look for songs with lyrics that seem to express an idea, event, or concept covered in the integrated study.

Create song lyrics. Create new lyrics for a known song incorporating interesting or important concepts from the integrated study.

Music for radio drama. Create a radio drama related to something in the integrated study (see Chapter 9). Look for music to use as an introduction or as background music for interesting or important parts.

Outstanding musicians. Create alternate assignments whereby musically talented students can compose a song or perform music related to concepts from the integrated study.

Visual Art

Period art. Study the art of the time period, place, or culture. What does the art tell you about the people and events? What values can you infer? What common themes do you see?

Images from popular culture. Collect pictures from magazines and newspapers that illustrate interesting or important ideas from the integrated study.

Creating art. Create art projects based on the integrated study. With middle school students, give them an idea from the integrated study, and then allow them the freedom to choose a medium and style to express that idea. For example, in studying civil rights, one middle school teacher asked her students to use a visual medium to express the idea of freedom.

Creative Dramatics

Basic creative dramatics. Creative dramatics uses no written dialogue and few props. Students find or are given an interesting or important event related to the integrated study. Their goal then is to bring that event to life using creative dramatics (see Chapter 9). These dramatic presentations should be relatively short with no written scripts (Johnson, 2000a).

Creative dramatics as problem solving. Find an interesting or important problem related to the integrated study. Use creative problem solving to generate solutions and pick the best one (see Chapter 10). Use creative dramatics to bring the problem and its solution to life.

Radio drama. Students take an interesting or important event or portion of a story and create written dialogue with narration.

Language Arts

Spelling lists. Create weekly spelling lists from words related to the integrated study. To extend this, have students pick the words they wish to study (Johnson, 1998).

Newspaper articles. Using an objective voice, write a newspaper account of events related to the integrated study.

Oral presentations. Create a short speech describing an interesting or important idea or event related to the integrated study (see Chapter 9).

Support-a-statement. Given a statement, students must look for details to support that statement (see Chapter 12). This activity often works best if you give students a minimum number of supporting details to look for. The support-a-statement can be used for an oral speech. It is also a good vehicle for teaching about paragraphs (an idea with supporting details), or it can become the basis for a longer paper. In a paper, each supporting detail becomes a paragraph or section.

Poetry. Poetry is using words to create pictures. It is an effective tool for advancing students' language skills, because poems call for careful observation and a precise use of words. Writers of poetry must be attuned to patterns, sounds, and the subtle effect of words. Start out with free verse poems before looking for rhyming patterns, syllable counts, or word sounds. Students who are not hindered by a particular form can focus on finding the best words to express their ideas. In free verse students use words or phrases, but not complete sentences, to create a picture of an interesting or important person or event related to the integrated study. Another way to use poetry is to have students use only words taken from a social studies or other textbook to create an interesting poem.

Super word web for vocabulary. The *super word web* (SWW) is a web to add depth and breadth to word knowledge. Students find or are given a new or interesting word in the context of a sentence (see Figure 5.4). Working in groups, students record synonymous words and phrases in the middle of a square or some other figure of their own design. It is helpful to have dictionaries or thesauruses available here. Along the outside, students list associations. Word webs can make interesting posters or can be used as a postreading activity.

Figure 5.4   Super Word Web

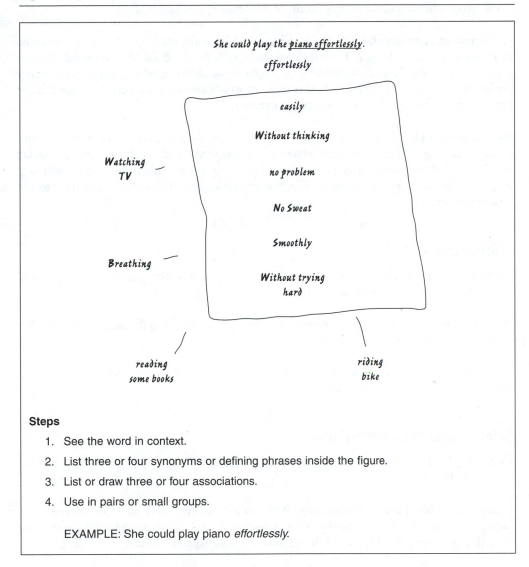

Steps

1. See the word in context.
2. List three or four synonyms or defining phrases inside the figure.
3. List or draw three or four associations.
4. Use in pairs or small groups.

    EXAMPLE: She could play piano *effortlessly*.

Grammar as inquiry. Using a text or trade book, have students do an inquiry search (see Chapter 10). For example, they would select two or three places in a text or trade book to get an example of nouns per hundred words (NPH) or some other part of speech or phrase. This activity leads naturally into a lesson on finding averages.

Grammar as sentence combining. In sentence combining, students are given or select two sentences from the integrated study. They must then combine the sentences while keeping the same ideas. The resulting sentence must be a complete sentence and use as few words as possible. This is a naturalistic approach to grammar as students naturally look for nouns, verbs, propositions, and connecting words to construct new sentences.

Grammar as sentence elaboration. In sentence elaboration, students are given a sentence from the text or trade book in the integrated study with the direction to elaborate it to make it more interesting. This allows students to see the basic structure of a sentence while using propositions, adjectives, verbs, and other types of words and sentence parts to make it more interesting. Creativity and humor should be encouraged.

Newspaper article. Using a more formal, academic style, students write an objective account of an interesting or important event related to the integrated study. Before writing, students should first list the important facts on a separate sheet of paper. This prewriting activity will help them create more concise, focused, and structured writing. It will also enable them to add missing information.

Mathematics

Averages. Use inquiry (above) or collect other types of samples related to the integrated study to look for averages or statistical trends.

Word problems. Create authentic problems using concepts found in the integrated study. Put students in small groups to solve them.

Describing in numbers. Ask students to describe an idea, item, concept, or event using numbers instead of words or pictures.

Science and Problem Solving

Concepts. Look for scientific concepts within an integrated study. Integrate these into the area of study.

Cause and effect: inductive reasoning. Within the integrated study, look for interesting or important events. Given a particular event (cause), ask students to use an infer-o-gram and inductive reasoning (see Figure 5.5) to infer what might happen (effect).

Cause and effect: deductive reasoning. Given a particular effect related to the integrated study, ask students to use deductive reasoning to determine the cause (see Figure 5.6).

Problems. Look for problems within a textbook, trade book, or the integrated study unit that need math to solve them.

Creating groups: inductive reasoning. This strategy reflects naturalistic or qualitative methodologies. In inductive reasoning students observe a field or an event in order to understand the groups in it. As data are collected and recorded, students organize or classify the groups. Finally, students describe the field or event in terms of the groups.

Figure 5.5   Infer-o-Gram

Inference Question: What will be the effect?	
What You Observe	What You Know
1.	1.
2.	2.
3.	
Inference:	

Figure 5.6   Deduct-o-Gram

Effect:	
Clues	Important Background Information
1.	1.
2.	2.
3.	
Probable cause:	

Problem solving. Look for problems related to the integrated study. Students are put into small groups and use either creative problem solving or means-end analysis to seek a solution (see Chapter 10).

Personal Connections

Personal connections. Look for ways that items related to the integrated study affect or connect with the students as individuals. For example, in studying the distributions of goods and services, students might choose a particular product from their lives and trace it back to its origin, looking at all the people and processes involved.

The metaphor. Use a topic related to the integrated studies as metaphor. For example, in studying alliances, students might be asked in a journal or writing assignment to describe a time when they made an alliance with others for some purpose. These types of writing activities are best shared in small group.

Double journal entry. The double journal entry is a method for making personal connections with a text or trade book. Students divide their note paper in half (Figure 5.7). On the left side (the objective side), students select and record one to four interesting or important passages from the book. One the right side (the subjective side), students describe the associations, ideas, and feelings that they experienced as they read the passage.

Figure 5.7   Double Journal Entry

Text	My Ideas
• Competition among sellers in a free market system keeps the costs low.	• There are many companies making DVD players. The prices seem to come down every year.
• Markets exist when buyers and sellers interact.	• There is a huge market for DVDs and DVD players because many people want them. Also, there are many places renting DVDs. Again, there seems to be a lot of people who enjoy watching DVDs.
• Greater demand usually means higher prices. Lower demand usually means lower prices.	• There are a lot of companies selling DVD players. This is what must keep the price low, as there is a big supply. We seem to have only one choice with our local cable TV, and that may be why the monthly rate seems to keep increasing.

Figure 5.8   Ranking Decisions

Situation	Possible Decisions	Rank in Order of Preference
• U.S. government wants to drill in Alaskan wilderness for oil in order to lessen its dependence on foreign oil.	• Drill for oil. • Improve energy conservation. • Ban/eliminate SUVs. • Enforce gas mileage standards. • Improve relationships with oil-producing countries • Look for alternative sources of energy (hydrogen).	1. Improve energy conservation. 2. Enforce gas mileage standards. 3. Look for alternative sources of energy. 4. Ban/eliminate SUVs. 5. Improve foreign relationships. 6. Drill for oil.

Reflected values: Our group values our natural wilderness lands. We want these preserved at all costs. This can be done very easily by improving our energy consumption.

Ranking decisions. Ranking decisions is a form of a values clarification activity (see Chapter 16). Students are presented with a description of a situation found in the textbook, trade book, or integrated study unit. As a class or in small groups, students then generate three to four possible decisions that could be made by one or more of the characters. Finally, students rank the decisions and describe the value or values reflected in their top choice (see Figure 5.8).

Feelings connectors. Feelings connectors are intended to connect students' lives and feelings with those found in the integrated study. In the first feelings connector in Figure 5.9, students describe an interesting or important event related to the integrated study and identify the main person involved. Students then use inference to identify that person's possible feelings or views related to the event. In the second feelings connector students go on to try to connect these feelings with similar feelings from their lives or experiences.

Using Expanded Views of Intelligence and Multiple Levels of Thinking

Howard Gardner's book *Frames of Mind* (1983) was instrumental in getting schools to begin thinking about intelligence in much broader terms. He defined intelligence as the ability to solve problems or create products that are valued within a culture. Instead of a single entity with many facets, Gardner has identified eight intelligences (Checkley, 1997), all of which work together as a system. These are described in Figure 5.10.

Figure 5.9   Feelings Connector

	Event and Person	*Feeling*
Integrated Study		
My Life		

Figure 5.10   Gardner's Multiple Forms of Intelligence

1. **Linguistic intelligence** is the ability to use words to describe or communicate ideas. Examples: poet, writer, storyteller, comedian, public speaker, public relations, politician, journalist, editor, or professor.

2. **Logical-mathematical intelligence** is the ability to perceive patterns in numbers or reasoning, to use numbers effectively, or to reason well. Examples: mathematician, scientist, computer programmer, statistician, logician, or detective.

3. **Spatial intelligence** is the ability to perceive the visual-spatial world accurately (not get lost) and to transform it. Examples: hunter, scout, guide, interior decorator, architect, artist, or sculptor.

4. **Bodily-kinesthetic intelligence** is expertise in using one's body. Examples: actor, athlete, mime, or dancer.

5. **Musical intelligence** is the ability to recognize and produce rhythm, pitch, and timbre; to express musical forms; and to use music to express an idea. Examples: composer, director, performer, or musical technician.

6. **Interpersonal intelligence** is the ability to perceive and appropriately respond to the moods, temperaments, motivations, and needs of other people. Examples: pastor, counselor, administrator, teacher, manager, coach, co-worker, or parent.

7. *Intrapersonal intelligence* is the ability to access one's inner life, to discriminate one's emotions, intuitions, and perceptions, and to know one's strengths and limitations. Examples: religious leader, counselor, psychotherapist, writer, or philosopher.

8. **Naturalistic intelligence** is the ability to recognize and classify living things (plants, animals) as well as sensitivity to other features of the natural world (rocks, clouds). Examples: naturalist, hunter, scout, farmer, or environmentalist.

Figure 5.11   Alternative Ways to Demonstrate Knowledge

• Create a poem. • Put important items on a time line. • Create a semantic web. • Put events or ideas in categories. • Create and give a speech. • Weigh or measure. • Plan and perform a newscast. • Design a crossword puzzle.	• Make a game or design a quiz show. • Create a sculpture or painting. • Create a radio drama. • Create a bulletin board. • Design a poster. • Design a survey. • Tape an interview. • Create a play. • Run an experiment.	• Make a commercial. • Use dance or mime to express an idea. • Create a rap song. • Design a reading guide. • Find related issues. • Describe an idea using numbers. • Describe multiple viewpoints. • Write a newspaper article.

An integrated study utilizing Gardner's theory of multiple forms of intelligence would include activities and topics that address as many of these areas as possible. Also, students would be given choices of how to demonstrate their learning (see Figure 5.11). That is, they would be encouraged to complete assignments or projects in ways other than writing reports or answering homework questions. For example, one student might write and perform a dramatic reenactment of an important event related to the integrated study, while another might demonstrate through visual art, while another might design a poster, while another might create a videotaped commercial.

Another expanded view of intelligence is Robert Sternberg's (1996) triarchic theory of intelligence. This theory recognizes three types of thinking that work together to solve problems, create products, or enable outstanding performance: (a) creative thinking, which is the ability to generate ideas and make associations; (b) evaluative thinking, which is the ability to monitor executive processes and analyze and appraise ideas; and (c) pragmatic thinking, which is the ability to recognize the context of the situation and adapt the idea to that context. Including activities that use these three types of thinking throughout the integrated study will enhance learning and also invite students to fully explore concepts within the integrated study.

In *Taxonomy of Educational Objectives* (1956), Benjamin Bloom described six levels of thinking (Figure 5.12). Without conscious effort, it is easy to use only lower-level questions, assignments, and activities, as these are usually the easiest to assign and assess. However, including all levels of thinking in an integrated study will enhance learning and move students away from the passive question-and-response operations that take place at the lower levels. You can use the six levels of thinking and specific operations for each level to guide the design of questions, assignments, or activities. For example, if you wanted to include thinking at the evaluation level in a social studies activity, you could have students support a statement, define a criterion, make a formal critique, compare and contrast, or use another operation at that level.

Figure 5.12   Taxonomy of Educational Objectives and Corresponding Operations

1. **Knowledge.** Recalls facts or remembers previously learned material.

   Knowledge level operations—define, describe, identify, list, match, name, tell, describe, show, label, collect, examine, tabulate, quote, duplicate, memorize, recognize, relate, recall, repeat, reproduce, or state.

2. **Comprehension.** Grasps the meaning of material.

   Comprehension level operations—interpret, explain, summarize, convert, defend, distinguish, estimate, generalize, rewrite, contrast, predict, associate, distinguish, estimate, differentiate, discuss, extend, classify, express, indicate, locate, recognize, report, restate, review, select, or translate.

3. **Application.** Uses learned material in a new situation.

   Application level operations—apply, change, compute, demonstrate, operate, show, use, solve, calculate, complete, illustrate, examine, modify, relate, change, classify, experiment, dramatize, employ, illustrate, interpret, operate, practice, schedule, sketch, or write.

4. **Analysis.** Breaks things down into parts in order to understand, organize, or clarify.

   Analysis level operations—identify parts, distinguish, diagram, outline, relate or associate, break down, discriminate, subdivide, analyze, separate, order, explain, connect, classify, arrange, divide, select, explain, infer, analyze, appraise, calculate, categorize, compare, contrast, criticize, differentiate, discriminate, distinguish, examine, experiment, question, or test.

5. **Synthesis.** Puts parts together to form a new whole.

   Synthesis level operations—combine, compose, create, design, rearrange, integrate, modify, substitute, plan, invent, formulate, prepare, generalize, or rewrite.

6. **Evaluation**. Uses a given criteria to determine the value of a thing or quality of a product or performance.

   Evaluation level operations—appraise, criticize, compare and contrast, support, conclude, discriminate, find main points, explain, infer, deduce, assess, decide, rank, grade, test, measure, recommend, convince, select, judge, explain, discriminate, support, argue, choose compare, defend, estimate, judge, predict, rate, select, value, or evaluate.

HOW DO I? Keep Track of Thinking Levels and Forms of Intelligence

The following charts combine the theories of Gardner, Sternberg, and Bloom. You can use these charts to plan activities and assignments and to keep track of thinking levels and forms of intelligences students use in the integrated study.

The GB Chart.* Using the GB Chart (Gardner/Bloom), you simply put a tally mark in the appropriate box after an activity or assignment has been planned or implemented. If any box seems to be filling up, it is a good indication that other types of activities should be designed and included in the unit.

Knowledge	Comprehension	Application	Analysis	Synthesis	Evaluation
Linguistic					
Math					
Spatial					
Kinesthetic					
Musical					
Art					
Interpersonal					
Intrapersonal					
Naturalistic					

Note: The GB chart was developed from an idea by Ginnette Boettcher, lead teacher at Bridges Elementary School in Mankato, Minnesota.

The GS Chart. The GS Chart (Gardner/Sternberg) uses the same idea as the GB chart above, but combines Gardner's and Sternberg's theories of intelligence and thinking.

Analytic Thinking	Creative Thinking	Pragmatic Thinking
Linguistic		
Math		
Spatial		
Kinesthetic		
Musical		
Art		
Interpersonal		
Intrapersonal		
Naturalistic		
Spatial		
Musical		

NCSS STANDARDS

Thematic Standards

The following NCSS thematic standards are addressed in this chapter. See Appendix A for a full description of the relevant thematic standards.

Early Grades

   I. Culture: c.

  II. Individual Development and Identity: a., g.

 III. Production, Distribution, and Consumption: b.

 IV. Global Connections: a., d.

Middle Grades

   I. Culture: c.

  II. Individual Development and Identity: a.

 III. Global Connections: a., d., f.

Pedagogical Standards

The following NCSS pedagogical standards are addressed in this chapter:

   I. Critical Thinking, Problem Solving, and Performance Skills.

  II. Active Learning and Motivation.

 III. Inquiry, Collaboration, and Supportive Classroom Interaction.

 IV. Planning Instruction.

  V. Assessment.

Essential Skills for Social Studies

The following NCSS essential skills for social studies are addressed in this chapter:

   I. Acquiring Information.
      A. Reading Skills.
         1. vocabulary

  II. Organizing and Using Information.
      A. Thinking Skills.
         1. classify information
         2. interpret information

3. analyze information
4. summarize information
5. synthesize information
6. evaluate information

B. Decision-making Skills.

Chapter Review: Key Points

1. Thoughtful planning of lessons
   - creates more purposeful instruction,
   - enhances learning,
   - enhances the effectiveness of teachers.

2. Lesson plans do not need to be overly complex to be effective.

3. The parts of a lesson plan include
   - objective,
   - introduction,
   - input,
   - activity,
   - closure/review.

4. The elements of effective skills instruction are
   - identification of procedural components,
   - direct instruction and modeling,
   - guided practice,
   - independent practice,
   - integration into the curriculum.

5. Social studies teachers can create their own units using the following steps:
   - Decide on a topic.
   - Gather material, information, or data.
   - Start organizing your data.
   - Break up the unit into specific lessons.
   - Look for specific activities or projects for each lesson.
   - Look for trade books and picture books for the unit.
   - Integrate parts of the unit across the curriculum.
   - Continue to review, get feedback, tweak, and refine.

6. Integrated studies focus on an area of study, then integrate it with as many related areas and ways of thinking as possible.

7. The integrated study avoids fragmentation and thus allows students to make greater connections and learn more deeply.

8. Expanded views of intelligence and multiple levels of thinking can be used to enhance any social studies unit as well as other curriculum units.

Making Connections

1. List three to five topics or areas that you would like to learn more about. For each topic, write an objective as if a lesson plan were being created specifically for you.

2. Select a topic or area about which you know a great deal. Design a lesson plan that includes an objective, introduction, input, activity, and closure/review.

3. List five to ten possible topics for a social studies unit.

4. Find a teacher's manual for social studies. Find five interesting or neat activities or ideas. Find five activities or ideas that you think you can improve.

5. Find a teacher's manual for social studies and describe how you might use it. What things might you add or change?

6. Select an area for an integrated study. Create a web to begin looking at creating possible connections and interconnections to others topics, areas of study, and activities.

7. In what ways do you see the three holistic learning ideas related to intrapersonal connections, interpersonal connections, and interconnectedness reflected here?

Chapter 6

ASSESSING STUDENT GROWTH

Thinking Ahead

1. What is learning? How should we assess and describe students' learning?

2. What have you learned in reading the five chapters of this book? How would you go about describing or demonstrating what you have learned to a friend or colleague?

3. Why do we give grades?

4. Other than assigning a letter grade, what might be some other ways to describe students' learning?

5. What do you see to be the strengths and limitations of standardized tests?

ASSESSMENT VERSUS EVALUATION

Although the terms *assessment* and *evaluation* are often used interchangeably, there is a difference. Assessment tends to be associated with diagnosis. The purpose here is to see how students are doing. Information is gathered with the intent of meeting the particular needs of a student or students. In contrast, evaluation tends to be associated with judgment. Here you are looking to see how well students have done and then making a judgment on their learning. The purpose is to use data to put students into a category, assign a letter grade, or place them on a normative scale.

In an ideal classroom, the emphasis is primarily on assessment. You regularly assess students' learning in order to discover their strengths and also to look for areas that need remediation. In this ideal classroom assessment is also used to diagnose your teaching. You collect data to see how well you are doing in helping students learn and you look for ways to become more effective in meeting students' needs. In this way assessment is used to inform your teaching practice.

GO THERE

- Article: "Student Assessment and Teaching": http://www.maec.org/educate/11.html
- Article: "What the Research Says about Student Assessment": http://www.ed.gov/pubs/IASA/newsletters/assess/pt4.html
- Performance-based assessment rubrics: http://school.discovery.com/schrockguide/assess.html
- Online journal: *Practical Assessment, Research and Evaluation:* http://pareonline.net/Articles.htm
- Middle grades assessment resources: http://www.middleweb.com/Assmntlinks.html

TRADITIONAL FORMS OF ASSESSMENT

Traditional forms of assessment are usually associated with written tests. In these tests students read a question or a short paragraph and either select the best answer from two or more choices or else search their long-term memory in order to retrieve a particular response or predetermined answer.

Standardized Tests

A standardized test compares all students who take the test to one standard. There is nothing inherently wrong with these tests. It is how they are used that determines their value and limitations (see Figure 6.1). A standardized test can be used effectively to provide a very

Figure 6.1   T-Chart Showing the Value and Limitations of Standardized Tests

Value of Standardized Tests	Limitations of Standardized Tests
1. Can be given to a large group.	1. Describe students only in terms of numbers.
2. Provide a very general sense of students' strengths and weaknesses.	2. Describe performance but do not prescribe remediation.
3. Can be used with other measures.	3. Measure only a very narrow type of thinking.
4. Can show certain patterns over time.	4. Can be scored on poorly by accident or circumstance.
5. Are cheap to administer and easy to score.	5. Do not reflect the kinds of problem-solving that occurs outside a school environment.
6. Are hard to score well on by accident.	6. Predict students' ability to score well on similar tests, rather than their ability to use what they have learned.
7. Provide a general sense of students' knowledge.	7. Teachers often feel forced to teach to the test.
8. Can be used to compare students to a relative group norm or criteria.	8. Exclusionary use creates a one-dimensional teaching and learning experience.

general sense of students' knowledge, vocabulary, skills, and thinking. But, as Gardner (1983) and Sternberg (1996) have pointed out, standardized tests measure only a very limited type of thinking; they do not reflect the kind of thinking and problem solving that students encounter in real-world, nontesting environments. Therefore, standardized tests, which include norm-referenced and criterion-referenced tests, should always be used with other types of measures for assessment and evaluation.

Norm-Referenced Tests

A norm-referenced test is a type of standardized test that describes students' performance relative to a group norm. Norm-referenced tests are associated with the bell-shaped curve (see Figure 6.2). The function of these kinds of measures is to describe how far the test taker is away from average. Here, all the scores are collected, a continuum is created, and students are placed on this continuum. These are tests like the SAT, LSAT, ACT, CAT, GRE, MAT, and the Iowa Test of Basic Skills.

Scores here are presented in terms of percentile rankings and grade equivalency scores. A percentile ranking in the 85th percentile means that when you compare your score to the scores of all others who have taken this test, you scored better than 85 percent of them. A grade equivalency score (GE) compares your score to all others who have taken the test and describes your performance compared to the average scores of each grade level. For example, a GE score of 3.5 means that this score is that averaged by students in their third year and fifth month of school. A GE of 3.5 would be a good thing if a student is in 1st or 2nd grade and a bad thing if that student is in 7th or 8th grade.

Standardized tests measure only a very limited type of thinking. They do not represent the type of thinking and problem solving encountered in the real world outside of school.

Figure 6.2   Bell-Shaped Curve

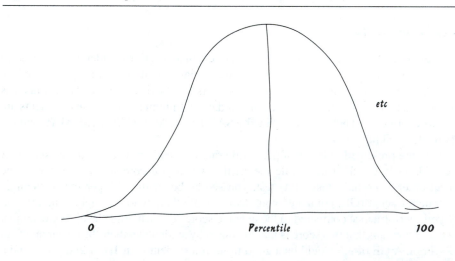

Criterion-Referenced Tests

A criterion-referenced test is a type of standardized test that compares students' performance to a given criterion. An example of this might be end-of-unit tests in math or reading. Here students must meet a certain criterion in order to achieve a passing score and move onto the next unit or grade. Scores are not compared to other students' scores; rather, they are used to demonstrate general knowledge or competency related to the ideas and skills covered in a particular unit or class.

HOW DO I? Increase Scores on Standardized Tests

It is very easy to make scores go up on standardized tests. Simply spend an hour a day practicing test-taking strategies using sample questions similar to those found on standardized tests. You could teach these using the following thinking frames.

Thinking Frames for Standardized Tests

Thinking Frame 1: Answering Story Problems

Students will read a story problem and select the best of several responses.

A. Read the problem and question.

B. Look at all the answers.

C. Eliminate those that do not fit.

D. Find one that seems right.

E. Reread and check.

Thinking Frame 2: Answering Math Problems

Students will read a math problem and select the best of several responses (always use scratch paper).

A. Read the problem.

B. Record the important numbers.

C. Decide on the operation.

D. Plug in the numbers and work.

E. Reread and check to see if it makes sense.

If this kind of practice were done each day of the school year, test scores would indeed go up (along with boredom and hostility), but real learning would go down, as students would be deprived of the joy of discovery and self-expression. However, it may be prudent to implement some sort of daily test-taking instruction before standardized testing occurs. This instruction should be relatively short and begin no sooner than two weeks before testing. But by preparing your students you are invalidating the standardized measure. This is one of the major deficits of standardized tests.

AUTHENTIC ASSESSMENT

There are a variety of ways for students to demonstrate their learning besides taking standardized tests. Authentic assessment asks students to apply knowledge and skills in ways they might in the real world outside the classroom (Burke, 1999). This type of assessment occurs over time as students create or design products and performances and solve real-world problems.

Data Collection

Your mindset using authentic forms of assessment should be that of a scientist. Here you are collecting data to find out how students are learning in your classroom. Collecting these data is not a snapshot of a single incident such as a test score. Nor should data collection rely on a single type of data, for example collecting only learning logs or only homework scores. Rather, the data collection used for authentic assessment is a series of quick looks taken at different times in a variety of ways. In this sense, data collection is much like collecting soil samples: you collect little bits of soil in different places over time. This means that you should not make the mistake of thinking that you have to collect, evaluate, and grade every homework assignment and activity that occurs in your social studies classroom.

Five different types of authentic assessment are described here: anecdotal records, checklists, student conferences, products and performances, and I-learned statements.

Anecdotal Records, Field Notes, or Written Observations

Anecdotal records are the written observations of what you see taking place in your classroom as students are working. Beginning teachers are often unsure of what sorts of things they should record here. The best advice for beginners is to just write what you see without evaluating. Once you start recording, you will begin to see things that are interesting or important. In this way anecdotal records or field notes help you to notice details you might not otherwise have noticed. And as you make many observations over time, patterns will begin to emerge from the data. While it is sometimes difficult to record your observations while you are teaching, you can make quick notes in the margin of your lesson plan to hold your ideas. Also, using cooperative learning groups and small group activities allows you to become a kid watcher and to record your observations in a notebook or journal.

EXAMPLE: Using Anecdotal Records

Pam Cassel is a 4th grade teacher. She keeps a file in her desk drawer for every one of her students. If something interesting occurs related to a particular student, she makes a quick note on the nearest scrap of paper, records the date, and puts it in that student's file. Along with observations and field notes, she also uses these files to collect representative samples of students' work, checklists, and test scores. The student file is a simple yet effective data collecting technique. It also helps Ms. Cassel become a more knowledge-able teacher when assessing growth, planning instruction, or speaking with parents about their child's progress.

Checklists

Checklists come in many forms. A checklist is a list that contains information about specific attributes such as behaviors, traits, or skills. When that attribute is seen, some method is used to either check it off or indicate the number of times it was present.

Student checklists. A student checklist is a list of skills in which students are asked to rate or describe their competency. The checklist in Figure 6.3 asks students to rate their ability to perform seven skills related to reading maps and globes. The purpose of the student checklist is to identify and define specific skills you want students to master and then to get them to reflect and honestly assess their level of competency. If you give grades on this checklist, make sure you tell students that their grade is based on an honest assessment of their level, not on how highly they rate themselves. The student checklist then becomes a way for you to assess and inform your own teaching as well.

EXAMPLE: Using a Student Checklist

Molly Szerbiak's 5th grade social studies class was studying a unit on economics that focused on manufacturing and production. As part of this class, students worked in small, cooperative learning groups to prepare a presentation for the class. Each student maintained a portfolio which included, among other things, a weekly checklist (see Figure 6.4). At the end of class each day, students used tally marks to indicate the activities in which they participated that day. They could also provide a variety of responses related to topics, skills, and questions in the bottom four boxes of the checklist, which were open-ended for this purpose. As the quarter progressed, these weekly checklists gave Ms. Szerbiak a good sense of where her students were spending the majority of their time, the skills learned, and the concepts and skills that needed to be taught. If students maintained their portfolios and checklists, they were given full points as part of their grade.

An open-ended student checklist contains a list of skills with enough space for students to describe their ability, understanding, or usage of each skill (Figure 6.5). This gives you a diagnosis of students' level of understanding and it enables you to plan instruction to meet specific needs.

Teacher checklists. You can design a checklist to indicate exactly what skills you introduced, what skills students have mastered, and when. Checklists like these are also helpful in guiding instruction and providing evidence that skills have been covered. Figure 6.6 contains a teacher checklist for student inquiry. You would keep one checklist for each student in a three-ring binder. Along the left-hand side, list the skills necessary for 3rd grade students conducting a successful inquiry. When students are working it is very easy to get the three-ring binder and make a quick assessment.

Figure 6.3   Student Self-Assessment Checklist

Map Skills—Grade 4

Student: _____

Rate yourself on the skills below using the following key: 4 = outstanding, 3 = very good, 2 = good, 1 = low.

Skill Level	
1. You can find states and cities on a U.S. map.	
2. You can find a position using latitude and longitude.	
3. You can use the scale to figure out the approximate distance between two points.	
4. You can use the scale to estimate driving time between two points.	
5. You can interpret map symbols.	
6. You know where most states are located on a U.S. map.	
7. You can name and identify the seven continents.	

Figure 6.4   Student Experiential Checklist

Weekly Checklist 11/1 through 11/5

Ask Questions	
Find Articles or Internet Sites	
Read and Take Notes	
Organize Notes and Look for Groups	
Talk and Plan With Group	
Create Visual Aids	
Plan and Practice Presentation	
Presentation topic:	
Special skills learned or used:	
Interesting things I learned:	
Skills I need help with:	

Figure 6.5   Open-Ended Student Checklist

Skill: Explain How You Use Each of These Skills

Web and Brainstorm	
Oral Presentation	
Time Line	
Support-a-Statement	
Rules for Discussion	

Figure 6.6   Teacher Checklist

Inquiry Checklist for 3rd-Grade Students

Student: _____

Describe the student's progress using the following: 4 = mastered, 3 = demonstrates competency, 2 = demonstrates some competency, 1 = demonstrates little competency.

Attributes	*Dates*							
1. Asks a question and uses data to answer the question.								
2. Records observational data accurately.								
3. Records numerical data accurately.								
4. Uses graphs and tables to display numerical data.								
5. Is able to use a data retrieval chart.								
6. Is able design a data retrieval chart.								
7. Is able to summarize data and make conclusions.								
8. Is able to write a lab report that includes the conditions, results, and ideas.								
9. Is able to use an objective, technical style of writing.								
10. Is able to use inductive thinking to find groups within a data field.								

Observations or Comments:

When using a teacher checklist, do not try to cover all attributes during a single session; rather, look for a few attributes during each observation. Also, one observation will tell you little; however, many short observations over time will tell you much. You can plan on using one checklist a quarter for each student.

Rating checklists. A rating checklist describes specific traits or skills you are looking for in a product or performance and allows the observer to assign levels of performance to each trait. This is similar to a rubric; however, while a rubric uses one or more sentences to provide a description of each level, a rating checklist uses one-word indicators (see Figure 6.7). Rating checklists are generally a more pragmatic method to use in collecting data for assessing students' growth in classrooms. The rating checklist in Figure 6.7 was used at the end of a 4th grade inquiry project in which students evaluated their own level of performance on one side and the teacher evaluated their performance on the other.

Student Conferences

A student conference is where one or more students talk about their work or some aspect of classroom functioning. Conferences can be conducted individually or in small groups. Data are collected in the form of notes related to your observations and assessments. These are then put into students' individual files.

Individual student conferences. Students should always do the majority of talking and lead the conversation in a student conference. The exchange is open-ended and teacher questions are used simply as prompts to get students talking. Conferences can last anywhere from two to fifteen minutes. Figure 6.8 contains a list of possible conference questions that can be used as prompts to initiate the conversation.

When conferencing with a student, take notes but do not try to get a verbatim transcript of the conference. Instead, record only information you think is important, such as strengths, weaknesses, general impressions, skills learned, progress, insights, or what the student is currently working on. You may wish to design some kind of a checklist to use for taking notes during conferences. It is normal to feel a little unsure of this process at first; however, after you have done a few you will get a good sense of what to record and how best to record it.

Individual conferences are also an effective way to touch base with each student in a personal way. Conferences such as these could be used across the curriculum. Conferences can be used to address social issues or interpersonal issues within your classroom as well.

Small group conferences. In a small group conference you meet with three to eight students at one time. This is an effective data-collecting method in that you are able to see a number of students fairly quickly and watch them interacting with each other. Group conferences also are a valuable teaching tool, as students are able to hear and respond to the thoughts of other students. Just as in individual conferences, you should talk as little as possible.

Figure 6.7 Rating Checklist for Inquiry Skills

Inquiry Skills		
Key: 4 = outstanding, 3 = very good, 2 = average, 1 = low.		
Student	*Skill*	*Teacher*
	Observe and describe.	
	Create a graph.	
	Use a data retrieval chart to collect data.	
	Create a survey.	
	Organize data—create groups.	
	Conclude.	
	Use a lab report.	

Student: _____

Grade Level: _____

Teacher: _____

Date: _____

Comments: _____

_____

_____

_____

_____

Figure 6.8   Questions for Student Conferences

- How's it going?
- What are you working on? (Tell me about it.)
- What is something that you seem to do well?
- What might be something that gives you problems? (Tell me about that.)
- Tell me what you do when you work in a cooperative group.
- What skills have you learned?
- What part of social studies is most interesting to you?
- What is something interesting or important that you have learned in our social studies class?
- What would you like to learn more about in our social studies class?

EXAMPLE: Student Conferences

For one quarter, the students in Mr. Madsen's 6th grade social studies class are conducting individual inquiry projects. He assigns students conference times to talk with him about their projects, which include a series of investigations using surveys, data retrieval charts, lab reports, and presentations. Knowing they are going to meet with him, his students are able to prepare and make sure they have something to say. In these short conferences, Mr. Madsen listens, takes notes, asks questions, encourages, and makes one or two suggestions for improving their inquiry projects. He schedules no more than three to five conferences in any day, as individual conferences can be wearing. This allows him to see each student in his class every two weeks. He uses the following type of checklist to keep track of students and conference times.

Student Conferences Dates

Billy A.	8/23	9/13	10/4								
Sally B.	8/23	9/13	10/4								
Amy C.	8/23	9/13	10/4								
Molly D.	8/24	9/14	10/11								
Michael E.	8/24	9/14	10/11								
Thomas F.	8/24	9/14	10/11								

Figure 6.9   Rules for Small-Group Conferences

Before	Responding
Before	*Responding*
1. Be prepared.	1. Ask a question.
2. Bring all materials with you.	2. Find something you like.
	3. Ask for clarification.
Speaking	4. Find something it reminds you of.
1. Only one person talks at a time.	5. Offer suggestions or ways to do it differently.
2. Say what you have to say; then let others respond.	6. No put-downs or personal remarks.
3. Do not dominate the conversation.	
4. Listen.	

Small group conferences can also be adapted for use in a variety of situations. For example, you may use them to discuss good books, current or historical events, research projects, writing projects, moral dilemmas, math skills, problem-solving skills, textbook reading assignments, homework problems, or personal issues. Do not assume, however, that students instinctively know how to function in small groups. You must provide structure so that they know how to speak and respond to each other (see Figure 6.9). When using small group conferences it is common to spend a few class sessions teaching students how to interact in small groups. Students can be used to help model this process.

Eventually, you can prepare the students in your class to have small group conferences without your presence. They would use a checklist like the one in Figure 6.10 to report their progress. This checklist helps the group focus on the key elements of successful group behavior and provides you with another form of assessment data.

Students' Products or Performances

Samples of students' work can be used as a data source for assessing students' growth. You do not need to collect every bit of students' work; rather, take only representative samples at different times to give you a feel for students' performances and their changes over time. It is often helpful to create a flexible schedule to determine when you will collect students' work before you begin each quarter.

Figure 6.11 shows a product and performance assessment form (PPAF). This rating checklist can be used to analyze and evaluate any type of product or performance, such as inquiry projects, inventions, advertising campaign, dramas, dances, presentations, creative writing, or service learning.

Figure 6.10   Checklist for Small Group Conferences

Group: _____   Date: _____

	Yes	No	Some
1. The group stayed on task.			
2. Everyone responded or asked a question.			
3. The group used time wisely.			
4. Everyone was prepared for the conference.			
Interesting or important ideas:			
1.			
2.			
3.			

Figure 6.11   Product and Performance Assessment Form

Student: _____   Age: _____

Grade: _____   Type of product or performance: _____

Key: 5 = very high; 4 = high, 3 = average, 2 = low, 1 = very low.

Rate the product or performance on the following criteria:

_____ 1. Creativity

_____ 2. Integration of ideas

_____ 3. Technical merit

_____ 4. Sophistication and level of detail

_____ 5. Aesthetics: artistic expression, emotion, feeling

_____ 6. Overall effect

Comments: _____

_____

_____

_____

_____

_____

_____

_____

HOW DO I? Rate Independent Writing and Research Projects

The following form can be used to rate any kind of writing assignment. It is also a good teaching tool in that it forces you to define exactly what is expected and it puts the onus on you to teach each skill associated with those expectations. Also, students appreciate knowing what the requirements are and getting the precise feedback that this form provides.

Writing Assessment Form

Writing prompt or topic:

Key: 4 = outstanding, 3 = very good, 2 = average, 1 = low.

Content—ideas	Mechanics—spelling, grammar, punctuation	Met deadlines—fulfilled assignment requirements
_____	_____	_____
Organization—structure	Fluency—communication	Appearance
_____	_____	_____

Ideas or insights:

Skills to work on:

The following rating checklist was used for 5th-grade students' independent research projects.

Name: _____

Question or area of investigation: _____

Key: 3 = trait is present to a high degree, 2 = trait is present, 1 = trait is present to a low degree, 0 = trait is not present.

_____ Asked a question, identified a problem, or defined an area of exploration.

_____ Data collection was systematic using surveys, interviews, formal observations, or other forms.

_____ Data were analyzed in a way that was credible and trustworthy.

_____ The results were described clearly and accurately.

_____ Graphs or tables were used to display data.

_____ Recommendations or conclusions were made based on the results.

_____ The research was communicated in a way that was understandable.

_____ The research project met all deadlines.

Focus of the research:

_____

_____

_____

Major results and conclusions:

_____

_____

_____

"I-Learned" Statements and Webs

Another interesting way to find out what students have learned is to simply ask them. An *I-learned statement* (ILS), asks students this, using the prompt, "What I have learned about [insert topic]." The ILS could be written at the end of each class in a learning log for a sense of lesson closure, or in a short paper at the end of a unit. Also, encourage students to use pictures or diagrams occasionally to describe their learning, thus honoring multiple forms of intelligence and other ways of seeing.

Related to the ILS is the *I-learned web* (ILW), in which students create a web to describe their learning in three areas: topic, myself, and humanity. In creating a web, write the words "I learned" in the center (see Figure 6.12). Then create three or more nodes branching off. The

Figure 6.12   I-Learned Web

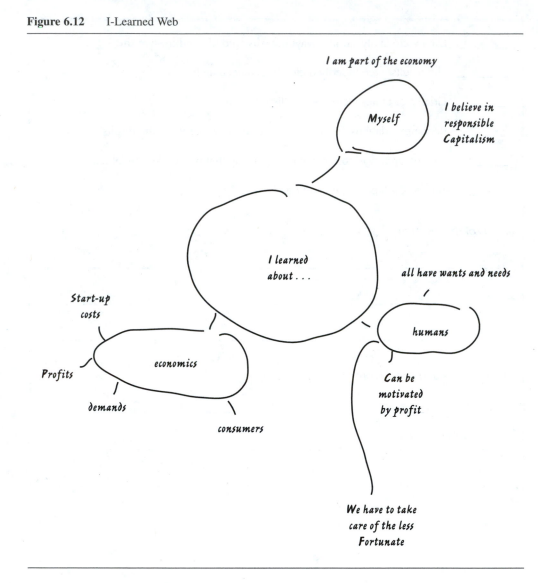

first node relates to the topic or experience. For example, if you were studying local government, this would be in the first node. The second node is labeled "humans" or "humanity." In
this part of the web students list three to five things they learned about humans in general. In
the third node, labeled "myself," students list three to five things they have learned about
themselves. The ILW helps students link areas studied to their own lives, enhances personal
reflecting by asking students to assess their own growth, and invites them to put their learning in the broader context of humanity.

TEACHERS IN ACTION: Conducting Student-Led Conferences

I have been doing student led conferences with my students for about 10 years. I do NOT do it the first time we have conferences, because I don't know enough about the child to be confident in what they tell their parents. Plus, I think parents want to talk to me the first time (I teach fifth grade). We keep data folders, which have all of their papers from the last four to five weeks in them (we purge them at interim and grade card time), plus charts of all of their test scores for the year. About two weeks before conferences, I have them fill out a form that covers a number of subjects (one per section). For instance: I have read _____ books this year and _____ was my favorite. It amounts to about five pages double spaced. I do two sections a day for the week and get them entirely filled in. Sections include math, spelling, handwriting, writing, reading, social studies, science, behavior, homework and tests. I read the paragraphs and explain what I mean by each blank, I also roam around the room, stressing honesty (at the conference their parent and I will know they are lying and it's embarrassing). Every once in a while I stop at a student's desk and say, "Is that really true?" if I see someone not being honest. Then the week before conferences, we practice at least 3 times with a partner—stressing looking up at the parent, speaking clearly, etc. I let parents know ahead of time that the student will be leading the conference and if they want to schedule one with me they can do so after their child is done. (I answer small questions, but direct most questions to the child.) Students are usually very nervous, but afterwards say it wasn't so bad and parents really like it. They like to hear their child tell them they have had 14 late papers, and then try to explain why. I sit in on the conference, but say little.

I only have the child present his or her grade card, not go over every little detail on it, because time doesn't permit it. My students have permission to start their conference without me in a nearby empty room if the one before theirs is running over. Good luck! It's a great way to make kids truly think about and honestly discuss their grades and behaviors with their parents.

—Karen, Fifth Grade

Author Reflection: I remember my first parent teacher conference. I was teaching 2nd grade at Greenwood Elementary School in River Falls, Wisconsin. I didn't have a clue about what to say at conferences, what kind of information to present, or how to interact with parents. So, I talked about what was safe and comfortable: I presented test scores, percentages, percentile rankings, and averages. Essentially, I described these children, these wonderful young human beings, in terms of numbers. These numbers certainly didn't tell much about their particular strengths or learning styles. Neither did they offer a prescription in terms of what parents might do to enhance learning at home. Instead, they simply delineated how far each child was from the mythical norm.

Sigh.

Conferences are a time to interact with families, to describe students' growth, and to celebrate learning and goal setting. With my 2nd grade students, I eventually learned to start conferences with a simple, "Well, how's it going?" I would then listen silently for a moment or two. That way, if parents had a particular question or concern they could talk about it up front. They wouldn't have to wait for an open spot to try to bring it up. It also

(Continued)

(Continued)

gave me a chance to learn more about my students. (The interesting thing about learning is that it usually involves listening or taking in information in some form.)

I also learned to keep a manila folder for each student. I would collect samples of the child's work in various areas to show growth as well as areas needing work. I began including checklists and ratings checklists that listed exactly what skill I was teaching and how each child was progressing. These checklists were never meant to be absolutely valid and reliable in the sense that a standardized test is; but they did provide a sense of where each a child was in terms of specific skills.

I never tried the student-led conference. Indeed, I never even heard about them until one of my graduate students described one in an action research project she conducted as part of one of my classes several years ago. These conferences seem to provide an opportunity for more authentic measures of students' learning. They also invite students to be a part of their own learning. Indeed, students of all ages can take part in selecting the work samples to include in their portfolios and in recording scores on spelling tests and other types of measures. And, these student-led conferences provide a forum for goal setting as well as an opportunity to talk about social skills.

Real learning should be something that students engage in, not something we do to students. The student-lead conference reflects the former. The teacher-led conference reflects the latter.

What is your response to the case? How do your reactions compare with the author's reflection?

Assessment should be used to describe students' strengths as well as identify areas for remediation.

PERFORMANCE-BASED STANDARDS

Performance-based standards define a set of skills to be mastered (Noddings, 1997). Ideally, these tasks should be specific enough to be measured, yet flexible enough to be used in a variety of academic situations (Reigeluth, 1997). In many states, school districts are required to use a set of state-mandated performance-based standards to create performance packages. Performance packages are a series of tasks that students must perform to demonstrate their level of mastery of each skill. In this way, performance-based standards compliment the idea of authentic assessment.

Demonstrating Competency

A performance-based standard describes what students should be able to do *as a result of instruction.* Explicit instruction is the important first step in helping students to demonstrate competency with respect to a performance-based standard. That is, you should not use performance-based standards merely as a series of assignments to give students. Instead, it is only after you have taught, reviewed, and reinforced the skill that you would document students' ability to use the skill. This documentation can be a product, performance, or rating checklist that can be kept in a student portfolio.

Figure 6.13 contains four NCSS essential skills for social studies related to thinking skills (see Appendix C.). The items are examples of performance-based standards in that they describe exactly what students should be able to do. Documenting students' ability to demonstrate their competency with respect to standards should always be kept as simple as possible. Do not mistake complexity for academic rigor. The checklist in 6.14 can be used to assess essential thinking skills.

Using Graphic Organizers to Rate Competency

To assess students' competence in thinking skills, you can use a variety of graphic organizers. For example, to assess their ability to see relationships among facts, you could use the finding causes (FC) graphic organizer (Figure 6.15). The FC chart helps students see the relationship between a current state (effect) and a previous condition (cause). Students first identify the current condition (effect), then list clues related to the condition in the column on the left. Next, students list any relevant facts or background information they know related to the condition or clues in the column on the right. Finally, they then make a reasoned judgment or hypothesis about the possible cause, based on the clues and background knowledge.

Figure 6.13   NCSS Essential Skills Standards Related to Thinking Skills

---

In classifying information, students will be able to

- identify relevant factual material,
- sense relationship between items of factual information,
- group data in categories according to appropriate criteria,
- place in proper sequence: (a) order of occurrence and (b) order of importance,
- place data in tabular form: charts, graphs, illustrations.

Figure 6.14   Checklist to Assess Essential Skills: Thinking Skills

Key: 4 = outstanding, 3 = very good, 2 = average, 1 = low.		
Student	Skill	Teacher
	T-chart: identify relevant factual material	
	cause-effect graphic organizer	
	finding causes graphic organizer	
	creating groups	
	ordering: chronology	
	ordering: importance	
	charts	
	graphs	
	illustrations	

Student: _____

Teacher: _____

Grade Level: _____

Comments: _____

_____

_____

_____

_____

Figure 6.15   Finding Causes Graphic Organizer

Condition:

Clues You See or Observe	Facts or Knowledge

Possible Cause:

EXAMPLE: Applying Performance-Based Standards

Below are examples of how to teach and then have students demonstrate their competence in the first two NCSS essential thinking skills: *identify relevant factual information* and *sense relationships between these facts.*

Identify Relevant Factual Material

As part of her social studies class, Ms. Olawakondi is studying editorials in local and regional newspapers. She uses the T-chart below to help her 6th grade students identify important facts and opinions. As the class reads through an editorial together, important facts are identified and listed in the left column on a large T-chart in front of the room. Opinions are listed in the right column. Over the course of the unit students work in small cooperative learning groups, in pairs or buddy groups, and individually to analyze editorials and opinion pieces. When Ms. Olawakondi feels students are ready to demonstrate their competency with respect to this standard, she gives each student an editorial and a T-chart to use to analyze it. (She has the editorial on an audiotape for ESL students and those who may have trouble reading.) She puts students' completed T-charts in their individual portfolios along with a rating checklist to demonstrate their ability to perform this skill.

T-chart: Identifying Relevant Information

Important Facts	Opinions

(Continued)

(Continued)

Interesting or important ideas you noticed:

_____

_____

_____

Sense Relationship Between Items of Factual Information

Mr. Hrbek uses the cause and effect graphic organizer below to help his 4th grade students identify relationships between an event (cause) and existing conditions (effects). He then helps his students to see the relationship between current events and future conditions. He does this first in a large group by asking students to list the effects rising gas prices will have on transportation costs, travel, farming, and the price of groceries and other goods that are shipped by truck. This is done in the column on the left. In the column on the right, he asks students to list or describe the consequences of these effects or the future conditions. For example, higher prices in gasoline may result in less travel, more fuel efficient cars, or more government money given for research and development of alternative fuel sources.

Cause and Effect Graphic Organizer

Cause: Rising gas prices

Effects	Future Conditions

Interesting or important ideas you noticed:

_____

_____

_____

You can use graphic organizers like the ones in these examples for whole class instruction with a variety of social studies topics. You also can design activities and assignments in which students use these graphic organizers in small cooperative learning groups, in pairs, and on individual assignments. Near the end of a quarter, you can ask students to demonstrate their competency in a skill by using one of the graphic organizers individually. Include each student's graphic organizer in his or her portfolio as a sample product to demonstrate skill competency. Also include a checklist in student portfolios to check off and rate each of the skills. By including students' ratings with your ratings, you allow students to be a part of the assessment process.

NCSS STANDARDS

NCSS Pedagogical Standards

The following NCSS pedagogical standards are addressed in this chapter:

I. Inquiry, Collaboration, and Supportive Classroom Interaction.

II. Planning Instruction.

III. Assessment.

Chapter Review: Key Points

1. Assessment is usually associated with diagnosis whereas evaluation is associated with a judgment.

2. Assessment should be used to inform our teaching practice.

3. Traditional forms of assessment usually include two forms of standardized tests: norm-referenced tests and criterion-referenced tests.

4. A norm-referenced test compares students' scores or performance to a group norm.

5. A criterion-referenced test compares students' scores or performance to a given criterion.

6. Authentic forms of assessment ask students to apply knowledge and skills in ways that reflect real-world situations.

7. Collecting data for authentic assessment is much like collecting soil samples in that you collect little bits of data, in different ways, over time and in different places.

8. Six forms of authentic assessment are anecdotal records, checklists, student conferences, student products or performances, and I-learned statements. Performance-base standards describe what students should do as a result of instruction.

9. Explicit instruction, followed by review and reinforcement, should occur before students are asked to demonstrate their competency with respect to a performance-based standard.

10. Sample products and checklists can be used to document students' mastery of performance-based standards.

Making Connections

1. Pick an assignment or project that you might have students do. Create a checklist that has the specific skills or attributes necessary to complete the assignment.

2. Create a short open-ended checklist to describe your learning thus far in your reading of this book. What are five characteristics of a good social studies lesson? Use these to create a ratings checklist. Then, evaluate a microteaching or classroom lesson using this ratings checklist.

3. Create a rating checklist for a student product or performance that you might use in your classroom.

4. Pick five to eight attributes you think you will need to succeed in your social studies classroom teaching (or student teaching) experience. Create a rating checklist of these skills. Rate your self on each.

5. Critics want to get rid of all standardized testing in your school district. Create an argument to support their case.

6. Critics want more standardized tests in order to hold teachers and students more accountable. Create an argument to support their case.

7. What other kinds of items might be included in a list of authentic assessment items in a social studies class?

8. Create an ILW for this chapter.

9. In what ways do you see the three holistic learning ideas related to intrapersonal connections, interpersonal connections, and interconnectedness reflected here?

Chapter 7

SPECIAL NEEDS STUDENTS IN A GENERAL EDUCATION SETTING

1. How might you go about meeting the special learning needs of gifted and talented students within your general education classroom?

2. Describe a skill, sport, or academic area in which you have trouble learning. How would you design instruction in this area to help you learn?

3. In your experience, what things make learning more difficult in a classroom? What things seem to make learning easier?

4. What do you know about meeting the needs of diverse learners in a general education classroom? What would you like to learn more about?

EDUCATION FOR ALL

One of the problems in education today is that the factory model is still used to guide our thinking about schools. With this model, all students step on the same educational conveyor belt in kindergarten and are carried along at the same speed, receiving the same educational parts until they come to the end 13 years later. This model assumes that one size fits all and that standardization is good. However, human beings are not standardized products and one size most certainly does not fit all. In most classrooms you can expect a diverse group of humans with varying degrees of ability, learning styles, emotional needs, backgrounds, socioeconomic status, religions, cultures, and interests. Presenting the same curriculum in the same way to them all might provide a nice distribution of scores that, in turn, form a lovely bell-shaped curve; however, this does little to help all students discover their unique talents and interests and reach their full potential. To do this, the curriculum and the learning experience need to be differentiated to meet the varying needs and interests of the diverse population of students in your classroom. This chapter describes some basic strategies that can be used to meet the special learning needs of students with learning disabilities, emotional behavioral disorders, and attention deficit/hyperactivity disorder, as well as gifted and talented children and second language learners in your social studies classes.

Public Law 94-142

In 1975, congress passed Public Law 94-142—Education of All Handicapped Children Act. It was later amended and is now called Individuals with Disabilities Education Act (IDEA). This law states that in order for schools to receive federal funds, they must provide free appropriate public education (FAPE) to all children with disabilities. Further, these students must receive special education services in the least restrictive environment (LRE). This means that to the greatest extent possible, students with special needs are to be educated in a general education classroom. Figure 7.1 contains a continuum of services for special needs students from most to least restrictive.

Figure 7.1   A Continuum of Services for Students With Special Needs

Most Restrictive ↑	• *Home or institution.* Students are provided special education services at home, or they reside in a treatment center in which education is provided.
	• *Special school.* Students go to a special school designed to meet their needs.
	• *Full-time special classrooms.* Students attend full-time in a special education classroom while in a general education school. This allows them contact with general education peers only during nonacademic periods.
	• *Part-time in special classrooms.* Students attend in a special education classroom but are pulled for part of the day to attend general education academic programs.
Least Restrictive ↓	• *General education with consultation.* Students attend full-time in a general education classroom. Educational specialists consult with the general education teacher to design instruction to meet their needs.

Inclusion vs. Mainstreaming

Two terms used in reference to the least restrictive environment provision are *mainstreaming* and *inclusion*. *Mainstreaming* assumes there is one main stream in which all should swim. To mainstream is to help special needs students adapt to the general education classroom curriculum, thereby getting them into this main stream. *Inclusion* honors the rich diversity of human experiences and conditions by acknowledging that there are many educational streams. Inclusion seeks to adapt the curriculum to meet the diverse learning needs of all students, thereby getting each into his or her particular stream. Here, the special education teacher takes the role of an educational specialist to work with the general education teacher to modify and design curriculum and learning experiences that are appropriate for special needs students in a general education classroom. Of the two, inclusion is more in keeping with the philosophy of this text.

SPECIFIC LEARNING DISABILITY

A *learning disability* is said to exist when there is a discrepancy between a student's expected ability and his or her achievement in one of seven areas: basic reading skill, reading comprehension, listening comprehension, oral expression, written expression, math calculation, and mathematics reasoning. The U.S. Department of Education's definition is in Figure 7.2.

A learning disability is not necessarily a thinking disability. Students with learning disabilities usually can think and reason; however, they often have trouble processing information in a specific academic area. To understand what it might feel like, think of a time when you were a less able learner. It may have been when trying to learn a sport, a musical instrument, a computer program, a financial plan, or some new area of study. What did it feel like? What would you have liked the teacher to do? What strategies could have been used to help you learn? This understanding will assist you in working with students with learning disabilities.

Inclusion honors the rich diversity of human experience and seeks to adapt the curriculum to meet the needs of students.

GO THERE

- National Dissemination Center for Children with Disabilities: http://www.nichcy.org/
- U.S. Department of Education (section for teachers): http://www.ed.gov/teachers/landing.jhtml
- History of IDEA: http://www.ed.gov/policy/speced/leg/idea/history.html?exp'0
- Public Law 107-110 No Child Left Behind, 2001: http://www.ed.gov/policy/elsec/leg/esea02/index.html

General Strategies to Enhance Learning for All Students

We often exacerbate learning difficulties for students with learning disabilities by teaching in ways in which they cannot learn. Bored or frustrated students whose emotional needs are not met learn less and exhibit more behavior problems. In their book, *Best Practice: New Standards for Teaching and Learning in America's Schools*, Zemelman, Daniels, and Hyde (1998) describe what has come to be known as *best practice*. These are the teaching strategies and educational practices that research has shown to be effective in keeping all students engaged in appropriate learning activities and enhancing learning. Figure 7.3 summarizes these best practices.

Figure 7.2   U.S. Department of Education Definition of Specific Learning Disability

---

IN GENERAL—The term "specific learning disability" means a disorder in one or more of the basic psychological processes involved in understanding or in using language, spoken or written, which disorder may manifest itself in imperfect ability to listen, think, speak, read, write, spell, or do mathematical calculations.

SPECIFIC LEARNING DISABILITY. "Specific learning disability" means a condition within the pupil affecting learning, relative to potential, and is manifested by interference with the acquisition, organization, storage, retrieval, manipulation, or expression of information so that the pupil does not learn at an adequate rate when provided with the usual developmental opportunities and instruction from a regular school environment.

Figure 7.3   Best Practices for Enhancing Learning

Best Practices Provide More . . .

- Experiential, inductive, hands-on learning.
- Active learning in the classroom, with all the attendant noise and movement of students doing, talking, and collaborating.
- Diverse roles for teachers, including coaching, demonstrating, and modeling.
- Emphasis on higher-order thinking; learning a field's key concepts and principles.
- Opportunity for deep study of a smaller number of topics, so that students internalize the field's way of inquiry.
- Reading of real tests, whole books, primary sources, and nonfiction materials.
- Responsibility transferred to students for their work: goal setting, record keeping, monitoring, sharing, exhibiting, and evaluating.
- Choice for students (e.g., choosing their own books, writing topics, team partners, and research topics).
- Enacting and modeling of the principles of democracy in a school or classroom.
- Attention to affective needs and the varying cognitive styles of individual students.
- Cooperative collaborative activity, developing the classroom as an interdependent community.
- Heterogeneously grouped classrooms where individual needs are met through inherently individualized activities, not segregation of bodies.
- Delivery of help to special needs students in regular classrooms.
- Varied and cooperative roles for teachers, parents, and administrators.
- Reliance on teachers' descriptive evaluation of student growth, including observational/anecdotal records, conference notes, and performance assessment rubrics.

Specific Strategies to Enhance Learning for Students With Learning Disabilities

In addition to general strategies, you can use specific strategies to differentiate the curriculum in a general education classroom to meet the needs of students with learning disabilities. Specific strategies include, for example, tiered assignments, modified assignments, agendas, graphic organizers, and literacy skill instruction.

Tiered assignments. Tiered assignments manipulate the same idea or input at different levels or tiers (Tomlinson, 2001). In tiered assignments the same lesson is presented to all students; however, you design two or more activities or assignments at differing levels of complexity. In this way each student still comes away with the important knowledge and understanding and at the same time is challenged at a level appropriate for his or her ability. The action words for Bloom's taxonomy of thinking skills can be used as guides to help you construct assignments at differing levels (see Chapter 5, Figure 5.12). Tiered assignments can be used to differentiate the curriculum for students with learning disabilities as well as for gifted and highly creative learners.

EXAMPLE: Tiered Assignments

Ms. Puckett's 4th grade class is studying a unit on American history in the twentieth century. As part of this unit she has created a series of lessons on sewage and waste disposal and the effect this technology has had on society. In one lesson she describes how sewage is treated in the city in which she lives, using pictures taken with her digital camera. At the end of the lesson students are given assignments at three different levels. At the first level, students are given a map that indicates the steps of the sewage treatment process. They are to label and describe each step of the process (Bloom's taxonomy—knowledge). At a second level, students are asked to list the steps involved in the treatment of sewage and then to create a map that indicates the process (Bloom's taxonomy—comprehension and application). At a third level, students are asked to list the steps used in the treatment of sewage and then to design a more efficient or effective sewage treatment process (Bloom's taxonomy—evaluation and synthesis).

Sometimes Ms. Puckett designates which students are to complete which assignment. But often, Ms. Puckett lets her students choose the assignment they wish to complete. This gives students the elements of choice and avoids the perception of MOTS. (MOTS is when gifted learners are given *more of the same* assignment as a way of differentiating their curriculum.) If you simply assign more work to gifted learners you will find that they soon learn to hide their giftedness. Instead, assignments for gifted learners should have higher levels of complexity. Also, advanced assignments are often more interesting than those at lower levels. Allowing students to choose their assignment gives all students opportunities to display thought processes that often are just as creative and complex as those of the students who have been formally identified as gifted learners.

Modified assignments. A variant of tiered assignments is to give a *modified assignment* or one that is shorter or more concise for special needs learners. Another way to modify assignments is to break assignments into manageable steps. For larger assignments, use a checklist or some other method to describe each step that must be completed. The goal of homework ideally is to reinforce learning; thus, it should involve practice of topics already covered in class (Good & Brophy, 1995). Unfortunately, many classroom teachers use homework as a measuring device to see if students have read the chapter or know the skill. Provide classroom time for students to work on the assignment. This allows you to structure the learning environment and help students individually.

Agendas. An *agenda* is a personalized list of tasks given to students (Tomlinson, 2001). The tasks are designed to accommodate their abilities and interests. Students are usually given two to three weeks to complete their agendas. You then act as a coach, helping students complete their agendas and providing short minilessons in both large group and small group settings. Agendas can also be used to differentiate the curriculum for gifted and highly creative learners.

EXAMPLE: Agendas for a Unit on Sewage Treatment

Personal agenda for: _____

Starting date: _____   Date for completion: _____

Student and Teacher Initial After Completion.

Student and Teacher Initial After Completion	Task	Special Instructions
	With a partner, read the article, "Sewage Treatment." Describe three interesting or important ideas.	Use reciprocal reading. Record the ideas in your learning log.
	Look on the Internet to find and describe health problems related to exposure to untreated sewage.	What is the name of the disease? What are the symptoms? Record your ideas in your learning log.
	Listen to the vocabulary tape that defines and describes each of the following words: sewage, treatment, recycle, sludge, aerobic, purification, chemicals, fecal matter, centrifuge, manure, dehydration, chemical, plant, refining, excrement, environment, ecology, purification, micro-organisms, bacteria, tertiary treatment, water.	Write five interesting or creative sentences. Each sentence should contain at least one vocabulary word. Record your sentences in your learning log.
	Complete the two sewage treatment worksheets.	Check your answers and put them in your portfolio.
	Choose two vocabulary words to include for study for your weekly spelling. Add eight of your own words that you wish to study this week.	Record the words and the definitions in your learning log. Look them up in the dictionary to make sure they are spelled correctly.
	Look on the Internet to find an interesting website related to sewage treatment.	Work with a partner to complete the website description sheet.

Graphic organizers. *Graphic organizers* are a visual representation of information to be presented in a lesson, displayed in a way that students can see the relationship of concepts, ideas, or items (Dye, 2000). Graphic organizers also assist students in making abstract ideas more concrete. Figures 7.4 to 7.6 contain three types of graphic organizers than can be used in social studies lessons. Other types of graphic organizers may include outlines, tables, graphs, charts, diagrams, or pictures.

Figure 7.4   Semantic Map

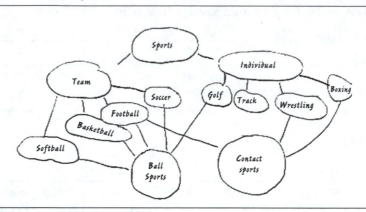

Figure 7.5   Flow Chart

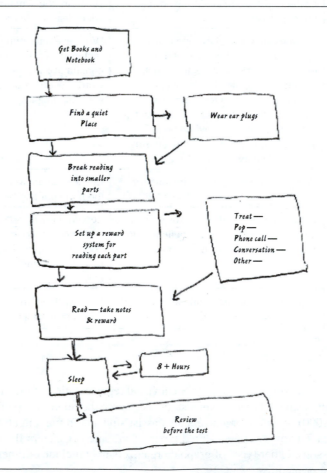

Figure 7.6   Venn Diagram

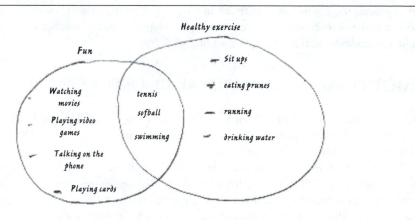

HOW DO I? **Use a KWL Chart**

Put a KWL chart on the blackboard or overhead. Before beginning the lesson, ask students to list what they know about a subject in the first column and what they want to know in the second column. This helps activate students' prior knowledge. At the end of the lesson ask students to make any necessary corrections in the first column and then to list what they have learned in the third column. Students also can use KWL charts individually as a prereading comprehension strategy for reading expository text.

KWL Chart

K—What Do You Know?	W—What Do You Want to Know?	L—What Did You Learn?

Expanded views of intelligence. Lessons and activities can be modified using Gardner's multiple intelligence theory (1999) and Sternberg's triarchic theory of intelligence (1996). This type of modification ensures multimodality of input and honors students' cognitive strengths (see Chapter 5).

Literacy Strategies. For low ability readers, teach comprehension skills to enable them to comprehend the expository text found in social studies and other texts (see Chapter 8). Also, design and use prereading, during-reading, and post-reading teacher-directed activities to enhance students' ability to create meaning with text.

EMOTIONAL OR BEHAVIORAL DISORDERS

An emotional or behavioral disorder exists when one's emotions or behaviors get in the way of learning and participating in the learning environment. The U.S. Department of Education's definition is in Figure 7.7.

There are both externalizing and internalizing emotional or behavioral disorders (Vaughn, Bos, & Schumm, 2003). Externalized behaviors include aggression, hitting, inability to pay attention, and impulsivity. Children who display these behaviors are more likely to be noticed and formally identified. Internalized behaviors include shyness, withdrawal, depression, fears/ phobias, or anxiety. Children displaying these are less likely to be noticed and identified.

Figure 7.7   U.S. Department of Education Definition of Emotional or Behavioral Disorders

"Emotional or behavioral disorders" means an established pattern of one or more of the following emotional or behavioral responses: (a) withdrawal or anxiety, depression, problems with mood, or feelings of self worth; (b) disordered thought processes with unusual behavior patterns and atypical communication styles; or (c) aggression, hyperactivity, or impulsivity.

The established pattern of emotional or behavioral responses must adversely affect educational or developmental performance, including intrapersonal, academic, vocational, or social skills; be significantly different from appropriate age, cultural, or ethnic norms; and be more than temporary, expected responses to stressful events in the environment. The emotional or behavioral responses must be consistently exhibited in at least three different settings, two of which must be educational settings, and one other setting in either the home, child care, or community. The responses must not be primarily the result of intellectual, sensory, or acute or chronic physical health conditions.

Strategies for Dealing With Externalized Behaviors

Strategies that focus on the outward behavior of students include social skills instruction and various behavior modification strategies.

Teach social skills explicitly. Often students may not have the social skills necessary to function well with others or even be aware of the need for such skills. Social studies provides an effective and appropriate context in which to teach social skills. In the context of this textbook, social skills are defined as purposeful strategies used to successfully interact with others in interpersonal and social situations. Teaching social skills involves purposeful instruction of positive behaviors so that students know how to act in important social and interpersonal situations. Some basic social skills are listed in Figure 7.8. Choose the skills that best apply to your grade level, students, and teaching situation. Add to this list as you observe

Figure 7.8   Social Skills

- Be willing to share with others.
- Be considerate of others. Do not take from, hurt, or embarrass other people.
- Respect others. Nobody is more or less important than anybody else.
- Smile or try to look pleasant.
- Greet people you meet or encounter in passing.
- Communicate. If somebody is hurting you or making you feel uncomfortable, tell that person. This is hard to do initially, but gets easier with time.
- Say no if you really do not want to do something. Do not allow yourself to be pressured.
- Wait patiently in line; take turns.
- Ask for help when you need it.
- Try to say only kind or positive things about others. Do not gossip, criticize, or condemn others.
- Encourage others in their efforts. Everybody is good at some things and not so good at others.
- Recognize and acknowledge when other people do a good job.
- Celebrate differences. Not everybody should be the same. Differences of opinion, experience, values, religions, and political views strengthen a society.
- Help others when you see that they need it.
- Identify and communicate your feelings when you feel angry, upset, or hurt.
- Make others feel important by paying attention to what they are saying. Do not let your conversation be disrupted.
- Cooperate with others in order to reach a shared goal.
- Learn when it is appropriate to put group needs ahead of self and when it is not.
- Seek synergy. Look for situations that work out to be in the best interest of all.
- Be fair and honest.
- Understand others. Look for the reasons behind their behaviors. Try to see things from the other person's point of view.
- Admit when you make mistakes.
- Apologize when you realize that you have made a mistake or hurt somebody.
- Look for the positive in others.
- Be a good listener. Encourage others to talk about themselves.
- Do not dominate the conversation.
- In conversation, talk in terms of the other person's interests.
- Try to find similarities and differences. Refuse to argue or debate as this seeks to create winners and losers and does not promote understanding.
- Asking somebody for a date: It is okay to be nervous. Be positive and considerate when asking somebody for a date. Ask well ahead of time (three days to a week). Respond politely if that person declines. Okay, well, thank you anyway. Also, in responding to a request, be polite and considerate of that person's feelings.
- Phone manners: Answer the phone by saying Hello, in a pleasant voice. As a caller, identify yourself and ask to speak to the individual you are calling.
- Be prompt. It is inconsiderate to make others wait.

your students interacting in the classroom and on the playground. Teach these social skills using direct instruction and by creating role-playing situations (see Chapter 9), and also by identifying and reinforcing positive or prosocial behaviors when you see students using them.

Behavior modification strategies. Behavior modification strategies involve rewarding behaviors that you wish to increase and ignoring or pairing with an aversive condition behaviors that you wish to decrease. There are a variety of methodologies that you can use. Among the easiest for classroom use are contingency contracts, token economies, and analysis of reinforcers (AR).

A *contingency contract* is a form of behavior modification that is effective in focusing on one or two specific behaviors that you wish to increase or decrease. Contingency contracts involve an if/then or when/then situation where receiving a reward or a privilege of some sort is contingent on a student's behavior. The contract provides a visual record and an external reminder for students. It also provides immediate feedback and holds students accountable for their behaviors.

EXAMPLE: A Contingency Contract

Mr. Brunansky, a 2nd grade teacher, used the contingency contract below with one of his students, Brad. Brad had trouble on the playground with other children, getting into fights and not being considerate. He also sometimes forgot classroom rules and acted out in class or did not complete his work. At conference time, Mr. Brunansky talked with Brad's parents and introduced the idea of a contingency contract. Mr. Brunansky identified two behaviors that he wanted to see more of: (a) being considerate of others on the playground, in gym class, and in the hallway, and (b) following classroom rules. With the approval of Brad's parents, Mr. Brunansky started a contingency contract where he gave Brad a rating on each behavior in the morning and in the afternoon. At the end of the week, Brad would take the contract home along with Mr. Brunansky's comments written on the back. If Brad had a score of 20 or better he would be allowed to watch TV that night. If he had a score of 25 or better he would be able to select a movie to watch at the video store. (When using contingency contracts it is best to start with low criteria to insure early success, then raise the criteria gradually.)

Key: 2 = good job, 1 = okay, 0 = let's try again.

	Monday	Tuesday	Wednesday	Thursday	Friday
A.M. Being Considerate of Others					
A.M. Follows Classroom Rules					
P.M. Being Considerate of Others					
P.M. Follows Classroom Rules					

This contract was taped inside of Brad's desk. Mr. Brunansky was able to give Brad fairly immediate feedback on his behavior twice a day. At the end of the week, Brad brought his contract to share with the principal or guidance counselor. This allowed Brad to get recognition for positive behavior or to explain where he needed to do better next time. After two weeks, Mr. Brunansky was able to raise the criteria slightly. After three weeks he moved to giving feedback just once a day, and eventually the contract was discontinued. The contingency contract also had the unanticipated benefit of improving Brad's number facts as he counted up his totals from day to day.

With a *token economy,* all students are able to earn a token, such as a chip, a star, or some sort of artificial money for outstanding performance related to academic performance, social skills, or friendship behaviors. Students are then able to use their tokens to buy some sort of reward or privilege such as eating lunch with the teacher, extra reading time, or prizes.

Analysis of reinforcers (AR) involves analyzing the behavior to try to determine what is reinforcing it, and then either eliminating it or strengthening a positive behavior by reinforcing it.

EXAMPLE: Analysis of Reinforcers

Sally calls out rude remarks in Ms. Gladden's 6th grade social studies class. This behavior appears to be reinforced by the reaction she gets from Ms. Gladden and from peers. After an analysis of the reinforcers, Ms. Gladden decides she can remove the reinforcement of this behavior by reacting calmly to Sally's remarks and by removing her from the immediate presence of peers, seating her at a table in the back of the room. If the behavior continues, Ms. Gladden may have to pair the behavior with an aversive conditioner. An aversive conditioner, sometimes known as punishment, is an unpleasant situation used to eliminate the behavior. The aversive conditioners that Ms. Gladden uses are asking Sally to talk with her at noon (thus removing her from her social group), or asking her to leave the room and spend time in the principal's office. In both situations, Ms. Gladden does not have to raise her voice or react in anger. She does not have to create a negative environment for other students. She is in full control and is focusing on the behavior, not the student.

You must be careful in the use of aversive conditioners. Avoid using them as the sole method of modifying behavior, for a variety of ethical reasons. Also, aversive conditioners are not effective in shaping behavior, as they do not teach or reinforce the correct behavior.

In Ms. Turkoglu's 4th grade class, Robert has been struggling with learning certain friendship behaviors. Ms. Turkoglu knows that when students are learning new behaviors she needs to reinforce them anytime she sees semblances of them. This reinforcer can be fairly quiet and simple. For example, when she sees Robert remembering to use one of the friendship behaviors, she quietly says, "Robert, I really like how you remembered to listen and let people talk in your small group today. Nice job." This reinforcer can also be made public. For example, after seeing Robert work well in a cooperative group, the teacher said, "Robert, you really worked well with your cooperative learning group today. I am going to let your group have first choice of activities during free time today."

Strategies for Attending to Emotions

Too often in working with students with emotional behavior disorders, teachers use strategies that focus only on external behaviors. This does nothing to attend to the emotions or the causes of internalized behaviors. Also, schools often reinforce problem behavior by separating these students from others and by trying to control them instead of building on their strengths or teaching positive behaviors. Peterson and Hittie (2003) recommend the following measures to prevent emotional disturbances from developing or escalating:

- Build a sense of community.
- Use engaging teaching practices.
- Teach appropriate behaviors instead of only punishing.
- Provide students with a sense of unconditional positive regard.

Three strategies for addressing emotional needs are the use of circle groups, learning logs, and "inner curriculum" activities. These can be used with all students to build a sense of community.

Circle groups. A *circle group* consists of three to five students who meet at a regular time, usually once a week, to share their thoughts or the experiences of their lives. Circle groups are based on the belief that humans benefit from engaging in authentic communication with others. The function of the circle group is to provide the structure for this honest dialogue as participants sit in a circle and share their insights and responses.

For each circle group session, give a self-reflective question or task to participants (see Figure 7.9). Give students the question or task before they move into their circle groups and ask them to record their initial ideas in a learning log or on a piece of paper. The act of writing allows them to generate insights, enhances reflection, and helps to organize their thinking. Some teachers even give the question or task a day or two ahead of time. Students then move into their circle group to share their ideas and insights.

Circle groups can play an important role in classrooms by helping students understand themselves and others. With primary students, use groups of three students, four with intermediate students, and five with middle and high school students. To establish trust, keep students in the same circle groups for at least ten weeks. Also, in working with circle groups, you will need to spend time teaching specific interpersonal and social skills and modeling appropriate circle group behavior.

Figure 7.10 contains seven tips to ensure the effectiveness of circle groups. You will need to teach students exactly what each tip means. It is helpful to create a poster with some or all of these tips to remind students how to function effectively in their circle groups.

Learning logs. Students can use *learning logs* as a place to record their thoughts, observations, interesting ideas, emotions, insights, and experiences. The learning log is a written version of their "thinking space" and thus should not be graded for spelling, mechanics, or content. Learning logs can be used to record general observations about students' lives and feelings as well as to record ideas or insights into a subject area. In a

Figure 7.9   Prompts or Tasks for Circle Groups

- What brings you joy and happiness?
- What special talents do you have? What are you really good at doing? What is something you are not very good at?
- How have you changed?
- What kinds of things do you like to learn about? How do you like to learn best?
- List five good things that have happened this week.
- Describe a lesson you have learned about life.
- What kind of person do you want to become?
- What do you like about you?
- What are you afraid of?
- List five interesting or important things that have happened in the last week.
- What do you wonder about? What would you like to know?
- What is something interesting or important that you noticed lately?
- What problems seem to come up often in your life?
- What things get in the way of what you want to do?
- What is most precious to you?
- Whom do you look up to? Why?
- List one or more songs that describe or relate to something going on in your life. What is the connection?
- Complete the following sentence: I feel [happy, sad, proud, angry, anxious, upset, excited, peaceful] when _____.
- Describe who you are, using only pictures and symbols, no letters or words.
- Complete the sentence: I will be happier when _____.

Figure 7.10   Tips for Circle Groups

---

1. Make sure everyone contributes.

2. Keep the conversation moving. (Do not spend too much time on any one person or issue.)

3. All views must be heard. Make sure that no person dominates the group.

4. Accept all ideas.

5. Seek always to understand. Never seek to disprove (or disapprove of) someone's idea.

6. Do not try to force others to accept your ideas or force your opinion on another.

7. Celebrate tangents! Everything is important. Allow the group to get off the subject.

social studies context students might record: (a) ideas related to lesson content; (b) ideas describing how the lesson content connects with their lives or experiences; (c) insights, observations, feelings, or associations related to the lesson; or (d) other observations about their lives (see Chapter 15).

Having others respond to learning logs greatly increases students' interest and improves the quality of their thinking and writing, as they receive feedback on how their ideas are perceived by others. Feedback also allows them to experience bits of each others' lives and emotions and, thus, helps them to understand each other better.

Inner curriculum activities. The *inner curriculum* is a school's plan for addressing the inner life of students. It consists of a series of experiences and activities that helps students examine their emotions, imagination, intuition, ideals, values, and sense of wonder (Johnson, 2005). The inner curriculum can be inserted into the social studies curriculum. It is composed of four elements:

- *Intrapersonal elements* involving students' emotions and intuition. In dealing with emotions, students identify feelings and then connect them to external events or situations. Drawing on intuition teaches students how to use their general impressions or sense of knowing apart from logic and emotion.
- *Expressions of the intrapersonal.* Students give expression to what they discover in intrapersonal activities. The arts are often used for this. Music, dance, visual art, drama, poetry, and creative writing can all be used as separate curricular elements or used across the curriculum. Also, personal metaphors, journal writing, and small group discussions where students are engaged in honest dialogue can also be used to express intrapersonal elements of the inner curriculum.
- *Interpersonal elements.* Students understand themselves in the context of a group, culture, or social setting. Activities include cooperative group activities, values clarification, moral dilemmas, and aesthetic responses to literature.
- *The human condition.* This element of the inner curriculum helps students to know themselves in the context of humanity. The goal is to begin to understand what it is to be human and to find similarities among people over time and across cultures. Comparisons using mythology, literature, and history as well as newspapers and current events can be used to this end. The inner curriculum activities, like the circle groups and learning logs with aesthetic responses, are effective strategies for attending to the emotions of all students.

ATTENTION DEFICIT/HYPERACTIVITY DISORDER

Students with attention deficit/hyperactivity disorder (ADHD) have a hard time concentrating or focusing. According to the DSM IV-TR (American Psychiatric Association, 2000), ADHD is a disruptive behavior disorder characterized by the presence of a set of chronic and impairing behavior patterns that display abnormal levels of inattention, hyperactivity, or their combination. The symptoms of ADHD are listed in Figure 7.11.

Figure 7.11   Symptoms of ADHD

An individual with ADHD may display some or all of the following symptoms:

- Difficulty sustaining attention.
- Easily distracted.
- Often does not seem to listen.
- Often shifts from one uncompleted activity to another.
- Often loses things necessary for tasks.
- Often interrupts or intrudes on others.
- Has difficulty awaiting turn in groups.
- Often blurts out answers to questions.
- Often engages in physically dangerous activities without considering the consequences.
- Often talks excessively.
- Has difficulty playing quietly.
- Has difficulty remaining seated.
- Often fidgets or squirms in seat.
- Has difficulty following instructions.

Peterson and Hittie (2002) describe the following strategies for creating engaging learning opportunities to help meet the special learning needs of students with ADHD:

1. Use expanded versions of intelligence.

2. Use workshops, authentic learning, and activity-based learning.

3. Provide opportunities for creativity, choices, and open-ended assignments.

4. Create working environments that involve social interaction.

5. Provide situations where students can be alone or have limited distraction, such as study carrels, in the back of the room, or with headphones and soft music.

6. Help students set goals, plan, break goals into short-term steps, and monitor their progress.

7. Help students organize their work by developing notebooks, filing systems, or computer organization.

8. Provide tools to assist in planning, scheduling, and tracking assignments.

9. Provide written as well as oral instructions.

10. Establish a time line for assignments.

11. Build on students' strengths.

TEACHERS IN ACTION: Accommodating Special Needs Students

I am a general education teacher and I have three MR students and one of those students has severe behavioral problems. Last year, 9 of my 32 students had special needs. You can do it! My classroom is self-contained, so I teach them social studies also. During my social studies time, they are expected to try their best to follow along in the books with us (they average a first or second grade reading level). I partner them with someone they like and who I feel will be able to help if needed. I ask both partners if they would like to have a partner and I ask the partner without special needs if he or she would like to be with the special needs student, etc. I don't always put the brightest children with them. It's who they feel comfortable with. During social studies I try not to do a lot of written work or independent readings. We dramatize a lot of the lessons and that enables all of the students to become involved. We also do a lot of drawings (we draw our visualizations from the reading). When it comes time to look up vocabulary words, I give my special needs students fewer words to look up. I also give them the page the word is on. What I do for each child depends on how low he or she is. On the tests, I read the test to them individually and I give them fewer questions. If the question has an A, B, C, D answer, I will eliminate two of the answers so they have fewer to choose from. I do not give them fill in the blank unless they have a word bank. If I am running short on time, I will give them an oral test. I hope I have helped you. Oh, yeah! I also let them listen to the lesson on tape. Good luck!

—Christi

Author Reflection: Creating an inclusive classroom is not something easily mastered by a beginning teacher. However, inclusive teaching is good teaching for all students. The goal in all good teaching is to find and develop each student's strengths. This is exactly what inclusive teaching seeks to do.

A complaint I often hear from people who are not familiar with inclusive education is that placing special needs students in a general education classroom will somehow take away from the general education students' learning, to which I would say, "Nonsense." First, if you understand inclusion and know how to use inclusive strategies, you will be able to design learning activities to meet the needs of all your students, including highly creative and intellectually gifted students. Second, the students in your inclusive classroom setting should still be in the least restrictive environment. This means that some special needs students will be in your room full time with the help of a special education teacher, while others will be there just some of the time. Finally, and perhaps most important, an inclusive classroom setting offers students the greatest of all possible lessons: the lesson of compassion and understanding. Although all humans may not be of equal ability, all are of equal value. All humans, regardless of their ability or physical condition, deserve friendship and care.

The worth of any society should be judged by how it cares for the least able of its citizens.

What is your response to the case? How do your reactions compare with the author's reflection?

Intelligence is the ability to solve problems or create products.

HIGHLY CREATIVE AND
INTELLECTUALLY GIFTED LEARNERS

Most definitions of gifted and talented children recognize five areas of giftedness: general intellectual ability, specific academic aptitude, creative or productive thinking, leadership ability, and visual and performing arts. The U.S. Department of Education (1993) offers the definition of gifted and talented shown in Figure 7.12.

Figure 7.12.   U.S. Department of Education Definition of Gifted and Talented

Children and youth with outstanding talent perform or show the potential for performing at remarkably high levels of accomplishment when compared with others of their age, experience, or environment. These children and youth exhibit high performance capability in intellectual, creative and/or artistic areas, possess an unusual leadership capacity, or excel in specific academic fields. They require services or activities not ordinarily provided by the schools. Outstanding talents are present in children and youth from all cultural groups, across all economic strata, and in all areas of human endeavor.

GO THERE

- National Research Center on the Gifted and Talented: http://www.gifted.uconn.edu/ nrcgt/resource.html#identification
- National Association for Gifted Children: http://www.nagc.org/
- Jacob K. Javits Gifted and Talented Students Education Program: http://www.ed .gov/programs/javits/index.html

We often think of gifted and talented students as those who perform well in school or have outstanding scores on standardized tests that claim to measure intelligence. However, intelligence involves much more than what can be measured on these tests. Howard Gardner (1983) describes intelligence as the ability to solve problems or to create things that are valued in one or more cultural settings. Since intelligence or problem solving comes in many forms, it is limiting to define intellectually gifted individuals by their ability to perform on tests that offer only a narrow selection of problems to be solved. However, by merging Gardner's conception of intelligence and the U.S. Department of Education's definition of gifted and talented children, a broader definition of giftedness can be created. Thus, a gifted individual might more accurately be defined as one who demonstrates the ability to solve problems, create products, or perform at remarkably high levels of accomplishment. These problems, products, or performances can occur in all areas, including the visual and performing arts, various academic areas, leadership and interpersonal skills, and other areas involving creativity and invention.

General strategies that can be used in a social studies class to meet the needs of gifted and talented students include tiered assignments and agendas, described above. As mentioned earlier, it is important not to simply give gifted and talented students more work to do. Instead, their special learning needs can be met by a curriculum that is differentiated to include three elements: choice, challenge, and complexity. Teaching strategies that include these elements are the use of expanded views of intelligence (see Chapter 5), problem solving (see Chapter 10), inquiry learning (see Chapter 11), and using creative and critical thinking skills (see Chapter 12). Other teaching strategies that can be used are curriculum compacting and differentiation, open-ended and complex activities, and alternative reading selections.

Curriculum compacting and differentiation. Streamlining the regular curriculum to eliminate the repetition of previously mastered material is referred to as *curriculum compacting*

(Renzulli & Reis, 1997). Students demonstrate mastery of basic skills or concepts by "testing out of" a unit or area of study. This provides them time for appropriate enrichment or accelerated learning activities.

Open-ended and complex activities. Design activities and assignments that are open-ended and allow students to go as far as they want. You will note that many of the activities in this book fit this description. For example, instead of having students complete a worksheet on sewage treatment, Ms. Hersch instead had some or all of her students design a more efficient, effective, or innovative sewage treatment process.

Alternative reading material. Instead of the regular chapter in the social studies textbook, provide alternative reading material that describes similar ideas at higher levels. For younger students you could use upper grade textbooks. For older students look for journal, magazine, or Internet articles. Always give gifted students a choice of which reading material to select.

STUDENTS WHO ARE BILINGUAL OR HAVE LIMITED ENGLISH PROFICIENCY

The last area of diversity described in this chapter examines bilingual students or those who have limited English proficiency (LEP). As more cultures assimilate into our communities, students with English as a second language (ESL) are becoming a greater part of our school culture. There are six types of language-ability students:

- Non-English speaking students who are monolingual in their home languages.
- Limited English speakers who are fluent in a language other than English.
- Student who speaks both English and another language fluently.
- Students who are limited in both English and their other language.
- Students who speak English fluently but are limited in their other language.
- Students who speak English fluently but no other language.

In her book, *Adapting Instruction to Accommodate Students in Inclusive Settings,* Judy Wood (2000) describes key concepts in second language acquisition. Below, nine of these are listed along with their implications for general education teachers.

1. Language acquisition is a process the human brain does well. Humans are naturally wired to learn language. This is something we do naturally starting at a very early age by being immersed in a language and having meaningful interactions with others. You should immerse your ESL students in the language of the classroom and create environments that are rich in stimulus and interaction with students and teachers.

2. Students learn a second language in different ways and at different paces. There is not a standard path or set of benchmarks. The pace at which ESL students learn a second language is related to their learning styles, level of education, parents' level of education, experience, and knowledge base.

3. Language acquisition is not easy for children. Children do not learn languages any more easily than adults, because they are having to learn new concepts as well as the labels for these concepts. (Adults have a knowledge base filled with concepts, and for them, learning a new language is simply a matter of putting the right label on the right concept.) So that ESL students do not fall behind in learning concepts, encourage them to continue to use and develop their first language.

4. Learning a second language takes time. Students are often learning about a new culture as well as a new language. Oral fluency can take from three to five years. Be patient, provide instruction that promotes English acquisition, and remember that a lack of English proficiency does not indicate a lack of intelligence.

5. Silence is sometimes needed. Do not be afraid of silence. Some English language learners go through periods of silence when they are inputting language. Allow your students to experience silence. Also, when they are ready to verbalize, create a risk-free environment where it is okay to experiment and make mistakes.

6. Students need context to learn English. Isolated drills or flash cards do not provide a meaningful context to learn English. In your classroom, work with the ESL teacher to provide a rich context by providing words to study that are part of social studies and other classes.

7. Students need meaningful interaction with native speakers to learn a second language. Provide opportunities for ESL students to interact with other students by using cooperative learning groups, literacy circles, and other classroom strategies that have students talking and interacting with others.

8. Errors in language production indicate progress. Errors are a necessary stage in language acquisition. Expect mistakes and correct them gently using modeling.

9. Receptive language skills are usually more advanced than productive skills. ESL students can understand, but cannot always use, written or spoken language to convey meaning. Consider using group assignments as well as modifying assignments by allowing for pictures or other forms of communication.

NCSS STANDARDS

Thematic Standards

The following NCSS thematic standards are addressed in this chapter. See Appendix A for a full description of the relevant thematic standards.

Early Grades

I. Culture: a., b.

Middle Grades

I. Culture: a., b.

Pedagogical Standards

The following NCSS pedagogical standards are addressed in this chapter:

  I. Learning and Development.

 II. Differences in Learning Style.

III. Critical Thinking, Problem Solving, and Performance Skills.

IV. Active Learning and Motivation.

 V. Inquiry, Collaboration, and Supportive Classroom Interaction.

VI. Planning Instruction.

Essential Skills for Social Studies

The following NCSS essential skills for social studies are addressed in this chapter:

I. Relationships and Social Participation.
   A. Personal Skills.
   B. Group Interaction Skills.

Chapter Review: Key Points

1. Curriculum and learning experiences need to be differentiated to meet the diverse learning needs and interests of all the students in your social studies classes.

2. Public Law 94-142 guarantees free and appropriate public education for all students in the least restrictive environment.

3. Whereas mainstreaming tries to adapt the student to meet the demands of the curriculum, inclusion adapts the curriculum to meet the needs of a diverse population of students.

4. A learning disability is a discrepancy between ability and desired achievement in basic reading skill, reading comprehension, listening comprehension, oral expression, written expression, math calculation, or mathematics reasoning.

5. Designing learning experiences that do not frustrate or bore students is an important first step in meeting the special learning needs of all students.

6. In a general education setting you can meet the learning needs of students with learning disabilities by using tiered assignments, short or modified assignments, agendas, graphic organizers, expanded views of intelligence, and direct instruction of reading and comprehension skills.

7. In an educational setting, an emotional behavioral disorder exists when one's emotions or behaviors prevent or interfere with learning.

8. In a general education setting you can deal with behaviors by teaching social skills and using contingency contracts or other behavior modification strategies.

9. In a general education setting you can address students' emotional difficulties through the use of circle groups, learning logs, and inner curriculum activities.

10. Students with attention deficit/hyperactivity disorder have a hard time concentrating or focusing.

11. Gifted and talented students are those who demonstrate the ability to solve problems, create products, or perform at remarkably high levels of accomplishment in any area, including the visual and performing arts, various academic subjects, leadership and interpersonal skills, or other areas involving creativity and invention.

12. Choice, challenge, and complexity can be introduced into the curriculum of gifted and talented students through the use of expanded views of intelligence, problem solving, inquiry learning, and creative and critical thinking skills.

13. In a general education setting you can meet the learning needs of gifted and talented students by using tiered assignments, agendas, curriculum compacting and differentiation, open-ended and complex activities, and alternative reading material.

14. Recognizing nine key concepts of second language acquisition will help you understand the special needs of English language learners and create an effective learning environment for them.

Making Connections

1. Why is social studies a good venue for addressing issues of diversity?

2. Describe a time when you were a less able learner.

3. Describe a time when your emotions got in the way.

4. When were you a more able learner? When did you know more and feel frustrated?

5. When you have to read a book or study, what things make it hard for you to concentrate? What do you do to help yourself?

6. Describe three interesting or important ideas that you will use from this chapter.

7. Create a picture, diagram, or symbol that represents one or more ideas found in this chapter.

8. Create a learning log entry for this chapter along with an aesthetic response.

9. Use two of the operations in Bloom's taxonomy to create a tiered assignment for this chapter.

10. What are the three activities from this chapter that you will be most likely to use in your classroom?

11. In what ways do you see the three holistic learning ideas related to intrapersonal connections, interpersonal connections, and interconnectedness reflected here?

Chapter 8

TEXTBOOKS AND SOCIAL STUDIES

Thinking Ahead

1. What strategies do you use to help read and understand a textbook?

2. How is reading a paperback novel different from reading a college textbook?

3. What are you going to do to help your low readers acquire the necessary knowledge from a social studies textbook?

4. After reading a chapter in a social studies textbook, what are some activities besides worksheets that you might use to help reinforce and expand ideas found in the text?

5. How do you learn new words?

6. What new words have come into our vocabulary in the last ten years?

HELPING STUDENTS COMPREHEND

Reading is the act of creating meaning with text. This section describes how to improve students' ability to comprehend their social studies and other textbooks through the use of comprehension skills.

What Is Comprehension?

Comprehension is the act of constructing meaning with text (Dole, Duffy, Duffy, Roehler, & Pearson, 1991). Meaning does not reside in the text alone waiting for the reader

Comprehension is the act of constructing meaning with text.

to passively absorb it. Instead, the reader plays an active role, using information in the head to filter, organize, interpret, and generate relationships with incoming information and to ultimately construct meaning (Reutzel & Cooter, 1996). Comprehension then is an interaction between word identification, knowledge, and comprehension skills (Cunningham, Moore, Cunningham, & Moore, 1995).

The Need for Comprehension Skills

Currently, little time is spent in most classrooms teaching students how to comprehend expository text (Reutzel & Cooter, 1996). Instead, much of reading instruction is spent developing accurate and automatic word identification skills and increasing oral reading fluency. This does not guarantee that students will develop the skills necessary to successfully read expository text. And simply exposing students to comprehension worksheets or other tasks requiring them to recall information found in a text also does very little to increase their ability to comprehend expository text (Dole et al., 1991). In order to improve students' ability to comprehend expository texts independently, explicit instruction is needed in the use of comprehension skills (Guthrie et al., 1996).

What Are Comprehension Skills?

Comprehension skills are the strategies a reader uses to construct meaning and retrieve information from text. Comprehension skills are very much like thinking skills. As described in Chapter 12, a thinking skill is a cognitive process that can be broken down into steps and taught explicitly. Comprehension skills are also cognitive processes that can be broken down into steps and explicitly taught. Three types of comprehension skills are described below: prereading skills, during-reading skills, and postreading skills. These skills can be easily learned and flexibly applied to a wide variety of reading situations.

Prereading Comprehension Skills

Prereading skills are used primarily to activate relevant schemata (Figure 8.1). Schemata are hypothesized knowledge structures in memory that contain elements of related information (Glover, Ronning, & Bruning, 1990). By activating these, the reader is better able to connect new knowledge to knowledge already in memory.

Preview and overview. Using this skill, the reader first notes the title and subheadings in the text to get a sense of the structure. Next, the first and final paragraphs are read to get a sense of the content. This helps the reader interpret the text as it is then read. Finally, the text is read.

Web and brainstorm. Here the structure of the text is used to create a semantic web. The title or topic of the chapter or text is used as a central node. The headings of each section are used as subnodes. The reader then brainstorms on each subnode to generate relevant knowledge. The web provides a visual organizer that shows the relationships between concepts, which are then used to help the reader interpret the text. This same web can also be used as a postreading skill. Here, the reader uses the information gleaned from the text to add to and refine the web.

Figure 8.1   Pre-Reading Comprehension Skills

Preview/Overview

1. Look at the title and headings.

2. Read the first paragraph and last paragraphs.

3. Read the article or chapter.

Web and Brainstorm

1. Look at the title and headings.

2. Create a web using the title or topics as a central node.

3. Using section headings as subnodes.

4. Brainstorm on each subnode.

5. Read the article or chapter.

6. Add to and modify the original web.

During-Reading Comprehension Skills

During-reading comprehension skills are used to monitor comprehension, to evaluate ideas gleaned from each paragraph, and to begin to organize ideas within the structure of the text (Figure 8.2.)

Figure 8.2   During-Reading Comprehension Skills

Paragraph Reread

1. Read each paragraph quickly.

2. Reread to find important sentences or ideas.

3. Continue.

Read and Pause

1. Read a paragraph.

2. Pause and check. (Do I understand?)

3. Return or resume.

Paragraph reread. This skill is used by many expert readers intuitively. First, a paragraph is quickly read to get a general sense of its content. Next, the paragraph is read a second time. Finally, the reader analyzes the structure and content of each paragraph and evaluates the information in order to find an important sentence or ideas. This also helps the reader to make connections with the other ideas found in the text.

Read and pause. This skill is designed primarily to monitor comprehension and develop metacognitive awareness. Here the reader pauses after each paragraph to see if there is sufficient understanding, then either returns to reread the paragraph or continues reading the next paragraph. Some readers find it helpful to use a three-by-five-inch index card to help focus and concentrate when reading. The card is moved to the bottom of each paragraph as it is being read.

Postreading Comprehension Skills

Postreading skills are used to reconstruct important ideas, organize those ideas, and evaluate those ideas (Figure 8.3).

Article reread. First, the text is read quickly to provide the reader with a sense of topic. This knowledge is then used to interpret, sort, and evaluate the information as the text is read a second time. Finally, interesting or important ideas are recorded.

Sequencing. First, interesting or important ideas are recorded as the text is being read. Then those ideas are evaluated and arranged in order of their importance. Finally, readers add their own ideas and interpretations to the list.

Figure 8.3   Post-Reading Comprehension Skills

Article Reread

1. Read the article or chapter.
2. Reread the article or chapter.
3. Note or record important ideas.

Sequencing

1. As you read, list important ideas.
2. After reading, arrange ideas in order of their importance.
3. Look for your own ideas to add.

Teaching Comprehension Skills

A review of the research indicates that students appear to benefit whenever cognitive processes are made clear and explicit (Adams, 1989; Bereiter & Scardamalia, 1992; Marzano,

1991). It makes sense then that explicit instruction be used in the teaching of comprehension skills. To do this, use the five *elements of effective skills instruction* described in Chapter 12: (a) direct instruction and modeling, (b) identification of the procedural components, (c) guided practice, (d) regular practice, and (e) application or use in other areas in order to ensure transfer.

As with any skills, students need regular practice with comprehension skills in order to be able to use them effectively. Any time students are asked to read expository text they should be reminded to use a comprehension skill. Having these comprehension skills displayed in poster form will allow you to quickly point to the steps. You should encourage students to use the comprehension skill with which they are most comfortable.

EXAMPLE: Reinforcing Comprehension Skills

Mr. Marino, a 3rd grade teacher, said to his class: "Before we get into our social studies class, we're going to quickly practice using a comprehension skill we've learned yesterday, *Read and Pause*. (Each student opens the text to the chapter which will be assigned that day.) With this comprehension skill, you read a paragraph, pause to see if you've understood what you've just read, and then either return and reread the paragraph or resume reading. Go ahead and try this with the first three paragraphs. When you're finished, record two or three ideas in your reading journal that you think are interesting or important. Be ready to share these. (Mr. Marino allows time for most of the students to read the text and record some ideas, then he continues.) Were there any paragraphs that you needed to read only once? What paragraphs did you have to read twice? Who has an idea from the text that they're ready to share?"

EXAMPLE: Integrating Comprehension Skills Across the Curriculum

Ms. Sanchez has just finished describing the solar system to her 8th grade students. Now she would like them to read the chapter in their science textbooks that reinforces the concepts covered in her lesson. She points to the chart which has the thinking frames for *Paragraph Reread* located on the wall near the front of the room. She says to her students, "For tomorrow you'll be reading Chapter 5, The Solar System. You have about 30 minutes in class today to start. That should be time for many of you to finish. Trying using our new comprehension skill, *Paragraph Reread,* to help you get ideas from this chapter. Remember the steps." (She points to the poster and quickly reviews each step.) "When you are finished reading this chapter, record four ideas that you think are interesting or important in your learning log and be ready to share with your group tomorrow."

TEACHER STRATEGIES TO HELP STUDENTS COMPREHEND

Most classrooms contain students of widely varying reading abilities. It is possible to have students who are reading two or more grade levels below their current grade level as well as

Comprehension skills help readers retrieve information from text and should be taught explicitly.

students who are reading two or more levels above. What can you do to insure a successful reading experience for all? One approach is the *Scaffolded Reading Experience* (SRE) in which a teacher creates a carefully orchestrated set of activities to assist students in successfully engaging in any reading they do (Johnson & Graves, 1997). Based on the concept of scaffolding (a temporary and adjustable support that allows accomplishment of a task that would be impossible without the scaffold's support), the SRE is a flexible framework designed to help all students get the most out of every literacy experience.

To implement a SRE, select pre-, during-, and postreading activities that help students comprehend what they are reading. In general, with less able readers and for more difficult selections, more scaffolding is needed. Conversely, with more able readers and for less difficult selections, less scaffolding is needed. The scaffolded reading framework is flexible and adaptable in that it presents a variety of options from which you will select those that are best suited for your students and situation.

Prereading Activities

Prereading activities prepare students to read the upcoming selection. Five strategies are described here.

Connect with students' lives or connect related new information to known information. This strategy helps to make the unfamiliar more familiar by connecting the information to be read to what students already know. The Comparison Chart described in Chapter 12 can be used here.

Use fluency to activate background knowledge. Use the thinking skill *fluency* to generate ideas and information about the upcoming selection (see Chapter 12). In a large group, brainstorm concepts related to the upcoming selection or chapter. Ask students what they know about the topic and to record their responses on the board. This is another way of connecting the new information to the known information.

Preteach important concepts. At times you may need to preteach important concepts in order to build text specific knowledge. The text would then be used to reinforce or expand upon concepts that are already familiar to students.

Preteach vocabulary. Before reading, define and describe key words that will be in the upcoming text. In this way, both the words and the related concepts will be familiar to students when they are encountered in the text.

Preteaching using a graphic organizer. Use a graphic organizer in the form of an outline, semantic web, or any visual display to enable students to see the structure of the information to be covered. Provide this in the form of an overhead, poster, or student handout, then briefly go over the concepts before reading.

During-Reading Activities

During-reading activities include both things that students themselves do as they are reading and things that you might do to assist them as they are reading. Avoid round-robin reading where one student reads a paragraph or section out loud and other students follow along. This strategy tends to put too much focus on successfully pronouncing words and too little focus on creating meaning. Besides, round-robin reading is an artificial form of reading. You are not very likely to encounter a group of people in a library, taking turns, reading the same section out loud.

Active outlining. Give students an outline describing the major sections of the chapter. On this outline, leave space for students to record ideas. After students read each section of the chapter, they record interesting or important ideas on their outline. This strategy works well with students who are working in pairs.

Chapters on tape. You can avoid having low readers fall behind conceptually by making chapters available for them to listen to on tape. During reading time have a tape recorder with headphones available on a table in the classroom. All students should be given the opportunity to listen to the chapter on tape with the requirement that they also follow along with their text. Many will soon find that they are able to read faster than they are able to listen. Also, these audio tapes can be created by older students for low readers at younger grade levels. This provides them the opportunity and justification to practice reading using easier text.

Group read. Group reading is a cooperative learning activity designed to meet the needs of low readers, yet it can also be opened-ended with creative activities designed to meet the needs of all students. Here students are put in heterogeneous groups of three to six students with high and low readers in each group. The task for each group is to read the assigned text and then produce some sort of product that demonstrates their learning. The following roles might be assigned.

- President—makes all decisions.
- Reader(s)—one or two people who read the text out loud.
- Note taker(s)—one or two people who record the important ideas.
- Idea pointer—points out the important ideas.
- Artist—demonstrates one or more of the important ideas visually using a diagram or pictures.
- Speaker—presents ideas to the rest of the class.

Students read the assigned text in small group and then hand in some sort of product. To make students individually accountable, have each record three to five interesting or important ideas in their learning log.

Modify the text. For low readers, look for ways to modify the text in order to create an easier version with just the main ideas (see Chapter 7). Conversely, for gifted readers, look for more complicated or high level texts that cover similar topics.

Postreading Activities

Postreading activities serve a variety of purposes. They provide opportunities for students to

- synthesize and organize information gleaned from the text so that they can understand and recall important points,
- reinforce or reformulate concepts and ideas,
- analyze and evaluate the information presented,
- respond to the text in a variety of ways,
- manipulate important ideas from the text,
- expand or extend the information from the text.

Any of the activities described in this text can be designed to be used as a postreading activity. Move beyond using only worksheets that ask students to regurgitate or replicate information found in the text. Worksheets can be used effectively as a postreading activity; however, their value is greatly diminished when they are the only such activity used and also when they are used solely for evaluation purposes. Below are some variations that you might consider for postreading activities.

Understanding windows. *Understanding windows* is a strategy for finding out what students know and what is unclear or fuzzy. Students here draw two large squares on a blank sheet of paper (Figure 8.4). The squares should take up most of the page. One window is the clear window. Students list three to five ideas from the chapter or text that seem clear here. In the unclear window, students list ideas that are still a little unclear or fuzzy. They then share their ideas in small groups. This allows students to converse about ideas in the text. Often, many of the things in the unclear window are moved to the clear window through this conversation. The understanding windows also provide you with a form of formative assessment, giving you a sense of what ideas you need to reteach.

Figure 8.4   Understanding Windows

Clear	Unclear

Double journal entry (see Chapter 5). Here students draw a line down the middle of their paper, then they record three to ten interesting or important ideas from the text on the left side. On the right side they record their personal interpretations, associations, or reactions to the idea.

Support-a-statement (see Chapter 4). Give students a statement related to the chapter or assigned text they have finished reading. They must then go back into the chapter to find ideas or information to support this idea. This can also be used as a prereading activity as it sets a purpose for reading.

I-chart. After reading a chapter in a text, students list what they consider to be the three to six interesting or important or ideas (see Chapter 6). Students then examine these to create a related inference or big idea (see Figure 8.5). This activity can be done individually; however, it works best with a buddy or in a small group. To extend this, students work individually and use the I-chart to list and examine interesting or important events that occurred in their lives, in current events, or in history during a certain time and place.

Four square (see Chapter 9). Here four students each write what they consider to be the most interesting or important idea from the chapter in their learning logs or on a separate piece of paper. They then meet with three other students. On a large sheet of paper, they create a square cut into four sections. Each student records his or her idea in one of the squares. Students then look for an inference or big idea related to the four ideas.

GO THERE

- Information and activities related to reading comprehension: http://www.literacy .uconn.edu/compre.htm
    http://www.reading.org/
- Research-based strategies and information related to improving comprehension: http://www.readingonline.org/articles/handbook/pressley/index.html
    http://www.ncte.org/collections/adolescentliteracy/resources/116835.htm

Figure 8.5   I-Chart

Interesting or Important Ideas:
Inference or Big Idea:

TEACHERS IN ACTION: Using Texts to Teach Successfully

I teach fifth grade. There is so much vocabulary and material in the book that I believe that if kids come out with general concepts about history they are doing quite well. My expectation is that students will remember main ideas. What caused the Civil War? Who was it between? How was the Civil War resolved? We also do the tapes in class. I also assign the textbook for independent reading after I go over the main ideas and vocabulary. You could try what I do: I give a quiz every week on the material we have covered that week. I let them use the textbook for quizzes. That way, they do pass the quiz.

   When I give a test, I spend a couple of days reviewing, then I give them my own test.

   One of the problems is that if you are using the publisher's test, you may be giving them something that is too hard for them. Your students' success may depend upon their reading comprehension levels. I make up my own quizzes and tests which I believe are suited for all grade levels. If you have children who are poorer readers, you can put a word bank after every few questions (if it's fill in the blanks). If it's multiple choice, maybe you can give them A, B, and C as choices instead of A, B, C, and D. I got this idea from a special education teacher. Some of the teachers have tried this with the low readers and special education kids. I have found that one of the reasons kids hate social studies so much is that they are expected to memorize so much stuff. Maybe you can just quiz them on the main ideas, as I mentioned

(Continued)

(Continued)

above. You can also give them a grade from a project, a skit, a poster, or even an essay test. Last year, I asked my fifth graders to write an essay on anything they could remember about the Civil War. I told them that if they filled one side of a piece of lined paper with the main ideas of the Civil War, they would receive an A on the paper. If they filled up ¾ of the paper, they would receive a B, etc. They ALL shot for the A. Every single one of my kids answered the essay question (the unit test, by the way) in a wonderful way! The work was outstanding, and they remembered so much about the Civil War that I was impressed. We proudly posted these, along with the Civil War posters that they also decided to do.

Good luck! I know you can help all students achieve success in social studies.

—Sarah, Fifth Grade

Author Reflection: In education, we need far more teachers and far fewer measurers. A measurer is one who simply gives a homework assignment, corrects it the next day, and records the scores. A teacher is one who designs activities and assignments to help students manipulate the information and understand new ideas to the best of their abilities. A teacher doesn't have to record the score on every homework assignment. A teacher tries to catch students being successful. A teacher knows that a paper and pencil test is only one of many ways for students to demonstrate their knowing (see Chapter 5).

One strategy that has worked successfully with my students from 3rd grade to graduate school is to allow them to use one page of notes (front and back) on any test or exam. They can use any form of notes they want, as long as they are contained on one sheet of paper. They can even type them up using six-point type and three-tenths-inch margins. Students soon find that the very act of organizing their notes helps them understand. Most do not even need to use them when they answer questions on the exam. Also, knowing that my students have notes invites me to make my exams more about understanding things and less about remembering things.

What is your response to the case? How do your reactions compare with the author's reflection?

ATTENDING TO STUDENTS' VOCABULARY

There is a cyclical effect between vocabulary, reading comprehension, and knowledge. Word knowledge affects reading comprehension, which in turn helps students expand their knowledge bases, which in turn facilitates vocabulary growth and reading comprehension.

While students know and can read newly acquired words, their knowledge is often partial, incomplete, or lacking deep meanings for many of these words. Thus, instruction is needed to strengthen students' depth and breadth of word knowledge and to move new words into their productive vocabularies.

Features of Effective Vocabulary Instruction

Susan Watts (1995) describes six features of effective vocabulary instruction:

- Students are provided multiple exposure to words in a variety of contexts over time.
- Words are taught in the context of a story, theme, or content area unit.
- Teachers help students activate prior knowledge when learning new words.
- Relationships are drawn between new words and known words and concepts.
- Students are taught to use context clues and dictionaries to enhance their word knowledge.
- Students are encouraged to interact with the words so they are able to process them deeply.

Strategies for Developing Students' Vocabulary

Based on the six features above, six strategies for developing students' vocabulary are described here:

Word walls. A word wall is a large sheet of butcher paper, hung on the wall or bulletin board, and used to display vocabulary words in context. New or interesting words can be arranged in categories according to a particular letter pattern, concept, or story. They might also be used in a sentence. This provides students with a context for seeing new words and presents a visual reference for ideas covered in previous lessons. Use games, riddles, or sponge activities with word walls words as well.

Semantic maps. Semantic maps or word webs can also be used to display new words and show their relationship to other words or ideas (see Figure 7.4). Here, words can be included with pictures, diagrams, labels, and charts.

Wide reading. Promote and encourage wide reading. Including 15 to 45 minutes of sustained silent reading each day is an effective use of instructional time. Wide reading exposes students to more words, increases word recognition and reading fluency, facilitates word learning, and helps to expand students' knowledge base.

Learning logs. Pairs of students identify interesting words found in a story or text. Learning logs are then used to record these words in the sentence in which they were found. Finally, students generate other possible words or phrases that might be substituted for the original word.

Teacher language. Model the use of new words and precise language when speaking in the classroom. Be conscious of bringing new words into the classroom vocabulary. When using a new word in class, link it with a known synonym and use it in a variety of settings throughout the day.

Interesting words. Recognize interesting word usage encountered in texts or in other places. Help students begin to notice how words are arranged to create varied effects. Point out interesting or effective ways that writers use words to create feelings, communicate an idea, or describe an event.

Moving Words Into Students' Productive Vocabulary

Michael Graves (1986) describes six word learning tasks:

- Learning to read known words.
- Learning new words representing known concepts.
- Learning new words representing new concepts.
- Clarifying and enriching the meanings of known words.
- Moving words into students' productive vocabularies.
- Learning new meanings for known words.

The strategies described below can be used to help with the last three tasks.

Word classifying. Word classifying can be used to support students' use and exploration of words. Classifying is used to arrange items or information into a given set of categories. The steps are to (a) look at the categories and their definitions, (b) look at the items, and (c) move items into groups according to similarities or association. For vocabulary, use the following steps.

First, prepare for the lesson by finding two or three words which may be new to the students. Ideally, these words are related to or found in a story being read or current theme being studied in another class. This provides a context for learning the new words. Second, find three to ten synonyms or associations for each of the new words and print them on three-by-five-inch cards. The synonyms can be words, phrases, or associations and should be fairly familiar to students.

Third, introduce each new word in the context of a sentence, either orally or in writing. The context helps students make inferences as to the word's meaning. Fourth, provide an explicit definition of the word and another example of that word being used. Fifth, when all the new words have been introduced in this fashion, put the new words used as category headings and displayed on the front board. Sixth, distribute the synonyms and associations written on the three-by-five-inch cards. Tell students that each of their words is related to the new words on the board. They must then decide which category to put their three-by-five-inch cards in and tell why it is related to that category. Finally, call on students individually to bring their cards up and put them underneath one of the two or three new category words. (This step can be done in a large group or small group.)

When all the words are posted in their correct categories, students have a visual reference showing the new words and various synonyms and association. To extend this, use a writing prompt (see Chapter 15), and ask students to write using at least two of the words found on the board.

EXAMPLE: Sample Lesson Plan for Using Word Classifying

Teacher: Mary Larkin

Grade Level: 6

Subject: Social Studies

Objective: Students will use *clarifying* to move new words into their productive vocabulary.

Introduction:

"Today we're going to learn new words that we can use to help describe ideas and situations."

Input:

1. The first word is *insolent* or *insolence:* The king was shocked by the man's insolent behavior. (Students volunteer three ideas about what they think insolent means.)
2. Insolent means disrespectful comments or behavior.
3. What are some things that come into your mind when you hear the word insolent? (Brainstorm and list ideas on the board.)
4. The second word is *devious:* The plan to replace the erasers was devious. (Students volunteer three ideas abut what they think devious means.)
5. This means to be sneaky or to have tricky plans.
6. What are some things that come into your mind when you hear the word devious? (Brainstorm and list ideas on the board.)

Activity:

1. In a large group or small group, students are given synonyms for the new words written on a three-by-five-inch card. They must decide which category the word goes into and explain why.
2. Students look at the list of associations for both words and are asked to describe a situation using at least 10 of the words on the board. This situation can be real or imaginary.
3. Bonus points can be given for (a) realistic ideas, (b) imaginative ideas, (c) the shortest paragraph that makes sense, (d) the most interesting idea related to a particular subject, or (e) the most unusual idea.

Word Box:

1. *Insolent*—haughty, snotty, rude, disrespectful, insulting, smart comments, wisecracks, rude, impolite, brash, brazen, cheeky, daring, impertinent, irreverent, ill-behaved, discourteous.
2. *Devious*—deceitful, guileful, covert, concealed, crafty, evasive, foxy, shifty, sly, sneaky, tricky, underhanded, wily.

Super word web. SWW was described briefly in Chapter 5 in the context of creating integrated units. It is a strategy which uses a visual organizer to develop depth and dimension of word knowledge. This can be used to handle new vocabulary words as either a prereading or postreading activity. For expository text, it is recommended as a prereading activity so that new words and concepts can be used to facilitate comprehension. For narrative text, it is recommended as a postreading activity so that students can use the context of the story to enrich their word knowledge. SWW can be conducted in large or small groups, although it should be modeled a number of times before students attempt to use it in small groups.

HOW DO I? Use a Super Word Web

- Introduce the target word, either orally or in writing, in the context of a sentence (see Chapter 5, Figure 5.4).
- Provide a definition of the target word for students. When they are working in pairs or small groups, have students use a dictionary.
- Students draw a figure in the middle of a blank sheet of paper. Butcher paper can be used to create large poster-sized figures for classroom display.
- Students list synonymous words and phrases inside the figure.
- Students list things they associate with the target word along the outside of the figure.

Word knowledge affects students' ability to learn and comprehend what they read. Social studies provides a rich context for exploring the meanings of many new words and concepts. Clarifying and SWW are two strategies that can be used to expand and strengthen students' vocabulary and to move new words into their productive vocabulary.

NCSS STANDARDS

Thematic Standards

The following NCSS thematic standards are addressed in this chapter. See Appendix A for a full description of the relevant thematic standards.

Early Grades

I. Culture: a., b.

Middle Grades

I. Culture: a., b.

Pedagogical Standards

The following NCSS pedagogical standards are addressed in this chapter:

I. Learning and Development.

II. Differences in Learning Style.

III. Critical Thinking, Problem Solving, and Performance Skills.

IV. Active Learning and Motivation.

V. Inquiry, Collaboration, and Supportive Classroom Interaction.

VI. Planning Instruction.

Essential Skills for Social Studies

The following NCSS essential skills for social studies are addressed in this chapter:

I. Acquiring Information.
   A. Reading Skills.
      1. comprehension
      2. vocabulary

II. Organizing and Using Information.
   A. Thinking Skills.
      1. classify information
      2. interpret information
      3. analyze information
      4. summarize information
      5. synthesize information
      6. evaluate information
   B. Metacognitive Skills.

Chapter Review: Key Points

1. The purpose for reading narrative text is different from that of expository text; thus, the strategies for reading and comprehending are also different.

2. Comprehension skills should be used only with expository text.

3. Too much time is spent in most classrooms on word identification skills and too little time is spend on teaching students how to comprehend expository text.

4. A comprehension skill is a strategy readers use to construct meaning and retrieve information from a text.

5. Comprehension skills should be broken into steps and taught explicitly to students at all levels and of all abilities.

6. Comprehension skills should be taught using the elements of effective instruction:
   • Direct instruction and modeling
   • Identification of the procedural components
   • Guided practice
   • Regular practice
   • Application or use in other areas in order to ensure transfer

7. Most classrooms have students of widely varying reading ability.

8. The Scaffolded Reading Experience (SRE) can be used to help students comprehend what they are reading.

9. SRE contains pre-, during-, and postreading activities designed by the teacher.

10. There is a relationship between vocabulary, reading comprehension, and knowledge.

11. Addressing students' vocabulary will improve reading comprehension and the acquisition of new knowledge.

12. Classifying and super word webs (SWW) are two strategies for moving words into students' productive vocabulary.

Making Connections

1. Which two comprehension skills are you more likely to use?

2. Select a chapter in an elementary or middle school level social studies textbook. Use a SRE to design pre-, during-, and postreading activities.

3. Design a postreading activity using one of the many activities described so far in this text.

4. Create an understanding window for ideas found in this chapter or in this text. Share in a small group.

5. Create an I-chart for this chapter.

6. What interesting or new words did you find in this chapter?

7. In a small group, create a SWW for one of the new or interesting words in this chapter.

8. Select a chapter in an elementary or middle-level social studies textbook. Design a word classifying activity for two words found in this chapter.

9. In what ways do you see the three holistic learning ideas related to intrapersonal connections, interpersonal connections, and interconnectedness reflected here?

Chapter 9

LEARNING THROUGH HUMAN INTERACTION

Thinking Ahead

1. When have you worked together in a group to complete the task or reach a goal? What things seem to have contributed to your success here? What things might have hampered your success?

2. How has the ability to work together in groups contributed to human development?

3. When have you had to work together or interact with others in a teaching and learning setting? What things did you enjoy? What things would you want to have done differently here?

4. What makes a good leader? Who are some of the important leaders in our society, in the world, and in your life? What skills or traits do effective leaders have?

5. What skills or traits do good listeners have?

THE IMPORTANCE OF HUMAN INTERACTION IN SOCIAL STUDIES EDUCATION

The National Council for the Social Studies describes six skills related to human interaction (NCSS, 1994). Students should be able to (a) contribute to the development of a supportive climate in groups, (b) participate in making rules and guidelines for group life, (c) serve as a leader or follower, (d) assist in setting goals for the group, (e) participate in delegating duties, organizing, planning, making decisions, and taking action in group setting, and (f) participate in persuading, compromising, debating, and negotiating in the resolution of conflicts and differences. This chapter focuses on human interaction as it relates to teaching and learning in social studies. Described below are four pedagogical strategies that involve human interaction: cooperative learning, creative dramatics, communication skills, and leadership.

When used as a *pedagogical tool,* human interaction enhances learning (Kauchak & Eggen, 1998; Johnson & Johnson, 1999). For example, getting your students to discuss ideas from a lesson or unit with others in a small group allows them to manipulate ideas and process them at deeper levels. Human interaction also exposes students to a variety of thoughts, perspectives, and thinking styles. Finally, interacting with others and working in groups increases student motivation (Johnson & Johnson, 2002), which is an important element in learning (Bruener, 1977).

Human interaction can also help students become better human beings. Humans who interact are more likely to understand each other. Humans who understand each other are also more likely to nurture, help, and cooperate. Human interaction also lessens the sense of isolation that some students feel. Social isolation is linked with many problems and disorders which may include drinking and drugs, depression, and forms of delinquency (Santrock, 2004). Finally, creating classroom learning experiences that involve human interaction teaches students how to function in a group and thus help them get ready to meet the challenges of interacting in a diverse society. If human interaction can do all this and at the same

Humans who interact are more likely to understand each other than humans who do not interact.

time enhance learning, it seems that these types of strategies should be emphasized in your classroom.

COOPERATIVE LEARNING

Cooperative learning can be used in your classroom to enhance learning in all curriculum areas and learning situations (Borich, 2004; Johnson & Johnson, 1999). Cooperative learning is a structured learning activity consisting of the following six elements:

Positive interdependence. In a cooperative learning group students perceive they are linked with other group members so they cannot succeed unless everyone does his or her part. This element is best achieved by designing activities in which each student has a specific role or task within the group. Various roles that can be used for cooperative learning groups are listed in Figure 9.1.

Individual accountability. You will need to structure cooperative learning activities so that every individual in the group is accountable for his or her performance in some way. Often average scores are used, or else one grade is given to the whole group based on the end product; however, these should be used with extreme caution and only on rare occasions. In cooperative learning groups the process is more important than the product. It is the process of working together that enhances learning. As such, not every activity should be graded. But if you insist on assigning a grade to a cooperative learning activity, evaluate your students on the process of working together (see Figure 9.3).

Figure 9.1   Roles for Cooperative Learning Activities

1. *President:* Makes final decisions. Appoints individuals to fill other roles.

2. *Reader:* Reads the material out loud.

3. *Recorder/Scribe:* Records ideas.

4. *Sociologist:* Checks to see how the group is doing on social skills (use matrix).

5. *Checker:* Checks to make sure everyone's voice or ideas are heard. Makes sure each person has contributed an idea. Sometimes uses a tally mark checklist to indicate who is speaking.

6. *Encourager:* Looks for good ideas to note and encourages full participation.

7. *Speaker/Explainer:* Describes the group's decision, explains.

8. *Summarizer:* Restates the group's major conclusions or answer.

9. *Artist:* Creates a visual image to correspond with knowing.

10. *Dancer/Mime:* Creates or performs movement to correspond with assignment.

11. *Musician:* Sings, performs, or describes songs or song lyrics that correspond with assignment or presentation.

12. *Materials Handler:* Gets necessary materials to finish the task.

13. *Idea Checker:* Checks on the learning by asking group members to explain, summarize material.

14. *Timekeeper:* Keeps track of time.

15. *Energizer:* Energizes the group when it starts to lag.

16. *Researcher:* Gets needed background information or material. Often, this person uses the Internet.

17. *Brain:* Helps think of answers/ideas.

18. *Sound effects:* Creates sound effects at appropriate times during a presentation.

HOW DO I? Achieve Individual Accountability

- Pick one person at random to explain the group's ideas.
- Students do assignments together; however, pick one group member's assignment at random and give that score to all.
- All students sign off on the project.
- Each person completes a different portion of an assignment.
- At the end of the activity each person in the group describes his or her role in the project on a separate sheet of paper.
- At the end of the activity each person describes what he or she has learned in a journal.
- Students use a checklist similar to that in Figure 9.3 to document each member's contribution to the group. Substitute individuals' names for group names here.

Social skills. Your students need to be taught the social skills necessary to function in a group (Figure 9.2). Before the cooperative learning activity, introduce one new social skill, teach it, and then model or demonstrate what it looks like. During the activity, use anecdotal records or checklists to look for that skill. Figure 9.3 contains an example of a checklist that can be designed for use with a cooperative learning activity. Keep checklists like these in a three-ring notebook to give you a sense of the cooperative learning performance of the class and of individual groups over time. Use the bottom of the checklist to note general observations and to list social skills to focus on next time. This checklist can also be used to help you recognize and reinforce outstanding social skills performance by individuals or groups at the end of the activity.

Figure 9.2   Social Skills for Cooperative Learning

Forming Skills

1. Move into groups quietly.

2. Stay with the group.

3. Use quiet voices.

4. Take turns.

5. Keep hands and feet to yourself.

Discussion Skills

1. Summarize or restate.

2. Describe feelings.

3. Criticize ideas, not people.

4. Ask for justification: Ask members to give facts and reasons.

5. Ask for clarification when you do not understand.

6. Look for areas of commonality.

7. Honor differences of perspective and philosophy.

8. Allow others to speak.

9. Make your points concisely.

10. Withhold judgment initially. Accept all ideas during discussion/brainstorming phase.

Functioning Skills

1. All group members need to share ideas.

2. Look at the speaker.

3. Use each others' names.

4. Express support and acceptance.

5. Ask for help or clarification when needed.

6. Energize the group when necessary

Working Skills

1. Contribute to the group.

2. Help the group reach its goal.

3. Complete his or her role or assignment.

4. Give a good effort.

5. Meet deadlines.

6. Stay on task.

7. Complete the group task.

Figure 9.3   Checklist for Social Skills

Task: _____

Date: _____

Key: ✓ = skill was present, ✓+ = skill was present to a greater degree, ✓– = skill was present to a lesser degree, # = let's talk.

	Group 1	Group 2	Group 3	Group 4	Group 5
I. Forming Skills					
1. Move quickly and quietly into groups.					
2. Stay with the group.					
3. Use quiet voices.					
4. Take turns.					
II. Functioning Skills					
1. Share ideas and opinions.					
2. Look at the speaker.					
3. Use each others' names.					
4. Express support and acceptance.					
III. Discussion Skills					
1. Make your points concisely.					
2. Look for areas of commonality.					
3. Allow others to speak.					
4. Ask for justification.					
IV. Working Skills					
1. Stayed on task.					
2. Completed individual assignments.					
3. Completed the group task.					

General notes/observations:

A specific task. The tasks you ask students to do in cooperative learning groups must be specific. Students should be able to answer yes or no when asked if they have completed the task. Examples of nonspecific and specific tasks for cooperative learning groups:

> *A nonspecific task.* As a postreading activity, ask groups to discuss Chapter 5 in the social studies text.

> *A specific task.* As a postreading activity, ask groups to list five interesting or important ideas from Chapter 5.

> *A very specific task.* As a postreading activity, ask each student to list two interesting ideas from Chapter 5 individually, and then to move into cooperative learning groups. Each group will rank all their ideas from most important to least important.

Face-to-face interaction. When your cooperative learning groups are functioning well students are seated "knee-to-knee and eye-to-eye" so that they can look at their group mates as they are working together.

Reflection and review. Allow time at the end of every cooperative learning activity for reflection and review. This is where groups examine how well they did in working together and completing the task. (These two are often related.) This is also the time for you to recognize outstanding social skills performance by individuals and groups.

HOW DO I? Get Students to Reflect on and Review Cooperative Learning Experiences

With the whole class:

- Describe those things you observed while students were working in cooperative learning groups related to the process.
- Ask students to describe the things that seemed to go well in their group.
- Ask students what they would do differently in their group to improve group functioning.
- Ask students to assess how well their cooperative learning group did in accomplishing its task.

In cooperative learning groups:

- Use a checklist similar to that shown in Figure 9.3 to help students focus on specific social skills.
- Ask groups to give themselves a grade on three to four social skills.
- Ask groups to describe three things they did well and three things they will try to improve in the next cooperative learning activity.
- For individual reflection and review, ask students to record their observations and ideas in individual journals or learning logs. Then have students share their ideas with the group.

Tips for Using Cooperative Learning

Be patient when beginning to use cooperative learning in your class. It takes a while to learn and become comfortable with the design and implementation of these types of activities. Also, students need time and practice to learn this process. Introduce cooperative learning initially by using short, simple tasks. It works best to begin by using groups of two and three students for primary grades and groups of four to six with intermediate and middle grades. If you find that students are having trouble working in cooperative learning groups, make the tasks less complex or the groups smaller.

Keep in mind when planning cooperative learning activities that they generally take more time than other kinds of activities. This extra time is offset by the fact that students learn more and learn more deeply. Thus, while you may not be able to cover as much, students will be able to uncover a great deal more. However, to make the best use of classroom time, keep cooperative learning groups on task. This can be done by specifying at the outset the amount of time students have to complete the task. Then, as groups are working, provide verbal mile markers by telling students how much time they have left.

How are members selected for cooperative learning groups? In most instances, you should choose members for cooperative learning groups or you should use some sort of random selection. Avoid having students select members for their groups as it creates undue social pressure on those who may not be perceived as popular. Student selection also tends to create groups that are homogeneous. Teacher-created groups will ensure diversity in terms of gender, ability, age, or other factors such as culture. Random selection to groups can produce some interesting dynamics such as when a student finds himself to be the only male in a group of females.

HOW DO I? Use Random Selection to Form Cooperative Learning Groups

- Use a deck of cards. All students are given cards. Their cooperative learning groups would be those who have the same card of another suit.
- Draw for names. Put students' names in a hat and have designated group leaders draw names to determine their groups.
- Look for similarities. This method creates random groups of random sizes. Here you ask students to find classmates who have the same color socks or shirt, a birthday in the same month, or some other factor.
- Form groups based on students' choice. This also creates random groups of random sizes.
- Here you write down the names of five to seven different items on the board such as dessert items, board games, fruit, or movies. Students then look at the list and write their favorite on a three-by-five-inch card. On the teacher's signal, they then hold up their cards and look for similar choices for their group.

Four-Square

Four-square is a cooperative learning activity that you can adapt for use in a variety of settings. One way to use it is as a postreading activity. Individually, students record one

Figure 9.4   Four-Square

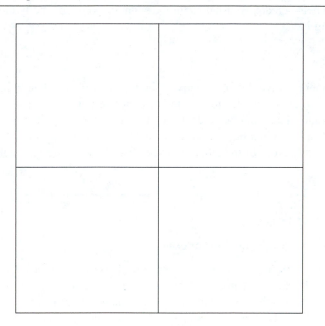

Big ideas, conclusions, or associations:

interesting or important idea from the assigned chapter or book. Next, they bring their ideas to their small cooperative learning groups. Each group member writes his or her idea in one of the squares on the four-square chart (see Figure 9.4). After initial ideas are recorded, students then examine them to see if there is a common element, a big idea, an interesting association, or a conclusion that can be made based on their four initial ideas. This may seem somewhat vague at first, but students quickly get the hang of it.

Four-square invites students to go beyond the knowledge presented, to synthesize, infer, and look for larger concepts or overriding ideas. It can also be used to help students make connections before a lesson. For example, at the beginning of a social studies lesson ask your students to write down two or three things they know about the subject to be studied. Then, in cooperative groups have them use four-square to share their knowledge, synthesize the ideas, and find a larger idea or conclusion.

Four members seems to work best here; however, sometimes you may have to have a three-square or a five-square group. The following roles can be used here:

- *President*—makes all final decisions and selects people for the other roles,
- *Scribe*—records all ideas on the four-square sheet or poster,

- *Speaker—presents* ideas and big idea or association to the class,
- *Artist or mime—*creates a visual picture, design, or nonverbal body movement to illustrate the big idea.

Jigsaw

Jigsaw is a cooperative learning activity in which students begin in a base group. Next, each group member moves to a different expert group where they develop specific knowledge in some area. Finally, students return from their expert groups to share their knowledge with their original base group in the creation of some product or performance. It is only by putting all pieces of the puzzle together that the base group is able to accomplish the task.

EXAMPLE: Using Jigsaw

To help students get ready for a text or exam:

After meeting in their base group, students move into expert groups. Give each expert group a study guide that contains questions for different sections of the upcoming test. The expert group works together to prepare answers and gather information for their section of the test. Finally, have students move back into their base groups where each expert shares his or her knowledge with other group members.

As a reading strategy for expository text:

After meeting in their base group, students move into expert groups. Each expert group is given a different section of a chapter to read. That section is read out loud by one or two readers as the others take notes. The expert group then creates an outline that describes the most important ideas from that section. Finally, students move back to their base group where they create an outline of the entire chapter.

Think-Pairs

Think-pair-share is a strategy where you ask your students a question and give them a minute to think. It sometimes works best to have them list or write down their initial ideas on thinking paper or in a learning log. Then ask students to turn to a neighbor to share their ideas. This is a quick and easy way to engage them in learning and for all students' ideas to be heard. It also creates an active learning situation by getting them to interact with the lesson material at a deeper level. You might also say, "Find somebody you have not talked with today." This invites students to interact with a variety of students, some of whom might be outside their normal social groups.

Pairs check is a strategy where students work in pairs to complete an assignment or to solve a problem. One student works to solve the problem or answers a question while the other one observes and checks. The checker can guide or give advice but cannot solve the problem. The conversation that occurs as a result of this dynamic allows students to hear the thoughts of others during the process of problem solving and thus enhances learning.

Perspectives on Learning: How to Use Cooperative Learning

Cooperative learning is a high level teaching strategy that takes knowledge, skill, and practice for a teacher to become fully proficient. It is beyond the scope of this text to present more than a cursory overview of this process. However, the information provided here should be sufficient for getting you started. It is recommended that you take a cooperative learning class as part of your professional development or that you obtain one or more of the following resources: *Cooperation in the Classroom* (Johnson, Johnson, & Holubec, 1991), *Classroom Teaching Skills* (Cooper, 1999), and *Joining Together: Group Theory and Group Skills* (Johnson & Johnson, 1999).

There is a wealth of research supporting the use of cooperative learning as an effective learning tool for all students (Johnson & Johnson, 1995; Johnson, Johnson, & Skon, 1979; Johnson, Maruyama, Johnson, Nelson, & Skon, 1981; Marzano, Pickering, & Pollock, 2001; Slavin, 1995; Springer, Stanne, & Donovan, 1998). Despite this, however, cooperative learning has been unfairly criticized by some. The claims are that one or two people, usually high ability students, end up doing all the work (Gallagher & Gallagher, 1994). Keep in mind that cooperative learning is a tool, and like any tool, it can be misused. One misuse of this tool is to use it only as a measurement device, that is, to grade every cooperative learning activity, or to assign major projects to small groups for which they will receive a grade. Cooperative learning used this way on a regular basis will likely put undue pressure on those who are highly motivated to achieve as well as on low ability learners.

As stated earlier, not every activity in a classroom should be evaluated and graded. The purpose of cooperative learning is to enhance learning. The process of working cooperatively in a group enhances learning by enabling students to manipulate concepts and ideas, to engage in higher level thinking, and to hear a variety of perspectives and thinking styles. The process of working cooperatively also makes learning more enjoyable, increases motivation, and helps students develop important social and interpersonal skills.

EXAMPLE: Using Cooperative Learning to Teach the Concept of Interpersonal Intelligence

Grade Level: 5

Objectives:

1. Students will find and describe examples of interpersonal intelligence in a newspaper.
2. Students will identify three interesting or important ideas related to interpersonal intelligence.

Introduction:

This week, we've learned about several different ways to be smart. Today we're going to learn about a new intelligence called interpersonal intelligence.

Input:

1. There are many ways to be smart.
2. Interpersonal intelligence is one way to be smart.

(Continued)

(Continued)

3. (Write *interpersonal* on the board.) Is there a part of this word that you recognize? What might give us a clue as to what it might mean?
   A. Help students to see *inter* and *personal*.
   B. *Inter* means between. *Personal* refers to a person.

4. This means you are very good at work between people or with people.
   A. You know how to organize them.
   B. You are aware of their feelings.

5. Examples: coaches, teachers, and managers all need to be able to organize and work with people.
   A. Ask students to list examples of people they know who seem to have strong interpersonal intelligence.

Activity:

1. Put students in cooperative learning groups of four.

2. Roles: (a) president, makes all decisions, appoints others, and keeps track of time; (b) scribe, records ideas; (c) speaker, shares group's ideas with large group, (d) artist, creates the poster to include on a class bulletin board.

3. Task: Students look through the newspaper to find at least four examples of people with strong interpersonal intelligence (allow 20 minutes). This could be examples of people who have used interpersonal intelligence in order to accomplish something or people who seem to be very good at working with other people. They will create a poster by cutting out the article and pasting it on a sheet of white paper. At the bottom of this, they will describe what this person accomplished and why they think this person has strong interpersonal intelligence. At the end, each group will share three interesting or important ideas with the whole class they discovered about interpersonal intelligence. Posters will be put on a class bulletin board.

Closure:

1. Ask students to identify two things that worked well in their group.

2. Recognize interesting and unique ideas and identify groups that worked well together.

TEACHERS IN ACTION: Cooperative Learning Activities

I think that, in social studies or any other subject area, the key to successful cooperative grouping is keeping the kids on task while they are working. If you make the group sizes reasonably small, no more than three, then you will have more constructive work time. I have found that when you have groups of more than three, somebody in the group is coasting, while others are carrying the weight of the work. I also make sure that the kids work quietly. The more noise there is in the room, the less it seems that gets done. Kids get off task so easily, especially when they get noisy and get into the chatting mode. I think that if you give the students a grade for their cooperative work, they will work more seriously. Elect a team leader, and make sure that each person in the group has an assigned job. I have successfully had kids create maps together. They can also work together in small groups to read the textbook. Each group can pick a section of the text, and then report it to the class. Sometimes I have had them get together as a small group to play reporter. They report the event as if it happened yesterday. For example, "In today's news, the colonists dumped tea into Boston harbor."

—Wanda, Elementary School Teacher

Author Reflection: It is sometimes okay for students to get off task. As a matter of fact, sometimes off task is really on task. Sometimes the best thing we can do for our students (who happen to be human beings by the way) is to invite them to sit in a small circle and talk to each other. And in doing this, our students might be able to understand other human beings living on the good planet Earth just a little better. And understanding others is always a good thing. Nothing bad ever came out of understanding. In contrast, misunderstanding has caused a lot of bad things to happen.

Social studies is the study of humans interacting. Hmmm . . . maybe we should provide opportunities for humans to actually . . . interact?

What is your response to the case? How do your reactions compare with the author's reflection?

GO THERE

- Office of Education Research and Improvement (OERI), U.S. Department of Education: http://www.ed.gov/pubs/OR/ConsumerGuides/cooplear.html
- Official website of the jigsaw classroom: www.jigsaw.org

The jigsaw website describes four problems that may occur in any classroom, and then gives a brief description of how the jigsaw technique addresses these problems. What are the problems and solutions described on the jigsaw website?

- Johnson and Johnson Cooperative Learning Center at the University of Minnesota: http://www.co-operation.org/
- Article, "What is the Collaborative Classroom?": http://www.ncrel.org/sdrs/areas/rpl_esys/collab.htm
- How can the cooperative classroom help students connect learning in school to everyday life? A teacher's web page on teaching social skills: http://home.att.net/~clnetwork/socialsk.htm
- Meta-analysis of research supporting cooperative learning: http://www.co-operation.org/pages/cl-methods.html
- A good overview of cooperative learning and a variety of cooperative learning strategies: http://edtech.kennesaw.edu/intech/cooperativelearning.htm

CREATIVE DRAMATICS

Creative dramatics can be thought of as a form of cooperative learning, as the six cooperative learning elements described above apply equally here. Creative dramatics can be defined as a structured drama activity that uses students' imagination and willingness to act or pretend to reinforce academic objectives (Johnson, 1998). Creative dramatics uses no written dialogue, making it different from doing a play. In a play, actors read or memorize the lines that somebody else has written. Instead, in creative dramatics, actors use their own words to convey meaning. Although a beginning structure is often provided, students using creative dramatics are encouraged to improvise or change the original form.

Components of Creative Dramatics

Creative dramatics has four necessary components: structure, open-endedness, a safe environment, and feedback.

Structure. While pretending is very natural for most students, improvising a short drama can be a difficult and abstract process. Students need structure to guide their actions and dialogue during the initial stages of creative dramatics. You can provide this structure by modeling and demonstrating the basic story, actions, possible dialogue, and characterizations. It is best to keep early dramas short and simple, using only two to four characters. Older students and those with experience in creative dramatics will need less structure.

EXAMPLE: Using Creative Dramatics for Social Skills

Ms. Berenguer plans a creative drama activity as part of her 6th grade social studies unit on social skills. The skills she is focusing on are courtesy and consideration. She creates a scene that takes place in a fast food restaurant where two people are waiting to give their orders. The restaurant worker is ready to take an order but does not know who is next in line. Ms. Berenguer provides structure by describing the initial situation, then models the drama up to the point where the worker turns and asks, *"Who's next?"* Drama groups are formed and asked to portray both the courteous and considerate responses as well as the rude and inconsiderate responses by each of the characters in the drama.

Openendedness. Creative dramatics is spontaneous and changeable. Although it works best when you provide a beginning structure, this structure should be flexible and open-ended. As your students become more comfortable with creative dramatics, they will begin to use ideas and experiences from their own lives to create unique variations on the original themes. Using a prepared script would not allow this to happen. Provide structure, but let students find their own words to carry the meaning and also encourage improvisation and alternate endings.

A safe environment. Creativity of any kind involves a certain amount of risk and disclosure. Creativity will be enhanced if you create a fun, safe environment. Close the classroom door during the initial learning stages of creative dramatics in order to develop a sense of safety and community. Be willing to take creative risks by modeling and participating in creative dramatics. This will prime the pump for further creative endeavors. Also, provide feedback that is positive and specific, and that acknowledges actors and their efforts, to ensure that creative behaviors continue. Finally, never force students to participate in creative dramatics; instead, always ask for volunteers.

Feedback. Students like to receive feedback, both formal and informal. Informal feedback is best given by your response during the drama. Laugh when it is appropriate and give other verbal and nonverbal responses. More formal feedback is given when a drama has ended. Here, you help students reflect and review the experience using the actors' elements (see Figure 9.5). This gives you a chance to recognize actors for those things done well. Feedback in creative dramatics is also a way to recognize students who may not be successful in other academic areas. As students become more familiar with the feedback process, they will be able to reflect upon these experiences and describe successful and less successful dramatic elements. Actors of all ages eventually develop a critical eye and become adept at giving each other positive feedback.

Figure 9.5   The Actors' Elements

- *Voice.* The actors use a loud, clear voice that varies in pitch and tone, and is at the appropriate rate.
- *Body.* The actors use their whole faces and bodies to create a character. They react with their bodies to the actions of other actors.
- *Character or imagination.* The actors create characters that are believable. Actors stay in character at all times.
- *Group work.* The actors work well with their group by staying on task, taking turns, sharing, and helping to create a drama.

Getting Started

There are four things to consider when beginning to use this powerful learning tool: First, allow your students to slowly become comfortable with this process. Use creative dramatics no more than two or three times a week. Second, consider using creative dramatics right before lunch or toward the end of the day when students are apt to be restless and need a chance to move. Third, students love to perform for other students. Send small groups of actors to other classrooms to do quick five-minute dramas. Finally, keep it light and make having fun the priority. Creative dramatics is meant to be an enjoyable learning experience.

Creative Dramatics Activities

Below are some simple ideas to use in designing creative dramatics activities.

Creative dramatics as problem solving. Invite students to find an interesting or important problem from their lives, history, or current events. Then use problem-solving strategies to generate ideas and find a solution (problem-solving strategies are described in Chapter 10). Use creative dramatics to bring the problem and solution to life.

Radio drama. Have students pick an interesting or important event from history, current events, or from a story. Have them create written dialogue with narration, sound effects, and music. (This is one place where written dialogue can be used.) Use audio tape to create and record these radio dramas.

Social skills. Design creative dramas to help teach social skills such as waiting in line, applying for a job, asking for permission, polite conversation, or how to act at a party.

Social situations. Use creative dramas to practice uncomfortable settings or situations such as: parent-teacher-student conferences, asking somebody for a date, getting a shot, settling arguments, apologizing, respecting somebody with a different opinion, or confronting a friend.

Moral dilemmas. Design creative dramas around real life issues, moral dilemmas, or ethical issues from school or real life (see Chapter 10 and Chapter 16).

Puppets. Use puppets for creative dramatics. With younger students, a popsicle stick with a figure glued to it is a good starting place.

TV interviews. Create imaginary interviews using a talk show format with famous characters from history, books, or current events.

Social studies is the study of human interaction, which includes oral communication.

COMMUNICATION SKILLS

Social studies is the study of humans interacting. An integral part of human interaction is the ability to communicate with others. It makes sense that this aspect of human interaction be included in a social studies curriculum both as an area of study and as a pedagogical tool. Human communication involves reading, writing, speaking, and listening. The section below describes how to use two of these, speaking and listening, in a social studies context. Strategies for reading and writing in social studies are described in Chapter 15.

Oral Communication

Oral communication can enhance learning in any subject area. It can be used to manipulate lesson input or to examine and explore lesson-related ideas. It also provides those students who may have difficulties reading and writing another way to demonstrate their learning. Finally, it is open-ended so as to provide choice, challenge, and complexity for highly creative or intellectually gifted students.

To use oral communication in a social studies context, first decide on three to five *Elements of Oral Communication* (EOC) on which to focus (see Figure 9.6). Then define each trait and demonstrate what it looks like. Use the elements of effective skills instruction to teach them.

Second, have students create a brainstorming web to find and develop a speaking topic (see Chapter 12). To do this, identify a topic and print it in a circle in the center of a blank sheet of paper. Then think of two to three nodes or subtopics and brainstorm to find interesting or important things about each. Students should use only single words or short phrases to hold each idea. You will need to model this process initially by thinking aloud and drawing on a blackboard, poster, or overhead to create a brainstorming web.

Third, students use their brainstorming web as a guide to give a short speech about their topic. The teacher should also model these speeches. These speeches should be no more than one minute in length for middle grade students and 30 to 45 seconds for primary students. This is much longer than most students think. To speak, students move into groups of three to five. One student stands and gives his or her speech to the small group. Another student in the group should be designated as the timekeeper and say, "time" when the allotted time is up.

Using this technique, four to six students speak to their small groups at the same time instead of one student speaking to the whole class. This is a much less intimidating way of developing oral communication. Also, the teacher is able to see many students give their oral presentations within a relatively short time span. Students generally need to do this two to three times a week for a couple weeks to get comfortable with the process.

Below are five different ideas for choosing oral communication topics:

1. **Free choice.** Students are free to choose any topic for their speech.

2. **Trade book postreading.** Students create a web and do a speech as part of a postreading activity. Here they describe something interesting or important that occurred in the story.

3. **Textbook postreading.** Students create a web and do a speech as an alternative to a worksheet or other kind of assignment related to a social studies textbook reading assignment. Here they would pick out three or four interesting or important ideas from the assigned chapter.

Figure 9.6   Elements of Oral Communication (EOC)

1. Look at your audience.

2. Use a moderate pace. Not too fast and not too slow.

3. Use inflection. Don't use just a monotone. Make your voice rise and fall to make listening more interesting.

4. Stand in a controlled stance. Don't lean or slouch.

5. Use your hands to emphasize points.

6. Pause at important parts.

7. Use visual aids.

8. Answer questions directly and succinctly.

9. Use correct grammar.

10. Use known words. Avoid slang or profanity.

11. Use words judiciously. Avoid nonwords and nonphrases such as: "um," "well," "you know," and "you guys." Do not use extra words if it can be helped.

12. Be concise and to the point. Do not ramble.

4. **Social studies topics.** Students create a web and do a speech on a theme related to social studies. This can be extended by having students get new information related to their topics.

5. **Persuasive speech.** As part of a discussion, students choose an issue related to social studies and make a case for a particular view.

HOW DO I? Prove Feedback and Assessment for Oral Communication

During the first weeks of oral communication, review the EOC but keep things very informal. Eventually, you can teach students how to respond and give feedback to each other; however, there needs to be quite a bit of trust built in small groups before you get to this point. It should be stressed that this is feedback and not criticism. It is used to improve oral communication and not as an evaluation or assessment. Also, all speakers, even the most polished professional speakers, use various forms of feedback to improve their skills.

The oral communication checklist below can be used as a guide in providing feedback. For this type of assessment, some prefer to use a rating checklist with the following key: 4 = *outstanding*, 3 = *good*, 2 = *average*, 1 = *low*. As students become more comfortable with the EOC and the process of creating and giving speeches, you can begin to include elements that focus at the content of the speech such as topic, length, use of visual aids, interest, or value.

Oral Communication Checklist

Speaker: _____

Topic: _____

Key: √ = skill was present, √+ = skill was present to a greater degree,
        √– = skill was present to a lesser degree, # = let's talk.

looks at audience	
uses a loud voice	
not too fast or slow (rate)	
controlled stance and hands	

Something done well:

_____

_____

_____

_____

Listening Skills

Effective communication involves both the ability to speak in order to accurately transmit your ideas and also to listen in order to receive what another has said. Often when people talk about listening skills they are really referring to remembering skills. That is, how to remember or recall something that was previously said. *Listening skills,* however, are those receiving skills that enable you to fully attend to what another person says with honest intent (see Figure 9.7). Honest intent means that you sincerely try to understand and respond to what the other person is saying; you are not simply waiting silently for a quiet spot to jump in with your own ideas. Listening skills are a form of social or interpersonal skills that can be introduced in the intermediate grades. They are especially relevant in the middle school grades as students are grappling with social and interpersonal elements.

In teaching listening skills, use direct instruction, modeling, and guided practice to teach each skill initially. For independent practice, move students into pairs. In pairs, one person describes a problem or situation from their life while the other person uses listening skills to listen and respond. After five to ten minutes, switch roles. Figure 9.8 has a variety of cues or prompts that can be used for listening practice.

Figure 9.7   Listening Skills

1. *Eye contact:* Look at the person.
2. *Be quiet:* It's not about you. Let the other person talk. Do not talk about yourself. Do not describe a similar situation in your own life.
3. *Use verbal and nonverbal RTA:* Received Transmission Acknowledgment. Nod, "yes . . . I see . . . okay . . . " etc.
4. *Clarify:* "Tell me more . . . I don't understand . . . Does this mean . . . I wonder about . . . "
5. *Paraphrase:* "What you're saying is . . . It sounds like . . . So you want to . . . It seems to be that . . . "
6. *Question:* "Why is it that . . . Do you want to . . . How is it that . . . What do you think would . . . What do you feel . . . What is it that you'd like to do . . . ?"
7. *Reflect outward:* "I'm feeling . . . I'm finding myself . . . I want to . . . "
8. *Respond:* If the speaker asks for your opinion, you should provide one. Don't do this unless asked specifically.
9. *Gently suggest:* "What would happen if . . . Have you tried . . . Do you think you might . . . ?"
10. *Show interest:* Show the other person that you are interested in what he or she has to say.

Figure 9.8   Cues for Listening Practice

1. Describe a time when something went wrong.
2. Describe a time when something went perfectly.
3. What seems to always get in the way of your being successful or doing what you want to do?
4. What kinds of things hurt your feelings? What kinds of things make you feel good?
5. Who has helped you? Who have you helped?
6. Describe the perfect friend. What traits does he or she have?
7. How are you different today than you were in the past?
8. What is something that you wonder about?
9. What do you doubt? What do you doubt about life, others, yourself, school, friends, or teachers?
10. Describe something you really like to do.
11. Describe something you do not like to do, but you know you have to.
12. Where would you like to be in the future? What would you like to be doing?
13. If you could fix something about your life or the way the world is, what would it be?
14. What are some changes you would like to make for yourself?
15. Describe some things that make you feel angry. What do you do when you are angry?
16. Describe some things that make you feel happy.
17. Describe at least two goals you would like to accomplish this year.
18. Describe somebody you admire or look up to.
19. What are some rules you think all humans should follow?
20. What do you believe? What do you believe about life, others, yourself, school, friends, or teachers?

LEADERSHIP

Leadership can be defined as an individual's ability to lead a group toward a common goal. Studying leaders and leadership skills as part of your social studies class will enable your students to understand the dynamics involved in group interactions and will also serve to enhance their own ability to lead groups. There are two types of leadership: Leadership by power and leadership by influence. Leadership by power occurs when a person uses physical strength, military power, money, manipulation, influence, or coercion to obtain an outcome regardless of the group consensus. History and current events are filled with examples of these types of leaders. Their desires and visions take precedence over those of the people they lead. They maintain control only as long as they have the most power. Conversely, leadership by influence occurs when a person operates within the consensus of a group to accomplish a shared goal. This is generally the most effective type of leadership to use within a democratic society.

Individual Leadership Characteristics

So what makes a good leader? There is not one effective leadership style; rather, there are many styles that exist in various combinations on three continuums (see Figure 9.9). Different situations call for emphasis on different points of these continuums. For example, the style of leadership used in a military situation usually calls for more of an autocratic emphasis and would be much different than the style of leadership that would be effective in a school, business, or community group. Leadership styles that work in one type of setting may not work in another.

Regardless of the particular style, an effective leader has some or all of the following characteristics:

- Is able to sense what needs to be done.
- Can communicate with people around him or her.
- Is able to direct people toward a common goal.
- Knows how to delegate responsibility.
- Is organized.
- Can finish a task.
- Can evaluate information and make decisions.
- Is able to evaluate the abilities of others and utilize their talents.
- Has effective critical thinking and problem-solving skills.
- Knows his or her own strengths and weaknesses.

Leadership, Interpersonal Intelligence, and Social Skills

Effective leaders are able to read the intentions and desires of others and act upon this knowledge in helping a group achieve a shared goal. In this sense, leadership involves a form of interpersonal intelligence (Gardner, 1983). Leadership also involves the use of social skills.

Figure 9.9   Leadership Continuums

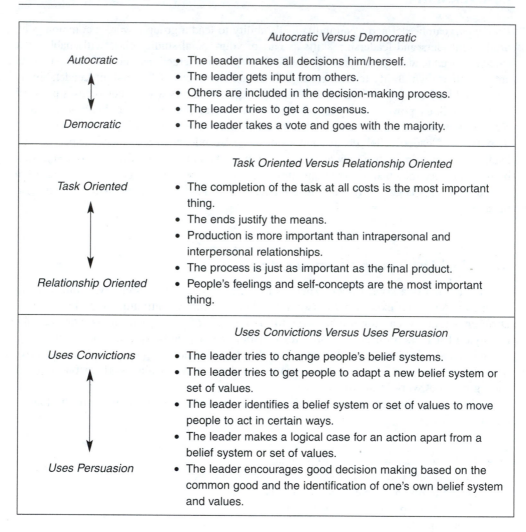

Autocratic Versus Democratic

Autocratic

- The leader makes all decisions him/herself.
- The leader gets input from others.
- Others are included in the decision-making process.
- The leader tries to get a consensus.

Democratic

- The leader takes a vote and goes with the majority.

Task Oriented Versus Relationship Oriented

Task Oriented

- The completion of the task at all costs is the most important thing.
- The ends justify the means.
- Production is more important than intrapersonal and interpersonal relationships.
- The process is just as important as the final product.

Relationship Oriented

- People's feelings and self-concepts are the most important thing.

Uses Convictions Versus Uses Persuasion

Uses Convictions

- The leader tries to change people's belief systems.
- The leader tries to get people to adapt a new belief system or set of values.
- The leader identifies a belief system or set of values to move people to act in certain ways.
- The leader makes a logical case for an action apart from a belief system or set of values.

Uses Persuasion

- The leader encourages good decision making based on the common good and the identification of one's own belief system and values.

The following social skills can be explicitly taught to enhance students' effectiveness as leaders:

- Remember and use people's name many times in conversation.
- Listen to the ideas of others. Consider other people's points of view. Why might they think the way they do? You empower people when you allow them into the process.
- Monitor facial expressions, body language, and vocal tone of others. Recognize the feelings of others.
- Use the problem-solving strategies described in Chapter 10 to achieve shared goals. Means-end analysis can be used to define the end state and identify ways to achieve that

state. Creative problem solving can be used to define a problem and generate a variety of ideas before choosing the best one.

- Use positive reinforcement. Recognize outstanding effort and those things done well. Encourage people who are struggling.
- Ask questions instead of giving direct orders. "Bill, can you get the paper?"
- Admit your own mistakes.
- Say only positive things about others. While you might describe how things might have been done better, do not criticize the person. In the same vein, always look for ways to legitimately compliment people in the group.
- Delegate responsibilities. Do not try to do it all yourself. Get all people to contribute by using their talents.
- Prioritize. Identify what is important in reaching the goal and what is not. Also identify those things that are urgent and need to be done first and those things that are less important and can be done later.

Leadership Activities

The following activities can be used to develop leadership skills and study leaders.

Study of leaders. Design a unit on leaders (see Chapter 5). This unit can be studied as a stand alone unit, or embedded within relevant subject area (Bisland, Karnes, & Cobb, 2004). For example, as a part of your leadership unit, in science class you could study important leaders in science. In your units, use biographies and autobiographies to understand the dynamics of leaders' lives as well as to get a sense of their values and thinking. Also look for their common characteristics. Include leaders from all cultures and all time periods throughout the world, focusing on those who have brought about positive change and also those who caused harm and destruction.

Local leaders. Within your community, ask leaders in community organizations, business, religious organizations, and government to come in and talk about their leadership styles.

Leaders in current events. Identify important leaders in current events. Create a leadership bulletin board and ask your students to bring magazine, newspaper, and Internet articles related to each leader.

Small group leadership activities. After studying the characteristics of leaders and leadership skills, put students in small groups to accomplish a task or to solve a problem. Working in small groups allows your students to practice leadership skills in a safe setting (Bisland, Karnes, & Cobb, 2004). With each task, randomly select one person to be the leader. Every student should have equal opportunities to experience the leadership role. The leader in each group is in charge of organizing priorities and delegating responsibilities in order to complete the task on time.

EXAMPLE: A Small Group Leadership Activity

What can be done to help students be kinder and more respectful of others at our school? Your group will need to find a solution for this problem, describe a plan for implementing this solution, and design a presentation. You will have two days to complete your task. Your solution and implementation plan will be presented to the class. The presentation should be between five and ten minutes in length and must include some sort of visual aid.

Key: 4 = outstanding, 3 = very good, 2 = good, 1 = low, 0 = did not meet criteria.

Rating Checklist for Kindness and Respect Activity	
Criteria	*Rating*
1. The group finished the project on time.	
2. The group was successful in finding a solution.	
3. The solution is practical and effective.	
4. The implementation plan is practical and effective.	
5. The presentation was easy to understand.	
6. The presentation included visual aids.	
7. Speakers used effective oral speaking skills.	
8. The presentation was five to ten minutes in length.	

Fishbowl. In a *fishbowl* activity, one group of students works to complete a task or solve a problem while the rest of the class watches. After the task is completed, the rest of the class discusses the group's process, its success in accomplishing the task or solving the problem, and the various social skills used. The individual leadership characteristics and the social skills described above can be used to help the class analyze and review the fishbowl interaction. In these fishbowl activities you sometimes might choose one person to be the leader and at other times you might allow for leadership to emerge. With any fishbowl activities, students should always be asked if they wish to volunteer.

GO THERE

- Leadership lesson plans and activities: http://humanityquest.com/ topic/art_activities/ index.asp?theme1=leadership
- Lessons on leadership and public service: http://www.studentsandleaders.org/dc/

NCSS STANDARDS

Thematic Standards

The following NCSS thematic standards are addressed in this chapter. See Appendix A for a full description of the relevant thematic standards.

Early Grades

I. Global Connections: b.

Middle Grades

I. Global Connections: b.

Pedagogical Standards

The following NCSS pedagogical standards are addressed in this chapter:

   I. Differences in Learning.

  II. Critical Thinking, Problem Solving, and Performance Skills.

 III. Active Learning and Motivation.

 IV. Inquiry, Collaboration, and Supportive Classroom Interaction.

  V. Planning Instruction.

Essential Skills for Social Studies

The following NCSS essential skills for social studies are addressed in this chapter:

   I. Acquiring Information.
    A. Study Skills.
      1. find information
      2. arrange information in usable forms

  II. Organizing and Using Information.
    A. Thinking Skills.
      1. interpret information
      2. analyze information
      3. summarize information
      4. synthesize information
    B. Decision-Making Skills.
    C. Metacognitive Skills.

 III. Relationships and Social Participation.
    A. Personal Skills.
    B. Group Interaction Skills.
    C. Social and Political Participation.

Chapter Review: Key Points

1. Human interaction can be used as a pedagogical tool to enhance learning and to help students be better human beings.

2. Cooperative learning is a pedagogical tool in which students work together to accomplish a task.

3. The six elements of cooperative learning are: positive interdependence, individual accountability, social skills, a specific task, face-to-face interaction, and reflection and review.

4. Creative dramatics is a structured drama activity that uses students' imagination and willingness to act or pretend to reinforce academic objectives and enhance learning.

5. A creative dramatics activity is structured, open-ended, done in a safe environment, and involves feedback.

6. Human communication, an integral part of human interaction, should be included in a social studies curriculum.

7. Communication involves both the accurate transmission of ideas (speaking and writing), and the accurate reception of ideas (listening and reading).

8. Speaking and listening are communication skills that can be used as pedagogical strategies in social studies and other subject areas to enhance learning.

9. A leader is one who is able to lead a group toward a common goal.

10. You can lead by power or by influence; however, leadership by influence is most effective in a democratic society.

11. There are a variety of leadership styles, each of which works best in a particular setting.

12. Certain skills can be explicitly taught to students to enhance their abilities to lead others toward common goals.

Making Connections

1. Why are some groups more successful than others? What social skills help people work together in a group?

2. Form a cooperative learning group with the following roles: *president*—makes all decisions, *scribe*—records interesting or important ideas, *resource manager*—gets books and other materials, and *speaker*—presents ideas to the class. Get a grade 1–9 social studies textbook or teacher's manual from a school or curriculum library. Design five cooperative learning activities that could be used with this material.

3. Use four-square as a postreading activity for one of the chapters in this book.

4. Design and perform a creative drama based on a social skill, a problem, or some area of current events.

5. Form a cooperative learning group with the following roles: *president*—makes all decisions, *scribe*—records interesting or important ideas, *resource manager*—gets books and other materials, and *speaker*—presents ideas to the class. Get a grade 1–9 social studies textbook or teacher's manual from a school or curriculum library. Design five creative dramatics activities that could be used with this material.

6. Describe an effective leader that you know. What traits does he or she have? Compare your traits with those listed by three others and look for similarities.

7. Form a cooperative learning group with the following roles: *president*—makes all decisions; *scribe*—records interesting or important ideas; *resource manager*—gets books and other materials; and *speaker*—presents ideas to the class. Get a grade 1–9 social studies textbook or teacher's manual from a school or curriculum library. Design five structured academic controversy activities that could be used with this material.

8. Give a one minute speech on a topic of your choosing to your small group.

9. Select a partner. Identify a problem in your life. Use listening skills to practice listening to each other's problem.

10. In what ways do you see the three holistic learning ideas related to intrapersonal connections, interpersonal connections, and interconnectedness reflected here?

Chapter 10

PROBLEM SOLVING
IN SOCIAL STUDIES

Thinking Ahead

1. What processes do you use when you have a major problem to solve?

2. What processes do you use when you are looking for an innovative new product, performance, or way of doing things?

3. Describe a person you know who seems to be innovative or good at solving problems. What characteristics does this person have that seem to help in this regard?

4. What are three major problems that you see in our society? How could these be examined in the context of social studies?

5. What do you think causes the most conflict in society and in the world?

6. What kinds of things seem to cause the most conflict in your life? What strategies might be successful here in each of these instances?

Life is a series of problems to be solved. These problems come in a variety of forms such as: How do I unplug the drain in the sink? What can I do to feel more comfortable in social situations? How can we solve the energy crisis? How can I get this little white golf ball in the hole using the fewest strokes? What can we do about the AIDS crisis in Africa? How can I meet the needs of my gifted math students? How can I get an A in this course? How can I get a job when I graduate? What is the best way to make social studies education interesting and relevant? How can I write a social studies text that provides readers with the knowledge and skills that will help them make a meaningful impact on students' lives?

A problem is a mismatch between the current and a desired state.

Students' problem-solving skills can be developed by directly teaching them effective problem-solving strategies and providing them with opportunities to practice these strategies (Armour-Thomas & Allen, 1993; Good & Brophy, 1995). Social studies provides a powerful context for this. This chapter focuses on problem solving and how problem solving can be used in social studies. The strategies described in this chapter can enhance students' problem-solving abilities in a variety of contexts. They can also be applied to the some of problems you may face as a teacher.

WHAT ARE PROBLEMS, AND HOW ARE THEY SOLVED?

A *problem* can be defined as a situation in which the present condition, product, or performance does not match the desired condition, product, or performance. Problem solving then is the process of moving from the present to the desired condition, product, or performance. It involves both creative thinking and critical thinking, both of which are described in Chapter 12. Sternberg and Williams (2002) identify seven steps in the problem-solving process. While these are listed in stepwise progression below, problem solving is often cyclical, with some steps repeated many times in varying order.

Step 1: Find the problem. Problems cannot be solved if they cannot first be identified. Identifying the problem occurs when a situation is observed and there is a recognition that things could be done better.

Step 2: Define the problem. Defining the problem involves seeking to understand the nature of the situation and discovering the possible causal factors. Here, you look to see why things are as they are.

Step 3: Represent and organize information about the problem. The next step is to visually organize the important information. Strategies used here include outlines, diagrams, brainstorming lists, and fact files.

Step 4: Create or select a strategy for solving the problem. Those who jump right into a problem without a strategy are less successful than those who take time up front to select or design an effective strategy (Csikszentmihalyi, 1990). This is why it is important to teach problem-solving strategies. Two problem-solving strategies described in this chapter are creative problem solving (CPS) and means-end analysis (MEA). Identifying one of these strategies before you start will improve your ability to solve the problem.

Step 5: Allocate resources for solving the problem. Is the problem solvable? Do the benefits outweigh the costs in terms of time, effort, and reward? What human and material resources are needed to find a solution? What human and material resources are needed to implement the solution?

Step 6: Monitor the problem solving. At this step, the problem-solving process begins. You are in the process of solving the problem while occasionally checking the progress in terms of resources and reaching a solution.

Step 7: Test and evaluate the solution to the problem. The final part of problem solving is to implement the solution in order to test it and make the necessary adjustments. Observe what part of your plan works and what part does not work and then tweak accordingly. Tweaking is a very important part of testing. Every new plan, program, or solution needs some adjusting during the implementation stage.

EXAMPLE: Problem Solving at Grantsburg Middle School

Finding the problem. A group of students in a 6th grade class at Grantsburg Middle School noticed that the lunch line in the cafeteria moved slowly, causing them to have to spend a lot of time waiting in line, which in turn cut into their noon break. For them, this was a problem.

Defining the problem. After making an initial observation, these students concluded that the line seemed to get congested at two points: where students paid for their meals and at the end of the line where students stop to reach for a carton of milk.

Representing and organizing problem information. These students made a diagram of the cafeteria and surrounding hall. They used this diagram to show the flow of the line and the congestion points. At this step it is also sometimes necessary to go get additional information. These students also did some research to find out when various classrooms were scheduled to go to lunch and when they actually went to lunch. All of this information was organized on a large white board.

Selecting a strategy. The 6th grade students decided that CPS (described in the next section) was the best problem-solving strategy to use with this particular problem.

Allocating resources. These 6th grade students determined the problem was solvable and that they would need the following: (a) 45 minutes at the end of the day to work on this problem, (b) access to a teacher for feedback and ideas, and (c) time to interview the cooks to get their insight.

Monitoring problem solving. Ms. Blyleven, a 6th grade teacher, agreed to work with these students. Every few days she met with them to see how close they were coming to a solution. She also helped them assess their ideas to see if they seemed feasible and pragmatic.

Testing and evaluating the solution. After a week, these students came up with an initial solution or plan. This plan had several parts: (a) each week one 6th grade student would volunteer to help collect lunch money, thereby creating two lines, (b) classroom teachers would be asked to be more punctual in terms of their assign cafeteria times, (c) each week one 6th grade student would volunteer to pass out cartons of milk as students were sitting at the tables, and (d) all students would be asked to speak loud and clear when talking to the cooks about selections and portion sizes. As this initial plan was implemented, three students observed, taking notes during the first two days. They kept meeting and refining their original plan until they felt they had most of the bugs worked out.

The Power of Real Problems

The example above was a powerful learning experience for these Grantsburg 6th grade students because it was a *real problem* that directly affected them. In social studies, students should, whenever possible, be engaged in real problems. Real problems, sometimes referred to as *ill-structured problems,* reflect real world events (Starko, 1995). Real problems are real, not riddles to be solved or mathematical word problems with one correct answer found in the teacher's manual. Real problems are those for which the teacher does not have an answer. One nice thing about real problems is that the real world is filled with them. Using these real-world problems in a social studies context thus serves to create a bridge between the curriculum and the real world that students live in. These real problems might be large societal issues that are addressed on the theoretical level such as: *How can we help the homeless?* They might also be local school or community problems such as the lunch line problem described above. Finally, real problems in a social studies context might also include problems that occur on the personal or interpersonal level. These are problems such as: *What can I do when my best friend is inconsiderate?*

The Importance of Redefining Problems

Sometimes an important part of finding solutions is redefining the original problem. This is where you look at the problem from another angle. For example, a societal problem we are currently facing is related to energy. The problem traditionally has been stated this way: *How can we get enough oil, coal, and natural gas so that we do not have to be reliant on other countries for our energy supply?* This problem redefined would be: *How can we develop hydrogen and other types of renewable energy so that we no longer need oil, coal, and natural gas?*

The problem: *How can we get tough on criminals and reduce crime?* The problem redefined: *What types of personal growth and empowerment programs, education, employment, and economic opportunities can we help develop so people are less inclined to commit crime?*

The problem: *How can we get the school board to allocate resources in order to provide more services for the gifted students in our school?* The problem redefined: *How can teachers differentiate classroom curriculums so that they meet the needs of the highly creative and gifted students?*

The problem: *How can I get the students in my seventh hour social studies class to be quiet and behave?* The problem redefined: *What can I do to create a social studies curriculum that is so interesting and relevant that students will want to be engaged and participate?*

Most real-world problems are not one dimensional and do not have one simple answer. Spending time up front redefining the problem allows all sides of the issue to be seen. It also helps you to see possibilities that had not been previously considered.

TWO PROBLEM-SOLVING STRATEGIES

Two very useful problem-solving strategies are *creative problem solving* and *means-end analysis.* There are many more complicated models; however, these strategies are fairly simple and can be used at all grades and levels.

Creative Problem Solving

In using Creative Problem Solving (CPS) first define the problem, and then generate as many ideas as possible for solutions. The key to successful implementation of this strategy is to produce a large number of ideas. There should be no evaluation of your initial ideas as this would prevent the full range of possibilities from being explored. It is only after all possible ideas are generated and listed that you should engage in any sort of evaluative discussion. This is where you look to choose one idea that seems to be the best. And often, two or three of the ideas will be combined for the final solution. This would not be possible had you not first generated a number of ideas. The final steps are to refine, implement, and evaluate the solution. The CPS steps are listed in Figure 10.1.

Figure 10.2 contains a graphic organizer used to guide students' thinking in the CPS process. Working alone, with a partner, or in groups, students first define the problem, then generate and list their ideas in the column on the left. The column on the right is used to list or record background information related to the problem. Both of these are used in choosing a solution and developing an initial plan.

Figure 10.1   Thinking Frame for CPS

1. Define the problem.

2. Generate as many solutions as possible.

3. Choose a solution that seems the best.

4. Elaborate and refine.

5. Implement the solution.

6. Review, evaluate, and refine as necessary.

Means-End Analysis

In using Means-End Analysis (MEA), begin by describing the desired state. "What is the goal?" "What outcome would I like to bring about?" "What would it look like if this problem were solved?" This is followed by an analysis and description of the current state. Next you identify important considerations or background information related to the problem situation. Then, you generate a list of steps or conditions necessary to get to the desired state. "What things need to occur?" "What do I need to do in order to make this happen?" These steps or conditions do not have to be in any order. Finally, a plan is constructed that will move you from point A (current state) to point B (desired state). The steps listed in this final plan should be in chronological order. The steps for MEA are listed in Figure 10.3.

The MEA graphic organizer in Figure 10.4 can be used to guide students' thinking processes. Just like the CPS graphic organizer above, students can work individually, with a partner, or in groups in using this. In doing real-world problem solving, you may wish to have your students submit a plan similar to that in Figure 10.4 before they begin their project.

Figure 10.2   CPS Graphic Organizer

Problem:	
Ideas:	Important Background Information:
Initial Solution/Plan:	
Things That Worked:	Things That Need Fixing/Changing:

Figure 10.3   Thinking Frame for MEA

1. Describe the desired state.

2. Describe the current state.

3. List important considerations or background information.

4. Generate a list of necessary steps or conditions.

5. Construction and implement a plan.

Figure 10.4   MEA Graphic Organizer

Goal/End State:
Current State:
Considerations or Important Information:
Necessary Steps/Things to Do:
Materials Needed:
The Plan:

EXAMPLE: Using CPS in 3rd Grade

Ms. Niekro's 3rd grade class was studying the history of the Mississippi River. In looking at how the river was used for transportation in the nineteenth century, the class discovered that paddleboats sometimes got stuck on sandbars. She thought that this would be a good time to use CPS. After presenting important information about paddleboats, she defined the problem: What would be the best way to get a large paddleboat off a sandbar? In a large group, Ms. Niekro and the class brainstormed to get some ideas going. She recorded students' ideas on a chart in front of the room. She also got students to think of things they knew about paddleboats. This information was also recorded on the chart.

Problem: The paddleboat is stuck on a sandbar.	
Ideas	*Important Background Information*
• Get horses to pull it off. • Dig a trench. • Use poles to push it. • Tie ropes around trees and pull. • Use dynamite to blow up the sandbar.	• The current is strong. • The river is sometimes deep. • Paddleboats are big. • Paddleboats are heavy. • Paddleboats have flat bottoms.

Students then moved into cooperative learning groups with four students in each group. The following roles were used:

- *President*—makes all final decisions and assigns roles and tasks.
- *Scribe*—records and remembers important ideas.
- *Artist*—draws a picture or diagram to show what their idea might look like.
- *Speaker*—shares the ideas with the class.

The task for each group was to come up with the best way to get a large paddleboat off of a sandbar. Each group could use one of the ideas on the chart in front of the room or find one of their own. Students were given 15 minutes to complete the task, after which each group presented their ideas to the class. Later that day, the class went to the computer lab. Ms Niekro had preselected five websites for students that had important information and diagrams related to paddleboats (see Chapter 14). Students worked in pairs at the computer to visit each site. Their task was to find information that might help them in solving their paddleboat/sandbar problem. When students went back to class, they were asked to record their best ideas in their social studies learning logs along with a picture or diagram.

EXAMPLE: Using MEA in 8th Grade

Mr. Reardon's 8th grade class was studying societal issues related to the economy. As part of this unit, he asked his students to envision their country as they would like it to be in 30 years in terms of jobs, production of goods and services, the distribution of wealth, and the economy. After generating some initial ideas, students moved into cooperative learning groups with five students in each. Their task was to describe their idea of a perfect society in 30 years in terms of the economy and the distribution of resources. What kind of economy would they like to see? What kind of society would they like to live in? Groups used the MEA graphic organizer in Figure 10.4 to guide their process. They used both their social studies textbook and the Internet to get information related to the current state of the society and other important background information. They were given a week to put together a presentation which was to include visual aids of some sort. Bonus points were given for unique or creative ideas that were also pragmatic.

GO THERE

- Basic information on the process of problem solving by the University of Michigan College of Engineering: http://www.engin.umich.edu/~problemsolving/
- The Osborne-Parnes Creative Problem Solving Process Manual: http://www.ideastream.com/create/
- Background information related to all aspects of problem solving, invention, creativity, and decision making by the Management Assistance Program for Nonprofits: http://www.mapnp. org/library/prsn_prd/prob_slv.htm

---

THINKING BROADLY

An obstacle often encountered in problem solving is a predisposition to think in limited ways (Sternberg & Williams, 2002). Good problem solvers are also those who are able to think outside the box, who are able to rise above traditional ways of thinking and seeing to generate ideas that are totally unique. Starko (1995) describes three strategies that can be used to help students think broadly: *FFOE, brainstorming, and SCAMPER*. These strategies can be used for finding problems and solving them.

FFOE

FFOE stands for *fluency, flexibility, originality,* and *elaboration.* Looking at a condition, product, or performance, have students divide a piece of paper into four parts and generate ideas in each of the following categories:

1. *Fluency.* Think of as many ideas as possible.

2. *Flexibility.* Think of a wide variety of different types of ideas.

3. *Originality.* Think of unusual, crazy, silly, or unique ideas.

4. *Elaboration.* Add things to original idea, condition, product, or performance.

Brainstorming

Students (and often adults), do not naturally know how to brainstorm; thus, they must be taught the process. Initially, this process should be modeled in a large group with the teacher writing down the ideas generated by the class. Later, students can move into small groups. Idea generation works best in pairs or small groups, as students are able to hear a number of ideas. These initial ideas, in turn, serve to generate more ideas. There are four rules for brainstorming. Put these rules in poster form to assist your initial instruction, and then use this poster for quick review at later times:

1. *All ideas must be accepted.* No criticizing or evaluation is allowed. At this stage, bad ideas are just as important as good ideas.

2. *Freewheeling is celebrated.* Creative, bizarre, unusual and silly ideas are welcomed along with smart aleck comments and random associations. All of these can be used to stretch our thinking and get us thinking more broadly.

3. *The goal of brainstorming is quantity.* The more ideas we have, the greater our choice is in finding a solution.

4. *Hitchhiking is welcome.* Hitchhiking is when you add to an idea that has already been stated or combine two or more ideas. This is a technique many creative problem solvers use. Encourage your students to do this as well.

SCAMPER

Using this strategy, you examine the original condition, product, or performance, then use the seven steps identified in the acronym to facilitate broad thinking. In some situations, it is not possible to generate ideas with every letter of the acronym.

1. *S—Substitute or simplify.* What substitutions can be made? How can the original be made simpler?

2. *C—Combine.* What combinations can be made? What would happen if two old things were combined to create something new?

3. *A—Adapt.* What can be adapted from something else? What else is like this and how can it be adapted for use with the original?

4. *M—Modify, magnify, or minify.* What things in the original can be changed? Is there anything that can be made bigger? Is there anything that can be made smaller?

5. *P—Put to other uses.* Can the original or some part of the original be put to other uses?

6. *E—Eliminate.* What part of the original can be eliminated or taken away?

7. *R—Rearrange or reverse.* What would happen if you rearranged parts of the original or reversed the sequence?

It is best to focus on only one of these broad thinking strategies at a time. Give students plenty of opportunity to practice them. You will find that the quantity of ideas generated and the quality both improve with use over time. These broad thinking strategies can also be used with creative writing, art, creative dramatics, poetry, inventions, and science fair projects.

TEACHERS IN ACTION: Problems in Education

I have no idea what the most important problem facing education is today, because I think it varies from school to school. I have been a teacher for almost three years, and my biggest problem has been administration: a lot of administrators (at least the ones I've worked with) have been so long out of the classroom, they have no idea anymore about how difficult teaching can be. They scream about test scores, yet never seem to take into account that teachers today have so much more to deal with than they did 40 years ago! We are not expected just to teach, but to be counselors, surrogate parents, cheerleaders, social workers, health and character teachers, etc.

I don't mind being all these things for the kids; I feels it's part of my job, but people need to realize it's hard to get the 3 R's in when Jane can't concentrate because she's homeless, or Joey has so many behavioral problems, you spend your whole day calming him down instead of teaching!

I think the biggest problem in education today is the attitude towards education itself: Many parents see school as nothing more than "babysitters" for their children, take no responsibility for their children's education, and do not make the children themselves take some responsibility for their education; and lawmakers who have never set foot in a classroom think they know what's best for our country's education. That's just a little too much like me telling a doctor what's best to do for a cancer patient!

—Alishia #29858

Problems in School

Some problems in school we have control over; it's the ones we have no control over that sometimes affect learning the most: Parents who are completely uninvolved. Parents who think teachers are glorified babysitters and give no support. Children who do not get fed at home or have a decent night's sleep. Attendance—kids who do not come to school, but we are still accountable for their learning. Parents who do not support what the teacher is doing in class and pass this on to their kids. Poverty and inequitable spending between the "rich" schools and the "poor" schools. Children with emotional problems who need serious counseling.

I believe the home environment is critical to the success of any child. It is very difficult to help children succeed when they are being abused or neglected at home. How do you teach a child who sleeps through class because the child has no bed time? How do you teach a child who comes to school crying every day because of situations at home? How do you teach a child who is absent at least one day every week and never makes up any work? These are the problems we see in our school on a daily basis.

—Doni #67231

Author Reflection: In education today we face a wide variety of complex problems that cannot be solved with one or two simplistic solutions. However, the problem-solving and broad thinking strategies described in this chapter could be successfully applied to many of these problems. The good news is that they already have been. There are millions of innovative, resourceful classroom teachers who have created and continue to create effective solutions for many of these problems. There are also thousands of researchers, theorists, and curriculum writers who offer research-based solutions and creative new ways of thinking about education that could be employed to effectively improve education.

The bad news is that the majority of these solutions are unheard or ignored. Instead, politicians have given us (forced upon us) No Child Left Behind (NCLB). This is a solution that is not based on research; rather, it is based on "I-think-isms," factory models of education, business paradigms, and political ideology. It provides simplistic solutions for complex problems; these solutions are validated only by popularity and perception. And when these simplistic solutions fail to reach their desired result, as they inevitably will, blame will once again be focused on teachers, parents, and students or that old standby punching bag, teachers' unions.

The basic essence of NCLB is this: Some schools are identified as failing schools (based solely on standardized test scores). Parents then have the option of moving their students to successful schools (based solely on test scores). This is it. This is the great NCLB innovation built upon a business paradigm by business-thinking people. The untested hypothesis is that all the happy successful schools will grow and prosper, and all the "bad" failing schools will disappear someplace, the "reasoning" behind this (if you want to call it reasoning), is that this system seems to work well with Wal-mart stores, McDonald's burger joints, and Kwick-E Mart convenience stores, so it must therefore work equally well with schools, with "competition" the successful prosper and "unsuccessful" fade away, or so they say. However, while this paradigm may work in the business world where profits are the bottom line, it does not transfer to education where the bottom line is people.

If we want fundamental change in the quality of education, then we must focus on the quality of education. A novel thought, yes? We need to take a qualitative look at the teaching methodologies and curriculums that are used in schools and classrooms and make changes in the way we do education. This bill does nothing to address the quality of education. It does not change how we go about the business of educating our children. Instead, it promotes a test-and-measure mentality that serves only to create winners and losers.

What is your response to the case? How do your reactions compare with the author's reflection?

PROBLEM SOLVING IN THE CLASSROOM

Problems can be embedded into all areas of the curriculum as well as into social studies to enhance learning. This section describes a variety of strategies for including problem solving in an elementary and middle school classroom.

Personal and Interpersonal Problem Solving

Working in small cooperative groups of three to five, ask students to find solutions for personal and interpersonal problems. The small group format provides a safe environment for them to explore options and alternative for the problems they may face or be experiencing in their own lives. It also provides students with a variety of ideas and perspectives. Below are five ideas for using these types of problems in small groups:

1. Find interpersonal problems or personal decisions from a story the class is reading, from history, or from current events. If possible, look for the kinds of problems that might be related to a problem or decision that students might encounter.

2. Choose a common problem that students at your grade level seem to face. For younger children this might be something like encountering a bully or teasing on the playground. For older students it might be something like dealing with peer pressure or an unfair situation involving a teacher or parent.

3. Have students choose a problem from their life to use as a creative writing prompt or journal writing activity. After writing, students share their individual problems and answers in small groups. To extend this, ask students to try their solutions and report back. A great amount of caution and discretion should be used here. This is not an activity to do the first month of a school year. You need to know your students well before you move into these types of activities. They also need to be able to trust and respect you and their classmates. Encourage your students to write only about those things they feel comfortable in sharing in a small group. Let them know that there are other times and places to talk about more personal issues.

4. Select problems found in "Dear Abby" or some other advice columns. At the end of the activity, small groups can compare their answers to the advice the columnist gave. Again, discretion and a thorough knowledge of your students should be used when selecting the types of problems to be examined here.

5. Ask students to volunteer to anonymously submit a personal problem in a problem box that can be used in small groups. No students ever should be forced to share a personal problem. Use a word processor to type the problems so that nobody knows whose it is before distributing it to groups. You will need to vet these carefully to avoid embarrassment or inappropriate disclosure. This can be a powerful learning activity; however, again use your discretion and knowledge of your students to guide you here.

HOW DO I? Design Independent Problem-Solving Projects

Problem solving can also be used for independent projects to be done individually or in small groups. The steps below will guide students (and you) as they go through this process. The rating checklist in Figure 10.5 can be used for feedback and evaluation.

1. Find a problem. What is something that irritates you? What is something that could be done better? What should be improved? Is there a product that has not been invented? Look for a need, a product, a condition, or a performance that needs improving. What is something about being at school or in your neighborhood that bothers you? Do you wish there were better shows on TV? Is there something in your life that you wish were easier or different somehow?

2. Gather data. Get information related to your problem. You may need to go to the library and get important background information. You can also get information by observing, recording, listening, asking questions, interviewing experts, surveying people, reading books or magazines, or using the Internet.

3. Select a strategy. Choose a problem-solving strategy to use in solving your problem (CPS, MEA, or some other strategy). Then go about solving your problem.

4. Communicate your idea. After the problem has been solved, present your findings or ideas to an audience. You can create a demonstration, speech, drama, commercial, report, video, drawing, sculpture, dance, research report, or experiment, or use graphs and tables.

Think Tank

A *think tank* is a small group that looks to find a solution to a specific problem. The problem can be real or imaginary. Think tanks might solve national problems, local problems, imaginary problems, problems or conflicts found in a story, or classroom or school problems. It is sometimes helpful to have the whole class brainstorm a variety of problems in a large group. Then, the students in each think tank can decide which problem they will work on. In small groups, the following roles can be assigned:

- *President*—Assigns roles and keeps the group on task.
- *Scribe*—Records ideas during brainstorming sessions.
- *Speaker*—Presents the final idea or solution to the class.
- *Brain*—Thinks of unique ideas.

In assigning roles for any activity, it usually works best to first pick the president at random and then allow the president to assign the other roles.

Figure 10.5   Rating Checklist for Independent Problem-Solving Activities

Key: 4 = outstanding, 3 = very good, 2 = average, 1 = low.

Criteria	*Rating*
1. *Responsibility:* The student was able to (a) come up with a problem and (b) solve the problem in the prescribed time.	
2. *Problem finding:* The problem (a) is a problem, (b) causes people difficulty, and (c) does not have a good solution.	
3. *Thinking:* The solution (a) is practical, (b) solves the problem, and (c) is likely to be used.	
4. *Communication:* The presentation (a) communicates the problem and solution clearly; (b) uses the elements of effective oral speaking; (c) is clear, logical, and organized; and (d) is interesting.	

Comments: _____

_____

_____

_____

_____

_____

_____

_____

_____

_____

_____

Decision Making

In *decision making*, students work in small groups to evaluate solutions for a particular problem. Given a problem, students first brainstorm to find a number of possible solutions. Next, they choose what they feel are their top three. They then use the graphic organizer in Figure 10.6 to list both the positive and negative consequences of each solution. All solutions must have at least one positive consequence and one negative consequence. Finally, the group comes to a consensus in deciding which solution they feel is the best. They must provide at least two supporting reasons for their choice. Their solutions are presented in a large group. This is somewhat similar to the strategies used in moral decision making described in Chapter 16.

Figure 10.6   Graphic Organizer for Examining Solutions

Problem:

Solutions	Positive Consequences	Negative Consequences
1.		
2.		
3.		

Decision:

Supporting statements:

1.

2.

3.

HOW DO I? Embed Problem Solving in a Social Studies Curriculum

Embedding problem solving into a social studies curriculum begins with teaching students the problem-solving process. CPS and MEA should be taught to students using problems or situations with which they are familiar. You might ask students to use them in inventing new products or in solving problems they encounter in their lives. It is always best to have students work in groups or pairs initially.

(Continued)

(Continued)

> Once students seem to have a grasp of these two strategies, begin to look for problems within the context of your social studies. These problems might be something explicitly stated or you might do as Ms. Niekro did above and create or define a problem that is related to something you are studying. In history, look for real-life problems faced by people. For example, "What could have been done to prevent the Dakota (Sioux) uprising of 1862 in New Ulm, Minnesota?" In studying current events use real-life problems. For example, "How should we protect our country from terrorists?" This could be a problem-solving activity that would lead to all sorts of interesting areas related to cultures, resources, global connections, and national responsibilities. If you are using literature in your social studies curriculum as described in Chapter 15, look for problems faced by the characters in the story.
>
> Problem-solving activities can range in complexity from simple classroom activities that are relatively short in duration and do not require additional resources to the more complex independent projects that require students to get background information, create supplemental materials, and design a formal presentation.

SERVICE LEARNING: PROBLEM SOLVING IN THE COMMUNITY

One of the goals of the social studies education is to promote knowledge of and involvement in civic affairs (NCSS, 1994). Problem solving that invites students to solve community problems can be effective in this regard (Starko, 1995). Service learning is a form of real-life problem solving. Service learning is an experience in which students learn through active participation in thoughtfully organized service experiences which meet a community need (Bussler, 2002). It is different from volunteerism or community service (Howard, 2001). To be service learning it must (a) provide relevant, meaningful service with the community, (b) enhance academic learning, and (c) prepare students for active civic participation.

In designing a service learning experience, four components need to be included: preparation, service, reflection, and celebration (South Carolina Service Learning, 1994). *Preparation* is used to provide students with the background information and skills necessary for the project. *Service* involves students in some type of meaningful, engaging work. *Reflection* is the act of thinking critically about the experience afterwards, and *celebration* is a concluding activity used to recognize a job well done.

There are three types of community service: First, *direct service* is where students have direct contact with the people in need. An example would be helping elderly people washing windows. Second, *indirect service* is where students channel resources to the problem but do not come in direct contact with people. An example here would be to collect food for homeless shelters. Third, *advocacy* involves lending a voice to a cause or bringing awareness to a problem. This might include creating posters to bring awareness to the dangers of smoking.

EXAMPLE: Two Service Learning Projects

KINDNESS CAMPAIGN

Grade: 2

Subjects: Social Studies, Art

Materials: art supplies, sign materials (plywood, paint)

Type of service: indirect/advocacy

Students' goals:

1. Students will develop and implement a kindness campaign to raise awareness of the importance of kindness, compassion, and understanding in the school and community, and to reduce bullying and teasing in the school.

2. Students will understand how kindness and compassion will lead to a better school and a better society.

3. Students will develop strategies for handling teasing.

Preparation:

The teacher will read *Simon's Hook: A Story About Teases and Put-Downs* (Burnett, 2000). In this book, Simon is teased by friends and feels hurt and confused. A neighbor helped Simon deal with teasing with a story about a fish who learned not to bite on teasing hooks.

Introduce the problem of teasing. Ask students why they think some kids pick on or tease others. Ask students what strategies they use when they are being teased. Brainstorm ways to prevent or stop teasing in schools. Get some ideas for what might go into a commercial, poster, video, website, or creative drama to get their ideas across.

Introduce and discuss with students the importance of kindness and making everybody feel welcome. Discuss and describe how developing kindness, compassion, and understanding are the best ways to eliminate many problems in our communities and help people live together. Brainstorm ways in which students might get this message out to the school and to the community.

Service:

Students will develop a kindness campaign where they create Be-Kind signs and video ads for school and community cable tv. The goal is to raise awareness of the importance of kindness, compassion, and understanding. The signs can be displayed in local grocery stores, libraries, and other public places. Students will also put together a short creative drama as described in Chapter 8 to illustrate the importance of teasing and kindness. These dramas will be presented by several groups of 2nd grade students to individual classrooms.

Reflection and extension:

After they implement their plan students reflect as to the impact and they examine other ways to improve their kindness campaign.

(Continued)

(Continued)

Celebration:

The class will celebrate a job well done with a beverage or party. Get a community leader to come in and acknowledge and honor the efforts of these students.

BABYSITTING

Grade: 7

Subjects: Social Studies and Health

Materials: babysitting room; babysitting course or unit; books, toys, and games for young children; animal crackers

Type of service: direct

Students' goals:

1. Students will identify the responsibilities of child care.
2. Students will understand some of the basic developmental levels and needs of young children.

Preparation:

Students will be involved in a unit or short course that teaches some of the basics of child development and child care. The problem will be introduced: Parents who come to school for school functions often have young children. If there was some sort of child care service at school, it would be easier for parents to be involved. How can we create a babysitting service at school? What needs to be done? How do we make parents aware of this service? Students will begin collecting books, toys, and games for use in a babysitting room.

Service:

Students will set up a volunteer babysitting service at PTA/PTO meetings, student-parent conferences, and other school activities involving parents. One adult may be needed to supervise.

Reflection:

Students will share their experiences and observations of children and their behaviors at various times of the year.

Celebration:

At the end of the year, a tea or coffee will be hosted by parents to recognize and honor students for their work.

A Powerful Learning Tool

Service learning can be a powerful learning tool that helps break down the barrier between school and real life. School becomes not something that is done in the abstract, but something real. Also, students feel empowered, able to make positive change within their school or community. And like all problem solving, it involves active manipulation of and interaction with the subject matter. Students are able to process information at deeper levels.

GO THERE

- The Corporation for National and Community Service: www.leaderschools.org/2002profiles/south.html
- National Service Learning Clearinghouse: http://www.servicelearning.org/
- National Service Learning Partnership: http://learningindeed.org/index.html

---

Conflict resolution is problem solving on an interpersonal level. Learning how to confront and solve conflict is an important part of students' development.

CONFLICT RESOLUTION: INTERPERSONAL PROBLEM SOLVING

Conflict resolution is problem solving on an interpersonal level. An *interpersonal conflict* is a state of disharmony between two or more people (Girard & Koch, 1996). People living together in societies who have a variety of values, beliefs, wants, and needs are naturally going to come in conflict on occasion. It makes sense, then, that conflict resolution be included in your social studies curriculum in order to help students understand the nature of conflict and human interactions. Also, inclusion of conflict resolution will provide students with the skills necessary to constructively deal with the conflict they will encounter in their own lives.

It is a mistake to think that all conflict should be avoided. Indeed, there are many benefits to conflict (Deutsch, 1973). Conflict prevents stagnation and creates the conditions for evolution and growth. Confronting conflict allows for the examination and airing of problems that might have gone unnoticed. Also, the conflict that sometimes occurs between students in schools at recess and other free time is normal and can play an important part in students' development. These situations provide opportunities for students to begin to learn how to manage their differences and resolve disputes. Often there is the temptation for you to jump in and solve these types of problems for students; however, this robs them of the learning experience. Instead, teach your students the knowledge and skills necessary to solve their own problems and resolve their own conflicts.

Sources of Conflict

Deutsch (1973) describes five sources of conflict: resources, preferences and nuisance, values, beliefs, and forces within a relationship. These types of conflict occur between individuals, families, groups, communities, societies, religions, and nations. Understanding the source of conflict is the first step in resolving it or sometimes avoiding it.

Resources. Conflict can take place when resources are limited or when they are perceived as limited and when two or more people or groups want them. For example, in the community of nations, conflicts are often created when one country hoards or controls resources such as land, oil, economic power, food, jobs, water, or access to natural resources. Cooperation and collaboration are the most effective ways to avoid these kinds of conflict. Likewise, countries that strive only to compete economically on the world market at the expense of others create winners and losers and thus ensure conflict. Conflict always costs a great deal in terms of time and resources.

On the interpersonal level conflict often arises when people mistakenly think that success, acceptance, or friendship are limited resources. You can avoid a great deal of interpersonal conflict in your classroom by helping students understand that these are in unlimited supply. There are three strategies to use here:

- Make sure that all students experience success in some area. Do this by expanding the definition of intelligence and including multiple ways for students to demonstrate their knowledge.
- Interact with all students using unconditional positive regard (Rogers, 1961). Let them know that they are accepted for being who they are.
- Teach students the social skills necessary to be a good friend so that they will have a world of friends with which to interact.

Preferences and nuisance. Conflict can take place when the activities or tastes of one group impinge upon another's preferences or when they become a nuisance or impediment to another's goal. For example, in the world community, this type of conflict is created when the corporate or economic interests of one country impinge upon the religious or cultural interests of another country. This type of conflict also occurs when what one person or group is doing gets in the way of what another person or group is trying to do—for example if you were trying to study and your neighbor was having a loud party. Strategies for these types of conflicts start with helping each party to respect the rights and dignity of the other. Resolution usually involves stopping the offending behavior or some type of segregation.

Values. A value is a trait, quality, entity, practice, or experience that one deems important. (Chapter 16 describes these more fully.) Conflict often arises when people's values are at variance with another's. However, simply having different values does not create conflict. Instead, conflict occurs when one's values are forced on another or when another's values are demeaned or depreciated. For example, a group may value the practice of daily silent meditation. Conflict would be created if this group were to insist that all should adopt this practice or if they were to demean or depreciate those who did not engage in or value this practice.

Values-based conflict occurs also when one person or group uses power or influence to ensure that their values are the predominant ones. An important point in regard to democratic ideals that is often missed in social studies education is that a democracy is different than majority rules. A democracy is designed to protect the rights of the minority and as such has a system of checks and balances. Even though the majority of citizens may agree with a particular issue, a democratic government protects the constitutional rights of all citizens, especially those in the minority.

Beliefs and belief systems. Conflict can occur when there is a difference in what people believe to be true related to data or perceptions. It is not the difference in beliefs or belief systems that causes conflict, rather, it is when one person or group insists that their beliefs are correct and that others must adopt them or adhere to a similar world view.

Forces within a relationship. Conflict is created when there are opposing views or desires within a relationship. Relationship here can be defined as two or more people coexisting as a unit. It could be an interpersonal relationship with two people, or a group, family, or society. Conflict occurs when groups or people want to go different ways or have goals that conflict with each others'.

Conflict Behaviors

There are five ways of dealing with conflict: competing, accommodating, avoiding, compromising, and collaborating (Girard & Koch, 1996; Vanzandt & Hayslip, 1995). For younger children, these can be represented as the shark, teddy bear, turtle, fox, and owl. These five behaviors vary on the dimensions of assertiveness and cooperation as well as on whether their primary emphasis is outcome or relationship (see Figure 10.7).

Competing. The shark seeks to resolve conflict by overpowering and attacking the other disputant who is seen as an opponent and not a partner. This conflict behavior can be the most destructive as it creates a win-lose situation with the primary emphasis on outcomes over relationship.

Figure 10.7   Conflict Behaviors and Dimensions

Behavior	Dimensions	Primary Emphasis
Competing—shark	assertive and uncooperative	outcome
Accommodating—teddy bear	unassertive and cooperative	relationship
Avoiding—turtle	unassertive and uncooperative	neither outcome or relationship
Compromising—fox	some assertion and some cooperation	some outcome and some relationship
Collaborating—owl	assertive and cooperative	outcome and relationship

Accommodating. The teddy bear seeks to resolve conflict by giving up his or her own goals in favor of those of others. This creates a lose-win situation with the teddy bear most often being the loser. Relationships are seen as more important than one's own needs or outcome. Sharks and teddy bears may appear to get along initially, however, only one party wins, and without meaningful conflict resolution, there is little change or growth.

Avoiding. The turtle seeks to resolve conflict by avoiding it. There are times when this is the most prudent course of action. However, in the long term turtle behaviors do not advance outcomes or relationships. In this sense, turtles can be just as destructive as sharks.

Compromising. The fox seeks to resolve conflict by giving up some of his or her original goals and by persuading the other disputant to do the same. This approach tends to value some outcome and some relationship.

Collaborating. The owl seeks to resolving conflict by confronting it as a problem to be solved in cooperation with an equal partner. Collaboration is the highest form of conflict resolution as it creates only winners and it allows programs, processes, and relationships to evolve.

Conflict-Resolution Strategies to Teach Students

This section describes six conflict resolution strategies that can be taught to students in elementary and middle school settings. The ultimate goal is for students to be able to transfer these skills to real-life situations (Woody, 2001).

Avoiding conflict. The best way to resolve a conflict is to avoid one when possible. Understanding the five sources of conflict helps in this. For example, insisting that others share your values will cause conflict. Knowing this, one would hopefully go forward in a manner that would respect the values of another group or person.

Resolving conflict using the six-step collaboration process. The six-step collaboration process works if both parties are willing to work together. The graphic organizer in Figure 10.8

Figure 10.8   Graphic Organizer for the Six-Step Collaboration Process for Conflict Resolution

Source of the Conflict:

Side A—wants and needs	*Side B—wants and needs*
Ideas	
Possible Solution #1:	
Side A—benefits and costs	*Side B—benefits and costs*
Possible Solution #2:	
Side A—benefits and costs	*Side B—benefits and costs*
Possible Solution #3:	
Side A—benefits and costs	*Side B—benefits and costs*

Eventual Solution:

can be used to guide students' thinking through each step: First, identify the source of the conflict. Second, both sides list their wants and needs related to the conflict. Third, both parties brainstorm in order to generate a wide variety of ideas for possible solutions. Fourth, identify the three best solutions. Fifth, evaluate each solution on the basis of costs and rewards for each party. And finally, select the solution that offers the most benefits and the least costs for implementation. Then implement the solution and revise and refine as necessary.

Negotiating resolution to a conflict. The steps to negotiating resolution of conflict here are based on Johnson and Johnson's (1991) conflict resolution model: First, confront the disputant.

Describe your view of the conflict, express your feelings, and invite the other to do the same. Second, jointly define the conflict as a problem that can be solved. Do not label or insult, rather, identify the source of conflict. Third, communicate positions and feelings. Both parties describe their view of the situation, their feelings relative to the situation, and what they see as points of agreement and disagreement. It is important that each listen respectfully as the other speaks. Fourth, communicate cooperative intent and explore possibilities. This is where you work together to generate ideas for a possible solution. The problem-solving strategies described in Chapter 10 are effective here. Fifth, take each other's perspective. During this step, both should take the perspective of the other in an attempt to understand what the other wants. This helps in evaluating possible solutions. And finally, reach an agreement. Decide on a solution or combination of solutions that seems to provide both persons or parties with what they seek.

Comparison web. The comparison web can be used to help parties find common ground upon which to find or build a resolution. It is based on the thinking skill *Comparing and Contrasting* described in Chapter 11. Using the comparison web graphic organizer (see Chapter 6), students identify and list similarities and differences related to values, opinions, wants, needs, or perspectives. An idea or plan is then created based on the similarities.

Conflict resolution bridge. The conflict resolution bridge works best with younger students. A bridge similar to that in Figure 10.9 is created on the playground or in the classroom. The playground bridge might be created with paint on a sidewalk or other hard surface. The classroom bridge might be created with tape. The bridge should be big enough for a student to stand in each space. Students with a conflict start on each side of the bridge. In the first square, students describe what they want in terms of the conflict. In the second square students describe their feelings. ("When you ___, I feel ___.") In the third square each student restates the position of the other. This square invites students to take the perspective of the other person in the dispute. In the fourth square students generate ideas for solutions. Finally, students pick an idea on which they both agree, meet in the middle, and shake hands.

Peer mediation. A peer mediation program is one in which groups of students are taught to mediate disputes among their peers (Willis, 1993). Students in conflict come to peer mediators to get help in resolving conflicts. The mediators work alone or in pairs and use many of the same skills as described above.

Conflict-Related Classroom Activities

This section contains a description of three activities involving conflict that can be used to enhance learning in your classroom: structured academic controversy, studying conflicts, and role play.

Figure 10.9   Conflict Resolution Bridge

I want	I feel	Restate	Generate Ideas	**Meet in the Middle**	Generate Ideas	Restate	I feel	I want
→	→	→	→		←	←	←	←

Structured controversy. A structured academic controversy is a strategy in which a conflict related to an academic subject is used to enhance learning (Johnson, Johnson, & Smith, 1991). It enhances learning by inviting students to think more deeply and critically about the concepts being addressed.

HOW DO I? Design a Structured Academic Controversy

1. Identify and introduce a controversy within the context of a lesson or unit. For example, in studying the U.S. constitution, the teacher might introduce the idea of passing a law that prohibits burning and defacing the U.S. flag.

2. Define the issue using a dualistic statement so that there are two specific sides. For example, "A law should be passed to make it illegal to burn or deface the U.S. flag." This is a statement with which one can agree or disagree.

3. Form base groups with four students in each. Within each group, pairs are formed. Each pair takes a different side of the issue. Sometimes you may want to give students a choice as to which side to support, while at other times you may want to assign students at random.

4. Each pair gathers and organizes information to support their position. Depending on how deeply you want to investigate the issue and how much time you have, this step can take 15 to 20 minutes or a couple of days. In the flag burning example, one pair would find information and opinions to support the law while the others would find information and opinions to oppose it.

5. Each pair reports back to their base group to present their views along with supporting arguments. Each pair then presents ideas to support their point of view. There should be no discussion or arguments as the initial ideas are being presented. After both sides have presented their cases, then there is a free discussion where students are able to ask questions and exchange ideas.

6. Students drop their advocacy roles within the base group and try to find a consensus position. Here they look to find common ground on one side of the initial issue or else they identify an alternative position upon which they can all agree.

7. Students report their group's position with two to five supporting ideas in the form of evidence or rationale. This report could take one of four forms: (a) one student is chosen at random within the group to describe the group's position and supporting ideas orally to the whole class, (b) each group identifies a speaker to share ideas orally with the whole class, (c) a report is written by the group that describes their position and supporting ideas, or (d) each person in the group is asked to write a report describing the group's position and supporting ideas.

8. The final step is optional. Here students describe their individual ideas related to the topic in a journal or learning log entry or in a short written response. Included in this are their observations relative to the process of working in the pair and in the group.

Figure 10.10   Graphic Organizer for Analyzing Conflict

Source of Conflict:	Identify which of the following conflict categories apply: (a) resources, (b) preferences and nuisance, (c) values, (d) beliefs, or (e) forces within a relationship.
Reason:	Write a detailed description (one to three paragraphs) of why the conflict is taking place.
Conflict Behaviors:	Identify the conflict behaviors that are being used by each party: (a) competing, (b) accommodating, (c) avoiding, (d) compromising, or (e) collaborating.
Rewards:	Describe who is being rewarded by the conflict state and what those rewards entail.
Costs:	Describe who is being hurt or negatively affected by the conflict state and what the specific costs entail.
Solutions:	List alternative behaviors or solutions that would negate, avoid, or resolve the conflict.
Best Solution:	Describe the solution that is the most pragmatic to implement and that results in the greatest rewards with the least costs.

Studying conflicts. Find interesting areas of conflict to analyze in current events, history, science, literature or trade books, or even in movies and on television. Use the graphic organizer in Figure 10.10 to help students organize their thinking and responses as they analyze conflicts.

Role-play. Role-playing in the form of creative dramatics as described earlier in the chapter can be used to help students understand conflict behaviors. Creative dramatics also gives students a safe place to practice a variety of conflict resolution options. To generate ideas for creative dramas involving conflict, ask the class to brainstorm a list of common conflict situations. Then form small groups to create dramas around one of the conflict situations to present to the class.

GO THERE

- PBS Teacher Source: Conflict Resolution: http://www.pbs.org/teachersource/ whats_new/health/apr01.shtm
- Websites for exploring conflict resolution in the classroom: http://www.education-world.com/a_curr/curr170.shtml
- David and Roger Johnson's conflict resolution page: http://www.co-operation.org/ pages/conflict.html
- Lists of conflict resolution program resources: http://www.doe.state.in.us/publications/ pdf_sservices/conf_resol_02.PDF

NCSS STANDARDS

Thematic Standards

The following NCSS thematic standards are addressed in this chapter. See Appendix A for a full description of the relevant thematic standards.

Early Grades

I. Global Connections: b.

Middle Grades

I. Global Connections: b.

Pedagogical Standards

The following NCSS pedagogical standards are addressed in this chapter:

    I. Critical Thinking, Problem Solving, and Performance Skills.

   II. Active Learning and Motivation.

  III. Inquiry, Collaboration, and Supportive Classroom Interaction.

Essential Skills for Social Studies

The following NCSS essential skills for social studies are addressed in this chapter:

  I. Organizing and Using Information.
    A. Thinking Skills.
      1. classify information
      2. interpret information
      3. analyze information
      4. summarize information
      5. synthesize information
      6. evaluate information
    B. Decision-making Skills.
    C. Metacognitive Skills.

  II. Relationships and Social Participation.
    A. Personal Skills.
    B. Group Interaction Skills.

Chapter Review: Key Points

1. Teaching problem-solving strategies explicitly helps students develop their problem-solving skills.

2. There are seven steps in the problem-solving process:
   - Find the problem.
   - Define the problem.
   - Represent and organize information about the problem.
   - Create or select a strategy for solving the problem.
   - Allocate resources for solving the problem.
   - Monitor the problem solving.
   - Test and evaluate the solution to the problem.

3. Real problems can be used in a social studies class to create powerful learning experiences.

4. Redefining a problem is where you look at it from another angle or see it in a new way.

5. CPS and MEA are two effective problem-solving strategies that can be easily taught to students in the elementary and middle school grades.

6. Being able to think broadly or think outside the box is a trait used by effective problem solvers.

7. FFOE, brainstorming, and SCAMPER are strategies that can be used to help students think broadly.

8. Problem-solving strategies can be used to help students address personal and interpersonal problems.

9. Service learning, a type of problem solving, is where students provide a service to the community in the context of a learning experience.

10. Including conflict resolution in a social studies curriculum helps students understand some of the forces that affect much human interaction and at the same time provides them will skills to constructively deal with the conflict in their own lives.

11. There are five sources of conflict: resources, preferences and nuisance, values, beliefs and belief systems, and forces within a relationship.

12. There are also five conflict behaviors: competing, accommodating, avoiding, compromising, and collaborating.

Making Connections

1. Define a problem you observe in society or in the community. In a small group, use one of the problem-solving strategies to create a solution.

2. Find a picture book or a chapter in a trade book that you might use with students. Generate a list of problems associated with each.

3. List five to ten real-life problems related to society. Describe where and how these might be integrated into a social studies curriculum.

4. Find a problem related to your daily life in some way. This could be an interpersonal problem, or a problem related to school, work, or some product or process. Use CPS to generate ideas and find a solution.

5. Find a problem specifically related to education. Use MEA to design a plan.

6. Find a problem in your personal life situation; then define it. Why is it occurring?

7. Find a solution to the problem you defined above. How might you evaluate that solution?

8. Find three problems in society, the community, the campus, or your personal life. Trade problems with someone from class and redefine each other's problems.

9. Do a MEA for your life. Where would you like to be in ten years? What steps will you take to get there?

10. Pick a grade level. With a partner, list ten problems related to social studies that you could use for problem-solving activities.

11. Your problem is this: How can you become the best possible teacher? What is the solution?

12. Which of the conflict behaviors do you tend to use when confronted with conflict?

13. Find an area of conflict in your own life. Use the graphic organizer in Figure 10.10 to analyze this situation.

14. Find a person with whom you disagree on an important issue. Use a comparison web to find differences and similarities related to this issue.

15. Identify a decision that must be made in your life. Use the decision-making strategy to evaluate three choices for a decision before identifying the best choice.

16. In what ways do you see the three holistic learning ideas related to intrapersonal connections, interpersonal connections, and interconnectedness reflected here?

Chapter 11

Inquiry Learning In Social Studies

1. What images, words, or other associations come to mind when you think of science?

2. What kinds of questions might a social scientist ask?

3. How do you think social scientists gather information and conduct inquiries?

4. How might you provide structure for an independent study in social studies?

5. How would you incorporate inquiry into a social studies class?

6. What are some interesting social questions that might be asked in the context of an elementary or middle school social studies curriculum?

Science is a subject, but it is also a process that is used to look at the world around us. Scientists are those who use various processes to ask questions and find answers. There is not one scientific method; rather, there are many methods of science that are used to ask and answer questions (Hodson, 1988). Inquiry is a teaching strategy that incorporates these various scientific methods into learning situations (Savage & Armstrong, 1996). It is a more advanced pedagogical skill and takes a little more planning. Inquiry moves students from passive receivers of knowledge to active creators of knowledge. It also reflects a thinking process that can be applied to a variety of situations and subject areas.

There are three methods of science described in this chapter: (a) *creating groups* or *inductive analysis,* (b) *surveys and interviews,* and (c) *inquiry experiments.* These are all examples of the types of inquiries used by real social scientists to find out about the world in which we live.

CREATING GROUPS: INDUCTIVE ANALYSIS

Creating groups reflects the methodology used by qualitative researchers in education and other social sciences. Here the researcher observes a field, a group, or an event in order to understand or explain it. Data are collected through observation. As data are collected and recorded, the researcher organizes them into groups or categories. Finally, the researcher describes the field, group, or event in terms of those groups. Sometimes groups or categories are determined before collecting data. This type of inquiry is used anytime you want to find out about the makeup of a field, group, or event. Here you are asking questions related to types or kinds of things that make up a larger whole (see Figure 11.1). For example: "What kinds of activities do students do during recess?" Below are three social studies–related inquiry activities that involve creating groups.

History or current events. What interesting or important events happened this week? At the end of the week, students work in small groups to brainstorm and record interesting or important world or national, community, or school events. These events are put in groups and described in terms of groups and numbers within each group. After a few weeks, students will begin to notice recurring groups. Eventually, students can create graphs to show change in the number and kinds of events over time. This can be extended with older students by looking for interesting or important events that happened the last year, in a particular decade, or in a particular century or other time period.

Figure 11.1   Questions for Inquiry Activity Related to Creating Groups

- What kinds of products are exported from China?
- What kinds of toys are sold in a particular store?
- What kinds of greetings do people use?
- What kinds of jewelry do you see people wearing at the mall?
- What kinds of TV shows are found in prime time on the major networks?
- What kinds of things in our daily lives use energy?
- What kinds of things seem to cause conflict on the playground?
- What kinds of stories are found on the front pages of most newspapers?
- What kinds of things are made out of metal in our school?
- What kinds of TV commercials are found during prime time?
- What kinds of ads are found in certain newspapers or magazines?
- What kinds of technology can you find at a particular place?
- What kinds of volunteer work are found in our community?

Playground behavior. During recess, students make an initial observation to determine the behaviors or types of activities and games that are present (a pilot study). These behaviors are then put into four to six categories or groups. Example: talking, chasing, using playground equipment, and group sports. These categories are used as headings on a *data retrieval chart* (DRC) (see Figure 11.2). A DRC is any graphic organizer that is used to gather and organize information.

The next day students observe the playground using the DRC. They put a tally mark in the appropriate category every time a behavior is observed. They then use this information to create a graph or table that describes the type and frequency of various playground behaviors. This activity can be extended by comparing playground behaviors at different times of the day, comparing boys' activities to girls' activities, or comparing the activities of older and younger students.

The story. What interesting or important things happened in a story? After reading a piece of historical fiction, historical nonfiction, or some other story related to social studies, have students brainstorm to create a list of 11 to 20 important or memorable events (use eight to ten events for primary aged students). Next, students analyze the list using inductive analysis to put the events into groups. Then the number of events in each group is recorded. These data can also be displayed in graph or table form (see below). To extend this activity, use the same groups to compare one chapter to another, one book to another book, or one author to another author.

Figure 11.2   DRC for Recording Behaviors

Behavior →	Talking	Chasing	Playground Equipment	Group Sports

SURVEYS AND INTERVIEWS

This type of inquiry is dependent on first asking or identifying a specific research question. Students then design some type of survey or create a set of interview questions to collect data and answer the research question. Surveys and interviews are effective ways for students to access information from their family and friends, the community, and others students in the class and school. This information can then be used to expand upon that found in the regular social studies curriculum.

Conducting Surveys

Survey activities can be designed for students as early as the primary grades by using surveys that have only one or two questions. Surveys for older students in elementary and middle school could have from six to a dozen questions. Survey data can be collected using two different types of survey questions: open-ended and closed-response.

Open-ended survey questions. An open-ended question allows respondents unlimited choices. Example: The inquiry question is, "What kinds of movies do students in our grade like to watch?" The survey question would be, "What kinds of movies do you like to watch?" Some respondents may report four or five different kinds of movies, while others may only report one. The researcher then creates categories out of all the movies listed using inductive analysis and then reports the number of movies in each category. These data can be reported using graphs or tables. Students then make inferences or predictions based on the data. These questions provide a more accurate sense of what respondents are actually thinking than closed-response questions. The problems with open-ended survey questions are that they are somewhat messy in terms of analysis and you can generally ask fewer of them in a survey.

Science is the process of asking questions and gathering data to answer them.

EXAMPLE: Open-Ended Survey Activities

Ms. Hamm's 4th grade class was studying media as part of their social studies curriculum. Ms. Hamm posed the question to her students, "What kinds of TV programs do you thinking students at Grantsburg Elementary School like to watch?" After a couple of hypotheses she asked, "As social scientists, how do you think we can get this information?" She then helped her students set up an inquiry activity using open-ended surveys. After coordinating with the rest of the teachers in the building, small groups of social scientists were sent to different classrooms with clipboards. They recorded the grade level and asked students in each classroom, "What TV programs do you like to watch?" They could record up to three programs for each student surveyed.

Over a period of three days, every classroom in the school was surveyed. After an initial look at the answers on their clipboards, students settled on the following categories: (a) prime-time comedies, (b) cartoons, (c) Nickelodeon kids' shows, (d) PBS learning programs, (e) animal shows, (f) nonfiction information shows, and (g) sports. The students then put the TV shows listed on their clipboards into groups and tallied up the numbers in each group. After totals were collected the class was able to describe the TV watching preferences of the students at Grantsburg Elementary in terms of categories and numbers within each category. As part of their language arts class, students were then asked to put this information in graph or table form, and to write a lab report. The lab report described the question, how the data were collected, the results, and what the results might mean.

Ms. Hamm told her class that this is one of the processes social scientists use to find out about the social world in which we live. She extended this activity by asking students if they thought older students watched different kinds of TV programs than younger students. Since each grade level was recorded when the initial data were collected, it was very easy to sort and compare. Graphs and tables were again created to show their results.

This activity could be extended many other ways, the easiest of which would be to ask students, "What else would you like to know? How could this be extended? Is there any more information we could get related to TV watching preferences? How should we set up another inquiry?" Students could find out if there were gender differences in students' TV watching habits. Using the seven categories already established, students could create a simple DRC where responses were recorded with a tally mark (see below). If students wanted to compare their school to another school, they could then talk about sample sizes and using percentages to make comparisons.

	Prime-Time Comedies	Cartoons	Nickelodeon Kids' Shows	PBS Learning Programs	Animal Shows	Nonfiction Information Shows	Sports
Females							
Males							

(Continued)

(Continued)

> Mr. Foudy's 2nd grade classroom was studying the community in his social studies class. He was looking at wants and needs and how food gets to the stores. As part of this, he asked his students the following question, "What do students in our class like to eat? What do you like to eat?" As each student responded, he recorded their answers on a large white board in front of the room. Once all the students' favorite foods were recorded, he asked his class to look at the list to see if they saw any groups. He reminded students that a group is two or more things that are the same. The class came up with the following groups: (a) desserts, (b) meat (hot dogs and hamburgers), (c) fruits and vegetables, and (d) bread things (pizza, french fries, pancakes). They counted the total number in each category. This information was put in graph form. As part of language arts, students wrote a simple lab report describing their question and what they found.

Closed-response questions. A closed-response question provides a number of choices for respondents to select. Example: "What is your favorite movie genre: (a) action/adventure, (b) comedy, (c) science fiction, (d) horror/thriller, or (e) nonfiction?" This type of question allows you to ask a number of questions and get quantifiable data on many types of issues fairly quickly. For example, after surveying a group of people with the question above, students could safely report that 84.4 percent of respondents surveyed preferred comedy as a movie genre. The problem with these kinds of questions is that they can be inaccurate, misleading, or controlling. What if the first movie choice of a respondent was not even listed on the question above? Or what if a respondent liked to watch three or four different kinds of movies equally well?

EXAMPLE: Closed-Response Survey Activities

Ms. Chastain asked her 6th grade students the following question, "What kinds of hobbies do students in our grade enjoy?" The survey question was, "Which of the following hobbies do you enjoy: collecting, crafts, sports, games, or music? Do girls like different hobbies than boys?" A DRC was created using these categories. Students and social scientists simply ask individuals to name their favorite hobby category. Tally marks were used to record the number of responses in each category. These data were quantified and communicated using a table or graph and lab reports were written. This inquiry was extended by comparing the hobbies of older and younger students, and the hobbies of students and parents or other adults.

Collecting		Crafts		Sports		Games		Music	
Male	Female	Male	Female	Male	Female	Male	Female	Male	Female

Mr. Wambach asked his 1st grade class, "What season does our class enjoy most: fall, winter, spring, or summer?" He created the DRC below on a piece of poster board. Each student came up and made a mark under his or her favorite season. As part of math class, students created a table using graph paper. The totals were counted and put under each column. Students also created a simple lab report describing their findings.

Fall	*Winter*	*Spring*	*Summer*

With a little imagination, survey inquiries can be designed to enhance almost any social studies unit. Some examples of the types of questions that might be asked are listed in Figure 11.3. Also, the Internet has surveys and polls on a wide variety of topics that can also be incorporated into social studies units to add depth and dimension to lesson content. To find these, use the Internet search terms *survey* or *poll* along with the topic of study for which you are looking (see Chapter 13).

Figure 11.3   Examples of Possible Survey Inquiry Questions

- What sport or game do most students enjoy playing?
- What do most students do on Saturday?
- What types of shoes do most people wear?
- What type of job or career do students want to have in the future?
- What kinds of TV shows are most popular?
- What radio station is most popular?
- What types of music do most students enjoy listening to?
- What candidate do students support for president, senator, governor, or some other political office?
- How many people are in students' families?
- Where do families get their groceries?
- What do students think is the most important event that happened this year?
- What kinds of pets do students have: (a) dog, (b) cat, (c) fish, (d) gerbil or other rodent, (e) bird, or (f) other?
- What kinds of problems do students have in their lives?
- What kinds of books do students in our class enjoy reading?
- What traits do students look for in a friend?
- Which citizenship trait do students think is most important: (a) honesty, (b) responsibility, (c) respect for others, (d) willingness to volunteer, or (e) other?
- Which citizenship trait do parents, other adults, or teachers think is most important: (a) honesty, (b) responsibility, (c) respect for others, (d) willingness to volunteer, or (e) other?

Interviewing

Interviews are used if you want to find out about people's experiences or perceptions. Here the researcher prepares a set of questions in advance and asks these in person. What you give up in quantity with the interview, you gain in depth. That is, while surveys allow researchers to get shallow information from many people; interviews allow researchers to get more in-depth information from a few people. Unlike the survey, the interview format allows the researcher to ask follow-up questions and to seek clarification, and it also enables the interviewee to expand on interesting or important information that comes up during the interview. Interviews are a good tool for use with oral histories.

Interviews are good ways to find out about family and community history and can be adapted for use as early as 1st grade. You will need to prepare the interview questions initially for younger students. A common mistake most beginning interviewers make is to have too many questions. The interview should contain five to ten questions with possible follow-ups for each question. Interviews for primary age students should contain one or two questions. Students should spend time practicing and conducting interviews in class with classmates before interviewing people from the community. Finally, it often works best if students use an audio tape to record the interview and then go back and take notes after the interview is completed.

INQUIRY EXPERIMENTS

The third type of inquiry, experiments, is the type of inquiry that most people associate with the scientific method. It is similar to surveys and interviews in that both ask specific research questions first, then gather data to answer the questions. It is different in that in conducting an experiment the researcher uses a test or procedure with independent and dependent variables. Experiments can be a lot of fun and can even get silly at times. The important thing to understand is that you are teaching the processes of conducting scientific inquiries. These processes are used in both the hard sciences and the social sciences. Also, with inquiry experiment activities, students will naturally begin to talk about validity, reliability, and sample size (see below). These activities then become excellent vehicles for teaching these advanced scientific concepts as well as discussions related to ethics in science. Three examples of this type of inquiry are described here.

Gender characteristics. The question is: "Do males and females perceive gender differently?" Without telling them the question, ask for four students to volunteer to be the research subjects and to step outside the laboratory (classroom). Select two females and two males. The other students in the laboratory will be the social scientists who will be observing and recording data. After telling the social scientists the inquiry question, ask them their initial thoughts on the issue, and get some predictions. Then, one at a time, bring a subject into the laboratory. Ask the subject to think of a female they know, famous or not, and to describe that person. As the subject describes, the researchers record the order of characteristics. That is, they would list what the subject describes in order, such as hair, height, personality, activities, physical stature, or some other characteristic. Each subject is then asked to do the same with a male they know of. Again, the characteristics described are listed in order. Do students perceive and emphasize different characteristics in males and females? Do boys and girls emphasize different characteristics in their descriptions?

This inquiry experiment works best with students in 5th through 8th grade. In conducting any kind of inquiry, always ask researchers why they think they got the results they did and what the data mean or tell us. Also include in the discussion whether they were generally able or unable to make generalizations based on the data, and ask how the experiment could be improved. These types of questions reflect the conclusion and discussion sections found in most research reports.

Where are the jelly beans? How long does it take for a student to learn where the jelly beans are? What paths do they take? Again, ask for four volunteers to be research subjects. Send the subjects out into the hall so you can set up the experiment in the laboratory/classroom. The research questions are, "How long does it take subjects to find the jelly beans? What paths do they take in their search?" Give researchers a map of the room to use as a DRC to record the path that each student takes. Put a jelly bean somewhere in the room. As each subject enters the room, that subject is asked to find the jelly bean. A stopwatch is started to record the time. Student researchers use lines on their maps to record the path each subject takes in the room. A different colored pencil or crayon should be used for each student. The times and the paths that each student takes are recorded along with other notes or insights.

This inquiry experiment works with students in 2nd through 8th grade. Again, this is used to learn the process of science and to explore ways in which social scientists sometimes look at human behavior. The times and paths the subjects take are not as important as the process of asking questions and collecting data to answer those questions.

Small group behaviors. What kinds of behaviors do individuals in a small group use to solve a problem? Does a leader emerge? If so how? This experiment is similar to the fishbowl activity described in Chapter 9. It works well if you are using cooperative learning activities in the classroom or if you are teaching social skills. The research questions are: "What social skills do you notice students using as they work to solve this problem? What seems to be effective?

Send four volunteer subjects out into the hall as you prepare the laboratory. When ready, ask all four to come in simultaneously. They are told that they are to create a TV commercial that is designed to get students to read a particular book. (They could also create a commercial related to some aspect of a social studies unit.) To successfully complete this project, they will need an actor and some sort of visual aid. After ten minutes, they will be asked to perform.

Many variations can be used for experiments with small group behaviors. With older students, you might ask the social scientist researchers to simply record the interesting or important things they observe about a task group. With a unit on leadership, you might create a DRC for researchers with specific leadership or small group social behaviors (see Figure 11.4). Students then would use tally marks to indicate the frequency of occurrences.

Figure 11.4   DRC for Small Group Inquiry Experiment on Leadership

Behaviors	Occurrences
Affirms Ideas of Others	
Clarifies Task or Idea	
Seeks Consensus	
Gets Group on Task	
Assigns Tasks	

If the class is studying creativity or creative thinking skills (see Chapter 12), researchers could look for specific types of thinking during the small group session (see Figure 11.5). For listening skills, you could create a DRC that lists the specific skills that you are teaching (see Figure 11.6). You could also design a DRC to record who does the talking (see Figure 11.7).

These types of inquiry experiment activities can be adapted for use in a variety of subject areas and at all grade levels. There are two things to keep in mind when doing this type of

Figure 11.5   DRC for Small Group Inquiry Experiment on Creative Thinking

Types of Thinking	Occurrences
Frequency	
Fluency	
Elaboration	
Originality	
Piggy-backing	

Figure 11.6   DRC for Small Group Inquiry Experiment on Listening Skills

Types of Thinking	Occurrences
Question	
Verbal RTA	
Nonverbal RTA	
Clarify	

Figure 11.7   DRC for Small Group Inquiry Experiment on Communication

Student	Number of Comments or Times Each One Talked
Student 1	
Student 2	
Student 3	
Student 4	

inquiry: First, always ask for volunteers to be the subjects or participants. In so doing, give these volunteers a sense of what they will be asked to do when they return to the laboratory. You will find after you have done a few of these that you have no trouble getting volunteers to participate (some students like the attention). Second, again, the process is more important than the product. That is, it is okay to do "bad science" as long as you reflect on the process afterwards, noting what would be needed to make it "good science." At the end of every inquiry experiment, always ask students, "What could have been done differently to make this experiment better? What other related research question might we ask? What other kind of experiment would you like to conduct?" These questions will, in turn, lead to new and interesting inquiry activities.

GO THERE

- Article: "Using the Internet to Promote Inquiry-based Learning": http://www.biopoint.com/inquiry/ibr.html
- The Inquiry Learning Forum for Teachers: http://ilf.crlt.indiana.edu/
- Inquiry learning process and activities: http://www.inquiry.uiuc.edu/
- Classroom applications of inquiry learning: http://www.teach-nology.com/current trends/inquiry/in_the_classroom/

Observing, asking questions, and looking for answers are naturally occurring human traits. It makes sense to use these to enhance learning.

BECOMING CRITICAL
CONSUMERS OF INFORMATION

Having students analyze and evaluate their own surveys, interviews, and inquiry experiments is an important part of helping them to become critical consumers of information. Once they are comfortable examining their own research, it is a very simple step to extend this analysis to the surveys, polls, and other research reports they may find on the Internet and from other sources. Below are some examples of some fairly basic questions that can be used for these discussions. As always, the questions should be adapted to the grade level with which you are working.

Sample size. Was there a large enough sample size? Why is a larger sample size more accurate than a smaller sample size? How many people do you think should be included? How might the researchers have found more people to respond to the survey? How might the researchers have changed the experiment to include more people? Do you think you would be able to make strong conclusions based on the data and number of people included? Do you think you would be able to apply the results to a larger population based on the data and number of people included?

Subjects or participants in the sample. Are there different kinds of people in the sample? Are there more males than females or more females than males? Why might this be important? Are there people of different ages in the sample? How might the results of the survey, interview, or experiment be different with different types of people included? Did the researchers select only certain kinds of people to be in the survey, interview, or experiment? Do you think the people in the survey, interview, or experiment might have given only certain types of answers?

Validity. Do the questions in the survey or interview reflect the research questions? Will the survey and interviews questions answer the research question completely and fairly? Which questions might be included or excluded? For experiments, does the data that are being collected adequately reflect the research question? Can the research question be answered using the type of data? Do the data accurately reflect the conclusions described? Do the data actually describe or represent what the researchers say they do?

Reliability. Do you think the answers, scores, or data are accurate? Would the same results appear if the measurement were made a second time? Was there something in the survey or experiment that caused a certain type of result?

Bias. Do the questions push people to answer in a certain way? Do you think the researchers were looking for certain types of answers? Is there a balance in the types of questions asked? Was the survey, interview, or experiment conducted fairly? Were the researchers looking for all types of answers or data? Did the researchers start with an answer and then look only for data that supported that answer?

Methodology. How might the survey, interview, or experiment be improved? Did the subjects or participants react as they normally would? Did the subjects or participants know what was going on? How else might data be collected? What other types of data might be collected?

ELEMENTS OF INQUIRY

This section describes the three elements that are common to any type of inquiry activity: knowledge, structure, and freedom.

Knowledge

You need to supply background knowledge so that the inquiry questions can be put in context. For example, if you design an inquiry activity related to American cities (Figure 11.8), students must first be provided with a certain amount of background knowledge about cities before they are given an inquiry question. Without this element, the inquiry is simply a matter of speculation and learning-by-guessing. A well-organized knowledge base guides the process of data retrieval and analysis.

Structure

Structure is used to guide students as they learn how to ask questions, collect data, answer questions, and communicate their answers. In the beginning stages of teaching the inquiry process, you can provide structure by asking the inquiry questions. However, as students become more familiar with this process they will eventually be able to ask their own inquiry questions. When collecting data, structure is provided in the form of a DRC (see Figure 11.8). DRCs come in a variety of forms, all of which can be used to help students organize data as they are collected.

Lab reports provide structure for students when reporting inquiry results. A lab report helps students communicate their ideas and can be used with any type of inquiry in any subject area. The lab report consists of three parts: the conditions (before), the results (after), and ideas or interpretations (see Figure 11.9).

The *conditions* section describes the research question; what went on before the observation, survey, interview, or experiment; and how students gathered information. The *results*

Figure 11.8   DRC for Inquiry Activity Related to Cities

Inquiry Question: What are the similarities and differences among major U.S. cities?

Cities	Climate	Population	Major Industries	Latitude and Longitude
Minneapolis				
Kansas City				
Boise				
San Diego				
Tampa Bay				

section contains the facts or the data that were collected. Here students report exactly what happened or present the data collected using as few words as possible. If students are doing an inquiry that uses numerical information, they can use graphs, charts, or tables to describe results (see tables and graphs below). In the *Ideas* section, students tell what they think the data might mean or describe how the data could be used.

Figure 11.9   Lab Report

Lab Report

Conditions

Our research group wanted to find out what kinds of movies 5th grade students like to watch. We also thought it would be interesting to see if boys liked different kinds of movies than girls do. We created a DRC that had five different kinds of movies: (a) action/adventure, (b) comedy, (c) science fiction, (e) horror/thriller, or (f) nonfiction. As they came out of the cafeteria after lunch, we asked students what kinds of movies were their favorites. We recorded students' answers using tally marks.

Action/Adventure		Comedy		Science Fiction		Horror/Thriller		Nonfiction	
Male	Female	Male	Female	Male	Female	Male	Female	Male	Female

Results

Type of Movie	Total	Males	Females
Comedy	42	18	24
Action/Adventure	22	18	4
Horror/thriller	15	4	11
Science Fiction	10	8	2
Nonfiction	0	0	0

Ideas or Conclusions

Comedies are the kinds of movies that most 5th grade students liked. Both boys and girls like this kind of movie. If we were going to have a party with both boys and girls, this is the kind of movie we would get. More boys than girls liked action/adventure. More girls than boys liked horror/thrillers. Nobody liked nonfiction movies.

Freedom

The third element of inquiry is freedom. If it is true inquiry, all answers must be accepted so long as there are data to support those conclusions. A good inquiry activity does not lead students to predetermined answers.

IMPLEMENTING THE INQUIRY PROCESS

In the classroom, the inquiry process starts when a teacher or student asks a question or states a hypothesis. Questions might include: What makes a good friend? What materials are used most often in manufacturing? What kind of bridge will hold the most weight? What things do major U.S. cities have in common? Next, students gather data. Then, the data are organized and used to answer the original question.

EXAMPLE: An Inquiry Lesson Plan and Lab Report

The following example of an inquiry lesson is based around the question, What is a hero? The input section of the lesson provides knowledge related to heroes. A DRC is used during the activity section to help students gather and organize their thinking, and students communicate their ideas in a lab report.

Grade: 4

Objective: Students will learn about heroes.

Introduction: Kurt Vonnegut, Lisa Leslie, Katherine Paterson, my father, and Jimmy Carter are some of my heroes or people I look up to.

Input:

1. Heroes are people we look up to.
2. They have some trait or talent that we think is important.
   A. We would like to have this same trait or talent.
3. Examples:
   A. Kurt Vonnegut is a very creative writer not afraid to be different (show picture, book).
   B. Lisa Leslie trains hard, works on skills, has good technique, and plays hard (show pictures).
   C. Katherine Paterson writes great books that are very touching (show pictures, books).
   D. Jimmy Carter was a president who stood up for what he believed. He tries to help people make their lives better (show pictures, magazine articles).
   E. My father was my hero (show picture). He always worked hard, respected people, and supported me.

(Continued)

(Continued)

4. Heroes can be famous and not famous.

5. Heroes aren't perfect. Nobody's perfect.
   A. They are just humans who have a trait or talent that we think is important or valuable.

Activity:

1. Inquiry question: What is a hero? What qualities do heroes have in common?

2. In small groups, find four heroes that are familiar to all or most.

3. Brainstorm to generate traits or experiences of each hero.

4. Use the data retrieval chart to list and organize ideas (show example below).

5. Each small group describes its general conclusions.

6. Individually, students write their conclusion in their learning logs.

Data Retrieval Chart

Hero →	Paul Wellstone	Mia Hamm	Lindsey Whalen	Malcolm X
Traits or Experiences →				

Conclusions:

Lab Report:

Conditions

Our group wanted to find out what made a hero. We listed four heroes that we all knew, brainstormed some describing words or traits for each of them, then looked to see if there were any common describing words or traits. Our heroes were Paul Wellstone, Mia Hamm, Lindsey Whalen, and Malcolm X.

Results

Our group found that most of our heroes worked hard, were very good at something, had some setbacks or failures, learned their skills related to their area, and spent a lot of time practicing.

Ideas

We think an important part of being successful is working hard, practicing, and not giving up.

Science Skills

Many inquiry activities call for students to master a set of skills related to science. These science skills, which also reflect NCSS essential skills (see Appendix C), include the following: observe, describe, create a diagram, create a graph, create a table, record, measure, weigh, use a database, keep a lab notebook, predict, make groups, ask a question, create a DRC, organize data, demonstrate, conclude, write a lab report. A checklist can be created and included in a learning portfolio along with lab reports to show students' progress in learning how to use these various methods of science (see Figure 11.10).

Figure 11.10   Checklist for Science Skills

Science Skills

observe _____	use a database _____
describe _____	predict _____
create a diagram _____	make groups _____
create a graph _____	ask a question _____
create a table _____	create a DRC _____
measure _____	organize data _____
record _____	demonstrate _____
use a lab report _____	conclude _____

Key: I = introduced, L = learned, M = mastered.

EXAMPLE: Using Inquiry With Independent Research Projects

Use the following information and guidelines to take students through all steps of the inquiry process. Modify these steps to fit the developmental level of the students. When students have completed their independent research projects, use the rating checklist below for assessment and evaluation.

Student Guide for Independent Research Projects

This project can be done individually or in small groups. This research allows you to investigate a topic that is of interest to you. Don't be concerned with a particular length, depth, or breadth of your research. Instead, find interesting topics and gather interesting supporting material. Some very good research is short and concise. The following steps will guide you through this process:

Steps

1. Ask a question. What do you want to find out about? What are you interested in? Look for questions. Talk to people. Read magazines or books, watch TV, or check the Internet to find ideas that you find interesting. Finally, put your interest in the form of a question.

(Continued)

(Continued)

2. Gather data. Get information about your question. Use at least two different sources. (Older students should use four to six different sources.) Read, record, listen, ask questions, interview experts.

3. Take notes and look for patterns. Record the interesting or important ideas that you find by taking notes. Look for common themes or patterns to appear. Organize your ideas into groups. Throw away information or ideas that are not important.

4. Answer your question. Use your notes to answer your original question. Add your own ideas or answers.

5. Communicate your idea. Present your findings or idea to an audience. You can create a demonstration, speech, drama, commercial, report, video, drawing, sculpture, dance, or research report or use graphs and tables.

Rating Checklist for Independent Research Projects

Key: 4 = outstanding, 3 = very good, 2 = average, 1 = low.

Criteria	Rating
1. Responsibility: (a) The researcher was able to come up with a question or idea, (b) the research was completed in the prescribed time, and (c) the researcher gathered appropriate sources for notes.	
2. Knowledge: The research (a) is interesting and informative, (b) demonstrates a knowledge base, and (c) uses an appropriate kind and number of sources.	
3. Thinking: The research (a) finds important ideas or themes, (b) uses knowledge (notes) to answer the research question, and (c) shows the researcher as a reflective learner.	
4. Communication. The presentation (a) communicates background knowledge and new ideas effectively, (b) uses the elements of effective speaking, (c) is clear, logical, and organized, and (d) is interesting.	

Inquiry Questions for a Social Studies Class

The chapter has outlined the inquiry process, described how to design inquiry activities, and provided examples of many different types of inquiry. Listed in Figure 11.11 are 89 inquiry questions that might be used with a social studies unit at various grade levels. Students should be encouraged to use interviews or other primary data sources to answer the questions. The Internet can be included as one of these data sources (see Chapter 14). Most of these questions will need some type of DRC to help students collect and organize data. Data can be described using tables, charts, bar graphs, pictographs, line graphs, diagrams, or time lines and presented using some form of a lab report.

Figure 11.11   Social Studies Inquiry Questions

1. What color socks did students wear today?

2. What kind of weather is it today?

3. What do we like to eat for dessert?

4. What size are our families?

5. What are things we like to do with our families?

6. What kinds of jobs do our parents have?

7. What kinds of pets do we have?

8. What is our favorite kind of garden food?

9. What is our favorite fruit?

10. Where do we buy our groceries?

11. What are our favorite TV shows?

12. Where does catsup come from?

13. Where does our water come from?

14. How many police officers are in our town?

15. What does a police officer do?

16. What does a firefighter do?

17. Where do we live?

18. What kind of job might we want when we get older? (Here, students collect data related to training, job prospects, and salary.)

19. What is our heritage?

20. What makes a good friend?

21. What was it like growing up in the 1940s, '50s, or '60s?

22. What do people remember about the Vietnam War?

23. What do people remember about the Korean War?

24. What do people remember about World War II?

25. Where is a good place to take a vacation?

26. What was Lincoln's childhood like?

27. What made Lincoln a good president?

28. What made Martin Luther King Jr. a great leader?

29. What is a good leader?

30. What is a compassionate person?

31. What traits are important in getting a job?

32. What is a good citizen?

33. What are the most important events that have happened in the last week? Month? Year? Decade? Century? Millennium?

34. What are the most important events of 1976?

35. Where and when did *The Bridge to Terabithia* (Paterson, 1977) take place?

36. What is a democracy?

37. What makes a good government?

38. How do people solve differences in families, classrooms, schools, communities, or countries?

39. What makes a good president?

40. What is the purpose of religion in our society?

41. What laws help keep us safe?

42. What are the important laws in our community, state, or country?

43. What are the important rules we have in our classroom, school, or family?

44. What kinds of jobs do our parents have?

45. What laws help protect our environment?

46. How do we get rid of wastes?

47. How much garbage does our family throw out each day/week?

48. What people have made a positive difference in our school, community, state, or country?

49. What is a hero?

Figure 11.11 (Continued)

50. Who are our heroes?

51. What values do we feel are important?

52. What kinds of problems do families sometimes face?

53. What kinds of problems are found in our classroom, school, community, state, or nation?

54. What should you do if somebody teases you?

55. How can you make somebody feel good?

56. How is your life different from that of somebody living in Japan, Russia, or South Africa?

57. How is your school different today than it was 10, 20, 40, or 100 years ago?

58. What inventions have changed our world?

59. What inventions have changed music?

60. What kind of music does our class, school, or community prefer?

61. Do girls like different kinds of music than boys?

62. Do older students like different kinds of music than younger students?

63. What kind of music do adults like? Older adults? Younger adults?

64. Where do most people get their news?

65. What are the wants and needs of people in our school, class, or community?

66. What do people in our class, school, or community like to do in their leisure time?

67. Where do we get our food?

68. How has transportation changed in the last 5, 10, 20, 50, and 100 years?

69. What products do we export? Import?

70. What important services are found in our community?

71. How far do students live from school?

72. How do students get to school?

73. What lakes, rivers, mountains, and deserts are found in our community, county, state, country, or hemisphere?

74. How many community members or parents were in the services?

75. What kinds of energy do we use each day?

76. What energy source is used to heat/cool our homes?

77. Where does our energy come from?

78. How is a desert different from a forest?

79. How did western pioneers get their food?

80. What were the most important inventions developed during the industrial revolution?

81. How have airplanes changed the way people live?

82. What Native American tribes lived in our region in the last 200 years? What happened to them?

83. What are the most important inventions of the last 5, 10, 50, 100, or 1000 years?

84. What was life like as a slave in 1800?

85. What problems did early settlers face?

86. What problems did Native Americans face before settlers came? After settlers came?

87. How did Christianity, Islam, Judaism, Buddhism, and Hinduism originate?

88. What are the similarities among the five major religions?

89. How do different countries protect religious freedom?

TEACHERS IN ACTION: Using Primary Sources in Inquiry Learning

My most successful lessons are my two Journal activities: one on the Lewis and Clark Journey and one on Aztec Daily Life. Most of the ideas I have generated myself and some characteristics were borrowed from the "History Alive!" series.

First, the kids make their own journals using construction paper and lined writing paper stapled together. Then, I place the students in mixed ability groups in which they will work for the next week to two weeks.

As soon as they enter class, they get into their groups and look to the board for directions and materials to gather (these are placed on a central table). The board instructions might look like this: "Please gather the following materials for your group: 1 set of markers, 2 photos, and 1 textbook per student."

Once everyone is settled with materials, I do a mini-lesson (about 5–7 minutes). This might include a dramatic reading from a primary source (Lewis and Clark's actual journals or a letter from Cortes describing the Aztecs), a list of facts, or a review of what was done the previous day. For example, "You are in the middle of an unknown continent. You have been traveling with Lewis and Clark for three weeks now and have seen many strange animals and plants. You have no idea if or when you will reach the Pacific. You suddenly encounter a group of hostile Native Americans . . ." Basically, I set the stage for that day's journal.

Now the students engage in hands-on, inquiry-based learning. They create their own historical theories and gather facts and data (using photos, reference books, textbooks, etc.). They place these discoveries and theories in their journals in the form of letters, pictures, and sketches based on guided questions that I have listed on the board.

Year after year, kids come back to me and remember these Journal lessons the most. It is a successful activity because it engages the children both in learning the historical/subject content and in the methodology of history itself. During these lessons, I NEVER have a behavior problem as they are so busy and engaged.

—Annie, social studies teacher, 5th–8th grades

Author Reflection: Annie has created a wonderful inquiry activity here. In doing so, she has her students engaging in the same sort of inquiry that real-life historians use. Notice that Annie uses all of the elements of inquiry described in this chapter. Plus, her students are reading, writing, drawing, and using a variety of media to get information. She is a master teacher.

Inquiry is a complex teaching strategy that takes a while to feel comfortable with and master. I believe, however, that it is well worth the time and effort as it has the potential to create very powerful learning experiences.

What is your response to the case? How do your reactions compare with the author's reflection?

TABLES AND GRAPHS

Tables and graphs are used to represent relationships among quantities. They are often used in inquiry activities to represent results or data collected. They can also be incorporated in all subject areas and at all grade levels.

Tables

Tables are a quick, very visual way to organize and report information. They are especially useful if you have a great deal of numerical data to report. Simple tables should be introduced in kindergarten and continued in more complex forms for a variety of purposes at all the grade levels. Nancy Kerr, a 4th grade student, conducted an inquiry project at her school to determine what kinds of books the students in the four 4th grade classrooms liked to read (see Figure 11.12). For her report, she put these data in table form. (Note that data in a table are listed in order from greatest to least in descending order.)

Tables also help to clarify and make comparisons among values for a variety of types of information. Tad Armstrong, a 7th grade student, used a table to organize her class presentation on the six most popular world religions (see Table 11.1).

Graphs

Graphs are also used to show comparison. Line graphs show change over time. Ms. Pippen was teaching social skills to her 5th grade class as part of cooperative learning. She had been

Figure 11.12   Leisure Reading Preferences
of 4th-Grade Students at Elm Creek Elementary School

Reading Preference	Totals
action/adventure	47
comedy fantasy	35
fantasy	22
mystery	21
biography	5
science fiction	3
historical	2
technical	0

Table 11.1   Table for World Religions

Religion	Date of Origin	Holy Text or Scripture	Numbers
Christianity	30–33 CE	Bible	2,215,000,000
Islam	622 CE	Qur'an and Hadith	1,300,000,000
Hinduism	4000–2500 BCE	Veda	900,000,000
Buddhism	560–490 BCE	Tripitaka	362,000,000
Judaism	2000 BCE	Torah	18,000,000
Sikhism	early 1500s	Holy Granth	16,000,000

working on getting students to say positive or encouraging comments in their cooperative learning groups. When working on cooperative learning tasks, Ms. Pippen assigned one student in each group the role of sociologist. It was the task of this student to observe group members interacting and to put down a tally mark every time a student made a positive or encouraging comment. One student, Molly Jordon, used a line graph to show how many positive or encouraging comments were made each day during the week as their cooperative learning group worked together. Figure 11.13 shows how the number of comments changed over time.

Figure 11.13   Molly Jordon's Positive Comments Line Graph

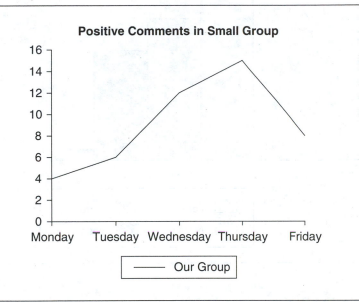

Positive Comments in Small Group

EXAMPLE: Using Tables and Graphs in Kindergarten

Mr. Cartwright asked his kindergarten students which kind of juice they like better: orange juice or apple juice. He had a big chart in front of the room with a picture of orange juice on one side and apple juice on the other. During the day, students were asked to use a magic marker to put an X underneath the one they like better. In this way, students could see that the marks on the chart represent a quantity of things in their world. Is it of critical importance that students know the juice preference of their class? Not really. However, this is an example of taking something that is familiar to students and using it to teach a skill. Mr. Cartwright creates these kinds of simple graph and table activities at least once a week throughout the year using a variety of topics. This simple activity prepares students to interpret tables and graphs and gets them ready for future math activities.

Bar graphs are used to compare two or more things. Figure 11.14 contains a bar graph that 2nd grade student Kanesha Longly used to show the vegetable preference of students in her classroom.

Figure 11.14　Bar Graph Showing the Vegetable Preferences of 3rd-Grade Students

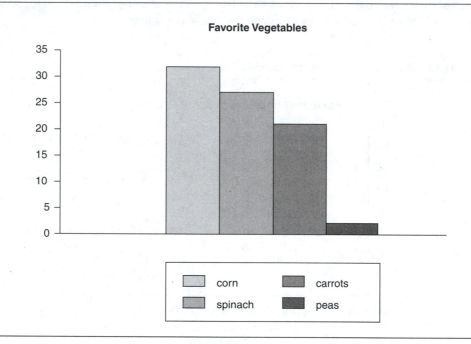

NCSS STANDARDS

Pedagogical Standards

The following NCSS pedagogical standards are addressed in this chapter:

I.　Critical Thinking, Problem Solving, and Performance Skills.

II.　Inquiry, Collaboration, and Supportive Classroom Interaction.

Essential Skills for Social Studies

The following NCSS essential skills for social studies are addressed in this chapter. See Appendix A for a full description of the relevant thematic standards.

I.　Acquiring Information.
　　A.　Study Skills.
　　　　1.　find information
　　　　2.　arrange information in usable forms

    B. Reference and Information-Search Skills.
       1. maps, globes, and graphics
       2. community resources

II. Organizing and Using Information.
    A. Thinking Skills.
       1. classify information
       2. interpret information
       3. analyze information
       4. summarize information
       5. synthesize information
       6. evaluate information

Chapter Review: Key Points

1. Science is a process of asking questions and collecting data to answer those questions.

2. Inquiry is a teaching strategy that uses methods of science to enhance learning.

3. Creating groups, interviews and surveys, and experiments are three types of inquiry that can be used in social studies and other curriculum areas.

4. Inquiry contains three elements: knowledge, structure, and freedom.

5. The steps of the inquiry are to ask a question, gather data, organize data, and communicate ideas about data.

6. Inquiry can be used for independent projects.

7. Teachers should always ask for volunteers to be subjects in inquiry experiments.

8. In inquiry, the process of doing science is sometimes more important than the actual product.

9. Helping students analyze and evaluate surveys, interviews, and experiments helps them to become critical consumers of information.

10. There are six areas to explore when analyzing surveys and interviews: sample size, subjects or participants in the sample, validity, reliability, bias, and methodology.

11. DRCs and lab reports can be used to provide structure.

12. Tables and graphs are used to represent relationships among quantities and can be used as part of inquiry as well as other social studies activities.

Making Connections

1. Do a quick survey using an open-ended question to ask at least 25 people to name the first thing or things that come to mind when they hear the term, "social studies." Use inductive analysis to find groups and numbers within each group. Report your data using a table or figure.

2. Create an interesting or amusing research question related to the topic of your choice. Conduct a quick survey using closed-response questions with at least 25 people to answer this question. Report your data and your conclusions using a lab report.

3. Using the same research question as above, create a survey using one to three open-ended questions. Give the survey to at least 25 people. Use inductive analysis to find groups and numbers, and communicate your findings using a lab report.

4. What would you like to know about teaching from an experienced teacher? Create a research question related to an area of teaching that might be answered by an interview. Create and conduct a three- to five-question interview with two classroom teachers.

5. Find a social studies textbook or teacher's manual at the grade level that is of interest to you. Using this, describe five kinds of inquiry activities you might use with this content.

6. Find an interesting unit or topic that might be included as part of social studies. Do a search on the Internet to find a survey or poll that might be used to enhance this topic.

7. Ask a question related to change over time and collect data to answer this question. Create a line graph to display your data.

8. In what ways do you see the three holistic learning ideas related to intrapersonal connections, interpersonal connections, and interconnectedness reflected here?

Chapter 12

CREATIVE AND CRITICAL THINKING SKILLS IN SOCIAL STUDIES

Thinking Ahead

1. Think of a skill you have learned. How did you best learn this skill?

2. How would you define critical thinking?

3. How would you go about teaching critical thinking?

4. What does it mean to be a creative thinker?

5. What do you think is of more value: being able to analyze ideas (critical thinking) or being able to generate ideas (creative thinking)?

This chapter examines the use of thinking skills within a social studies curriculum. Explicit instruction of thinking skills is the most efficient way to help students learn higher and more complex ways of thinking. Embedding thinking skills into a social studies curriculum enhances learning.

DEFINING THINKING SKILLS

A *thinking skill* is any cognitive process broken down into a set of steps which are then used to guide thinking (Johnson, 2000b). For example, inferring is a cognitive process that is one of the essential skills for social studies as defined by the NCSS (1994). To infer one must integrate observed clues with background knowledge in order to make an informed guess or prediction. This cognitive process can be made into a thinking skill by breaking it into the following steps: (a) identify the question or point of inference, (b) identify what is known or observed, (c) identify related knowledge that is relevant, and (d) make a reasoned guess based on b and c. Then it can be taught explicitly.

There are three terms that are often used synonymously with thinking skills: *high-level thinking, complex thinking*, and *critical thinking*. However, they are quite different. Each of these is described below.

High-Level Thinking

High-level thinking is any cognitive process that places high demands on the thinking and sorting of data taking place in short term memory. In looking at Bloom's taxonomy, these are the kinds of thinking processes that take place at the top: evaluation, synthesis, and analysis. However, students do not benefit from being exposed to high level thinking tasks unless there is explicit instruction first. For example, a teacher could ask students to compare and contrast the Iraq conflict to the Vietnam War. Students who are already fairly adept at high level thinking might be able to do this easily while other students will probably become frustrated. Unfortunately, this is what often happens under the guise of developing high level thinking: Teachers simply present high level tasks. In these situations there is no actual teaching, very little learning, and a great deal of student frustration.

Thinking skills instruction, on the other hand, makes learning this cognitive process fairly simple by making it a thinking skill. If you want students to be able to compare and contrast, you must first break this cognitive process into the following steps: (a) Look at the whole, (b) find the similarities, (c) find the differences, and (d) describe. Then, teach it using explicit instruction. With instruction, high-level thinking becomes relatively easy. This is the major premise of thinking skills instruction: Complicated things are made easy by breaking them into parts and teaching them explicitly.

Complex Thinking

Complex thinking is any cognitive process that involves many steps or parts. The difference between high level thinking and complex thinking sometimes is very slight. The best example of complex thinking is the thinking process that takes place when planning a lesson. Here you must (a) define the information or skill to be taught, (b) organize the knowledge or break the skill into manageable parts, (c) decide how to convey this knowledge or teach the skill to students at a level they can understand and in a manner that will keep them focused, (d) create active involvement (e) consider a variety of learning modes, (f) attend to individual differences, (g) manage student behaviors, and (h) design an activity to reinforce the skill or concept. These processes, of course, vary with the teacher and the situation.

In undergraduate teaching methods courses, students often struggle when they are first asked to design lessons. Indeed, it is not reasonable to expect them to know how to engage in the kinds of complex thinking needed to adequately design learning experiences without providing them with explicit instruction. Thus, lesson plan design should be broken into a few well-defined steps and taught explicitly (Johnson, 2000b). In this way, lesson planning becomes a thinking skill that enables preservice teachers to master this type of complex thinking more quickly and with less frustration.

Critical Thinking

Critical thinking is a type of thinking that converges on a single thought or entity. Here one must organize, analyze, or evaluate information; all of these processes could become thinking skills if they were broken into parts and taught explicitly. The opposite of critical thinking is creative thinking. This is thinking that diverges from a single point or entity. Here one must generate, synthesize, find alternatives, adapt, substitute, or elaborate. Each of these operations could also become thinking skills if they were broken into parts and taught explicitly.

GO THERE

- Instruction framework: Introduction to thinking skills: *http://www.aea267.k12.ia.us/cia/framework/thinking/*
- Thinking skills vocabulary and definitions: *http://www.adprima.com/thinkskl.htm*
- Georgia critical thinking skills program: *http://www.glc.k12.ga.us/pandp/critthink/homepg.htm*
- Many articles related to thinking skills: *http://www.newhorizons.org/strategies/thinking/front_thinking.htm*

We can improve children's ability to think by explicitly teaching thinking skills and embedding thinking skills into the curriculum.

ELEMENTS OF EFFECTIVE SKILLS INSTRUCTION

Thinking skills should be taught using *thinking frames* and the *elements of effective skills instruction*. A thinking frame is used to initially guide students' thinking (Johnson, 2000b; Perkins, 1986). A thinking frame is concrete representation of a particular cognitive process broken down into specific steps and used to support the thought process. Thinking frames can be constructed in poster form and placed in the classroom for teaching and easy review of thinking skills. Examples of thinking frames can be seen in Figure 12.1.

Thinking skills are of little use if they are not taught in a manner in which students can understand and learn to use them. Effective skills instruction of any kind incorporates four components: identification of the procedural components (steps), direct instruction and modeling, guided practice, and independent practice (Johnson, 1999; Pressley, Harris, & Marks, 1992). Each of these is described below.

Figure 12.1   Examples of Thinking Frames

Inferring	Comparing and Contrasting
1. Identify the question or point of inference.	1. Look at the whole.
2. Identify what is known or observed.	2. Find the similarities.
3. Identify related knowledge that is relevant.	3. Find the differences.
4. Make a reasoned guess based on 2 and 3.	4. Describe.

Identification of the procedural components. First, students are introduced to the skill, and the specific steps involved are identified. When teaching a thinking skill, this is where students are introduced to the thinking frame used to guide their thinking during the other steps.

Direct instruction and modeling. Next, the teacher gives explicit instruction as to how the skill might be used and models it by thinking out loud while going through each step. This element, which is used to provide students with an overview, should be relatively brief.

Guided practice. Guided practice is sometimes referred to as *scaffolded instruction* (Johnson & Graves, 1997). Here, the teacher takes the whole class through each step of the skill several times. The goal is to provide the support necessary for students to use the skill independently.

Independent practice. The teacher designs an activity so students can practice the skill independently. This may include homework. If the first three components have been taught effectively, students should be able to complete this with a 95 to 100 percent success ratio (Good & Brophy, 1995). Independent practice is not meant to be challenging. It is meant to practice those skills already covered in class.

EXAMPLE: A Thinking Skills Lesson Plan

Teacher: Andrew Johnson

Grade: 3

Subject: Social Studies

Objective: Students will use the thinking skill *creating groups* to put current events into categories.

Introduction:

Boys and girls, today we are going to learn how to use a new thinking skill called *creating groups*.

Input:

1. Thinking skills are the skills we use to help organize our thoughts.

2. They have specific steps to follow.

3. They make complicated thinking seem easy.

4. *Creating groups* is a thinking skill.
    A. Scientists often use this.
    B. Look at animals, organisms, rocks, etc.; look for patterns, and make sense of them by putting the items into groups (show example with animal pictures).

(Continued)

(Continued)

5. These are the steps of *creating groups*:
   A. Look at the whole.
   B. Identify reoccurring themes or patterns.
   C. Arrange into groups or categories.
   D. Describe.

6. Guided Practice: As a class, brainstorm to list 10 interesting events that have happened at school in the last week.
   A. Think out loud (cognitive modeling) to help students organize into groups.
   B. Example: Are there things that are the same here?

Activity:

1. In a small group, students list at least 20 current events that have happened this year.

2. Use *creating groups* to find categories.

3. Describe these events in terms of the groups.
   A. What does this tell you about this year?
   B. How does this year compare to last year?

Closure—Review:

Students will share their ideas with the whole class.

HOW DO I? Teach for Automaticity

As with any skill, students need to revisit and review *creating groups* even after it becomes part of their cognitive repertoire. Regular practice helps in developing efficiency and *automaticity*. Depending on age and ability, it might take as few as one or two lessons or as many as ten or more lessons for students to learn a new thinking skill and be able to use it independently. Also, the new thinking skill should be integrated through the curriculum wherever possible. This allows the teacher to provide regular practice. It also enhances all curriculum areas, raises the level of thinking, augments learning, and creates a more interesting, student-centered learning environment.

Depending on the level of the students, you should identify four to ten thinking skills to incorporate into your classroom each year. It is most effective to focus on one skill at a time and use it in a variety of situations and settings. You will need to spend anywhere from two weeks to a month on a single skill. Also, continue to review and use past thinking skills throughout the year.

APPROACHES TO THINKING SKILLS INSTRUCTION

How should thinking skills be taught? There are three approaches used in teaching thinking skills: the stand-alone approach, the immersion approach, and the embedded approach (Prawat, 1991).

The Stand-Alone Approach

The *stand-alone approach* consists of teaching thinking skills separately from subject-matter content (see Figure 12.2). Here a general set of thinking skills is identified and taught as a separate course or subject. The problem with this approach is that students do not have a context in which to learn and use acquired skills. The skills are viewed as puzzles with little relevance to academic or real-life tasks. Also, thinking skills learned in isolation do not transfer well to academic or real-world situations (Johnson, 2000b).

If you were to use this approach to the teaching of thinking skills, students would spend a great deal of time looking at a series of puzzles, word problems, or exercises presented in a book or in an isolated context. It would be assumed that students would be able to transfer these skills to other situations. However, this would happen in only a few instances.

The Immersion Approach

The *immersion approach* does not involve teaching thinking skills; rather, it allows good thinking to develop naturally as a result of students being fully engaged or immersed in content-related activities which call for high levels of thinking (see Figure 12.3). Here, students are provided with repeated practice in high level questions and thinking activities with the assumption that they will eventually develop the necessary cognitive skills to successfully engage in this kind of thinking. However, simply immersing students in high level thinking activities is not an effective teaching and learning technique: High ability students reinforce those ways of thinking already acquired while other students become frustrated.

If you were to use this approach to the teaching of thinking skills, you would simply assign complex tasks. It would be assumed that over time, students would be able to discover the steps necessary to complete these complex tasks and develop the appropriate thinking skills. Again, this would happen in only a few instances.

Figure 12.2   The Stand-Alone Approach

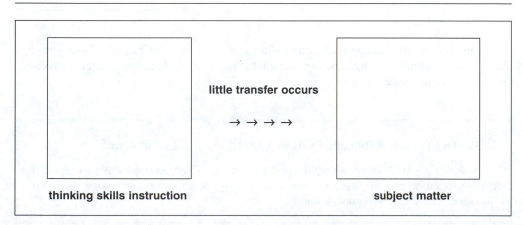

little transfer occurs

→ → → →

thinking skills instruction

subject matter

Figure 12.3   The Immersion Approach

subject matter

no thinking skills instruction

The Embedded Approach

Using the *embedded approach* you would teach thinking skills within a subject matter context (see Figure 12.4). Students would then apply these skills directly to the particular subject matter being studied. This allows them to use the thinking skills in a meaningful context and also helps students learn matter more deeply by manipulating subject area concepts (Marzano, 1991).

Figure 12.4   The Embedded Approach

thinking	*more*	subject
skills →	*learning*	← matter

If you were to use this approach you would teach thinking skills as part of social studies class using direct instruction, modeling, and guided practice. Students would then be asked to apply these skills to some aspect of the lesson.

HOW DO I? Embed Thinking Skills in a Social Studies Curriculum

1. Identify a body of knowledge or unit to be covered. For example, as part of a 3rd grade geography unit, Ms. Stockton was studying lakes, rivers, dams, and bridges and their impact on the surrounding environment.

2. Identify two to five thinking skills (see Figures 12.5 and 12.6), that can be used to create interesting classroom activities or assignments with the unit. Ms. Stockton chose the following skills based on the information to be in the unit and the concepts and skills she wanted her students to learn: flexibility, elaboration, comparing and contrasting, and ordering.

3. For each skill, look for activities, assignments, or discussion questions that could be used with the unit. Ms. Stockton came up with the following questions that could be used as discussion points or to create activities:

- **Flexibility:** What are some other ways to get across a river? What are some other ways to stop or divert the flow of water? What are some other uses for dams and bridges? What are some other kinds of things that we could use dams for? What are some other ways in which we could use rivers?
- **Elaboration:** How could the dam be made better? What could be added to the dam or bridge to make it more efficient or effective?
- **Compare and contrast:** Compare and contrast the different types of bridges and dams to find similarities and differences.
- **Ordering:** Put dams and bridges in order from strongest to weakest, most environmentally friendly to least, most practical to least practical, or most useful to least useful.

4. Make an initial plan of where each skill might be used within the unit. Ms. Stockton looked at her outline of the unit and the concepts and skills she wanted to cover. She decided where she wanted to introduce a thinking skill, and then identified cooperative learning and other types of classroom activities that could be designed using that skill, and she inserted them at different points in the unit.

5. Teach one skill at a time using ideas or concepts from the unit. Ms. Stockton taught no more than one thinking skill a day during the course of this unit. She introduced each thinking skill using thinking frames and the elements of effective skills instruction. She used each thinking frame to create a poster which was used to remind students of the steps before they engaged in an activity or assignment using the particular thinking skills.

6. Review and reinforce throughout the year. Ms. Stockton found that she could use these thinking skills in other subject areas. She continued using them for classroom activities and assignments and continued to refer to the thinking frame posters.

Thinking Frames

Creative thinking skills utilize divergent thinking: thinking that diverges from a single point. The following types of cognitive processes are used here: generating ideas, integrating ideas, or seeing things in new ways. The thinking frames for seven creative thinking skills are outlined in Figure 12.5. Each of these can be used to design activities and assignments in social studies.

Critical thinking skills involve convergent thinking: thinking that converges on a single point. It utilizes one or more of the following types of cognitive processes: organizing, analyzing, evaluating, or using given information to come to a specific conclusion. The thinking frames for eight critical thinking skills are outlined in Figure 12.6. Each of these can also be used to design activities and assignments in social studies.

Figure 12.5   Thinking Frames for Creative Thinking Skills

Fluency: Generate as many ideas as possible without evaluating.

Thinking Frame

1. Look at the idea or problem.
2. Do not worry about good or bad ideas.
3. Add as many ideas as quickly as you can.

Flexibility: Create a variety of different approaches.

Thinking Frame

1. Look at the original.
2. Find other ways for it to be used, solved, or applied.

Elaboration: Embellish an original idea.

Thinking Frame

1. Look at the idea.
2. Add things to it to make it better or more interesting.

Originality: Create new ideas that are unusual or unique.

Thinking Frame

1. Find an idea or problem.
2. Think of solutions or applications that nobody else has thought of before.

Integrate: Connect, combine, or synthesize two or more things to form a new whole.

Thinking Frame

1. Look at several things.
2. Select interesting or important parts from each.
3. Combine to describe a new whole.

Brainstorming Web: Create a web to generate ideas relative to a given topic.

Thinking Frame

1. Look at the original ideas.
2. Analyze to identify two to five related ideas for subheadings.
3. Brainstorm to generate ideas for each subheading.
4. Describe.

Generating Relationships: Find related items or events.

Thinking Frame

1. Look at the item or event.
2. Generate attributes.
3. Find items or events with similar or related attributes.
4. Describe the relationship.

GO THERE

- Graphic organizers that support thinking skills: *http://www.somers.k12.ny.us/intranet/ skills/thinkmaps.html*
- The thinking classroom: *http://learnweb.harvard.edu/alps/thinking/ways.cfm*
- Thinking skills activities for geography: *http://www.geographypages.co.uk/thinking .htm*

Figure 12.6   Thinking Frames for Critical Thinking Skills

Inferring: Go beyond the available information to identify what may reasonably be true.

Thinking Frame

1. Identify what is known.

2. Identify similar situations or important knowledge.

3. Make a reasonable guess based on 1 and 2.

Compare and Contrast: Find similarities and differences between/among two or more items.

Thinking Frame

1. Look at all items.

2. Find the similarities.

3. Find the differences.

4. Conclude and describe.

Analyze: Break an item or event down into its component parts.

Thinking Frame

1. Look at the item or event.

2. Identify important parts.

3. Describe each part.

4. Describe the whole in terms of each part

Supporting a Statement: Use appropriate reasons, detail, or examples to support a statement, idea, or conclusion.

Thinking Frame

1. Make a statement or claim.

2. Gather information/data to support the statement.

3. Organize the information.

4. Describe the original statement in terms of the new information.

Decision Making: Examine the options and alternatives in order to decide on a course of action.

Thinking Frame

1. Identify the problem or decision.

2. Generate decision options.

3. Evaluate costs and rewards of options.

4. Make a choice based on the above.

Ordering: Arrange events, concepts, or items in sequential order based on a criterion.

Thinking Frame

1. Look at or define a criterion.

2. Look at the whole.

3. Arrange items within the whole according to the criterion.

4. Describe the whole in terms of the new order.

Evaluation/Critique: Make a formal critique based on a set of criteria.

Thinking Frame

1. Look at or define a set of criteria.

2. Look at the subject.

3. Compare the subject to the criteria.

4. Describe the subject relative to the criteria.

Creating Groups (inductive analysis): Impose order on a field by identifying and grouping common themes or patterns.

Thinking Frame

1. Look at the whole.

2. Identify reoccurring items, themes, or patterns.

3. Arrange into groups.

4. Describe the whole in terms of groups.

TEACHERS IN ACTION: Thinking

I know we often feel that the kids should just be able to think through the questions, but this is a skill that does need to be taught. I have found that although we do try to do as much as we can in the younger grades, we are working on a lot of basic skills. A lot of the "deeper" thinking tends to begin in grades 3 upward, so by grade 5 they are still learning a lot about the process of thinking. And of course it depends on what happened in the previous years.

The great thing about teaching is that we can take a step back—see what is missing and revise our goals and plans. I think it's a great idea for you to begin to teach them "thinking skills." Plan for a problem solving time every day and not just math problem solving but word puzzles. Put up a unique word puzzle of the week and make it into a contest.

Demonstrate and model how you think through problems. Thinking is the fun part of learning—there are so many ways to challenge your kids and they will love being in your class.

And even we adults love to have the answer right there for us; it's less work. So the challenge now will be to have them realize that just because it is more work doesn't mean it is less fun.

Some other things you might want to try:

- Mystery stories—do a mystery novel study.
- More science and math problems.
- Open-ended questions where there are many "correct" answers.
- A lot of discussion times.
- Games like *Outburst Jr.,*—makes you realize how many possibilities there are for answers.

And don't let them get you stressed out. The first month of school is hard for everyone to get back into the mode of school. The kids are tired, they also are more into socializing with everyone they haven't seen since June. By October they will settle back into the routine of being in school and you'll find that their thinking skills will also start to return.

—Cathy-Dee #19925

Author Reflection: If we want to improve students' ability to think, we must teach them how to do so explicitly. This is the essence of thinking skills instruction. Students at all grades and of all ability levels can improve their ability to think if we teach them. However, I often wonder if the educational system truly wants good thinkers. Good thinkers may just challenge the status quo and demand change. Good thinkers may demand to be taught instead of tested. Good thinkers may lower the profits of the testing corporations. Instead, it appears as if our educational system seems to value students who can passively read a paragraph and fill in the appropriate bubble with their #2 lead pencils.

Do you agree with the author?

Source: Excerpt "Thinking: Posted by Cathy-Dee #19925" used with permission of ProTeacher Community. PERMISSION TO COME.

CREATIVE THINKING IN SOCIAL STUDIES

Presented here are some examples of how the thinking skills above might be integrated into social studies. These examples can be adapted for use at any grade level, with varying levels of ability, and in a wide array of teaching situations. For further information and strategies related to thinking skills, see *Up and Out: Using Creative and Critical Thinking Skills to Enhance Learning* (Johnson, 2000b).

Fluency. Fluency, sometimes known as brainstorming, is used whenever students need to generate a great many ideas. It can be used as a prewriting strategy or when looking for possible solutions to problems. The important thing here is to teach students not to evaluate ideas initially. Evaluating ideas comes only after a great number have been generated.

Flexibility. This thinking skill helps students to generate a variety of ideas looking for a number of different ways or approaches. For example, what are some other ways we might be able to get a telescope into space? What are some other ways in which we could educate students in our society, move products from factories to consumers, or generate power for our homes?

Elaboration. Elaboration looks to make the original better, more interesting, more detailed, more complex, or more refined.

Originality. This thinking skill is used to design or create something new such as a product, poster, or performance.

Integration. This thinking skill is used to create something new and interesting by integrating the salient elements of two or more existing things. To do this, students must first identify what those salient elements are and then combine some or all of them to create the new thing.

Brainstorming web. This thinking skill works well to create structure and generate ideas around that structure. Chapter 9 showed how it can be used to generate ideas for oral speaking. It can also be used as a prewriting activity to help students structure their ideas, or as pre- and postreading activities.

Generation of relationships. With this skill, students look for similarities between one or more persons, items, or events. This thinking skill works especially well when trying to make personal connections with subject matter. The visual organizer in Figure 12.7 can be used to guide students' thinking here.

Figure 12.7   Generating Relationships

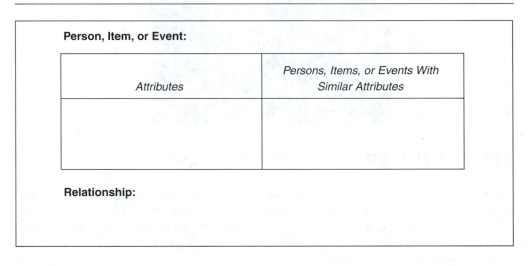

EXAMPLE: Using Fluency, Elaboration, Originality, and a Brainstorming Web

Fluency as a prereading strategy. Before reading a chapter in their social studies textbook, Mr. Malone had his 2nd grade students generate ideas *(Fluency)* on related topics prior to reading to activate relevant schemata. Their ideas are listed on the front board. To extend this, he asked his students to create groups (creating groups) and describe their lists in terms of groups and number in each group.

Fluency as a postreading strategy. For a postreading activity, Mr. Malone's students brainstormed to create a list of interesting or important ideas found in the chapter. As before, these are recorded and can be used to create groups, or students can list the items and put them in some sort of sequential order *(Ordering)*, such as most interesting to least interesting, most likely to impact their lives to least likely, most recent to least recent, or closest to furthest away.

Elaboration as a creative writing strategy. Ms. Bryant used *The True Confessions of Charlotte Doyle* (Avi, 1990) as a text for her 6th grade social studies class that was studying the history of the nineteenth century. To bring students' creative imagination into the learning experience, she had them examine characters, events, scenes, or items in a story and (a) add interesting details; (b) describe other items that might be included; (c) add details or descriptive adjectives to a sentence found in the story; (d) add other interesting characters, events, or items not included in the story; or (e) draw a scene or event adding details the author did not describe.

Using originality to find and solve problems. As part of a unit on science, technology, and society, Mr. O'Neil's students worked in small cooperative groups to create new inventions. They started by looking for a problem in their lives or in society. They then looked for new applications of existing technologies or other solutions to design their inventions.

Brainstorming web as a prereading activity. Mr. Fischer used this thinking skill to activate relevant schemata before reading. He announced a theme or topic found in the upcoming story selection. The theme was written on the front board and a circle was drawn around it. Students then were asked to think of three items or subtopics related to the original theme. Nodes off the circle on the board were created for the subtopics (see Figure 12.8). Students then brainstormed to add ideas to each node. After reading the story, students added to the original web.

Figure 12. 8   Brainstorming Web

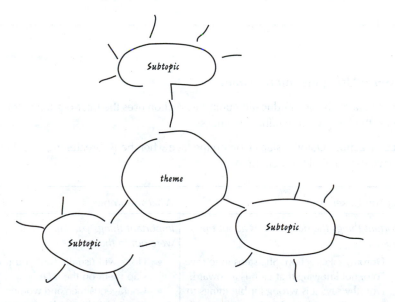

Brainstorming web as a postreading activity. As a postreading activity, Mr. Fischer had his students do this instead of worksheets: His students created brainstorming webs to describe the interesting or important events in a chapter or story. This is also an example of the thinking skill *analyze,* as students must break the whole into its component parts and describe it.

CRITICAL THINKING SKILLS IN SOCIAL STUDIES

Inferring. Inference is the act of using observed clues and background knowledge to make some sort of informed guess or conjecture as to what may be true. This can be used with persons or events in a story or in history, and it can also be transferred to personal and real-life situations (Johnson, 1996). The infer-o-gram in Figure 12.9 is a graphic organizer that can be used to guide students' thinking here.

Figure 12.9   Infer-o-Gram

Question:	
What You Observe—Clues	*What You Know—Background Knowledge*

Your inference:

EXAMPLE: Using the Infer-o-Gram

In her 7th grade character education unit, Ms. Walton uses the infer-o-gram below to guide students' thinking when making inferences.

Choice or action: Dorothy slaps Lion on the face when he is threatening Toto. What value may have determined this action?

What You Observe	*What You Know*
Important things the story tells us about the character:	*Important things you know that were not in the story:*
• Dorothy takes action. She steps in to save Toto, not knowing that Lion is a coward. • Dorothy says it is wrong for big things to pick on little things. She is standing up for a principle here. • After hurting Lion, Dorothy tries to comfort him when he cries.	• Lions will usually hurt you if you slap them on the face. • Courageous men and women throughout history have stood up for what they believed, even though they may have been hurt: Malcolm X, Martin Luther King Jr., Rosa Parks.

What You Observe	What You Know
Important things the story tells us about the situation: • Dorothy does not know Lion is cowardly. • Lion is growling and trying to scare Toto. • Scarecrow and Tin Man do not take action. They only cringe. • Lion threatens Scarecrow and Tin Man. Makes fun of them. Says he wants to fight. • Lion is brave until he's challenged.	• Cowardly men and women throughout history change their mind, retreat, or don't stick to their guns when threatened or challenged. • In books and movies, the hero or heroine often displays the traits that Dorothy does. • Many of the traits described by Joseph Campbell in *Hero With a Thousand Faces* (1968) apply to Dorothy.

Conclusion: Dorothy had courage and stood up for what she believed. She was willing to take action based on a principle even though she may have been hurt. Dorothy represents many of the traits that other heroes have in real life, movies, and books, such as Luke Skywalker, King Arthur, Nemo, Rosa Parks, Mohammad Ali, Malcolm X, and Martin Luther King Jr. To be heroic, we should identify what we believe, and then to try to stand up for it.

Compare and contrast. This thinking skill asks students to find common elements and differences. The comparison chart (Figure 12.10) can be used to guide students' thinking.

Figure 12.10   Comparison Chart

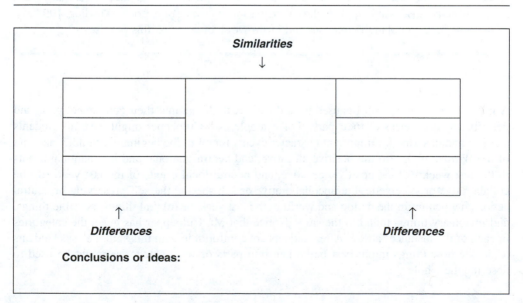

EXAMPLE: Comparing and Contrasting

In his character education unit, Mr. Culpepper uses the comparison chart below to help students compare and contrast different kinds of heroes. These heroes can be taken from a book, movie, history, or recent events, or from students' lives.

Luke Skywalker from Star Wars		Dorothy Gale from The Wizard of Oz
Differences	*Similarities*	*Differences*
a boy	both are teenagers	a girl
happens in the future	both live with aunt and uncle	happens in the past
evil character is male	both confront evil	evil character is female
in space	both find magical powers within themselves	on earth
	both have friends who help	
	both have creatures or animals who talk	
	both have helping characters: Obi-Wan Kenobi and Glinda the Good Witch	

Conclusions or Ideas: Heroes and hero stories have many similar characteristics. Many of these characteristics also apply to the characters in the *Harry Potter* books (Rowling, 1998), and to figures found in the religions and myths we studied earlier this year.

Analyze. This thinking skill is used to find and break things into their component parts and describe them in terms of their parts. For example, Mr. Culpepper might have his students analyze and describe (a) important character events found in the beginning, middle, and end of the *Wizard of Oz;* (b) the positive, negative, and neutral national and international events in the last week; (c) the positive, negative, and neutral local events of the last year; (d) the collaborative or synergetic, the uncollaborative or selfish, and the self-preserving or neutral actions happening in the nation and world in the last year; or (e) real things, possible things, and imaginary things found in the story. Notice that Mr. Culpepper has given the categories in each of the instances above. After students are comfortable with this skill, he asks students to decide how things might best be broken into parts or what categories might be used to describe the whole.

Supporting a statement. Here, students make a statement, then use clues or sentences to support it. The graphic organizer in Figure 12.11 can be used to organize students' thinking here. This could be used as a postreading activity where students are given a statement and then asked to look for clues in the chapter or text that support that statement. It could also be used to organize an independent study. Here students are given or make a statement related to the unit of study. They then look for data to support the statement. Finally, this thinking skill is also a good way to teach paragraphs in technical writing. A paragraph is usually an idea or statement with support or elaboration.

Decision making. Decision making is a thinking skill that was introduced in Chapter 10. Here students must first identify a problem or a decision that must be made, then generate ideas for a solution or decision. Next, the costs and rewards of each of these are evaluated before a decision is made as to the best course of action. Students could use this thinking skill in small groups to examine a situation or a problem in which a decision must be made. This could be a problem related to society, science, school, history, or a personal problem. The small group then generates a list of two to five possible solutions, listing both the positive and negative consequences of that solution. Finally, the group comes to a consensus as to the best solution and the reasons to support their decision. Using this as a small group activity also exposes students to multiple perspectives and the reasoning of others.

Ordering. Ordering can be used to rank any item, event, person, experience, or trait according to a given criteria. The orderizer in Figure 12.12 can be used here. First, students use the left side of the orderizer to generate a list of things. Then they examine or define a criterion. The criterion is then used to analyze the list. Students then put the items in order in the right column. For example, students could generate a list of (a) inventions from the 1970s and order them from most significant to least significant to their immediate lives, (b) things they have done in the last week and order them from positive to negative, (c) current events and order them from most important to least, (d) things to do on a weekend and order them from exciting to boring, (e) things to say when asking somebody out on a date and order them from most usable to least, or (f) solutions to a problem and order them from most pragmatic to least pragmatic.

Figure 12.11   Supporting a Statement

Statement/Claim:	Supporting Information
	1.
	2.
	3.
	4.
	5.
	6.

Figure 12.12   Orderizer

Things: Generate a list.	Criteria: Put them in order.
	1.
	2.
	3.
	4.
	5.

Evaluation/Critique. With this thinking skill, students must first generate criteria for an item, then rate or evaluate the item based on those criteria.

HOW DO I? Teach Evaluation Skills

The key to this thinking skill is to have students first identify the criteria. A good way to introduce this thinking skill is to have students evaluate books, movies, or TV shows. They can then easily move on to evaluate scientific products, inventions, decisions, solutions, their own learning, their own performances or products, or almost anything else. The first figure below is an example of a rating chart for a single thing. The second figure is an example of a rating chart that can be used for *Evaluating* many things.

Rating Chart for a Single Thing

Criteria	Rating
Interesting or fun characters.	
Likeable characters.	
Interesting adventures.	
The story is imaginative.	

Key: 5 = very high, 4 = high, 3 = average, 2 = low, 1 = very low.

Rating Chart for Evaluating and Comparing Many Things

Criteria:

A. Interesting or fun characters.   C. Interesting adventures.

B. Likeable characters.   D. The story is imaginative.

Stories	Criteria				Total
	A	B	C	D	

Key: 5 = very high, 4 = high, 3 = average, 2 = low, 1 = very low

Creating groups. Creating groups is a form of inductive analysis where you examine a field and try to induce or create order by organizing the things observed into groups. Here you look for recurring items, themes, or patterns to emerge from the field. Similar things are coded and moved into initial categories. Younger students can begin looking for groups or similarity in any kind of data. One simple primary activity is for everyone to put one shoe in a circle. Students are then asked to pick two shoes that are the same somehow and tell why they are the same. Older students could use this thinking skill when analyzing data of any kind. One example would be when conducting a survey using open-ended questions as part of an inquiry activity. Here students would get a variety of responses that would create a field. They would then create groups to put order on that field. This data could then be expressed quantitatively, put on a graph, and be used to make comparisons.

EXAMPLE: Creating Groups in an Inquiry Project

As part of an independent inquiry project, Sarah, a 7th grade student, was studying humor in American society. She decided to analyze a Three Stooges video in order to understand the Stooges and their humor. She watched a short 15 minute episode on video tape called *Grips, Grunts, and Groans* (Columbia Pictures, 1937) and began to look for instances of humor. As she watched, she used field notes to record those things done for comedic effect. In examining her notes, she came up with the following categories of humor: silly things, human-to-human violence, things-to-head violence, and self-mishap. She was able to quantify the instances of humor in each category (see table below), and put these data in the form of a bar graph. She could then use the data to make comparisons to other comedians of the era and to comedy movies of today.

(Continued)

(Continued)

Silly Things	Human-to-Human Violence	Thing-to-Head Violence	Self-Mishap
Total: 33	Total: 22	Total: 21	Total: 9

NCSS STANDARDS

Pedagogical Standards

The following NCSS pedagogical standards are addressed in this chapter:

I. Critical Thinking, Problem Solving, and Performance Skills.

II. Active Learning and Motivation.

III. Inquiry, Collaboration, and Supportive Classroom Interaction.

Essential Skills for Social Studies

The following NCSS essential skills for social studies are addressed in this chapter:

I. Acquiring Information.
   A. Study Skills.
      1   find Information
      2. arrange information in usable forms

II. Organizing and Using Information.
   A. Thinking Skills.
      1. classify information
      2. interpret information
      3. analyze information
      4. summarize information
      5. synthesize information
      6. evaluate information
   B. Decision-Making Skills.
   C. Metacognitive Skills.

Chapter Review: Key Points

1. A thinking skill is any cognitive process that is broken down into steps.

2. Thinking skills make complex and high level thinking easy.

3. Creative thinking is thinking that helps students generate ideas and relationships.

4. Critical thinking is thinking that converges on one point and helps students organize, analyze, or come to conclusions.

5. Thinking skills instruction should be embedded within the social studies curriculum.

6. Direct instruction, modeling, guided practice, and individual practices will help students learn thinking skills and transfer them to other situations.

7. Thinking skills can be used to help students learn more and learn more deeply.

8. Teachers can use thinking skills to design activities and enhance classroom instruction.

Making Connections

1. Find a teacher's manual for social studies. Use one or more of the thinking skills described above to create activities and assignments.

2. List five interesting or important ideas from this book that seem to stick in your mind. Use *ordering* to put them in order from most likely to be used to least.

3. In small groups, generate a list of at least 20 important terms or ideas related to teaching and learning in social studies. Use *creating groups* to put your list into groups. Describe your list in terms of groups and numbers within each group. Create a graph or table to display your data.

4. Find at least five ideas to support the following: Social studies could be the most important part of an elementary or middle school curriculum.

5. Use the graphic organizer for *comparing and contrasting* to compare yourself to another person.

6. Identify somebody in your life who did a good job of teaching you a skill. This could be a coach, director, teacher, or friend. Which elements of effective skills instruction did this person use?

7. In small groups, identify a skill that you know (sewing, cooking something, cleaning a fish, etc.). Use the elements of effective skills instruction to teach this skill in your small group.

8. In what ways do you see the three holistic learning ideas related to intrapersonal connections, interpersonal connections, and interconnectedness reflected here?

Chapter 13

CURRENT EVENTS AND CLASSROOM DISCUSSION

Thinking Ahead

1. Where do you get most of your news?

2. What ideas do you have for using a newspaper in a social studies curriculum?

3. What makes a really good or interesting classroom or small group discussion?

4. What things drive you crazy in a classroom or small group discussion?

5. What are some hot topics you try to avoid in discussions with friends or in a social situation? Why do you try to avoid these?

DIRECT AND INDIRECT METHODS OF APPROACHING CURRENT EVENTS

According to the National Council for the Social Studies (1994), "The primary purpose of social studies is to help young people develop the ability to make informed and reasoned decisions for the public good as citizens of a culturally diverse, democratic society in an interdependent world" (p. 3). Citizens who are able to make these informed decisions need information about a variety of topics, including current events. Incorporating current events in social studies education helps develop an interest in news and current events. It also helps young children make sense of the world around them and it serves to connect school life to life outside the classroom. This chapter describes a variety of strategies and activities for including current events in an elementary and middle grade social studies program.

Current events can be addressed both directly and indirectly. An indirect method would be to examine current events as part of the regular day in the elementary and middle grades (Ellis, 2002). Ask students to look for interesting and important news to report as part of the morning ritual. This news can be used as part of a general classroom discussion to raise awareness of these events. Some teachers create current events bulletin boards and ask students to find interesting or important pictures and stories from newspaper and magazines. These bulletin boards often have themes or sections such as international news, presidential elections, space, pollution, crime, sports, entertainment, energy, education, and the economy. You could also address current events indirectly by looking for connections and comparisons to subject matter in all curriculum areas. Finally, simply reading headlines or parts of a newspaper to students each day is a simple and effective way to foster an awareness of and interest in the news.

A direct method to use for current events would be to create units around topics in the news. This often requires teachers to get background information and create related activities (see Chapter 5). Current events could also be taught directly by creating a unit on newspapers or the media and then using current events within this context. Finally, current events could be used as part of a speech class or forensics program. Here students would be asked to give persuasive speeches or to debate using current event topics.

Current events can be addressed indirectly simply by making it a part of morning meetings or classroom conversations.

STRATEGIES FOR WORKING WITH NEWSPAPERS

With a little imagination and planning, newspapers can become an excellent source for creating lessons and activities in social studies as well as all other curriculum areas.

Elaboration. Find a product in a newspaper ad and have students look for ways to improve the product or ways to make the ad better. Also, pull sentences or paragraphs from the newspaper and have students add to them or make them more interesting.

Flexibility. Use a sentence or paragraph in the newspaper, and have students generate as many different ways to express the same idea as they can.

Originality. Students find a product from a newspaper ad and design their own video commercials, signs, or newspaper ad for that product.

Integration. Using newspaper ads for different products, students combine them to create a brand-new product or device. Then, they create a newspaper ad for this new product.

Creating groups. Record newspaper headlines over a period of time and put them into groups. The types of groups and frequency of items in each group are reported. These data can be graphed and comparisons can be made with other newspapers, types of publications, or time periods. Also, these data can be used to show how the news changes over time.

Ordering. Examine the newspaper stories across several days. List the headlines in the first column (see Figure 13.1). Then, put them in order according to some criteria. Criteria might include: (a) most important to least important, (b) good news to bad news, (c) most likely to affect you to least likely to affect you, (d) most important five years from now to least important, (e) most interesting to least interesting, or (f) other.

Figure 13.1   Graphic Organizer for Ordering

Criteria:

Headlines	*Order*
	1.
	2.
	3.
	4.

Graphing headlines over time. Find a newspaper to examine over time. Record the top headline every year. Find some criteria and rate that headline based on that criteria (see "Ordering"). Then create a line graph to show how the headlines and news change over time (see Figure 13.2).

Compare and contrast newspapers. In a newspaper, the placement of stories and the size of the headline are determined by the importance of the story. Examine two or more different newspapers from the same day. Compare the stories that appear on the front page and in what order on a given day. What does this tell you about that newspaper or editor?

Figure 13.2   Line Graph for Headlines

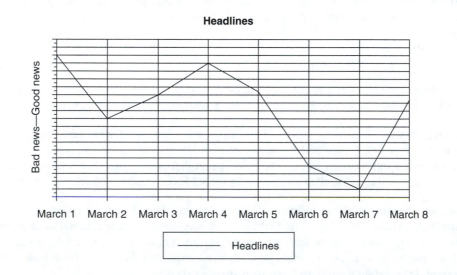

Headlines

Compare and contrast writing style. Compare the writing style of a section of a headline story to a section of a sports story. What is similar? What is different? Extend by making comparisons to a section from a textbook or a narrative book, or by comparing one newspaper to another.

Investigation of writing style. Examine a 100-word section of newspaper text. Design an inquiry project by asking one of the following questions: What does this section consist of? How many sentences? How many adjectives? How many adjectives per sentence (APS)? What is the average length of each sentence? This data can be graphed and comparisons can be made to other types of text.

Comic strip inquiry. Design an inquiry project that uses a survey to answer one or more of the following questions: What makes a good comic strip? What are the favorite comic strips? Do females like different comic strips than males? Do younger children like different comic strips than older children? Who are the most popular comic strip characters? What type of humor is most popular?

Facts and opinions. Students select an editorial and use a graphic organizer (Figure 13.3) to list the facts and opinions. Use the data to come to a conclusion.

Inference. Students select a letter to the editor and use the infer-o-gram described in Chapter 12 (see Figure 12.9) to make inferences about the author. The inference question might be: How might we describe the writer of this editorial? Who is this author? What political party does this author belong to? What other views might this author hold? Using the infer-o-gram, list the clues gleaned from the editorial on the left, then list important background knowledge that students might have related to this topic on the right. These two sets of clues are combined to make an inference.

Figure 13.3   Graphic Organizer for Sorting Facts and Opinions

Issue:

Facts	*Opinions*

What might you conclude?

Support-a-statement. After reading a news story, the student or teacher makes a statement relative to that story. For example, after reading a story about the war in Iraq, a statement might be: This is a very costly war. The students then search the newspaper article to find details to support that statement. These supporting details are listed using the support-a-statement visual organizer described in Chapter 12 (see Figure 12.11). This is a good activity for developing critical reading skills.

Creative problem solving. Students identify a problem found in the newspaper. In small groups, students use CPS to find a solution (see Chapter 10). Their solutions are presented to the class. Examples of possible problems: How can we reduce crime in our neighborhood? How can we prevent teenage smoking? How can we avoid police car chases? What can we do to improve schools?

Decision making. In this activity, students are presented with a problem taken from the newspaper. In a large group, solutions are generated. Students then move into small groups of three to six students. Each group picks the top five solutions and lists them on the graphic organizer for decision making (see Figure 13.4). Each student within that group ranks the solutions from highest to lowest. The total ranking score for each solution is tallied and a decision is made based on that score. This decision is elaborated and presented to the whole class.

Figure 13.4   Graphic Organizer for Decision Making

Each group member ranks the solutions from 1 to 5, with 5 being the highest and 1 being the lowest ranking. Totals for all students' rankings are tabulated in the far right column.

Problem: Local businesses need to attract more customers.

Decisions/Solutions	Jim	Mary	Sue	Pat	Total
Put up more signs around town.	4	1	2	5	12
Lower prices.	1	5	1	4	11
Build additional restaurants, movie theaters, and entertainment venues.	2	4	4	3	13
Change the types of items sold.	3	3	3	2	11
Use more advertising in newspapers and television.	5	2	2	1	10

Decision: Local business owners should try to encourage the development of restaurants, movie theaters, miniature golf, video arcades, and things that people would come to for entertainment. This would increase the number of visitors and amount of business.

Movie review/critique. Students first define the criteria for a good movie. This naturally leads to discussions about movie genres. Then, newspaper ads are found for movies students have seen. These movies are rated on students' criteria (see Figure 13.5). This can be extended by looking at several movies and rating them or by ranking them according to a criterion (Figure 13.6). This activity can also be used to review and critique books as part of a reading or literature class.

Figure 13.5   Evaluation—Rating Movies

Movie: *The Wizard of Oz*

Key: 4 = very high, 3 = good, 2 = average, 1 = low.

Criteria	Rating
Has a good plot or story.	3
Has plenty of action.	4
Has interesting lead characters.	4
Has a happy ending.	3

Total: 14

Figure 13.6   Evaluation and Ranking of Movies

Key: 4 = highest rating, 1 = lowest rating.

	Criteria				
Movies	*1*	*2*	*3*	*4*	**Total**
The Wizard of Oz	2	2	2	4	10
Jurassic Park	3	4	1	1	9
Star Wars	4	3	3	2	12
ET	1	1	4	3	9

Criteria

1. Has a good plot or story.
2. Has plenty of action.
3. Has interesting lead characters.
4. Has a happy ending.

Other perspectives. Find a news story that involves more than one person or groups of people. After generating some inferences about each of the people involved, use creative writing to describe the event from each person's perspective. How might each perceive and describe the story? For example, a story about a demonstration at a World Trade Organization meeting could be described from the point of view of the protestors, police, community members, local business owners, or members of the WTO. Creative dramatics could be used for dialogue, individual speeches, fake debates, or even imaginative interviews done in character.

HOW DO I? Use Journalism to Extend or Enhance Learning

A powerful form of learning occurs when the line between school life and the real world becomes invisible. That is, learning is enhanced when students are able to engage in real-life activities in the context of a subject being studied. Social studies lends itself well to the use of journalism to explore current and historical events.

• First, discuss the role and responsibility of a free press in a democratic society. Compare this with societies that do not have freedom of the press. Explore the reasons for including this in the Bill of Rights to the U.S. Constitution.

Amendment I—Freedom of Religion, Press, Expression.

Congress shall make no law respecting an establishment of religion, or prohibiting the free exercise thereof; or abridging the freedom of speech, or of the press; or the right of the people peaceably to assemble, and to petition the Government for a redress of grievances.

• Discuss and explore the ethics of journalism:

Seek truth and report it. Be honest, fair and courageous in gathering, reporting and interpreting information.

Minimize harm. Treat sources, subjects and colleagues as human beings deserving of respect.

Act independently. Be free of obligation to any interest other than the public's right to know.

Be accountable. Be accountable to your readers, listeners, viewers and each other.

—Society of Professional Journalists, 2004,
http://www.spj.org/ethics_code.asp

• Teach students the importance of finding and describing a story or an event using the five W's: who, what, where, when, and why:

Who—Who is involved? Who is affected? Who did what? To whom?

What—What happened?

Where—Where did this happen? Was there more than one location involved?

When—When did it happen? In what order did events take place?

Why—Why did it happen? What caused it?

- Ask younger students in grades kindergarten through two to first describe things as they happened using both written and oral communication. This is a prerequisite skill for more advanced journalism activities. Students can be asked to describe interesting or important things that happened in their school or in the community. Also, you can use a digital camera to take pictures of events and activities that occur in the school or community. Download these on a computer and print them off on a sheet of paper. Then have students write the descriptions or the stories that go along with them.

- Teach older students about bias, objectivity, and the role of a journalist. The role of the journalist is to represent (or *re-present*) reality so that that the consumer of the news has an accurate picture. This means one must get all the facts in order to describe what happened as accurately as possible, and one must not let opinions or flowery descriptions get in the way.

- Teach students to use technical writing. Technical writing uses concise, objective, third person language to explain and describe. Also, good technical writing is as concise as possible. In the real world, memos, descriptions, and news stories are more apt to be read if they are concise and to the point, rather than meandering with flowery language.

- Write news stories about important historical events. Students should get all the facts using at least two sources before beginning to write. One rule in journalism is to verify all facts using at least two sources. This is a good place to discuss this and explain why this is important.

- Write news stories about current events. Use the Internet (see Chapter 14), television, and other media to get the facts using at least two sources before beginning to write.

- Get older students to conduct interviews with interesting or important community figures (see Chapter 11 for interviewing skills). Their interviews can be used to create news stories that can be included in class newspapers or in school or community cable TV broadcasts.

GO THERE

- The Write Site—interactive journalism website for middle school students: http://www.writesite.org/
- Schoolnet News Network (SNN) journalism/social studies lesson plans for middle school: http://www.snn-rdr.ca/snn/cr_lessonplans/senior_lp.html
- Schoolnet News Network (SNN) journalism/social studies lesson plans for elementary school: http://www.snn-rdr.ca/snn/cr_lessonplans/junior_lp.html
- *USA Today* lesson plans and activities for middle school: http://www.usatoday.com/educate/home.htm
- Newspapers in education: http://nieonline.com/detroit/index.cfm
- Journalism lesson plans: http://eduref.org/cgi-bin/lessons.cgi/Language_Arts/Journalism
- Grades 4–6 student newspaper project: http://www-ed.fnal.gov/linc/fa1195/projects/butcher/Internetproject2.html
- Code of Ethics: Society of Professional Journalists: http://www.spj.org/ethics_code.asp

USING OTHER NEWS MEDIA

Most people today get their news from a wide variety of sources. Other news media include television, radio, news magazines, and the Internet. Most of the activities described above can also be used with other media.

The Internet. Stories that appear on the Internet should be read critically as these often do not have the same checks and balances in terms of editors and fact checkers that stories in other media do. However, websites created by major media are usually a little more trustworthy (see Chapter 14).

GO THERE

The following web sites are good news sources for elementary and middle school classrooms:

    www.usatoday.com

    www.cnn.com

    www.bbc.com

    www.newsweek.com

    www.msnbc.com

Comparing broadcasts. Keep track of the news stories presented on CNN, CNBC, FOX, PBS, and one of the networks (CBS, NBC, ABC) for one week. Record the stories and in what order they appear. Make comparisons and inferences based on the data.

Mock broadcasts. Create videos of news broadcasts for replay on school or local cable TV. Broadcasts might include international, national, and local news, as well as sports, weather, and entertainment.

Buzzwords and value statements. Often, news broadcasts use two or more guest analysts to present different sides of an issue. These can be recorded and presented in class. Students then analyze them to look for facts, opinions, buzz words, and value statements.

Discourteous speakers and uncivil debates. One of the marks of a civil and democratic society is the ability to recognize and respect differences among people in regard to philosophy, opinions, and values. We live in a pluralistic society where diversity and a multitude of views are viewed as a strength, not a weakness. While each of us may hold certain values to be very important, we must be able honor the values of others with whom we may not agree, and learn to disagree respectfully if we are to live up the ideals, principles, and practices of citizenship in a democratic republic. (See NCSS performance expectations related to *Civic Ideals and Practices,* Appendix B.)

Too often the "debates" that occur on cable network news programs are examples of what not to do in this regard. Here you will see uncivil behaviors such as frequent interrupting, laughing while another person is making a point, talking over other people, speakers talking as long as possible so that others cannot make a point, or cutting off people while they are talking. These things are done by program hosts and moderators as well as by guest speakers. And sadly, at the end of the discussion, the parties involved are no closer to developing a shared understanding or identifying areas of commonality. These televised arguments serve only to further polarize and to coarsen the national dialogue.

In the elementary and middle grades, an important part of social studies education is to teach students how to engage in civil discourse with people who have differing views. As part of this process, you can record these television news "debates" and use them in social studies classes as examples of what citizens living in a democracy should not do in discussing their views.

TEACHERS IN ACTION: Current Events

Here's my guidelines for sharing current events:

1. Each student will share one current event per week. A day is assigned that will be their day for the entire year.

2. The current event must be current and something in the news. It cannot be something that they just want to share with us, because it's not "show and tell."

3. They can get the news from the newspaper, television, radio, or from a parent. They may bring in the article, but it is not required.

4. Weather is not considered a current event. Sports may be used; however, only the score of the game is not enough for credit. They must add something important along with the score.

5. If the current event is forgotten, students need to write about it on a form that I have ready for them. They may turn that in the next day for complete credit. If that is forgotten, then they receive a zero for that week.

I do not give the students a grade on their current event, but I do keep track of whether they remembered or not. I usually tally these in my Social Studies grade book as a responsibility grade. Missing current events will hurt their social studies grade. I also use this time to teach others how to listen to their classmates. We make sure we are listening with our ears, eyes, and HEARTS! We make sure that desks are cleared off so the presenter knows we are interested in what s/he has to say. The activity only takes about 10 minutes. I love this time of day. It's a real community builder, and we get to learn about what's going on in our world!

—Anonymous, Elementary School Teacher

Author Reflection: In social studies, the world is our curriculum. There are five things I love about the wonderful ideas for sharing current events described here. First, knowing that they will be asked to report news one day a week invites students take more notice of it. Second, it's a simple yet effective idea. The best ideas are usually the simple ones. This one doesn't take a lot of time. Third, the teacher recognizes and honors a variety of news sources, including parents. She might want to include the Internet as another news source. Fourth, it sounds like a great way to build community in the classroom. And fifth, the students here are asked to listen with their ears, eyes, and hearts. I really like the hearts part. We don't talk enough about emotions in our classrooms.

What is your response to the case? How do your reactions compare with the author's reflection?

QUESTIONS AND CLASS DISCUSSION

Classroom discussions enhance learning by (a) helping students to clarify, apply, and manipulate ideas and extend their thinking, (b) allowing teachers to see how students are processing new concepts, so they can adjust instruction accordingly, (c) enabling students to hear the thinking of other students, and (d) providing opportunities for students to participate and be actively engaged in the learning experience (Sternberg & Williams, 2002). Classroom discussions are included in this chapter because they work particularly well with current events; however, they should be used with all subject areas.

Effective discussions do not happen by accident; you need to prepare. This is often a matter of designing three to five questions as part of your lesson plan. This ensures that your questions are purposeful instead of being used just to get students to talk. It is very hard to think of good questions on the spur of the moment. Having discussion questions prepared means that you have fewer things to think about and you are able to focus more of your attention on students' responses and the teaching moment.

"Does everything have to be scripted? Can't I be spontaneous?"

Yes and yes. Having your questions listed does not mean that you have to ask them. Good teachers are prepared, but at the same time they are flexible and spontaneous. It is very common to prepare a set of questions and then to ask some completely different questions once you get into the lesson. Also, if you find that one question or topic seems to be creating some interesting discussion, allow your students the freedom to explore to it. Intellectual curiosity is always a good thing. And, tangents often lead to powerful incidental learning that is sometimes remembered far after your carefully planned lesson has been forgotten.

Questions for classroom discussion should be prepared ahead of time; however, you should also be flexible and spontaneous.

Figure 13.7   Hierarchy of Discussion Questions

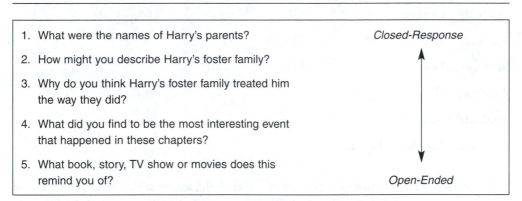

1. What were the names of Harry's parents?   *Closed-Response*

2. How might you describe Harry's foster family?

3. Why do you think Harry's foster family treated him the way they did?

4. What did you find to be the most interesting event that happened in these chapters?

5. What book, story, TV show or movies does this remind you of?   *Open-Ended*

Preparing Questions

When creating a discussion question, always test it out on yourself first by trying to answer it. This allows you to see if it is a good question. If you have trouble answering it, chances are that students will be confused and have trouble answering it as well. Also, questions used for discussion should have some *lower-level* or *closed-response questions* as well as some *higher-level* or *open-ended questions.* Closed-response questions are those that have a specific answer. Open-ended questions are those for which the teacher does not know the answer. Figure 13.7 shows some discussion questions that might be asked after reading the beginning chapters of *Harry Potter and the Sorcerer's Stone* (Rowling, 1998). Bloom's (1956) levels of thinking as described in Chapter 5 (Figure 5.12) can also be used to help in creating different levels and types of questions.

Evaluating Responses

A discussion should be a place to explore ideas and not an interrogation. As such, avoid asking only low level questions simply to determine if students know the correct answer. These are known as *IRE questions* (Cazden, 1998; Lukinsky & Schachter, 1998). Here the teacher *initiates* the question, the students *respond,* and the teacher then *evaluates* that response. IRE questions put teachers in a position of power and control instead of the preferred position of influence and structure. Below is an example of an IRE discussion:

Teacher: Children, what's the capital of Wisconsin?

Student: Eau Claire.

Teacher: No.

Student: Milwaukee.

Teacher: No.

Student: Madison.

Teacher: Right. And what's Wisconsin's state animal?

Student: Gopher.

Teacher: No.

Student: Deer.

Teacher: No.

Student: Badger.

Teacher: Yes. And what's the . . .

If you respond to questions simply in terms as an evaluator, creativity and the free flow of ideas will be stymied. One way to avoid IRE questions is to ask questions for which you do not know the answer. Another interesting example of IRE questioning can be seen in Ben Stein's character of the economics teacher in the movie *Ferris Bueller's Day Off* (Paramount Pictures, 1986). Here he uses low-level questions in an IRE pattern in a futile attempt to engage his class in a discussion.

> *In 1930, the Republican-controlled House of Representatives, in an effort to alleviate the effects of the . . . Anyone? Anyone? . . . the Great Depression, passed the . . . Anyone? Anyone? The tariff bill? The Hawley-Smoot Tariff Act? Which, anyone? Raised or lowered? . . . raised tariffs, in an effort to collect more revenue for the federal government. Did it work? Anyone? Anyone know the effects? It did not work, and the United States sank deeper into the Great Depression. Today we have a similar debate over this. Anyone know what this is? Class? Anyone? Anyone? Anyone seen this before? The Laffer Curve. Anyone know what this says? It says that at this point on the revenue curve, you will get exactly the same amount of revenue as at this point. This is very controversial. Does anyone know what Vice President Bush called this in 1980? Anyone? Something-d-o-o economics. "Voodoo" economics.*

Valuing Responses

It takes a certain amount of risk for students to answer questions in class as part of a teacher-initiated discussion. Instead of simply evaluating responses, learn to value them so that students will be more apt to risk answering questions. To do this, look directly at the student who is speaking. Nod, smile, or give some sort of nonverbal or verbal prompt that shows you are listening. One way to show you value and are processing student responses is to do a *sounds-like*. Here you rephrase and provide a brief overview of the student's point. For example:

"Sounds like you think the speed limit should be raised."

"Sounds like you liked the part in the story where Charlotte Doyle climbed the mast."

"Sounds like you have some very strong feelings on this subject."

What if a student says something that is totally wrong or off the point? How do you value that kind of response? Below are some examples:

"Interesting."

"There's a unique perspective."

"There's an idea I haven't heard before."

"Tell us why you think that way?"

"Okay, sounds like our class may need to get a little more information on that. Would you like to volunteer to do that? Thank you."

The point is, students should never be slighted or be made to feel stupid for responding to a question or participating in a class discussion. Also, effective class discussions should be very much like the discussions you might have with a group of friends; they should be places to share insights and explore ideas. They should not turn into contests, examinations, or quiz shows.

Wait Time and Processing

It is a very common mistake to ask a question and then immediately call on a student, or to do what Ben Stein's character did above: jump right in with an answer. Even though we are sometimes uncomfortable with silence, it can be used to enhance learning by allowing time for processing and reflection (Good & Brophy, 1995; Jensen, 2000). The period of silence before and after a student answers a question is called *wait time* (Sternberg & Williams, 2002). Wait time gives all students a chance to think and respond. Teachers should use a wait time of five to seven seconds before calling on a student to answer a question, even if hands go up in the air immediately. Some teachers silently count to themselves before calling on students in order to ensure they are providing adequate wait time. Also, when asking complex or high level questions, prove more wait time for additional processing and reflection (seven to fifteen seconds or more).

HOW DO I? Give Students Time to Process Answers

Below, four strategies are described that provide students with extra time to process and think before answering a question or engaging in a discussion.

Journal or thinking paper. Before discussing, have students write their responses or list their ideas in a journal or on a piece of paper. The act of listing and seeing one's ideas on paper helps them to generate more ideas. Also, paper can act as an extension of short term memory, allowing students to consider many ideas and associations. As an example of this, a teacher might say, "Today we're going to look at how to have a civil discussion in a democratic society. In your journal, list at least three polite behaviors that all people should use when in a discussion or conversation, and three things that really bug you when you are in this situation. Be ready to share your ideas with others." During the sharing of ideas, students could then add to their original lists as they hear interesting or important ideas from others.

(Continued)

(Continued)

Preview questions. Ask a question or give a discussion prompt well before the discussion begins. For example, in a lesson on dragons, mythology, and early cultures, a teacher might say, "In just a minute I'm going to ask you to describe a dragon, so you might want to start thinking about it now." The teacher would begin the lesson. When it came to share ideas, students would have had plenty of time to think about dragons.

Neighbors. Before opening up a question or idea for classroom discussion, have students turn to a neighbor and share their thoughts. Sometimes it works best to provide a bit of structure in this. For example, "Turn to your neighbor and share two interesting or important things you remember from yesterday's discussion of the role of local government."

Small groups. Put students in small cooperative groups of three to five students. Give them a question and allow five to ten minutes for them to share ideas and come to a consensus. A spokesperson is then chosen from each group to share their ideas with the whole class. This type of cooperative learning approach to answering questions often takes more time than the typical group discussion; however, students are exposed to a much larger range of ideas, they engage in higher levels of thinking, and they learn at much deeper levels (Johnson & Johnson, 1999).

Hot Topics

What about some of the hot topics? Do you need to avoid them in your classroom? No. However, you must consider your position of influence and thus respect the rights of parents to raise their children according to their beliefs, values, and principles. As teachers, we do not have a right to get on a soapbox or advocate for our causes. If a student asks for your opinion on an issue, share your ideas without being an advocate or having the last word.

EXAMPLE: Handling Hot Topics

The issue of prayer in public schools came up in a discussion in Ms. Ming's 7th grade social studies class. She has some very strong opinions on this subject; however, she does not want her ideas to influence students' thinking and discussion. Also, she respects the rights and perspectives of parents and students who may differ from her on this topic. Just as she would not want teachers of her own children forcefully advocating a position with which she strongly disagrees, so she does not advocate or push her ideas on her students. She allows the discussion to unfold in a way in which students do not know her stand on this issue. She asks probing and clarifying questions to students who seem to be on both sides of this issue. When the discussion gets heated or when a student responds to a statement with a personalized attack, Ms. Ming steps in and reminds students of the importance of civil discourse in a democratic society and the benefit of having multiple perspectives on every issue.

When a student asks her opinion, Ms. Ming responds, "I'm more interested in what you have to say right now. I'll share my ideas later." If she decides to share her views, it is only after students have had a chance to fully discuss the idea. She reminds her students that people of good character are found on both sides of this issue.

TEACHING DISCUSSION SKILLS

T-Talks

In classroom discussions there is always a danger that one or two people will dominate and not all voices will be heard. The *T-talk* is a technique adapted from an idea by Donna Alvermann (1991), which provides an opportunity for all students to express their ideas. It also promotes discussion and allows for multiple viewpoints to be expressed. With adaptation, it can be used in kindergarten through high school. These are the steps:

1. After reading a chapter, article, or story, or after discussing an event, the teacher finds a dualistic statement. A dualistic statement is one with which students have to either agree or disagree. For example: "The United States should drill for oil in the Arctic National Wildlife Refuge." "The drinking age should be lowered from 21 to 18." "Native Americans should have exclusive rights to the resources on their lands." "Reading class should be in the afternoon instead of the morning." "There should be a moment of silent prayer every day in our school." "Dick should take Sally to the party." "Jane should have Spot put to sleep."

2. In pairs, students create a T-chart on a sheet of paper and list a minimum of three ideas to support each side (see Figure 13.8).

3. Each pair then combines with another pair to form a four-person small group or quad. The quad shares ideas on both sides of the T, then looks to reach a consensus in creating a new dualistic statement. This new statement should be something with which all or most group members can agree. This new statement is sometimes very different than the original statement. There will be times when a consensus cannot be reached; however, all members will get a chance to describe their individual ideas later during class discussion or in their journals.

4. One speaker from each quad shares his or her group's conclusion and supporting ideas. The speaker has two minutes to share and must give at least two reasons to support the group's new statement.

5. Individually students then describe their opinions in their learning logs.

6. The issue is opened for class discussion.

T-talks can be adapted for use with younger students in grades one and two by using it only in large group. Here, the teacher records all of the students' ideas on a large chart or the front board. Steps 3 and 4 above are skipped.

Small Group Discussions

We cannot assume that students know how to communicate respectfully in small group discussions. Indeed, many adults have trouble with this. Use explicit instruction to teach students to use *positive discussion elements* (PDE) in discussions (see Figure 13.9). Focus on no more than four PDE initially and add others as they are needed. Display the PDE in poster form and remind students to use them whenever they move into a discussion of any kind. The

Figure 13.8   T-Talk

Dualistic statement:

Ideas to Support Agreement	*Ideas to Support Disagreement*

Consensus statement: _____

_____

_____

_____

list of PDE in 13.9 is not meant to be complete. You will find other PDE to add to this list once you start watching your students conversing in small groups. Also, notice that the PDE are an expanded version of the cooperative learning discussion skills described in Chapter 9.

To make small group discussions work initially, provide structure in the form of a question. An example of lack of structure would be for a teacher to simply say, "Get into your small group and discuss heroes and values." This lack of structure and clarity would make discussion difficult even for most adults. Instead, create structure by providing a clear task that will result in a specific product. An example of structure would be for a teacher to say, "At your desk, identify a hero or somebody you look up to. List some of this person's characteristics that make you look up to him or her. Move into small groups and share your heroes and their characteristics. After ten minutes, see if your group can identify at least two common characteristics of heroes. When you are done, choose one person to share with the whole class." Or even more simply, "Move into your small group. Try to identify at least two

Figure 13.9   Positive Discussion Elements for Small Group Discussions

1. Try to understand each other, not to win a debate.
2. Find areas of agreement and disagreement.
3. Make your point concisely. Do not ramble.
4. Let others into the conversation.
5. Support your points with credible ideas or reasons.
6. Affirm the ideas and presence of others through verbal or nonverbal communication.
7. Look at the person who is speaking.
8. Look at all members of your discussion group.
9. Include everybody in the discussion.
10. Always use polite, respectful language.
11. Respect differences others have related to values and opinions.
12. Analyze and disagree with the idea, not the person.

characteristics of heroes or people we look up to. You've got about ten minutes to do this. Choose one person to share your ideas with the class."

Initial discussions usually work best in groups of three to five students. After the discussion, have students reflect on how they did using PDE in their groups. Some teachers use PDE to create checklists for students to use to reflect on the success of their discussion. As students become more comfortable with small group discussions, the questions do not have to be as structured.

EXAMPLE: Using Positive Discussion Elements in a Fishbowl Exercise

In teaching discussion skills, what students discuss is not nearly as important as how they discuss. You are teaching the process of having a discussion. One way to examine this process is by using a technique called the *fishbowl,* which was introduced in Chapter 9. Remember that the fishbowl is where a small group has a discussion on a given topic in the center of the room while the rest of the class observes. This should be done only after a class has become fairly comfortable with small group discussions. Use the following steps:

1. Ask for volunteers for a fishbowl. Explain that students will be having a discussion in front of the room while other students watch. Tell them the topic of discussion.

2. Select three to five volunteers and set up a discussion area for participants consisting of desks or a table. This should be in front of the room or in the middle of the classroom with students on the outside.

(Continued)

(Continued)

3. Present the topic to be discussed in the form of a dualistic statement. For example, "School should be opened all year long with a shorter day. What do you think and why?" If discussions seem to be stagnant, you may sometimes need to ask students to see if they can find consensus or an area in which all can agree.

4. Give students some time parameters; however, do not be afraid to cut a discussion short if students have said everything they have to say, or extend it if the discussion really seems to take off.

5. Ask the students observing to record what they notice in regards to the PDE. That is, what things were done well? What things could be done differently?

6. At the end of the discussion ask students on the outside of the fishbowl to describe their observations or ideas related to the group's use of the PDE. Then ask students in the fishbowl to share their observations and insights.

7. Ask observing students if they have any ideas to add to the topic of discussion.

8. Extend by having students record their own ideas or views related to the topic of discussion in a journal or learning log.

9. You can make this an inquiry project (see Chapter 5) by creating some sort of Data Retrieval Chart (DRC) related to PDE for use here.

NCSS STANDARDS

Thematic Standards

The following NCSS thematic standards are addressed in this chapter. See Appendix A for a full description of the relevant thematic standards.

Early Grades

I. Global Connections: a., c., d., f.
II. Civic Ideals and Practices: c., d., g.

Middle Grades

I. Global Connections: a., c., d., f.
II. Civic Ideals and Practices: c., d., g.

Pedagogical Standards

The following NCSS pedagogical standards are addressed in this chapter:

I. Critical Thinking, Problem Solving, and Performance Skills.

II. Active Learning and Motivation.

III. Inquiry, Collaboration, and Supportive Classroom Interaction.

Essential Skills for Social Studies

The following NCSS essential skills for social studies are addressed in this chapter:

I. Acquiring Information.
    A. Study Skills.
        1. find information
        2. arrange information in usable forms
    B. Reference and Information-search Skills.
        1. special references
        2. maps, globes, and graphics
        3. community resources
    C. Technical Skills Unique to Electronic Devices.
        1. computer
        2. telephone and television information networks

II. Organizing and Using Information.
    A. Thinking Skills.
        1. classify information
        2. interpret information
        3. analyze information
        4. summarize information
        5. synthesize information
        6. evaluate information
    B. Decision-Making Skills.
    C. Metacognitive Skills.

III. Relationships and Social Participation.
    A. Personal Skills.
    B. Group Interaction Skills.
    C. Social and Political Participation.

Chapter Review: Key Points

1. Helping students become aware of and understand current events is an important part of social studies education.

2. Current events can be linked to all curriculum areas and can be addressed both directly and indirectly.

3. Newspapers are a good source to use for news and current events, but other sources include televisions, radio, news magazines, and the Internet.

4. Information from the Internet should be read very critically, as the Internet often does not have the checks and balances that other media do.

5. Respecting diverse perspectives and philosophies and being able to engage in civil discourse with people of opposing views is important in a democratic society.

6. Classroom discussions can enhance learning.

7. Discussion questions must be planned and should include a variety of questions.

8. An ideal classroom discussion should be very much like the type you might have with your friends.

9. Discussions that become a test or interrogation stymie creativity and the free flow of ideas.

10. All student responses must be valued.

11. Wait time is the period of silence before and after a question is asked.

12. A wait time of five seconds or more is needed for all students to be able to reflect and answer questions.

13. Hot topics should be a part of normal classroom discussions, however, a teacher has a responsibility to not be an advocate for a particular point of view.

14. T-talk is a discussion strategy to use to ensure that all voices are heard.

15. Students need to be taught how to have a civil discussion using the positive discussion elements.

16. Fishbowl is a strategy where one group has a discussion in the middle of the class while the rest of the class observes.

Making Connections

1. How do you see yourself using current events in your classroom? What are some new strategies that you wish to include?

2. Pick a topic. Create three to five good discussion questions. Then lead your small group or a class in a discussion.

3. What are some of the hot topics you think you would want to avoid in an elementary classroom?

4. Create a list of topics and a dualistic statements for T-talks.

5. Where do most of your friends or colleagues get their news? Create and conduct a survey. See if there are any differences related to age or gender.

6. Do one or more of the activities described in this chapter.

7. Identify an area of interest related to any current event. Go to the Internet and get enough information and varied perspectives to become a knowledgeable source. Present your information to the class in a short, three to five minute lesson. Create at least three discussions.

8. Watch cable news to find examples of uncivil discussions. Collect data using a DRC (Chapter 10) to determine the rudest person on cable news.

9. Create and implement a T-talk for you class. After, identify and describe your impressions.

10. In what ways do you see the three holistic learning ideas related to intrapersonal connections, interpersonal connections, and interconnectedness reflected here?

Chapter 14

USING THE INTERNET TO TEACH SOCIAL STUDIES

1. In what ways do you use the Internet to find out about the world in which you live?

2. How do you see the Internet being used as a learning source in a social studies curriculum?

3. How did you learn to use the Internet?

4. What sources on the Internet do you use to get information?

THE INTERNET

The *Internet* has changed the way we view the world. For the first time in human history an almost unlimited amount of knowledge is literally available at our finger tips. The Internet can be a powerful tool to enhance learning in the social studies and other curriculum areas; however, like any tool its effectiveness is dependent on how it is used.

BENEFITS AND LIMITATIONS OF ONLINE LEARNING

The Internet provides an abundance of information that includes many thousands of educational resources such as government documents, research reports, databases, historical documents, newspapers, and magazines (March, 1997). This information can be used to enhance or provide background information related to stories, textbooks, or various class topics. The Internet also provides worldwide access to resources such as directories, informational websites, academic journals, books, directories, guides, handbooks, blogs, academic units, lesson plans, teacher resources, live webcams, news broadcasts, discussions, and a variety of other informational sources. Students can communicate with people around the world and with experts on any subject. The Internet also allows you to go on virtual field trips to a variety of places including space missions, museums, monuments, the U.S. Senate, the White House, and famous historical sites, all of which can be used to enhance your social studies curriculum.

Besides the sheer volume and variety of information, one advantage the Internet has over other information sources such as books, magazines, and newspapers is its immediacy. On the Internet, ideas and information move very quickly into print form. A book can take six months to two years to move into print form, an academic journal can take several months, a magazine can take one or two weeks, and a newspaper can take a day. The Internet can move ideas and information from an author's head into print and then be dispersed to the masses in a matter of minutes. Indeed, the latest breaking news, often with accompanying video, can be found on www.cnn.com, www.msnbc.com, www.bbc.com, or some other news oriented websites.

The Internet is also personal in that students are able to extend their learning by exploring Internet sites of their choosing. The information they get is directly related to the clues or data they first put in. And, the Internet provides students direct answers to their specific questions.

However, there are limitations to the Internet as an educational tool, the primary one being that it is not a teacher. It cannot construct learning experiences, guide learners' inquiries, help

The Internet can be an effective tool to enhance learning. Its effectiveness is dependent upon how it is used.

them synthesize ideas, or enable them to make sense of new information. It also cannot create activities that allow students to manipulate, elaborate, extend, or apply information. By itself the Internet is not able to connect knowledge to personal experiences, motivate students, explore feelings, or address affective dimensions. Finally, the Internet is not able to develop students' decision-making and moral reasoning abilities. While there are programs available that can approximate all of these things, a teacher is ultimately needed to personalize and extend the learning experience.

HOW DO I? Choose Websites for Students

While there may be occasions when it is appropriate for students to conduct independent searches on the Internet, the majority of times students should be directed to websites that you have selected, at least initially. In this way, learning is more targeted and appropriate and students do not spend time surfing aimlessly around the Web. This also allows you to shape the learning experience to augment specific aspects of a curriculum, lesson, literature, or textbook. You will need to preview and evaluate potential websites. *Yahooligan's Teacher's Guide* (Yahoo! Inc., 2001) suggests that the *Four A's* be considered when teachers evaluate websites: accessibility, accuracy, appropriateness, and appeal.

Accessible. Check to see that the website is still there and that it downloads in a reasonable amount of time. You will also need to check to see that all the links still work.

(Continued)

(Continued)

Accurate. Is the information correct? Is it from a credible source? Who is the author? What are his or her credentials? If the website is from a nationally recognized organization, check to see what their goals or agenda are, and thus, their potential biases. Accuracy and credibility are also enhanced if there is a peer review process such as that for an academic journal, or if multiple sources are used to compile the site, such as the information journalists are required to use when writing for major newspapers, magazines, and television media.

Appropriate. You will need to determine if the website is appropriate in terms of content and complexity. Make sure websites do not include inappropriate references to sex, violence, racism, sexism, political propaganda, or extremist ideology of any kind. Also check to see if the content is at the appropriate reading level and complexity for your students. Younger students need websites that contain more pictures than words. Intermediate and middle school students should have access to websites that have familiar concepts and words that are in their vocabulary, and which are not overly long and difficult to comprehend. Figure 14.1 contains a list of websites and search engines that have filters to ensure that they are appropriate in terms of content. These search engines are also more likely to lead to websites that are appropriate in terms of complexity and reading level. You could also feel reasonably safe in allowing your students to use them when they conduct their own Internet searches.

Appealing. This final element is somewhat related to the idea of appropriateness above. The websites you select for your students need to be interesting and easy for them to read and understand. Headings and subheadings should be used to organize the text and allow the reader to see the structure. Pictures, diagrams, and illustrations should be used to enhance comprehension and help carry meaning to the reader.

Figure 14.1   Websites and Search Engines for Kids

http://www.timeforkids.com/TFK/
www.yahooligans.yahoo.com
www.ajkids.com/
http://www.rcls.org/ksearch.htm
http://www.awesomelibrary.org/
http://www.kidport.com/
http://sunsite.bereley.edu/KidsClick!/
http://www.surfnetkids.com/
http://www.thinkquest.org/library/
http://www.kids.net.au/
http://www.csun.edu/~hcedu013/cevents.html

INTERNET LITERACY SKILLS

Just like writing and reading, skills related to Internet literacy should be taught and reinforced in all curriculum areas. Internet literacy is the ability to access and evaluate information on the World Wide Web. Specific skills related to *Internet literacy* include the ability to conduct searches, evaluate sources, post information, and participate in online communications using e-mail, chat rooms, and discussion groups. Some would also include constructing websites as an essential skill here. An excellent source for understanding all aspects of Internet literacy in a classroom is *Yahooligan's Teacher's Guide* (Yahoo! Inc., 2001) at http://yahooligans.yahoo .com/tg. This site contains a wealth of information related to teaching Internet literacy, developing acceptable use policies for schools, citing Internet sources, and evaluating websites. It also contains a variety of teacher lesson plans, activities, and other sources for all curriculum areas.

Teaching Students to Conduct Internet Searches

One skill related to Internet literacy is the ability to use search engines to find information on the Internet. Like any other skill, this should be taught using the elements of effective skills instruction described in Chapter 12 (see Figure 14.2).

The specific steps for conducting an Internet search are listed in Figure 14.3. These should be displayed in poster form or on the computer for reference, reinforcement, and reminders. Most older students probably know the basics of conducting an Internet search; however, their searches can be made more effective and efficient by using these steps.

Figure 14.2   Elements of Effective Skills Instruction

1. Identify the steps.
2. Give explicit instruction and model its use.
3. Allow students to practice the skill under your guidance.
4. Allow students to practice the skill by themselves.
5. Reinforce by integrating it, reviewing, and using it in a variety of contexts.

Figure 14.3   Steps for Conducting an Internet Search

1. Enter one or more terms or key words.
2. Search.
3. Check and skim the list of website titles.
4. Briefly enter and preview sites that might be important or helpful.
5. Select only helpful or important sites for in-depth reading.
6. Expand or repeat as necessary using different terms or key words.

HOW DO I? Teach Students How to Do a Keyword Search

Below are teaching instructions for early and intermediate students. These can be modified for use with middle grade students.

- Ideally you will be able to teach Internet skills in a situation where all students can view a monitor controlled by the teacher. This enables you to demonstrate the skill as you are teaching it. This could be in a computer lab or in a classroom where the monitor is projected onto a larger screen. If this is not available, you can teach students in small groups of three to five using one computer or, in the worst case, you can use a large poster depicting what the search engine looks like. (Because of limited resources, teachers sometimes have to be adept at worst case scenarios.)

- Tell your students that Internet searches are used to help quickly find the exact information they are looking for. Use word clues very much like a detective uses clues to solve a mystery. These clues are called *key words* or *terms*. For example, if you wanted to find out what life was like for a soldier in the Civil War, two key words might be "civil war" and "soldier." Put these words into the search engine, press return, and see what you get. (Demonstrate this for your students.)

- Next you will see a list of titles for websites. Skim the list and check for titles that seem appropriate. Do not waste time on sites that are obviously not what you are looking for. (Show students the list of Civil War sites that appeared on the screen. Have them evaluate and discuss the sites that seem to be the most interesting or helpful.)

- Briefly enter the websites you think are interesting and helpful. Preview them quickly to see if they contain information that is helpful. For example, some of the Civil War websites that we have chosen have interesting pictures, diagrams, stories, and descriptions, while other do not. Select and enter only those sites that you feel are helpful. (In class, go into each site that students have selected above and ask them to evaluate and discuss to determine if the site is worthy of more focused reading.)

- Very often the sites you visit will give you other ideas for terms or key words to use in the search. You may also choose to expand your search to look more broadly at your topic or to look at different parts of it. Keep expanding and repeating your search using different words until you get the information you need. For example, you might also try "civil war," "soldier," and "daily life" to find out about our Civil War soldiers. These sites may provide ideas for other interesting things to look at such as uniforms, entertainment, health, sickness, music, or gambling. These are all clues that help you begin to piece together what life may have been like for a soldier in the Civil War. (Ask students to brainstorm to think of three to five expanded terms they might try to get more information about the life of a Civil War soldier. Try one or two of these to see what you get.)

- The next step is to practice doing a search together with students (guided practice). They should be sitting with another person in front of a computer that is connected to the Internet. Have two students work together to allow for the natural dialogue, questions, and discussion that all serve to enhance understanding. Ask students what terms they might use if they were interested in finding out what life might have been like for a pioneer living in the American West in the eighteenth or nineteenth century. As the class brainstorms possible ideas, list these on the board or a place where all students can see them. Decide on two terms, put them in the search engine, and see what sites come up.

- With the whole class, go through the steps for conducting an Internet search (Figure 14.3).

- For individual practice, give students a list of topics that are related to the social studies lesson or unit you are studying. Still working in pairs, allow students to choose one topic for an Internet search. After completing the search, students should hand in a list containing three to eight interesting or important new things they learned about their topics.

- Reinforce this skill throughout the year by asking students to look for additional information on a particular topic. Always ask for some sort of simple product as a result of their search. Before the search, always review by pointing out the steps for conducting an Internet search.

Teaching Students to Evaluate Websites

Because there is so much information available on the Internet, students must also be able to evaluate sources. For this, they should know the type of website and its purpose. There are generally six types of websites, each of which serves a different purpose. These are listed in Figure 14.4.

The second part of evaluating websites involves assessing the quality and credibility of the information found. Five criteria can be used for this evaluation: authority, accuracy, objectivity, currency, and coverage (Kapoun, 1998).

Authority. In establishing authority you are looking to establish the expertise and experience of the author. Questions to ask in establishing authority include the following: How credible is the author? Are the author's credentials listed? What makes him or her expert? Is this person qualified to write this document? Is the author affiliated with a recognized school, university, or national organization? Are there references cited? Does the site contain a bibliography? Can you contact the author? Does the site contain links to other sources you consider credible? Has the website been reviewed or vetted by others?

Accuracy. Accuracy is the degree to which the information on the website is correct or true. Questions to ask here include: Can the information be verified using another source? Is the information provided in its proper context? Is any important information missing? Are the facts consistent? Does the information agree with other information you know to be true? Is it believable?

Objectivity. Objectivity is the degree to which bias is used to select or present the information on the website. In an unbiased website the author presents the information as he or she finds it. The information then serves to form the author's beliefs. In a biased website, the author selects information to support a particular point of view. Here one's belief systems are used to determine what information is presented. This is where it is important to know the type and purpose of a website. Question to ask here include: Is the website trying to persuade

Figure 14.4   Types of Websites

One clue for identifying the type of website can be found in the suffix at the end of the website address. An ending suffix of ".edu" indicates an educational institution such as a school or college; ".gov" indicates a governmental agency or bureau; ".com" indicates a commercial site; ".org" indicates a nonprofit organization or personal page; ".mil" indicates a military agency; and ".net" indicates a site owned by an internet service provider.

Information website. The purpose of the information website is to present factual information. These compose the majority of websites.

Resource website. Resource websites are used to work as a tool or resource. These would include sites that provide mapping and driving directions, databases, conversion charts, statistical analyses, software programs, dictionaries, thesauruses, satellite weather images, and directories of records, addresses and telephone numbers.

News website. News websites provide the latest news or descriptions of current events. These include sites for well-known sources such as *Newsweek, USA Today,* the BBC, CNN, MSNBC, and any of the major newspapers in any city. There are also news websites developed by lesser-known sources. Because these sources rarely have the resources to hire professional reporters to do thorough reporting or to verify facts, they should always be a bit suspect in terms of their credibility.

Advocacy website. The purpose of the advocacy website is to promote a cause or organization. These vary across the political, religious, and social spectrums. When looking for information or news, make sure you are not using an advocacy website. Sometimes these are purposefully confusing in order to promote a particular agenda.

Business or marketing website. Business or marketing websites are designed to sell or market products or services. When looking for information or news, make sure you are not using this type of website. Having a commercial interest greatly diminishes the credibility of the information provided.

Personal website. A personal website is developed by an individual who is not affiliated with an institution or trying to sell a product. They are developed for a variety of reasons which may include making a personal statement; enhancing or facilitating communication; promoting a personal cause, service, or product; or simply to provide a creative outlet or a form of expression.

you or sell you something? Does it promote a particular religious, social, or political point of view? Does it contain emotional buzzwords that are designed to appeal to your emotions? Does it contain opinions?

Currency. In establishing currency you are looking to see when the information was written. Depending on the topic, the latest information is generally better than older information. Question to ask include: When was the page first placed on the Web? When was the information written? Are there any dates on it? Is there anything to indicate that the material is updated or kept current?

Coverage. Coverage is the degree to which the information presented is complete. Questions to ask include: Is the website still under construction? Is it clear what topics the website seeks to address? Does the site succeed in addressing these topics? Does the site provide you with the information you are looking for? Does it answer your questions? Are the ideas that are presented well stated, explained, and supported? Do you feel like you understand?

HOW DO I? Teach Students to Evaluate Websites

The goal in teaching students how to evaluate websites is not to have them do a formal evaluation of every site they visit. This would greatly impede the speed at which students are able to access information. Rather, the goal is to build awareness and to make automatic the thinking processes that go into evaluating sources of information found on the Internet. This evaluation of sources can be extended to other sources of information as well.

- Your teaching situation should be such that all students can view a monitor controlled by the teacher. First, spend time teaching students about each of the five elements of credibility. As you go over each area, find websites that show good and poor examples of each element.

- Preselect three to five websites on the same topic. In your preview, look for sites that are both credible and not very credible.

- Give students a copy of one of the website evaluators found in Figures 14.5 or 14.6. You may choose to put this in poster form and use it as you teach. In this way, students can always refer to it when they are searching the Internet.

- As you visit each website, get students' ideas on each of the criteria and get their overall impressions, ideas, or conclusions.

- To practice, have students work in pairs or in small groups to evaluate one or two preselected websites using a website evaluator.

- To reinforce this skill, remind students to consider these five elements of credibility every time they are going to do an Internet search or any time they consume information of any kind.

Communicating Safely and Effectively Online

There should be some basic rules established in your classroom for using the Internet. It is best if these are linked with a schoolwide *acceptable use policy* (AUP). These rules should address issues related to the content that students access as well as their mode of communication. The search engines listed earlier should filter the majority of content; however, it is still important to define and talk about the types of websites that would not be allowed in a classroom. These would include those with sexual, racist, violent, or derogatory (angry or insulting) content. Rules should also be created to address communication etiquette. Students should always be polite and courteous and never give false or misleading information when communicating.

The classroom is a good place to discuss issues related to Internet safety. Figure 14.7 contains a set of basic Internet safety rules for kids related to chat rooms, discussion groups, and e-mail communication.

Figure 14.5   Website Evaluator for Older Students

WEBSITE EVALUATOR

Website:

Topic:

Key: 3 = outstanding, 2 = average, 1 = low, 0 = poor or can't tell.

Authority

　1. The author is a credible source _____.

　2. The author has experience and expertise in this area _____.

　3. The author is with a recognized school, university, or national organization _____.

　4. The website contains references or a bibliography _____.

　5. The website is linked to other credible sources _____.

Accuracy

　6. The information seems to be correct or true _____.

　7. The facts are consistent within the website _____.

　8. The information seems to support what I know to be true _____.

Objectivity

　9. Information is presented without bias _____.

　10. The site contains facts (no opinions) _____.

　11. The language is objective (no emotional buzzwords) _____.

　12. The site is neutral (it does not try to promote, sell, or persuade) _____.

Currency

　13. The website was written recently _____.

　14. The information seems current _____.

Coverage

　15. This website seems complete _____.

　16. This site contains the information that I need _____.

　17. My questions are answered and I understand the topic _____.

　18. The ideas are explained and supported _____.

Impressions, ideas, or conclusions:

Figure 14.6   Website Evaluator for Younger Students

WEBSITE EVALUATOR

Website:

Topic:

Key: A = outstanding, B = average, C = low, F = poor or can't tell.

    Authority. The author seems like an expert _____.

    Accuracy. The information seems to be correct or true _____.

    Objectivity. The information contains just facts and does not try to persuade _____.

    Currency. The information is new _____.

    Coverage. The website is complete and helps me understand _____.

Impressions, ideas, or conclusions:

Figure 14.7   Basic Internet Safety Rules for Kids

---

1. Never give out your password to anybody on the Internet.

2. Ask a parent or teacher before you give out any personal information on the Internet. This includes your name, e-mail address, information about friends or family, pictures, your school, your telephone number, or your mailing address.

3. If somebody writes something that is rude or makes you feel uncomfortable, leave immediately and do not respond.

4. Ask a parent or teacher before you fill out any forms or buy anything on the Internet.

5. Ask a parent or teacher before you download anything from the Internet.

6. Never agree to meet in person anybody you meet on the Internet.

7. Always be polite and courteous when communicating on the Internet.

Internet Ethics

The Internet is still relatively new in terms of its impact on our societies. Many of the ethical issues are still evolving. However, the Computer Ethics Institute (CEI) (http://www.brook .edu/its/cei/default.htm), which is a branch of the Brookings Institution (http://www.brook .edu/default.htm), has created the "Ten Commandments of Computer Ethics." Some of these are related to Internet use. They also reflect the types of things that might be found in a school's AUP for the Internet. These CEI commandments are paraphrased here:

Do not use a computer to harm other people. Hurting other people might include hurting their reputation through vicious rumors or distorted innuendos. It is not ethical to engage in any form of communication or action that would cause pain, loss of employment, or financial hardship for another person or group. Also, it is not ethical to create or contribute to websites and programs that would promote harmful or violent actions.

Do not interfere with other people's computer work. This involves sending spam or computer viruses, as well deliberately harming files, programs, and databases.

Do not snoop around in other people's computer files. Unsolicited entry into somebody's computer is the same as physically breaking into an office and rummaging through somebody's files. Also, you should not access and read other people's e-mail communication without their permission.

Do not use a computer to steal. Getting things for free on the computer that are supposed to be paid for is the same as shoplifting or stealing in a store. Internet stealing also involves illegally downloading software, DVDs, or music.

Do not lie or engage in libel. This involves writing things that are not true. It also has to do with distorting the truth, presenting information out of context, intentionally misleading readers for personal or political gain, or putting out opinion pieces in the form of news articles.

Do not copy or use software for which you have not paid. It is not ethical to copy software or download programs onto your computer for which you have not paid. When you buy software programs, they are for individual use unless otherwise stated. You cannot put programs onto your computer that others may have bought for their individual computers.

Do not use other people's computer resources without authorization or proper compensation. This means you should not use others' computers or websites without their permission.

Do not appropriate other people's intellectual output. This is known a *plagiarism*. Plagiarism involves using somebody else's words or ideas as your own. This is especially relevant in academic environments where students are often asked to write reports. Students need to be told explicitly that they are not to cut and paste somebody else's words when preparing documents to be handed in as their own writing. Instead, teach them how to take notes, paraphrase, and cite their sources.

Think about the social consequence of the programs you write or systems that you design. It is not ethical to design or create any program, website, or communication that would have adverse consequence in the real world. Always use a computer in ways the ensure consideration and respect for others.

While it is appropriate to create websites to promote a cause, it is not ethical to use a computer or the Internet in ways that would purposely seek to defame, embarrass, humiliate, or offend others. This would include putting people's pictures or other personal information on the Internet without their permission, or sending e-mail that is disturbing, upsetting, or distasteful to the people receiving it.

Internet literacy involves developing a set of Internet ethics.

ONLINE STRATEGIES TO ENHANCE LEARNING

This section describes six pedagogical strategies for using the Internet to enhance learning in social studies.

Topic Hotlist and *Extend and Infer*

The *topic hotlist* is used to create a focused Internet learning experience. Here students review specific aspects of websites that you have previewed and selected in order to develop or reinforce specific ideas related to your social studies curriculum. This is a good introductory activity that can be used with students at all grade levels. There are three steps in creating this kind of activity: First, bookmark or create a handout that lists three to ten websites that enhance a concept or topic you are studying in social studies. Second, create a handout with specific tasks or questions related to each website. You can use thinking skills found in Chapter 12 to design tasks and questions. Finally, have students work in pairs or small groups to visit each website and complete the handout.

Extend and infer is designed to extend background knowledge related to a specific topic. It invites students to go beyond the facts to describe what they might mean. This activity is more appropriate for intermediate and middle-school students.

HOW DO I? Develop an Extend and Infer Online Activity

- Identify a topic related to social studies currently being studied that you wish to enhance or extend.
  - Find three to ten websites that hold information essential to understanding this topic.
  - Create one key question for each website.
  - Create a handout that lists each website address and the key questions.
- Using the graphic organizer below, have students work in pairs to list important things they already know about the topic in the column on the left. This is done before getting on the computer.

Topic:	
Things We Know About the Topic	Answers to Key Questions
	1. 2. 3. 4. 5.
What does this tell you about the topic?	

- Students then enter the websites and answer the key questions. One person is the surfer and the other person is the recorder. Their answers are recorded on the column on the right.
- Students examine their background knowledge and synthesize it with the information they get from the websites to answer the key questions. The goal is to extend what they know about the topic and then to infer to a greater conclusion. In the bottom box students describe what the information in the two columns tells them about their topics.

Internet Inquiry

The *Internet inquiry* uses the same inquiry process described in Chapter 11 and allows students to investigate a topic that is of interest to them. It can be conducted as an independent study individually or in small group.

HOW DO I? Conduct an Internet Inquiry

• Students ask a question. If students are not used to asking their own questions, you may need to provide some structure here by providing a list of questions from which they can choose. However, you want to encourage students to ask their own questions just like scientists and scholars do in real life. One way to help them identify a question is to have them work with a partner or in a small group to identify three to five topics that interested them. Then, they should pick one topic and put it in the form of a question.

• Students gather Internet data. They get information or data related to their questions by visiting websites. Primary students should visit two to five websites, intermediate students three to eight websites, and middle school students should visit five to ten websites.

• Students take notes and look for patterns. They use notes to record the interesting or important information they find on the websites. After all the websites have been visited, they examine their notes to look for common themes or patterns in order to create groups. The important ideas from their notes are then organized into groups, and unimportant ideas are discarded.

• Students use the notes (data) to answer the original question. They should be encouraged to add their own insights, ideas, or additional findings.

• Students present or communicate their findings or idea to an audience. They can create a demonstration, speech, drama, commercial, report, video, drawing, sculpture, research report, experiment, website, or poster display using graphs and tables.

• Use the rating checklist in Figure 14.8 to guide students' inquiry and to provide feedback and assessment on their final projects. (Modify this for use with primary age students.)

Subject Sampler

The *subject sampler* exposes students to a variety of websites organized around a particular theme or topic taken from your social studies curriculum. They respond to each website from a personal perspective. A personal response is one that does not have a correct answer (see Figure 14.9).

HOW DO I? Use a Subject Sampler

• Each student identifies a theme or topic related to social studies.

• Students find a variety of interesting, unique, or intriguing websites that are related to their topics or themes. They bookmark these websites or list them on a sheet of paper.

• Students meet in a small group and decide which sites they will visit. Allow them to choose which sites they wish to visit; however, give them a minimum number for which they are required to respond.

• Individually, students visit the websites and record their responses in a learning log or on a separate piece of paper.

• Students meet again in a small group to share their personal responses. To extend this, have students do a four square as described in Chapter 8 for each website.

Figure 14.8   Rating Checklist for Independent Internet Inquiry Projects

Steps:

    a. Ask a question.

    b. Gather data.

    c. Take notes and look for patterns.

    d. Answer the question.

    e. Communicate important ideas to others.

Key: 4 = outstanding, 3 = very good, 2 = average, 1 = low.

Criteria	Rating
1. *Responsibility.* (a) The researcher was able to come up with a question or idea, (b) the research was completed in the prescribed time, and (c) the researcher gathered appropriate sources for notes.	
2. *Knowledge.* The research (a) is interesting and informative, (b) demonstrates a knowledge base, and (c) uses an appropriate kind and number of sources.	
3. *Thinking.* The research (a) finds important ideas or themes, (b) uses knowledge (notes) to answer the research question, and (c) shows the researcher as a reflective learner.	
4. *Communication.* The presentation (a) communicates background knowledge and new ideas effectively, (b) uses the elements of effective oral speaking, (c) is clear, logical, and organized, and (d) is interesting.	
Comments or ideas:	

Figure 14.9   Personal Response Questions for Websites

For each website, students should respond using only *one* of the prompts below:

    1. What did this site remind you of or make you think of?

    2. What did you find interesting or important?

    3. What ideas or things from this website might you use or see in your everyday life?

    4. What ideas or pieces of information were most interesting or important?

    5. What new thing or things did you learn here?

    6. What old thing or things did you remember here?

    7. List three interesting or important things you found on this website. Rank them from most interesting to least interesting.

    8. What would you like to know more about?

    9. List three new or interesting words you found on this site.

Internet T-Talk

The *Internet T-Talk* is used to explore and discuss both sides of an important or controversial issue. This is described in detail in Chapter 13 and below.

EXAMPLE: Conducting an Internet T-Talk

Identify a controversial issue or topic. The first step in conducting an Internet T-talk is to identify an issue or topic. This issue or topic could be related to your social studies unit or it could be a current event. In Mr. Gaetti's 7th grade class, one of his students brought up the case of Judge Moore in Alabama during a discussion of current events. Judge Moore put a stone monument containing the Ten Commandments in front of his courthouse in Alabama. Since this topic seemed to generate a lot of interest among his students, Mr. Gaetti decided to create an Internet T-talk activity with this issue.

Provide students with basic background information related to the issue or topic. The next day, Mr. Gaetti provided some basic background information on the Judge Moore case to make sure that everyone understood the situation.

Put the issue or topic in the form of a dualistic statement. A dualistic statement is one that can be answered yes or no in relation to one's agreement. Mr. Gaetti used the following dualistic statement: The Ten Commandments should be allowed to be displayed in front of the courthouse in Alabama.

Have students form pairs to find and record supporting ideas. Mr. Gaetti randomly assigned students to pairs. Each pair created a T-chart on a sheet of paper. They then went to the Internet and plugged in key words to find information on this issue. Their task was to find and list a minimum of three ideas to support each side regardless of their current position (see below).

For/Yes	Against/No

Each pair combines with another pair to form a small group. On the third day, the pairs in Mr. Gaetti's class formed small groups. Each pair shared their ideas with the other pair. They were directed not to give their opinions until both pairs had had a chance to share all their supporting ideas on both sides of the dualistic statement.

Small groups work to reach a consensus. At this stage, students in the small groups were invited to share their positions. The task was then to work to come to a consensus on a new

---

(Continued)

(Continued)

statement to which all or most could agree. The 7th grade students discussed vigorously for about 30 minutes. When he sensed that most group discussions had run their course, Mr. Gaetti gave a verbal mile marker indicating that groups had 5 minutes left to find a consensus statement and at least two ideas supporting their statement.

Representatives share consensus statements and supporting ideas. One person from each of the small groups in Mr. Gaetti's classed shared the group's consensus statement and the supporting reasons with the whole class. One of the groups could not reach a consensus, although Mr. Gaetti kept urging them to find something that they could all agree on. Finally, students were asked to write their individual views and supporting reasons in their learning logs.

Internet Activism

Internet activism is designed to get students to act in regard to a social issue. Here they use background information and problem-solving skills to find a solution, make a recommendation, or develop a plan of action. What differentiates Internet activism from problem-solving activities is that Internet activism results in some sort of action.

HOW DO I? Develop an Internet Activism Activity

- Find an area of social concern.

- Provide students with initial background information related to the concern. Put the social concern in the form of a problem statement.

- Have students visit websites to develop background knowledge.

- Direct students to use the creative problem-solving strategy found in Chapter 10 to develop a solution to the problem or a set of recommendations to address the social concern.

- Have students develop a plan of action. The plan of action might be letters or e-mail to state or national congressional representatives or other government officials, letters or e-mail to companies, advertising or posters, websites, or video commercials to air on school or community cable broadcasts. It might also involve doing some sort of community service or some other activity.

- Have students put their plan into action.

GO THERE: Professional Organizations
Related to Using Technology to Enhance Education

- Computer-using Educators: http://www.cue.org/
- International Society for Technology in Education: http://www.iste.org

TEACHERS IN ACTION: Using the Internet to Teach Social Studies

I am thinking about my most successful lesson this year. The activity came out of our "We the Children . . ." online project. For this project, my students worked alongside a Grade 6/7 class from Magan International School in Tel Aviv, Israel. The students exchanged e-mails, but I wanted them to get a feel for the reality of life in Israel. So, one morning, I pointed them to an extensive photo essay presentation on the CNN Web site. Up to this point, my students viewed their Israeli peers as they would any other 12- or 13-year-old. This was largely because the e-mails from Israel were void of any mention of the suicide bombings and violence that were part of daily life in Israel.

You could have heard a pin drop in the room as my students flipped through the CNN pictures of a war-torn country and read the accompanying explanations. After they were done, we met together and discussed what we had seen, the implications for their new foreign friends, and their overall impressions and feelings. The students were somber as they talked about how different they felt about terrorism since they now knew someone in Israel, how they watched the evening news with concern, wondering if one of the suicide bombings had occurred in Tel Aviv, and if so, had it touched the lives of one of the kids from the Grade 6/7 class.

We discussed some of the "We the Children . . ." writing that the Israeli students had sent us, the writing that spoke of the fear and terror that they felt (but couldn't seem to discuss in their e-mails). We discussed why it may be easier to write their feelings in poem form as opposed to in their e-mails.

As I looked at their serious faces and passionate words, I realized that Internet access had not only broadened my student's worldview, but that learning and compassion had penetrated their hearts.

—Brenda Dyck, Middle School Teacher

Author Reflection: When I was teaching 2nd grade in River Falls, Wisconsin back in 1985, we thought it was a big deal to have an Apple IIe computer with its green screen and five-inch floppy disks. Being computer literate back in those olden days meant knowing how to use a word processing program. Our classroom computers were used mostly for drill and practice activities. They were flash cards with bells and whistles.

Today, at the beginning of this new century, we're still at the beginning stages of our technological revolution. We have yet to imagine the full potential of the Internet and other types of technology. However, I have to admit that I'm a little fearful of rushing too far too fast. I am fearful of human disconnection at an even greater level than exists today. Already, it seems like humans don't spend enough time talking with each other. I walk by college classrooms and see humans sitting in darkened rooms peering up at a Power Point presentation. I see rows upon rows of humans sitting in computer labs staring at screens. We read e-mail messages on screens, or we hear voices on our cell phones. We watch DVDs. We play computer and video games. We need to connect more with real humans in the real world.

That said, Brenda used technology above to increase human connection, to help her students understand others at a much deeper and more personal level. I guess it's not the tool that we should worry about; it's how the tool is used.

What is your response to the case? How do your reactions compare with the author's reflection?

NCSS STANDARDS

Thematic Standards

The following NCSS thematic standards are addressed in this chapter. See Appendix A for a full description of the relevant thematic standards.

Early Grades

I.   Science, Technology, & Society: a., c.

II. Global Connections: c.

III. Civic Ideals and Practices: a., c., d.

Middle Grades

I.   Science, Technology, & Society: a., c.

II. Global Connections: c.

III. Civic Ideals and Practices: a., c., d.

Pedagogical Standards

The following NCSS pedagogical standards are addressed in this chapter:

I.   Critical Thinking, Problem Solving, and Performance Skills.

II. Active Learning and Motivation.

III. Inquiry, Collaboration, and Supportive Classroom Interaction.

Essential Skills for Social Studies

The following NCSS essential skills for social studies are addressed in this chapter:

I.   Acquiring Information.
  A. Study Skills.
    1. find information
    2. arrange information in usable forms
  B. Reference and Information-search Skills.
    1. special references
  C. Technical Skills Unique to Electronic Devices.
    2. computer

II. Organizing and Using Information.
  A. Thinking Skills.
    1. classify information
    2. interpret information
    3. analyze information

      4. summarize information

      5. synthesize information

      6. evaluate information

   B. Decision-Making Skills.

III. Relationships and Social Participation.

   A. Social and Political Participation

Chapter Review: Key Points

1. The Internet is an abundant source of information; however, its effectiveness as a learning tool is dependent on teachers' ability to use it effectively to support or enhance learning goals and objectives.

2. Developing Internet literacy is an important part of teachers' roles in the twenty-first century, and it should be taught and reinforced in all subject areas.

3. Internet literacy is the ability to access and evaluate information on the World Wide Web and includes the following skills: conducting Internet searches, evaluating sources, posting information, and participating in online communication.

4. Teachers should evaluate websites using four criteria: accessibility, accuracy, appropriateness, and appeal.

5. Students should be taught how to conduct Internet searches using the elements of effective skills instruction:
   - Identify the steps.
   - Give explicit instruction and model its use.
   - Allow students to practice the skill under your guidance.
   - Allow students to practice the skill by themselves.
   - Reinforce by integrating it, reviewing, and using it in a variety of contexts.

6. There are six different types of websites, each with a different purpose: informational websites, resource websites, news websites, advocacy websites, business or marketing websites, and personal websites.

7. Students should be taught how to evaluate the quality and credibility of information found on websites using five criteria: accuracy, authority, objectivity, coverage, and currency.

8. Website evaluators can be used to help students develop an awareness of the credibility of the information they find on websites; however, the goal is not to do a formal analysis of every website they encounter.

9. A teacher should establish classroom rules for using the Internet that address the kinds of websites accessed and communication etiquette.

10. The classroom is a good place to talk about Internet safety.

11. Five pedagogical strategies for using the Internet to enhance learning in social studies include topic hotlists, extend and infer, Internet inquiry, subject sampler, Internet T-talk, and Internet activism.

12. The community offers a variety of resources that can be used to extend or enhance learning in social studies.

13. You can teach students to use interviews and surveys to get information from their community just like real social scientists often do.

Making Connections

1. Visit Yahooligan's Teacher's Guide (Yahoo! Inc., 2001). Find and describe five interesting or important teaching ideas you will use in your social studies classroom.

2. Identify an interesting or important topic that you would like to address in your social studies classroom. Use one of the search engines to find five to ten websites to use with this topic.

3. Pick a topic of interest to you. Find a website that you find to be very credible and another that you find to be not very credible on this topic.

4. Find a website related to a controversial social, political, or religious topic of the day. Use the website evaluator to make a formal assessment of that website.

5. What additional rules might you include for school or classroom Internet use?

6. What, if any, additional safety precautions should be included in the basic Internet safety rules for kids?

7. Identify a social studies unit you teach or will be teaching. Use one of the six Internet strategies described in this chapter to design a learning experience.

8. Conduct an Internet inquiry on some question related to teaching in general or teaching social studies specifically.

9. Use the Internet to find websites that contain social studies lesson plans.

10. Conduct an Internet T-talk related to the following dualistic statement: Standardized tests are poor indicators of teachers' effectiveness or teaching abilities.

11. In what ways do you see the three holistic learning ideas related to intrapersonal connections, interpersonal connections, and interconnectedness reflected here?

Chapter 15

LEARNING THROUGH LITERATURE AND LANGUAGE ARTS

Thinking Ahead

1. Describe a favorite trade book that you read in elementary or middle school. What social studies concepts might be connected with this book?

2. How do you think literature can help students understand themselves and others? How might it be used to help students understand social studies concepts? In what ways might literature serve to help meet the goals and purposes of social studies education?

3. How might personal or reflective writing serve to enhance social studies education?

4. What connections do you see between social studies and writing?

USING LITERATURE TO TEACH SOCIAL STUDIES

There are many very good social studies texts and commercial curriculums that can be used in elementary and middle school classrooms. Unfortunately, teachers sometimes find themselves forced to use social studies texts and curriculums that are outdated, poorly written, or badly designed. In these cases, you can hear an audible groan when students are asked to take out their social studies texts. There are two very simple solutions to this: The first is to creatively adapt the social studies text using only those parts that you find worthwhile while adding to the other parts as if it were an integrated unit (see Chapter 5). The second is to use literature in the form of picture books and trade books for social studies class. This section focuses on the second option.

The Magic of Books

Picture books rely on pictures to carry the story and are usually used with primary students. However, many picture books can, with a little creativity and imagination, also be used with older students. A *trade book,* sometimes called a *chapter book,* is a story that is broken into chapters and relies on text, instead of pictures, to carry the story. Why should literature be used with a social studies curriculum? Four reasons:

Learning through stories is a natural way to learn. Throughout history humans have used stories, mythologies, and legends to carry important ideas from one generation to another (Campbell, 1988). Stories are far more interesting than a list of facts. Also the human mind seems better able to absorb and remember stories. This is because a story line pulls things together in a logical sequence. Stories also elicit or draw upon our emotions and personal experiences, enabling us to make associations to our own lives. Through story, facts and concepts become more relevant and we are able to learn things at a much deeper level.

Literature helps us to experience and understand other people, times, and situations. Louise Rosenblatt (1983) says that literature makes known the many ways humans meet life's possibilities. Reading books and hearing stories allows us to hear the thoughts of others, and to make contact with their values, dreams, and philosophies. Also, through literature we can have vicarious experiences of people in different times and places. In this way a good book can be a powerful field trip of the mind.

Literature can enhance students' ability to engage in moral reasoning and can help clarify their own values. Hearing the thoughts of literary characters struggling with issues and situations is much like what happens with moral dilemmas and values clarification activities (see Chapter 16). Children are exposed to the reasoning and thought processes of others and it is this process that gives insight into their own reasoning. Literature can be used then, not to teach particular values or behaviors, but rather, to expose students to the values and moral reasoning of others who are searching for what they consider to be the best action or behavior in a given circumstance. Being exposed to literary characters working out their principles and values creates the conditions whereby students are better able to reflect upon and gain perspective on their own. Also, as described in Chapter 16, the problems and situations faced by characters in the story can be used as problem-solving and moral-reasoning activities for the students in your class.

Literature helps children make sound choices. In a story we encounter the imaginative trials and errors of others. Here we are able to vicariously experience the logical consequences of certain actions without having to experience the actual actions or consequences. Literature can also help people view their own problems and situations more objectively. For example, if a child was going through an abusive situation, reading about the abusive situation of another may provide a context for that child to make sense of the situation and provide some ideas as to possible courses of action. Similarly, if students are making decisions related to drugs, alcohol, sex, gangs, or crime, experiencing the full impact of possible decisions through the actions of some literary characters can help to provide insight.

Using literature is an effective way to enhance social studies.

HOW DO I? Use Literature in Social Studies

Trade books and pictures books can be used to augment lessons from a social studies curriculum or textbook. This is the *textbook-driven* approach outlined in the column on the left below. Social studies units can also be built around trade books and picture books. This is the *literature-driven* approach outlined in the column on the right.

Textbook-Driven Approach	Literature-Driven Approach
1. Start with a topic or unit.	1. Find a good book.
2. Find a book (narrative text) related to the topic.	2. Teach social studies lessons based on things found in each chapter
3. Get a copy for each student.	3. Use textbooks as a reference source for students to get specific information for activities and assignments.
4. Use literature circles or reading workshops where students are reading different books or read different chapters at their own pace.	4. Create minilesson to teach social studies concepts.
5. Create minilessons to teach textbook concepts.	5. Students spend the majority of class time reading or engaged in literacy discussions.
6. Use textbooks as a reference source for students to get specific information for activities and assignments.	

The Literature-Driven Approach

So how do you create a social studies unit around a trade book or picture book? These are the steps:

1. **Find a good book.** Good books are those books that people find interesting and engaging. Chances are, if the book is interesting to you, your students will also find it interesting. In looking for trade books you will find that young adult literature is often better written than adult literature. This is because the writers of young adult books do not rely on death, violence, or sex to carry the story as writers of adult stories often do. With primary students you can build a unit around one or more picture books.

2. **Read the book or books.** Read the book and start to look for areas in the story where you might create lessons related to geography, time, government, society, science and technology, human interaction, or other areas related to social studies. For example, if you are using *Bridge to Terabithia* (1977), you might research important events of the 1970s, geography or events related to the time and place, music and cultural traditions of the period, transportation of the era, or important technological innovations that occurred during that time.

3. **Do research; get information.** Part of teaching is providing students with information that is well organized and in a form that they can easily assimilate. Good teachers teach. That is, they recognize there are times when it is necessary to tell students about the world in which they live. Even teachers who might describe themselves as holistic, child-centered, or constructivist understand that there are instances where it is appropriate to provide students with information using visual aids and spoken words (speech) in a structured format. Based on the ideas in Step 2, conduct research in order to get the background information necessary to create and teach effective lessons.

4. **Create activities to go with each chapter.** All of the activities described in the preceding chapters can be used with trade and picture books to design prereading activities or postreading activities. The goals of the activities are to manipulate, expand upon, or explore the ideas found in the chapter or in the information provided by you during the social studies lesson.

5. **Decide on the approach for reading and the reading schedule.** Create a very flexible general outline of the chapters, the information that you will provide with each, and activities that might go with each chapter. With chapter books, do no more than a chapter or two a day. This allows the slower readers to keep up with the class. A typical class period might include one of the following approaches:

   • Provide a prereading activity, allow students to read the assigned chapter or chapters silently or with a reading partner, and then assign a postreading activity based on that chapter to be done in class or as homework or during social studies class.

   • Create an activity to do at the beginning or end of the class and let students spend the majority of time reading.

   • Provide information related to the book and then create an in-class activity or assignment for students to do. Here you would not assign chapters, but simply provide information (lecture), relate this information to things happening in the book, and then design activities to manipulate the information or ideas presented.

6. **Differentiate instruction for high- and low-ability students.** With younger students, it may be appropriate for you to read the assigned chapters and then do classroom activities. With older students, you will need to accommodate to meet the special needs of readers of differing abilities. For low-ability readers, use one of the strategies described in Chapters 7 and 8. Also, as described in Chapter 8, you can meet the needs of low-ability readers by having the chapters on audiotape. Have a center with headphones where students can come to listen to the chapter. Make this acceptable by telling all students that it is okay to sometimes simply listen and let the ideas flow.

Should you let students read ahead? Generally yes. It is hard to say no to a student who has a passion for reading. If students finished the book, provide them with books written by the same author or other books on the same topic. However, be careful not to make this extra reading extra work. That is, if they read extra books they should not have to be held accountable for these books. The goal here is to simply enjoy the stories.

Books and Genre

What kinds of books and genres should you use in a social studies class? The genre is not as important as the content. Almost any book that has humans interacting can be used for a social studies class. For example, there are some very good fantasies or science fiction books such as *A Wrinkle in Time* (L'Engle, 1962) and *Eva* (Dickinson, 1990) that can be used to cover topics such as good and evil, heroes, feeling different, future technology, or problem solving. There are realistic fiction books that depict real-life situations that can be used to examine interpersonal and social issues such as *The Goats* (Cole, 1990) and *Maniac Magee* (Spinelli, 1990). Historical books and historical fiction such as *A Long Year of Silence* (Doty, 2004) and *Girl in a Cage* (Yolen & Harris, 2003) can be used to examine time periods. An excellent source for lists and brief descriptions of a variety of trade books that can be used in a social studies curriculum can be found at the NCSS and CBC websites below. The NCSS has a website that identifies notable social studies trade books for young people along with the related thematic strands of the NCSS curriculum standards for social studies. The Children's Book Council (CBC) is a nonprofit organization that promotes the use and enjoyment of children's trade books and related materials. You can get information about a variety of books from many different publishers at these two websites.

GO THERE: Lists of Trade Books for Use in Social Studies

www.socialstudies.org/resources/notable/

www.CBCbooks.org

http://teacherlink.ed.usu.edu/tlresources/units/byrnes-literature/lit.html

http://www.udel.edu/dssep/literature.html

http://www.udel.edu/dssep/articles.htm

http://www.nancypolette.com/litguides.asp

TEACHERS IN ACTION: Story Line Method for Teaching Social Studies

This method aims to teach a social studies unit just as you would teach a novel. You begin with the setting, which is your state (Indiana) at some point in history. Have the kids research what Indiana would have looked like at that time (characteristics of the communities, sources of income, natural resources, etc.). You can use the textbook or the internet for this, with each small group focusing on one portion of the setting, and reporting what they learn to the class. After you have gathered a sufficient amount of information, the class works together to make a huge mural of an Indiana town with a lot of history. (Or, you could divide the class into small groups and ask each group to design a different mural map.) When this is complete, have the kids take you on a tour.

Next, begin the character development. Each child invents his/her own character that s/he thinks could live in that town and writes (in a journal) every small detail about the character: appearance, name, job, family, dislikes, etc. Next, the students make models of their characters (similar to a paper doll) using fabric scraps, yarn, ribbon, etc. The characters turned out so interesting and unique in my grade two classroom.

For plot, you can introduce an event that happened in history. Each child writes "in character" to describe the effect of the event on the character. They may also role play to discuss events with others in the town.

Next, for the climax, have the kids research an important aspect of the local history. Each student continues to write in his/her journal. I also had them hold a class debate and put together speeches to discuss what "should" be done about the problem. My class got so into this. It really brings social studies to life for them.

Finally, for the resolution, the community came to some sort of consensus. You then compare your story to what really happened in history. The last journal entry is reflectively written from the student's (not the character's) point of view to talk about what s/he has learned from the experience. I love this approach. It gets the kids out of the textbook and teaches them in a way they can really relate to.

—Melanie, Teacher, Grade Two

Author Reflection: One of my mottos for teaching and for life is this: Dream big and start small. (You can really do anything you want if you are willing to commit to the task.) Melanie's ideas seem like a fun and interesting way for students to learn about history (and a lot of other things as well); however, I would encourage you to start small and keep it simple when you first try this. You may need to start with a very short experience done as a whole class activity. This will enable you to provide a lot of modeling and guidance. Then you can move to small groups and pairs. And finally, after some weeks or months, depending on the age of your students, they might be able to do this as an individual activity.

I agree with Jerome Bruner who said that anything can be taught at any level. It's just a matter of understanding where your students are and breaking things down appropriately.

Another good motto for teaching and for life (when you really get into teaching you will find that they are actually the same thing) is this: Adopt and adapt. All teaching ideas you encounter in this textbook and elsewhere should be adopted and adapted to meet the particular demands of your teaching situation and tailored to fit your teaching style.

What is your response to the case? How do your reactions compare with the author's reflection?

THE LANGUAGE ARTS AND SOCIAL STUDIES

The language arts can also be used as an effective learning tool in social studies. The language arts encompass the expressive parts of reading, writing, speaking, and listening. Reading, speaking, and listening have all been covered in previous chapters. This section will focus specifically on writing and writing activities as they relate to social studies. *Expository writing* can be used to explore ideas, to organize thinking, and to communicate ideas and information to an audience. *Creative writing* can also be used to explore a variety of intrapersonal dimensions and to communicate ideas through the use of art and metaphor. Both forms of writing can be used to enhance learning in all subject areas at all levels.

The Process of Writing

Writing is the process of using print to create meaning. It is best taught and learned using the five-step process writing approach first described by Donald Graves (1983):

Step 1: Prewriting. The goal in prewriting is to generate ideas without regard for evaluation. Listing, brainstorming, outlining, silence, conversation with a neighbor, or power writing (described below), all are ways to generate ideas. What writers do before writing is just as important as what happens during the writing process.

Step 2: Drafting. Drafting is the writer's first attempt to capture ideas on paper. Quantity is valued over quality. If done correctly, the draft should be a rambling, disconnected accumulation of ideas.

Step 3: Revising. This is the heart of the writing process. Here a piece is re-visioned and reshaped many times. The draft stage is like throwing a large blob of clay on the potter's wheel. The revising stage is where you shape the blob of clay, adding parts, taking parts away, and continually mold and change until you get it just right. You look for flow and structure. Writers at this stage spend a lot of time rereading paragraphs and moving things around.

Step 4: Editing. This is the stage where the mechanics of writing are attended to. This is where grammar, spelling, and punctuation errors are corrected. Make sure you do not move editing to an earlier stage. Many good ideas and a great deal of good writing have been stymied by teachers who insist that Step 4 be Step 1 or Step 2. If writers are editing or overly concerned with mechanics at the prewriting, drafting, and revising stages, the flow of ideas and the quality of writing will suffer. Precious brain space that should be devoted to generating and connecting ideas will instead be utilized to attend to writing mechanics.

One last thing about the editing phase: Real writers edit their writing at the end. Real writers also rely on editors or friends to read their work and give them feedback, and the spell check and grammar check functions of their word processing programs to find and correct errors. In teaching our students to become authors and composers of authentic writing, teach them to approximate the writing process used by real writers.

Step 5: Publishing. This is where students writing is shared with an audience. At this stage, writing becomes real. You can publish students work using class books, collections of writing based on a theme, student newspapers, student magazines, posting writing on websites, displaying short samples of writing in the hall or out in the community, or having students read out loud in small groups, to another classmate, or in a large group setting.

Choice of Writing Topics in a Social Studies Class

Students are more motivated to write and take greater pride and ownership in the final product if they are given choices as to their writing topics. However, choice does not mean total choice all the time; rather; it means that you use a continuum of options, sometimes giving students more choice and sometimes less. A continuum of choices is presented here:

- **Choose a variation on a topic.** Give students a theme or topic and allow them to interpret it and respond to it or explore a facet of it that they find of interest.

- **Choice within a set of topics.** Give students a menu or list of possible topics to explore through writing and let them make a choice. Students with similar topics might even be encouraged to work together to gather information related to their topics.

- **Choice within a set of parameters.** Give students a set of parameters within a subject and then allow them to choose a writing topic within those parameters. Example: When studying science and technology, you might ask students to find a topic they are interested in related to technology, become an expert, and tell the class about it using writing.

- **Choice related to personal or reflective elements.** Include personal or reflective writing assignments and activities as well as more formal expository writing assignments. Here students tell their stories or describe their ideas, insights, or personal experiences related to a theme or subject.

Provide opportunities for students to select writing topics that they care about, topics that invite them to say what it is they want to say, and opportunities for them to share their writing and ideas with others. This will create a greater motivation to write which, in turn, will improve students' writing and communicating skills and result in a more interesting and engaged classroom.

EXAMPLE: Choosing a Topic Within Parameters

Ms. Gagne had to force herself to read the papers she had assigned her 8th grade social studies class. After one major assignment it became very apparent that her students cared little for the writing topic that she had selected for them. They had as much interest in writing a meaningless paper to please their teacher as Ms. Gagne did in responding to their meaningless papers to please her students. It seems as if the only thing this writing assignment accomplished was to create a situation whereby a whole lot of people spent a whole lot of time doing something that created a whole lot of meaningless misery, just so that Ms. Gagne could have some sort of measuring device to use in sorting people into grading categories. A great deal of time was being spent by students writing their papers, and Ms. Gagne spent countless hours reading, responding, and grading these papers. With all the time and energy going into this writing assignment, she really questioned how much learning was taking place.

(Continued)

(Continued)

The next quarter, Ms. Gagne decided to try something different. Instead of assigning students a writing topic, students were asked to select a topic related to a unique or interesting aspect of the social studies unit they were studying. They were given a menu of possible writing ideas as well as the option of choosing their own idea with the approval of the instructor. The papers were to be two to four double spaced pages, but no more than five, and students were to use a minimum of two sources. Grading was based on five criteria: (a) content, (b) depth of thinking, (c) organization and readability, (d) writing mechanics, and (e) professionalism (meeting deadlines and handing in a product that looks professional).

The result of this was that students were able to find topics that were much more meaningful to them than the very narrow topic that Ms. Gagne had assigned the previous quarter. Some students wrote about topics that Ms. Gagne had not even considered. Also, in reading them, she was able to see their minds at work as they grappled with ideas and topics that were of interest to them.

EXAMPLE: Using Reflective Writing to Enhance Social Studies

Mr. Kelly's 5th Grade Class

Mr. Kelly's 5th grade class was studying the Midwest region of the United States as part of their social studies class. He introduced the concept of change, showing his class how this region had changed over the last 300 years in terms of the environment, the plant and animal life, and the lives of the people living there.

He then used the following two writing prompts: "What would you like to be doing if you had lived in the early 1800s? What things have changed in your life in the last couple of years?"

Students wrote for three to four minutes and then shared their ideas in a small group. Mr. Kelly also wrote and joined in one of the small groups, sharing his ideas as an equal member of the group. As a result of this activity students were able to make some personal connections with the material being covered. They were able to connect their very subjective feelings and experiences to the very objective material and thus learn at a much deeper and more personal level. Also, as Mr. Kelly listened to them share their ideas in a small group, he was able to see beyond the faces that stared up at him each day in class, to see the very real person beyond the face. At the end, he asked each group to come up with one big idea or something interesting they noticed to share with the class.

Ms. Newman's 2nd Grade Class

Ms. Newman's 2nd grade class was studying rules and laws as part of their civics and government unit. Before social studies class, she used the following writing prompt: "If there were no rules in school, what kinds of things would you like to do?"

Students wrote for two to three minutes, then moved into small group to share their ideas. Next, students moved back into a large group. Ms. Newman asked a few students to share their ideas. Ms. Newman was then able to link their writing to the importance of having school rules and laws and then societal rules and laws.

GO THERE: A Variety of Social Studies Lesson Plans, Many of Which Contain Writing Activities

http://www.csun.edu/~hcedu013/plans.html

http://www.col-ed.org/cur/social.html

http://jc-schools.net/write/write-socst.html

http://www.rcas.org/techconnect/socialstudiesunits.html

JOURNAL AND REFLECTIVE WRITING IN SOCIAL STUDIES

A journal in a social studies class can provide a place for students to record their thoughts, observations, and interesting ideas. The journal becomes a written version of their thinking space, a place to explore ideas, and should not be graded for spelling, mechanics, or content. Some might think that this type of reflective writing should be done only in a literacy class; however, remember that social studies is a study of people interacting. Sharing ideas and experiences through writing is a powerful way for students to begin to understand themselves in a greater social and human context. It can also be a vehicle to help students know and understand others. This knowledge and understanding contributes to their ability to make informed and reasoned decisions just as much as knowledge and skills related to history, geography, civics and government, economics, and psychology.

Responding to Journal Entries

Having others respond to a journal greatly increases students' interest and improves the quality of their writing. These responses provide students feedback as to how their ideas are

A journal provides a written version of children's thinking space. It is a place to record thoughts and observations, and to explore interesting ideas.

being perceived by others. Students should always be given a choice as to which entries they want to share with others. Paper clips can be used to denote the specific entries here. Also, students need to be taught how to respond to each other's journal entries using aesthetic responses. An aesthetic response is one in which you describe the effect the writing has on your imagination, emotions, or associations. The aesthetic response questions in Figure 15.1 can be displayed in poster form as a guide in teaching students how to respond to the writing of others.

EXAMPLE: Using Journals

Mr. Portugal, a 2nd grade teacher in St. Paul, Minnesota has his students write in their journals first thing every day. As soon as school starts, students get their journals from the journal space on the shelf. Knowing that they will be writing every day, students notice things and think about what they might write about on the way to school. In their journals students are encouraged to use words or pictures to hold the idea. During this time Mr. Portugal also records his thoughts and observations in his journal. When he notices the writing energy diminishing around the room (usually after two to five minutes), students are asked to find a new friend to share their writing. (The rule is that you cannot read to the same friend twice during the same week.) In a short time, his students are engaged in an authentic writing activity, they are provided an audience for their writing, and they are able to listen and share with others the things that are going on in their lives. As the year goes on, Mr. Portugal experiments, using groups of three and four students for these early morning sharing sessions.

In Ms. Lombardozzi's 8th grade social studies class, a small part of her students' quarter grades is based on their journal entries. If students make the required number of entries, they receive all the participation points. Knowing that middle school students can forget or lose their journals, she keeps the journals in a box in her classroom (in a secure location). On those days when she wants students to use their journals, she lays them out on a table for students to pick up as they enter her classroom. She does not use the journals every day; however, when she does, students are asked to make personal connections to that day's topic using five types of journal prompts (see below). She always has her journal prompts written on the board at the beginning of class. This enables students to select and process relevant information during class to use in responding in their journals at the end of class.

Journal Prompts

Five types of journal prompts that might be used in social studies class are described here.

3-I prompt. The 3-I prompt asks students to describe two to five *I*nteresting or *I*mportant *I*deas that they will take with them from that class.

Personal relevancy prompt. This prompt asks students to pick an idea from class and describe how it affects or touches their lives.

Figure 15.1   Questions That Elicit an Aesthetic Response

---

1. What did it make you think about?

2. What is something it reminded you of?

3. What book, movie, TV show, or historical event is this like?

4. What images were painted in your head as you read?

5. What did you want to know more about?

6. What is one idea that you liked?

7. What were you feeling as your read this?

8. What experience in your own life has triggered similar feelings or situations?

9. What events in your life are similar to those described?

10. What do you want to say to the writer/author?

Personal metaphor prompt. Here students are given a metaphor related to that day's topic and asked to describe how it manifests in their lives. For example, after studying wars, you might ask students to describe a time when they were at war with themselves or somebody else or to describe a time when they experienced great conflict.

Artistic prompt. The fourth type of journal prompt is the artistic prompt. Here, students are asked to draw a diagram or picture that describes something related to that day's class. This allows students to use artistic and visual-spatial intelligence in coming to know and describe an idea from class. Students are also given the option of recording a song lyric, describing music, or composing poetry that might illustrate or enhance an idea from the class.

Wide open prompt. Some days you might simply ask students to describe something that is going on in their lives. Upper elementary and middle school students should always be advised to consider the level of disclosure, as you are obliged to take action if you discover something illegal or harmful.

Sharing Journal Entries

Sharing journal entries with others helps students see a certain universality of experience and helps them to understand each other at a deeper level. Sharing also has a certain cathartic effect in that it allows students to identify things that they may have been harboring in their unconscious, and to record these things, share them with others, and then get some kind of response or feedback. Again, students should always be advised to consider the types of things they will be sharing and the level of disclosure, as other people will be reading them. Students can share journal entries with other students in a variety of ways.

Partner oral response. This is the type of sharing Mr. Portugal used in the example. Here students find a neighbor and read a journal entry orally or simply describe some of the main ideas. Partners then respond orally to the ideas, again, using an aesthetic response.

Small group oral response. In small groups, students read or describe a journal entry. These entries become natural vehicles for small group discussions as members of the group respond orally with aesthetic response questions and comments.

Trade and respond. Students trade journals with a partner and write their responses right on the journal page. In this way the journal becomes a living entity and a collection of perspectives. In groups of three or more, students can keep rotating journals until everybody has responded to each.

Whole class. Two or three volunteers sign up to share an idea or journal entry with the whole class each day. Do no more than three of these whole class kinds of sharing in a given class period as students naturally get distracted after a few minutes of listening passively.

Other Writing Ideas

This section contains other writing ideas that can be used to enhance a social studies curriculum and promote deeper learning in all subject areas.

Power write. In *a power write,* students try to catch as many ideas they can in a three-minute period (use two minutes for younger students). This is different from a *free write* where students write whatever they want in an extended period of time. The goal in the power write is to get students to bypass the logical mind through free association, catching the first thought that pops into their minds. A stopwatch should be used here so that students know they are writing for a specific amount of time. Ask them to keep their pencils moving, writing down the first thing that comes to their minds.

Students' power writing is apt to be very disjointed. It helps if you model this sense of disjointedness by showing and reading a copy of a power write (see Figure 15.2). Encourage students to use scribbles, scratch marks, arrows, diagrams, single words, incomplete sentences, and quick impressions. If done correctly, the power write will help writers discover a wealth of images and impressions of which they may not have been aware.

The power write can serve two purposes: First, it can be used as a prewriting tool for students to discover ideas for writing. By generating a pile of ideas students are usually able to find a couple of good writing nuggets that they had not thought about previously. Second, power writes help students discover insights, ideas, or issues of which they may not have been aware.

Figure 15.2   Example of a Power Write

Cold, cold, cold . . . Glasses fog up when I come inside . . . Got a pair of new pants . . . Can't wait to wear them . . . Good music . . . I like the songs we're singing in choir . . . Spinning wheels . . . Reminds me of yellow circus peanuts my grandma used to give me when we went to her house . . . I'll be going there with my brother on Saturday . . . My brother is bugs me sometimes . . . Do I bug people? He plays basketball . . . I love watching the games . . . The loud noise . . . I plan on going out for basketball when I'm older . . . Left the basketball in the garage . . . Doesn't bounce . . . Bill's coming over after school . . . We sometimes play basketball in the snow . . . Fun . . .

Students can do power writes directly in their journals or they can use a separate piece of paper and then record only the interesting or important ideas from the power write in their journals. Power writes become more powerful when they are shared with a partner or in a small group. When sharing here students should always be given the option of reading their writing in its entirety or simply describing a few interesting or important ideas.

FREE VERSE

Poetry uses words, sounds, and phrases to paint a picture. Free verse is a kind of poetry that paints this picture without the use of rhyme, meter, or other defined poetic devices. This form of poetry allows students to concentrate on the sound of the poem and on recreating a feeling or event. Free verse is a good starting point for writing poetry, as feelings and ideas are not sacrificed for form. Other poetry forms will naturally develop from here as students begin to experiment with different sounds and their effects.

Poetry can also be used to bring other ways of seeing to other subject areas. This is an important point for social studies. Instead of writing assignments, worksheets, or other types of homework, you can make learning more interesting and creative by giving students the option of creating poetry or other kinds of art related to the concepts being studied in social studies class. It need not be long or elaborate. Often, a few simple words can best capture the feeling or ideas related to a person, place, situation, or event. Figure 15.3 contains a free verse poem that was created for a middle school unit on the history of music.

Figure 15.3   Free Verse: Music

Music

A skin stretched over a hollow log.
The ancients, pounding.
Vibrations, traveling through the air.
Moving outward, invisible through space.
Sounds,
Coming one after another.
Repeating, pulsating.
People moving now,
Moving in time with sound.
Responding to sound.
Transforming by sound.
A chant,
A prayer, repeated over and over.
The sound becomes line.
The line takes shape, moving here and there, fluttering about,
A butterfly,

A dancing butterfly of sound.
The dancing line, now joined by another.
Line upon line, intertwining, one upon the other.
The other upon the one.
Many together to produce blend.
Chord.
Colors of sound, perfectly matched.
Harmonies knit,
A bridge from here to there.
Between inner and outer.
Sound.
The sound of the mother's heart within the womb.
The sound of life.
And the sound of silence.
A pounding silence then.

NCSS STANDARDS

Thematic Standards

The following NCSS thematic standards are addressed in this chapter. See Appendix A for a full description of the relevant thematic standards.

Early Grades

   I. Culture: a., c.

   II. Individuals, Groups, and Institutions: a., b., c., d., e., f.

   III. Individual Development and Identity: a., b., f., g.

   IV. Global Connections: a.

Middle Grades

   I. Culture: a., c.

   II. Individuals, Groups, and Institutions: a., b., c., d., e., f.

   III. Individual Development and Identity: a., b., c., e., f.

   IV. Global Connections: a.

Pedagogical Standards

The following NCSS pedagogical standards are addressed in this chapter:

   I. Critical Thinking, Problem Solving, and Performance Skills.

   II. Active Learning and Motivation.

   III. Inquiry, Collaboration, and Supportive Classroom Interaction.

Essential Skills for Social Studies

The following NCSS essential skills for social studies are addressed in this chapter:

   I. Acquiring Information.
      A. Reading Skills.
         1. comprehension

   II. Organizing and Using Information.
      A. Thinking Skills.
         1. classify information
         2. interpret information
         3. analyze information
         4. summarize information

5. synthesize information
6. evaluate information
   B. Decision-Making Skills.

III. Relationships and Social Participation.
   A. Personal Skills.

Chapter Review: Key Points

1. Literature in the form of picture books and trade books can be used to enhance social studies.

2. Learning through stories is a natural way to learn.

3. Literature can help students experience and understand other people, times, and situations; enhance their ability to engage in moral reasoning and clarify their own values; and help children make sound choices.

4. Literature can be used to augment or enhance a social studies textbook or curriculum that is already in place.

5. Social studies units can be designed around picture books and trade books.

6. Books of almost any type and genre can be used in a social studies class.

7. Informational or expository writing can be used in social studies to help students organize their thinking, explore ideas, and to communicate ideas with others.

8. Creative writing can be used to explore a variety of interpersonal and intrapersonal dimensions related to social studies.

9. Writing should be taught using the five-step process, which consists of prewriting, drafting, revising, editing, and publishing.

10. Students are more motivated to write and create better writing if they are given choices of writing topics.

11. Journals provide students a place to record, explore, and examine their own ideas.

12. Sharing ideas and experiences through reflective writing helps students understand themselves and others, which in turn can help them make better and more thoughtful decisions.

13. Students should respond to each others' journal and reflective writings using aesthetic responses.

14. Students can begin to perceive a certain universality of experience and understand each other at deeper levels by sharing journal entries.

15. Power writes and free verse can both be used to enhance learning in social studies.

Making Connections

1. Describe the best book or some of the best books you have read.

2. Describe a book that has helped you understand a person or people, a situation or condition, a time period, a culture, or an event.

3. Why is it important to include writing as part of social studies?

4. Visit one of the websites listed in this chapter and find three to five books you might use with a social studies unit.

5. What approach to using literature in social studies appeals to you more: the textbook-driven approach or the literature-driven approach? Why?

6. What idea related to this chapter would you like to explore and write about?

7. Do a power write using the prompt: social studies and learning. Share your ideas with three others in a small group. After sharing, look for one large idea, insight, or inspiration to share with others.

8. What are two to five interesting or important ideas you will take from this chapter?

9. Create a picture or a diagram to hold or describe an idea from this chapter.

10. Create a free verse poem to illustrate an idea related to education or learning.

11. In what ways do you see the three holistic learning ideas related to intrapersonal connections, interpersonal connections, and interconnectedness reflected here?

Chapter 16

CHARACTER EDUCATION

1. What do you associate with character education? What do you associate with values education?

2. What values should be taught to our students to help them become good citizens?

3. What is a good citizen?

4. How would you define morality?

5. How might the issue of morality be addressed in a public school?

The schools should be helping the children to look within themselves, and from this self-knowledge derive a set of values.

—Maslow, 1971, p. 185

DEFINING CHARACTER AND CHARACTER EDUCATION

Any discussion about *character education* starts with a definition of *character*. The operational definition used for this chapter focuses on *ethics* or the positive moral qualities that motivate and guide one's life. Most would agree that people of good moral character have qualities such as honesty, generosity, courage, fortitude, acceptance, and compassion. (Positive character traits are called *virtues*.) These are all qualities that serve to nurture oneself and others. Most would also agree that people of bad moral character have qualities such as selfishness, sloth, greed, anger, hatred, ignorance, and pride. These are qualities that serve to take from or harm oneself and others. To develop character then is to develop ethics that are used to guide one's thoughts, words, and actions. Exactly what these ethical qualities are will always be open to discussion; however, as will be seen below, there are certainly plenty from which to choose.

Another term that comes up in relation to character and character education is the word *integrity*. Integrity comes from the word *integrate*. Integrity is the integration of one's *values* with one's thoughts, words, and actions. People who act with integrity have defined their values and have integrated them into their *philosophy*. A philosophy is one's personal belief system about how to live and deal with situations. To act with integrity is to align yourself with your values and operate from your philosophy. Thus, an important first step in character education is to help students define and describe what it is they value.

Here is the sticky wicket in this whole business of character education: Character and integrity are internal states reflected outward. Too often "character education" is perceived as an external state reflected inward. That is, people think it is simply a matter of telling students how they must behave and what they must do or refrain from doing. The mistaken assumption here is that students will internalize and embrace a set of values based on their conformity to an external set of behaviors. Instead, if the focus is on embracing positive values first, it is much more likely that positive behaviors will follow. And, while it is important to describe and pass on our values to students, ultimately they must come to identify and embrace their own set of values. In this way, they will be more apt to act on these values in all aspects of their lives.

Character education then can be defined as instruction, planned experiences, and activities that are designed to help students identify and integrate a set of positive character traits and to develop ethical qualities based on their values. And to be teachers of character, we must first be students of character. That is, we need to identify our values and ethics, then look to see how and to what degree these are manifest (or not) in our behaviors. This is part of being a reflective teacher, one who continually asks, "What are my values? What ethical qualities reflect my values? Are my behaviors in alignment with my values? What is my educational philosophy? Is my educational practice in alignment with this philosophy? Are my thoughts, words, and actions reflective of the values and ethical qualities I have embraced? Do the curriculum and my educational practice represent my values?"

Character education helps students identify and integrate a set of positive character traits and develop ethical qualities based on their values.

VIRTUES AND ETHICAL CODES

The terms *virtues* and *values* are often used interchangeably; however, a value is more encompassing. It is anything that you find of worth or importance (see below). A virtue, as described above, is a positive character trait such as bravery, courage, compassion, or respect. World religions serve as good sources to use in identifying virtues or ethical codes to use for character education. And, as described in Chapter 2, you can address religions in a public school setting; but you cannot promote or denigrate a particular religion or religious view. Below are some of the virtues and ethical codes taken from various religions and from other sources as well. It is helpful in presenting a global view for students to see that ethics and morality are not germane to, or the privileged domain of, any one particular religion or religious view.

Hinduism—The Yamas

The Yamas are an ethical code that arises out of Hinduism.

1. **Ahimsa—Nonviolence**. *Nurture and sustain all living creatures.* This is the practice of doing no harm. Abstain from injuring other living creatures. Avoid negative or harmful thoughts, words, or deeds that may harm or cause pain to another.

2. **Satya—Truthfulness**. *Be truthful in word and thought.* Your words and thoughts should conform to the facts. Do not conceive or unnecessarily keep secrets.

3. **Asteya—Non-stealing**. *Use only what belongs to you.* Do no take from others, steal, enter into debt, or covet what another has. Do not gain at the expense of another.

4. **Brahmacharya—Continence**. *Seek always to give to another in relationships.* Control lust when single and be faithful when married. Be restrained in thought, word, and deed. Reject sexuality that uses or degrades.

5. **Kshama—Patience**. *Be patient in regard to people and circumstances.* Do not be ruled by time; function in the here and now. Remain poised and good-natured. Do not dominate conversations or interrupt others. Let others behave according to their nature. Accept people for who they are; do not try to change them.

6. **Dhriti—Perseverance or fortitude**. *Be steadfast in pursuing a goal or completing a task.* Develop willpower, discipline, and persistence in working toward that which you are trying to achieve. Do not give up or be distracted. Do not give up or be put aside by fear or failure.

7. **Daya—Compassion**. *Practice compassion and be compassionate.* Seek to understand others without judgment. Be kind to all people, animals, and plant life. Assist the weak, the poor, the sick, the elderly, and the very young. Stand up for those who are suffering. Oppose those who abuse or take advantage of others. Stand against cruelty and hate.

8. **Arjava—Honesty**. *Be honest in your daily work.* Act with honor and dignity at all times. Obey the laws. Do not cheat, accept bribes, or try to take shortcuts. Be honest to yourself as well as to others. Admit your mistakes. Take responsibility for your shortcomings without blaming others.

9. **Mitahara—Moderate appetite.** *Be wise and moderate in your diet.* Eat fresh, wholesome foods that vitalize the body. Avoid junk foods. Eat in moderation, at regular times, and only when hungry. Eat at a moderate pace, never between meals, and never in a disturbed atmosphere.

10. **Shaucha—Purity.** *Be pure and positive in mind, body, and speech.* Think positive, nourishing thoughts. Speak only to edify or uplift others. Do not use negative or harsh language. Do not gossip or speak ill of others. Keep a clean body, home, and workplace.

Buddhism—The Noble Eightfold Path

Buddhism tells us that joy, or the elimination of suffering, can be attained by following the Nobel Eightfold Path.

1. **Right view—Optimistic.** We perceive the world as a positive, nurturing place, both internally and externally. We are hopeful. We are able to distinguish between that which is positive and nurturing and that which is negative or destructive.

2. **Right thinking—Positive attitude.** We cultivate only positive thoughts that nurture self and others. We do not think negatively about ourselves, others, or situations.

3. **Right mindedness—Acceptance.** We are nonjudgmental in our attitudes. We accept without judgment ourselves and others. Also, we do not use our belief systems to determine what data or information is true; rather we determine what we believe based on data and information.

4. **Right speech—Nurturing words.** We speak only to edify or we say only positive things. Does speech build up self and others? We do not criticize, gossip, or tear down another.

5. **Right action—Nonviolence.** We seek to nurture in all that we do. We avoid that which causes harm to self and others.

6. **Right diligence—Fortitude.** We do not give up in pursuing those tasks we consider worthy. Also, our actions are motivated by that which is best for our selves, others, and the environment.

7. **Right concentration—Contemplation.** We are able to focus on the moment. We do not hold onto past thoughts, hurts, or transgression. We are able to calm the mind. We allow silence both internally and externally.

8. **Right livelihood—Integrity.** We find a way to live or earn our living in which we do not transgress our ideals. We love and nurture through our occupation.

Buddhism—Wholesome and Unwholesome Seeds

The Buddhist mystic, Thich Nhat Hanh (1998) says we have both positive and negative traits within. He describes it as having both wholesome and unwholesome seeds within our store consciousness. The wholesome seeds uplift and help us transform our suffering. These are traits such as humility, self-respect, noncraving, nonanger, concentration, diligence, equanimity, and nonviolence. The unwholesome seeds are heavy and imprison us. These are traits such as anger, greed, hatred, ignorance, pride, and doubt.

We have a choice in every situation as to which seeds receive our attention and thus, become watered. Seeds create emotional states from which thoughts arise. Thought precedes action, thus, the fourth step of the Buddhist Noble Eightfold Path, right action (good), is dependent on our attention (right-mindedness and contemplation). Focusing on internal states is an important part of helping people to acquire the behaviors that nurture the self, others, and the environment.

Christianity and Judaism—The Ten Commandments

The Ten Commandments are accepted by both Judaism and Christianity as being of divine origin. In looking at the first three commandments of the traditional version (see Figure 16.1), you can see why it is problematic to have these displayed in a secular setting. Figure 16.1 contains the traditional version of The Ten Commandments as well as several other variations.

Christianity—The Beatitudes

The beatitudes in Christian tradition are very similar to the Noble Eightfold Path in Buddhism in that it contains advice for addressing disposition or state of mind.

1. *Blessed are the poor in spirit, for theirs is the kingdom of heaven.* **Inner-directedness.** We have an internal locus of control. We are not consumed by chasing external rewards or possessions. We do not covet what another has. We are satisfied to live in the moment. We know that happiness ultimately comes from within.

2. *Blessed are those who mourn, for they shall be comforted.* **Empathy.** We notice, understand, and feel the suffering of others.

3. *Blessed are the meek, for they shall inherit the earth.* **Humility.** We do not think we have all the answers. We are humble and willing to listen to others.

4. *Blessed are those who hunger and thirst for righteousness, for they shall be satisfied.* **Self-reflection and integrity.** We seek to discover our values and our philosophy and we try to align our thoughts, words, and deeds with our values and philosophy.

5. *Blessed are the merciful, for they shall obtain mercy.* **Forgiving.** We nurture those around us in thought, word, and deed and we do not hang on to perceived wrongdoings.

6. *Blessed are the pure in heart, for they shall see God.* **Positive thinking.** Our mind and our words generate unconditional positive regard (love) for all. We water positive seeds within stored consciousness. We do not dwell on negative things.

7. *Blessed are the peacemakers, for they shall be called sons of God.* **Harmony.** We seek collaboration, cooperation, and relationship instead of competition and gain at the expense of others.

8. *Blessed are those who are persecuted for righteousness sake, for theirs is the Kingdom of Heaven.* **Courage and fortitude.** We identify and stand up for our values and ideals. We speak out and act against that which is harmful to others.

Figure 16.1   Various Versions of the Ten Commandments

*The Traditional Version
of the Ten Commandments*

1. Have no other gods before Me [the God of the Hebrews].

2. Make no images of anything in heaven, earth or the sea, and do not worship or labor for them.

3. Do not take God's name in vain.

4. Do no work on the seventh day of the week.

5. Honor your parents.

6. Do not kill.

7. Do not commit adultery.

8. Do not steal.

9. Do not give false testimony against another.

10. Do not covet or desire anything that belongs to another.

Native American Ten Commandments

This has been published in many places on the Internet. The author is unknown:

1. Treat the Earth and all that dwell thereon with respect.

2. Remain close to the Great Spirit.

3. Consider the impact on the next six generations when making decisions.

4. Work together to benefit all humanity.

5. Freely give help and kindness wherever needed.

6. Do what you believe to be right.

7. Look after the well-being of your mind and body.

8. Contribute a share of your efforts to the greater good.

9. Be truthful and honest at all times.

10. Take full responsibility for your actions.

Ten Commandments of Solon

Solon was an Athenian who is believed to have been born around 638 BCE. Some would also believe him to be the founder of Western democracy.

1. Trust good character more than promises.

2. Do not speak falsely.

3. Do good things.

4. Do not be hasty in making friends, but do not abandon them once made.

5. Learn to obey before you command.

6. When giving advice, do not recommend what is most pleasing, but what is most useful.

7. Make reason your supreme commander.

Ten Commandments for Humanists

This is believed to have been written by the Long Island Secular Humanists in 1999.

We, the members of the human community speak these words, saying

1. We shall not limit freedom of thought.

2. We shall not cause unnecessary harm to any living thing or the environment.

3. We shall be respectful of the rights of others.

4. We shall be honest.

5. We shall be responsible for our actions.

6. We shall be fair in all matters to all persons.

7. We shall be considerate of the happiness and well-being of others.

8. We shall be reasonable in our actions.

(Continued)

Figure 16.1 (Continued)

Ten Commandments of Solon	Ten Commandments for Humanists
8. Do not associate with people who do bad things. 9. Honor the gods. 10. Have regard for your parents.	9. We shall nurture these values by word and deed in our children, family, friends, and acquaintances. 10. We shall not limit inquiring or testing by their consequences, on any matter, including these Commandments.
	A Secular Version of the Ten Commandments 1. Recognize the interconnectedness of all things. 2. Do not make a god of human endeavors or other things such as work, money, status, fame, power, religion, rock stars, movie stars, politics, government, academia, logic, or science. 3. Use your intuitions, as well as your emotions, knowledge, and reason in solving problems, making decisions, and coming to know the world. 4. Take time for rest, relaxation, and play. 5. Honor your parents. 6. Do not seek to harm others with your thoughts, words, and deeds. 7. Be honest and seek only to nurture in your intimate relationships. 8. Do not take what is not yours or seek to gain at the expense of another. 9. Be truthful to yourself and others in your communication, seeking never to deceive or mislead. 10. Happiness is found within, not in the possessions or position of another.

Islam—Character and Life Skills

In their conceptual framework for Islamic education, the Islamic Education Strategic Unit (2004) identified the following life skills related to character and character education:

Early—Primary Grades

1. Obey your parents.

2. Respect and listen to elders.

3. Help and serve others, at home and in the community. This is part of developing community and giving to the greater whole.

4. Be honest and truthful with others.

5. Be polite and kind to others.

6. Share what you have with others.

7. Be courageous and brave in doing what must be done and standing up for what is right.

8. Be willing to give to those in need.

9. Be clean (hygiene: body, clothes), and orderly (put things away).

10. Eat only food that is good for you.

Basic—Intermediate Grades

1. Know yourself. Know and understand your emotions, intuitions, strengths, and limitations. This is related to intrapersonal intelligence, self-actualization, self-acceptance, and self-esteem.

2. Keep a positive attitude. Be optimistic and accepting in thought, word, and deed. Avoid negative thoughts, gossip, or cutting humor. Be cheerful and hopeful, and be a good sport.

3. Care for others. Develop the habit of giving and service. Be kind and generous with your talents, your time, and your resources.

4. Be clean. Cleanliness is related to habits, neatness, personal hygiene, and thoughts.

5. Respect others. Be polite and courteous to all.

6. Honesty. Be fair and trustworthy. Be sincere and genuine in what you say and do.

Teens—Middle School

1. Find a purpose. Develop vision or goals for your life, both short term and long term. Decide to stand for something.

2. Make good choices and be accountable for your actions. Make decisions based on your values, accept the consequences, and be responsible for your choices.

3. Be responsible. Honor your commitments. Do what you promise to do. Be organized and punctual so that others can depend on you.

4. Develop positive relationships. Be honest and kind to all. Devote time and attention to family, friends, yourself, and others.

5. Solve problems. Learn to solve your own problems. Be resourceful and self-reliant in making decisions and solving problems.

6. Be self-disciplined. Develop discipline and self-control, avoid things that are harmful, and do those things that nurture self and others.

7. Be healthy. Choose activities and habits that are healthy for you physically, mentally, and emotionally.

8. Be conservative in your use of resources. Be thrifty and moderate in your use of money, material, and other resources.

Baha'i Faith—Six Virtues

Below are six virtues described in the Baha'i faith (Esslemont, 1980):

1. Service to others.

2. Courtesy and reverence.

3. Nonjudgment. Abstain from faultfinding.

4. Humility.

5. Truthfulness and honesty.

6. Self-realization. Find and give full expression to one's true inner nature. Find and develop your talents.

Native American—Teaching Virtues

In their book, *Teaching Virtues: Building Character across the Curriculum* (2001), Don Jacobs and his daughter, Jessica Jacobs-Spencer, present a holistic approach to character education from a Native American perspective. In this book, they have identified nine virtues and then created activities that go across all curriculum areas. These nine virtues are

1. **Fortitude.** This virtue allows a person to endure pain or adversity in order to complete a task. This is about not quitting or giving up, about sticking to something that is worthwhile.

2. **Courage.** Courage is a trait that keeps you moving forward even if you are afraid. It enables you to meet danger and take risks for a higher purpose. It also allows you to live your values regardless of the consequences.

3. **Patience.** A person who is patient is able to delay gratification or to wait good-naturedly for an intended outcome. Patient people are more understanding and forgiving of others as they make mistakes, and thus more understanding and forgiving of themselves.

Patience is also the disposition or mind-set that allows one to take baby steps to a larger goal without losing hope.

4. **Honesty.** An honest person is truthful about what he or she says, does not willingly mislead others, does not take that which belongs to another, and tries to conduct personal or business transactions in a way that is open and does not deceive. An honest person is truthful about things that matter, and honest people are willing to reflect and be truthful with themselves.

5. **Humility.** A humble person does not assume he or she is better than or knows more than others. A humble person is therefore willing and able to listen to others. Humility allows one to let go of preconceptions and avoid arrogance, pride, and boasting.

6. **Generosity.** Be generous or give to others. Do not cling to material possessions or put their value over people and relationships. Avoid greed and selfishness.

7. **Spirituality.** Become aware of and respect the mysterious connections between self, others, nature, the environment, and all aspects of the universe. Recognize the sacred nature of these relationships and interconnections.

8. **Integrity.** Integrate your values and beliefs with your thoughts, words, and deeds. Adhere to the virtues described here even when nobody is looking.

9. **Peacefulness.** Calm the mind. Avoid that which causes agitation. Allow for moments of quiet, contemplation, or meditation. Look for peaceful relationships in all things. Avoid confrontation and militarism at all costs.

Unitarian Universalist—Statement of Principles

Unitarian Universalists seek to affirm and promote the following:

1. The inherent worth and dignity of every person.

2. Justice, equity, and compassion in human relations.

3. Acceptance of one another and encouragement in spiritual growth.

4. A free and responsible search for truth and meaning.

5. The right of conscience and the use of the democratic process.

6. The goal of world community with peace, liberty, and justice for all.

7. Respect for the interdependent web of all existence of which we are part.

Humanist—Five Ethical Principles

Humanism is not a religion; rather it is a philosophy or a worldview. Humanists have five ethical principles that they believe should be the basis of ethical conduct:

1. Abstain from conduct injurious to life and the physical well-being of persons. **Nonviolence.**

2. Abstain from the theft of property of others. **Honesty.**

3. Abstain from sexual violence and misconduct. **Continence.**

4. Abstain from falsehood, fraud, and deception. **Truthfulness.**

5. Abstain from drunkenness, narcotics, and mind-bending drugs. **Sobriety, contemplation,** or **right-mindedness.**

Moral Intelligence—Seven Virtues

In her book, *Building Moral Intelligence* (2001), Michele Borba has identified seven virtues that she feels are essential in helping children build moral intelligence. She defines moral intelligence as the capacity to understand right from wrong and the ability to act on that understanding. However, as we will see below, right and wrong are not always easily determined. The virtues that Borba depicts as essential for moral intelligence include the following:

1. **Empathy.** Ability to identify with other people's feelings and concerns.

2. **Conscience.** Knowing the right way to act and acting that way.

3. **Self-control.** Regulating your thoughts and actions to avoid internal or external pressure to act in ways you know are not right.

4. **Respect.** Treating yourself and others in a kind and considerate way that shows they are of value to you.

5. **Kindness.** Words and actions that demonstrate you care about the feelings and welfare of others.

6. **Tolerance.** Respecting the rights and dignity of all people, even those who have different beliefs and value systems.

7. **Fairness.** Being nonjudgmental and open-minded, acting impartially, and seeking justice.

TEACHERS IN ACTION: Character Education Quilts

I created a classroom quilt using ideas from character education and incorporated them into my discipline plan for the year. This was a great way to start the first week of school. After developing and discussing our discipline plan, each student received two quilt pieces. On each piece they needed to write three to five sentences and illustrate how they could show respect on one and responsibility on the other. The ideas ranged from respect to one another and other adults to responsibility for taking care of their work, homework, and things in school. When the pieces were finished, we mounted each square onto a colored and slightly larger square of construction paper. Students then laced yarn through pre-punched holes on the construction paper squares. From there, we joined our quilt together on a bulletin board with the title, "Character Counts!" This was a spur-of-the-moment idea that "popped into my head" the day before school started. I wasn't sure how it would turn out, but it was really a lovely bulletin board display that I kept up until conference time in November! (Also, it was a great way to refer students back to their September commitments.)

—Anonymous Teacher, Fourth Grade

Author Reflection: We don't have to make this whole character education thing so gosh darn complicated. Keep it simple. Just pick three to eight virtues or positive character traits and then focus on them during the year (it's always good to include parents in this selection). It works best if a whole school can commit to a set. Teach the virtues specifically, then incorporate them into lessons including history, current events, art, music, literature, and any other place in the curriculum that seems appropriate. Character education then becomes a continued conversation throughout the year and at all grade levels throughout the school.

Selecting and defining a set of virtues also helps your classroom or your school stand for something. You can then say, "These are our values. These are the ideals that we think are important. This is who we want to be. We want our words and our actions to reflect these things."

There is a difference between building character and insisting on conformity and compliance. People of good character act on a set of virtues. Sometimes these actions cause them to reject the norm, to be noncompliant and even defiant. Some people of character even manage to get quite a few people angry at them. Imagine that. Martin Luther, Maya Angelou, Maria Montessori, Rosa Parks, Martin Luther King, Dian Fossey, Malcolm X, and Hillary Clinton have all raised the ire of certain groups at different times. (Note that having character is different than being a perfect human being.) All of these people were willing to stand up to those who tried to silence them or make them conform in some way.

What is your response to the case? How do your reactions compare with the author's reflection?

VALUES EDUCATION

As alluded to above, a *value* is a trait, quality, entity, practice, virtue, or experience that you deem important or of worth. A virtue is one form of a value. It is a positive character trait or a *personal value* related to ethics. Part of values education is teaching students about virtues. Which ones? It is possible for schools to identify certain virtues with which most would agree and then teach them (Hoffman, 1993). These might include any of the virtues described above or others such as creativity, loyalty, hard work, cooperation, participation, responsibility, humor, imagination, friendship, confidence, loyalty, assertiveness, dignity, freedom, equalitarianism, equality of all, or resourcefulness. These are all virtues that can be taught explicitly without alienating most groups within a community.

In teaching about virtues, you cannot assume that your students have full knowledge of these words or concepts; therefore, teaching should always begin with a definition and direct instruction (Ellis, 2002). Figure 16.2 shows an example of a values lesson related to a virtue.

Eight Values Clarification Activities

Values clarification is a pedagogical strategy that can be effectively used within a values education context. There has been much confusion and misunderstanding about this strategy in recent years. Contrary to what some groups report, values clarification activities are not

Figure 16.2   Values Lesson Plan

A Values Lesson on Compassion

Grade Level: 5

Objective: Students will learn about compassion.

Introduction:

A value is a trait or characteristic that a person thinks is important. Compassion is one value that many people think is important.

Input:

1. Compassion means caring and wanting to help people in need.

2. Compassionate people notice people who need help.
   A. They understand or can image what it is like to be in a similar situation.
   B. They want to help them.

3. Compassionate people understand and care for others.
   A. They care for the feelings of others.
   B. They care for the health and safety of others.

4. Compassionate people will not tease or make others feel bad.

5. Compassionate people try to understand others.
   A. They are friendly.
   B. They like all kinds of people.
   C. They have lots of friends.

6. Compassionate people make good doctors, teachers, and friends.

Activities:

Small Group Activity

1. In our story *Bridge to Terabithia* (Paterson, 1977), you've encountered several characters so far.
   A. Jess, Leslie, May Belle, Miss Edmunds, and Mrs. Myers.

2. In your group, which of the characters would you like to encounter if you were in trouble or need? Which would you least like to encounter?
   A. Be prepared to describe the traits of each character.
   B. Tell why you picked them.

Individual Activity

1. In your journal, write the statement, "Jess Aaron is a compassionate person."

2. Gather information to support that statement.

3. Describe a real-life person who you think is compassionate.

4. (If time)—Describe an example of compassion that you have witnessed or experienced in your life.

values-free. That is, this strategy does not put forth the idea that there is no right or wrong. It also does not dismiss or demean virtues, ethics, or personal accountability. Instead, values clarification activities help students identify, analyze, and elucidate their own values. This is much more powerful and lasting than simply telling students what they should value or how they should behave, although there are times when it may be appropriate to do just this.

Values clarification activities usually involve defining, listing, ranking, or rating things that students value. These activities come in many different forms, but they should have some or all of the following four characteristics:

- Students' insights and ideas are respected. Teachers do not correct, evaluate, or validate students' responses.
- Students are free to make choices. Teachers do not lead students toward a predetermined choice or response.
- There is a discussion or sharing of ideas either before or after the activity.
- Students are encouraged to consider both the positive and negative consequences of their choices.

Below are ideas for possible values clarification activities. Keep in mind the developmental level of your students in adapting each activity to your particular students and teaching situation.

Define that which is valued. Students list or define five to ten things that they value. You could do this in a number of different categories such as: material things, virtues, personal characteristics, experiences, activities, or people. A common starting activity is to have them list five physical objects they value. After sharing their lists, in small groups or in a journal, ask students what their valued objects might say about them or who they are.

In subsequent lessons, have students list or define what they value related to friendship traits, jobs or occupations, social skills, amendments in the U.S. Bill of Rights, citizenship responsibilities, student responsibilities, student rights, human rights, topics of interests, leisure activities, entertainment options, books, TV shows, or movies. These should always be followed by some sort of processing activity where students are asked, "What does this tell you about who you are and what you value?" Any of these activities can be extended by asking students to rank the items in their lists from most important to least important and having them justify or support their top choices.

Ranking personal values or virtues. Given a list of personal values or virtues such as honesty, compassion, and hard work; ask students to rank them from most important to least. They should then describe their reasons for picking their top two values. This works well as a small group activity because it always invites great conversation. The answers students come up with are not nearly as important as the preceding conversation. It is in conversation that students must clarify and communicate that which they value as well as listen to and learn from others.

Ranking experiences. In a large group, generate a list of present or future experiences that students find enjoyable such as playing football, getting a driver's license, eating dinner with the family, or talking with friends. Individually or in a small group, ask students to rank them from most important to them to least important. They should then describe their reasons for picking their top two experiences. This kind of activity helps you to understand your students and see what is of value to them. Make sure you do not diminish students' choices here.

Ranking decisions. Present your students with a description of a problem or a decision that must be made in a particular situation. This problem or decision can be taken from current events, history, or science, or from a trade book, story, television show, or movie (see Chapter 10). Then give students three to eight solutions or decisions relative to this problem. Ask them to rate or rank the decisions and to describe the value reflected in their top choice. This lesson can be extended on subsequent days by having students generate a list of their own solutions or decisions. They can also rank their solutions from most compassionate to least, most effective to least, most economic to least, most enjoyable to least, etc.

Virtue reflected by choices. Give or have your students find an example of a choice or an action made by a person or character in a story, in history, or in current events. Using the thinking skill *inference* (see Chapter 12), have students describe the virtue reflected by the choice or action. For younger children, you may need to provide a list of virtues from which to choose.

Virtues determine choices. Give or have your students find an example of a choice or action that must be made by a person or character in a story, in history, or in current events. Then give them three personal values or virtues. In small groups, have students determine and describe a choice that would reflect each virtue. For example, what would the compassionate choice be? What would the humble choice be? What would be a courageous choice?

Considering the consequences. Present your students with a description of a problem or a decision that must be made in a particular situation. Give or have students identify three solutions or choices and ask them to describe both the positive and negative consequences of each (see Chapter 10, Figure 10.6). Then have students rank the decisions or solutions.

HOW DO I? Extend Values Clarification Activities

The values clarification activities above can be done individually by students. They can also be extended for use in small groups. When doing small group values clarification activities, have your students generate and list some of their own ideas on a sheet of paper or in a learning log before joining the group. This ensures that each group has a diverse set of ideas with which to work. The group is then able to generate additional ideas and come to a consensus as to their top choice or choices. For example, after sharing their own lists of personal traits that they value, students would then try to find three or four important traits with which their whole group can agree. Keep in mind that the lists or answers students come up with is not as important as the thinking and discussion that occur during the decision-making process. By being actively engaged in this thinking and reasoning process, students are able to identify and define their own sense of values.

Thinking Skills Applications in Values Education

Chapter 12 describes how to use both creative and critical thinking skills to enhance learning. The following activities incorporate thinking skills to help students begin to form or identify their own personal values or virtues.

Fluency. In small groups, ask students to brainstorm to find different examples of a particular virtue from their lives, literature, history, or current events. Example: Self-discipline is a virtue. Generate examples of instances where you or other people have demonstrated this trait.

Flexibility. Using an action from literature, history, current events, or students' lives, have students find alternative actions which demonstrate a particular virtue. Example: In the story "The Three Little Pigs," what might have happened if all three of the pigs had all cooperated in building their houses?

Originality. Have your students create an advertising campaign along with brochures, posters, or TV commercials to promote a particular personal value or virtue.

Compare. Have your students find an example of people who embody a particular virtue. These people can be selected from students' lives, literature, history, or current events. Use the compare-o-graph in Figure 16.3 to have students list interesting or important traits, life events, or experiences in the column under each person's name. Then look for commonalities.

Figure 16.3   Compare-O-Graph for Looking at Common Experiences

Virtue	Sally Ride	Leonora Marie (Kearney) Barry	Margaret Mead
Courage			

Commonalities:

1.

2.

3.

Compare and contrast. Give your students or have them find an example of a person who embodies a particular virtue. This person might be famous or local, currently living or from history, real or from a book, movie, or TV show. Then students use a comparison chart to examine the similarities and differences in life events or traits between themselves and the selected person (see Chapter 12, Figure 12.10).

Support a statement. Make a value statement regarding a famous person found in current events, literature, or history. For example, "Ruth Bader Ginsburg has great fortitude." Then have students find clues or information to support this statement. Use the support-a-statement graphic organizer to help students gather and organize information (see Figure 16.4).

Figure 16.4　　Support-a-Statement

Statement	Supporting Information
Judge Ginsburg has great fortitude.	

GO THERE

- Character Education Network: http://www.charactered.net/
- A variety of lesson plans and web sites for character education: http://www.uen .org/utahlink/activities/view_activity.cgi?activity_id'5399
- Character education resources: http://www.goodcharacter.com/
- Center for the Advancement of Ethics and Character: http://www.bu.edu/education/ caec/
- Character based lessons: www.choiceskills.com
- Teaching compassion: TEACHkind.org

Teaching for Wisdom

Robert Sternberg (2001) advocates that teaching for wisdom be a part of our curriculums. He defines wisdom as the application of tacit knowledge, mediated by values, toward the goal of achieving a common good through a balance of interests. To expand on this slightly, wisdom could be defined as the ability to solve problems or create products that nurture self, others, and the environment. In teaching for wisdom, all students would learn to develop their talents and abilities for this purpose. Sternberg's suggestions for developing wisdom in the classroom are listed in Figure 16.5.

Figure 16.5   Sternberg's Suggestions for Teaching for Wisdom

1. Provide students with problems that require wisdom to solve.

2. Help students think in terms of the common good when solving problems.

3. Teach students to balance their own interests with those of other people and institutions.

4. Provide examples of and analyze wise thinking in the past.

5. Use think-alouds or verbal protocols to model wisdom for students.

6. Help students think dialectically (think on both sides of an issue).

7. Show students that you value wise problem solving through recognition and reinforcement.

8. Link learning to students' lives by encouraging them to carry their learning outside the classroom.

Moral behavior is that which nurtures or gives to self, other people, and the environment.

MORALITY IN EDUCATION

Values and virtues are different from morality. *Morality* is a code of behavior based on a set of values. Just as each individual has different values, so there are many different concepts of morality and moral behavior. This section examines how morality might be addressed within a public school setting.

Defining Moral Behaviors

A traditional definition of morality is that it is the act of conforming to the rules of right conduct. *Moral behaviors* then are those actions that fall within the boundaries of what has been defined as correct behavior by a person, group, or institution. But the big question is who determined which behaviors were correct and which were incorrect. What criteria did they use? What were their motivations? How did the time period and the social customs of the day affect their thinking?

This big question leads to lots of little questions such as: Are there any behaviors that can be thought to be universally right and universally wrong in every situation? Is it okay to steal to save your family from starving? If a tax is unfair, is it okay to cheat on your tax returns so as not to pay it? If it is wrong to break a law, is it okay to drive 56 miles per hour when the speed limit is 55? If being thrifty or economical with our money is a good thing, is it okay to buy things made by prison labor in China? If capitalism is good, is it okay to destroy a wooded area to make profits through building a housing development? What should be done if only the affluent can afford proper drugs or medical care? If you are to be humane to plant and animal life, is it right to kill a turkey so that humans can enjoy a Thanksgiving dinner? Should you ignore or assist people in distant countries who are being oppressed and killed by their governments? Is it right to enforce the borders around our country so that we can keep all the jobs, money, and food while others on our planet starve?

As you can see, it gets very messy when you try to define morality strictly in terms of behaviors. One fairly objective definition of morality that can be used in a classroom is this: Any thought, behavior, or action can be said to be moral or right if it serves to nurture the self, others, and the environment (Johnson, 2003b). Any thought, behavior, or action can be said to be immoral if it serves to take from or harm the self, other people, or the environment. However, things are seldom black and white. In most situations you must determine what is the greatest good for the greatest number in order to determine a moral course of action.

Theories of Moral Development: Kohlberg and Gilligan

This section examines two theories of moral development: Lawrence Kohlberg's *Levels of Moral Reasoning* and Carol Gilligan's *Stages of the Ethics of Care.* Both of these theories have come under criticism in recent years for a variety of reasons. The usual complaint is that the studies upon which they are based were not valid or reliable. However, these theories should not be used to predict behavior, but to understand behavior. They can also be used to shape our discussion and subsequent thinking about moral reasoning.

Kohlberg's Levels of Moral Reasoning

Lawrence Kohlberg (1984) spent more than 20 years researching the moral development of children in different cultures throughout the world. Instead of behaviors, he looked at the reasoning or motivation behind those behaviors. He discovered moral sensitivity to be a characteristic found in all humans that develops through six stages. While these stages or levels are hierarchical, nobody responds from any one stage consistently; rather, responses fluctuate depending on circumstance. However, patterns of thought and behavior may indicate at which stage one's moral reasoning or motivation seems to predominate.

Level 1—Punishment. At this level of moral reasoning, your actions are determined by punishment and how to avoid it. Here morality is under external control. People are motivated not by what is right and good, but rather by what will help them to avoid an aversive conditioner or a bad circumstance. The problem with operating at this level is that when a belief system based on punishment disintegrates there are no internal structures in place to regulate behavior. That is, when the punishment is removed, behaviors appear again that had been controlled by it.

Level 2—Rewards. At this level, right action is determined by what will bring the greatest reward. People engage in behaviors in order to earn some sort of gratuity. Morality here is still under external control. The problem here is similar to that above. When the external rewards are extinguished, one's whole way of thinking, acting, and being are threatened. People operating at this stage experience extreme dissonance or a sense of meaninglessness when life suddenly becomes devoid of reinforcing external stimuli.

Level 3—Social approval. This is sometimes called the good-boy/good-girl stage. Here, right and wrong are determined by that which is approved by others or by social conformity. This level is prevalent in middle school and high school. Belonging to groups here can provide adolescents with a sense of identity and belonging; however, they are then dependent on the group for the development of a belief system and the related sense of self. And as you have seen in many instances, belief systems that arise out of groups tend not to nurture the self, others, or the environment. Instead, belief systems at the group level are more often aimed at conformity and allegiance.

Level 4—The law. Right and wrong at this level are determined by the laws and rules of a particular person, social group, institution, or religious order. The law or rule is the final say, the ultimate authority. However, morality here is still externally dependent. Autonomous thought is conceded to the law. Here, a computer could easily answer the great moral questions of the day. Behaviors either do or do not fall within certain parameters. You can also excuse wrongdoing or shed responsibility for your behavior, as the Nazis did after World War II, by saying they were just doing their duty or following the rule of the day. And, as you have seen time and again in our own country, laws are often wrong. What is legal and what is moral are often two different things.

Level 5—Social contract. This is the beginning of autonomous thought. People at this level agree to obey rules and laws in order to preserve social order; however, they realize the fallibility of these rules and laws. Laws are created based on what is perceived to be the greatest good for the greatest number of people at a particular time and place. However, lawmakers' perceptions are often influenced by other things, and situations often change. Thus, people operating at this level are usually willing to adhere to certain portions of the law for the betterment of society even though they may not necessarily agree with them. They recognize that every rule or law is meant to be a dynamic, changing entity and that they have a responsibility to work within the system so that the laws continually evolve in order to meet our highest good.

Level 6—Universal principle. This is the highest level of moral reasoning. Here you realize that truth is the final reality. Right action is determined by your conscience in accordance with a set of universal principles (or virtues) regardless of the consequences. These principles are generally those that accord honor, dignity, and worth to all humans, plant life, animal life, and ecosystems. Very few people operate at this level consistently, and those who do seem not to be tolerated by systems or institutions. Martin Luther King Jr., Malcolm X, Abraham Lincoln, and Gandhi are some examples here.

Gilligan's Stages of the Ethics of Care

One major criticism of Kohlberg, first made by Carol Gilligan (1982), is that his research excluded and devalued women's ways of moral reasoning. She asserted that his theories on moral development were put forth by a male, in a male dominated society, using only male subjects (Gilligan, 1998). Thus, his research often showed that females were inferior to males in their levels of moral reasoning. Using extensive interviews of females, Gilligan found that women have differing moral and psychological tendencies than men have. According to Gilligan, women tend to think of morality in terms of caring and relationships whereas men tend to think in terms of rules and justice. She argues, however, that it need not be an either/or proposition; rather, society should come to value both ways of thinking and seeing.

Stage I. Preconventional morality. The goal is individual survival. You look at what is best for yourself. For growth to occur there must be a transition from selfishness to responsibility to others.

Stage II. Conventional morality. At this stage, self-sacrifice is seen as goodness. You learn to care for others and that selfishness is wrong. For growth to occur there must be a transition from goodness to holistic truth. You realize that you are a person too.

Stage III. Postconventional morality. At this stage, you embrace the principle of nonviolence. You do not hurt others or yourself. You learn that it is just as wrong to ignore your own interests as it is to ignore the interests of others. You see that a connection or relation involves two people, and if either one is slighted, it harms the relationship. Many never reach this.

Activities for Stimulating Moral Reasoning

This section describes activities that can be used to enhance students' moral reasoning.

Behavior chart. Have your students look for examples of behavior on each of Kohlberg's or Gilligan's levels in a trade book, narrative text, textbook, current events, or history. The charts in Figure 16.6 are then used to record the behaviors. Using inference, students generate a conclusion or big idea based on their data.

Line graph. When reading a story in a trade book, ask students to list the actions of the lead character. Then use inference to decide the level of moral reasoning or stage of the ethics of care associated with each action. Finally, have students create a line graph to show these levels and how they changed over the course of the book.

Figure 16.6 Behavior Charts

Kohlberg Chart

Levels of Moral Reasoning	Behaviors
1. Punishment	
2. Rewards	
3. Social Approval	
4. The Law	
5. Social Contract	
6. Universal Principle	

Conclusions or big ideas:

Gilligan Chart

Stages of the Ethics of Care	Behaviors
1. Concern for Self	
2. Concern for Others	
3. Concern for All	

Conclusions or big ideas:

Analyzing levels, stages, and actions. Ask students to analyze a specific action found in books, current events, or history. Ask them to discuss and infer the possible moral reasoning the person or people might have used to decide on this action.

Moral dilemmas. Moral dilemmas are based on the idea that children develop the capacity for moral reasoning and advance more quickly to higher levels by practicing their reasoning skills and by hearing the thoughts and moral reasoning of other students. A moral dilemma is where students are given a real-life situation in which there is a dilemma, a decision, or a problem that must be solved. Students are then put into small groups of two to five students and asked to come to a consensus in finding an answer, solution, or decision. The answer is not as important as the reasoning that goes along with it. Teachers should float as unobtrusively as possible to get a sense of where students are at. Whenever possible, try to construct a moral dilemma that pertains to students' lives. And just as with the values clarification activities described above, teachers should not correct, evaluate, or validate students' responses and they should not lead students toward a predetermined choice or response.

EXAMPLE: Plagiarism Moral Dilemma

Mr. Atherton gives the following moral dilemma to groups of students in his 8th grade social studies class:

Pat has been getting up early to deliver newspapers in the mornings to make some extra money to buy some new basketball shoes. After school, Pat goes to basketball practice. This makes for a very long day and Pat is usually pretty tired by the time the family has finished supper in the evening. There is a big report due in Pat's social studies class; however, Pat has forgotten about it until the night before it is due. Pat is in a panic because this report is a big part of the final grade for the quarter. Pat's grades in other classes are not very good. If Pat doesn't earn a passing grade in this class, Pat will not be eligible to play basketball for the rest of the season because of academic eligibility requirements. In desperation, Pat goes on the Internet and finds a website that contains a report that meets most of the requirements of the assignment. It could easily be downloaded and copied, and with just a few changes Pat could hand it in. What should Pat do? What would your advice to Pat be?

When creating these types of moral dilemmas, Mr. Atherton tries, whenever possible, to use a gender-neutral name and to avoid including gender-identifying pronouns. Also, he uses a deck of cards and has students draw for groups of four. In this way, there are a variety of different types of groups, some fairly heterogeneous in terms of race, gender, and ability, while others are more homogeneous.

Students are given about 15 minutes to read through the problem and decide what they think Pat should do. At the end, one person is chosen to share their group's advice and supporting reasons with the class. After each group presents their ideas, Mr. Atherton opens this up for a whole class discussion.

> **GO THERE**
>
> Web sites containing moral dilemmas:
>
> www.friesian.com/valley/dilemmas.htm
>
> http://www.globalethics.org/resources/dilemmas.htm
>
> www.haverford.edu/psych/ddavis/p109g/kohlberg.dilemmas.html

Decision making. This is similar to some of the values clarification activities described above. Students examine a situation in which a decision must be made. They generate a list of possible decisions along with the positive and negative consequences of each. Students come to a consensus as to the best action and describe three reasons to support their decision. One student from each group shares their group's decision with the class. This activity exposes students to multiple perspectives and allows them to see the reasoning of others. This also helps them move more readily from one moral reasoning stage to another. The decision-making chart in Chapter 10, Figure 10.6, can be used here to gather and organize ideas.

NCSS STANDARDS

Thematic Standards

The following NCSS thematic standards are addressed in this chapter. See Appendix A for a full description of the relevant thematic standards.

Early Grades

I. Global Connections: f.

Middle Grades

I. Global Connections: f.

Pedagogical Standards

The following NCSS pedagogical standards are addressed in this chapter:

I. Critical Thinking, Problem Solving, and Performance Skills.

II. Reflection and Professional Growth.

Essential Skills for Social Studies

The following NCSS essential skills for social studies are addressed in this chapter:

I. Organizing & Using Information.
    A. Thinking Skills.
        1. classify information
        2. interpret information
        3. analyze information
        4. summarize information
        5. synthesize information
        6. evaluate information
    B. Decision-Making Skills.

II. Relationships & Social Participation.
    A. Personal Skills.

Chapter Review: Key Points

1. Ethics are the positive moral qualities used to guide and motivate one's life.

2. Positive character traits, called virtues, are those traits or dispositions that serve to nurture self, others, and the environment.

3. Integrity is the integration of one's values with one's thoughts, words, and actions.

4. One's philosophy is his or her personal belief system about how to live or deal with situations.

5. To act with integrity is to align yourself with your values and to operate from your philosophy.

6. Character education is the instruction, planned experiences, and activities that are designed to help students identify and integrate a set of positive character traits and to develop ethical qualities based on these values.

7. A virtue is a positive character trait such as kindness, courage, or discipline.

8. Many descriptions of important virtues or ethical codes can be found in various world religions and used in character education.

9. Values education is designed to help students identify, develop, and define their own sets of values.

10. A value is a trait, quality, entity, or experience that you deem important.

11. It is possible to identify a set of values with which most would agree and to teach them.

12. Values clarification activities have students define, list, rank, or rate some value or value-related entity such as a trait, quality, entity, or experience.

13. Morality is a code of behavior based on a set of values.

14. Just as individuals differ in what they value, so do individuals have different concepts of moral behavior.

15. According to Lawrence Kohlberg, moral reasoning occurs at six stages or levels: punishment, rewards, social approval, the law, social contract, and universal principle.

16. According to Carol Gilligan, there are three stages in the ethics of care: preconventional where one cares primarily for self, conventional where one cares primarily for others, and postconventional where one cares equally for self and others.

Making Connections

1. What are three individual ideals that you feel are important for a democratic society?

2. Pick one of the values and create a lesson plan that contains an objective, input, and an activity.

3. What is it exactly that you value? What experiences do you value? What traits do you value? What physical objects do you value?

4. Do one of the values clarification activities described in this chapter.

5. Design a lesson that uses one of the values clarification activities described in this chapter.

6. List eight rules for moral behavior that you think people should follow.

7. What general moral guidelines do you try to follow? Use a comparison chart to compare your guidelines with a classmate's.

8. Create or find a moral dilemma that could be used with middle school students.

9. Create or find a moral dilemma that could be used with 5th or 6th grade students, 3rd or 4th grade students, or 1st or 2nd grade students.

10. Find examples in your life when you have behaved at each of Kohlberg's six levels.

11. Find examples in your life when you have behaved at each of Gilligan's stages.

12. Look for an example of someone's behavior in the newspapers or news magazines. Speculate as to the person's motivation. Why did that person behave in that way? Which of Kohlberg's levels were they at?

13. If you had to create a list of ten positive behaviors that you would like all of humanity to display, what would they be?

14. In what ways do you see the three holistic learning ideas related to intrapersonal connections, interpersonal connections, and interconnectedness reflected here?

EPILOGUE

THE TEACHING QUATRAIN

The goal of this text is to enable you to become an effective teacher of social studies as well as other curriculum areas. Effective teaching involves four components: knowing, planning, doing, and reflecting.

Teaching = knowing + planning + doing + reflecting

1. Knowing. Having a cohesive body of knowledge related to social studies education as well as to teaching and learning will enable you to make thoughtful decisions about learning experiences. This body of knowledge will also help to ensure that the instructional approaches and teaching strategies you use are aligned with research-based theory and thus will be more likely to be effective in enhancing students' learning. Teacher preparation programs help preservice teachers begin to build an initial base of knowledge; however, more is needed. Inservice teachers often use professional journals, workshops, conferences, action research projects, professional dialogue and discussion groups, and graduate courses to expand and refine their base of knowledge. Master teachers continue to build and expand their knowledge bases throughout their teaching careers.

2. Planning. Effective lessons rarely happen by accident. Effective teachers plan their learning experiences. This planning allows you to link the knowing and doing parts of this equation. One cannot be effective without the other. And while it is important to be flexible by going with the teachable moment and allowing for interesting tangents, these teachable moments and interesting tangents are more likely to occur when there is purpose and a plan. Planning creates more purposeful and effective instruction and results in fewer behavior management issues.

3. Doing. The third element involves the effective implementation of the lesson plan. In the planning phase you defined a body of information, important concepts, or a set of skills that you want students to learn. In the doing phase you must decide how students can best learn these things. How can you present things in a meaningful way? How will you get students actively involved in learning? What activities will you use to reinforce or practice these things? How much instruction will you give? What will you do to ensure understanding? How will you differentiate instruction to meet the special needs of the very able learner and the less able learner? Master teachers have a toolbox full of pedagogical skills, strategies, techniques, and classroom activities that can be used toward these ends. Every chapter of this book contains a variety of strategies and activities that can be used to enhance the implementation and effectiveness of your lessons.

4. Reflecting. Finally, reflection allows teachers to make changes in the other three components and thus enhance their effectiveness (Watts & Johnson, 1995). It is the act of reflection that separates a very effective teacher from a less effective teacher. Being an effective teacher does not mean that you do not make mistakes or have bad lessons. (If teachers never make mistakes it often means that they have not experimented or tried anything new.) Effective teachers reflect in order to determine what went wrong and how the lesson might be changed. Less effective teachers simply blame the students, the curriculum, the weather, or parents when a lesson goes badly. Knowing that effective teachers make mistakes and have bad lessons on occasion, hopefully you will feel more comfortable in experimenting with some of the new ideas and techniques in this book.

IMPROVING EDUCATION

Teachers are the most significant variable in determining the quality of education students receive; yet, this variable is often ignored when it comes to discussions about improving the quality of education. To improve education, we do *not* need more tests, expensive programs, elaborate curriculum, or more externally imposed mandates. Instead, we need more caring and knowledgeable teachers. As teachers improve, so too does education. Best wishes to you. I would be most interested in hearing from you. Send your comments to:

Andrew P. Johnson, Ph.D.
Minnesota State University, Mankato
313 Armstrong Hall
Mankato, MN 56001
Email: andrew.johnson@mnsu.edu
www.teachergrowth.com

APPENDIX A

Disciplinary Standards for History, Geography, Civics and Government, and Economics

I. History

STANDARDS IN HISTORICAL THINKING FOR GRADES K–4

Standard 1. Chronological Thinking

    A. Distinguish between past, present, and future time.

    B. Identify the temporal structure of a historical narrative or story.

    C. Establish temporal order in constructing students' own historical narratives.

    D. Measure and calculate calendar time.

    E. Interpret data presented in time lines.

    F. Create time lines.

    G. Explain change and continuity over time.

Standard 2. Historical Comprehension

    A. Identify the author or source of the historical document or narrative.

    B. Reconstruct the literal meaning of a historical passage.

    C. Identify the central question(s) the historical narrative addresses.

    D. Read historical narratives imaginatively.

    E. Appreciate historical perspectives.

    F. Draw upon data in historical maps.

    G. Draw upon visual and mathematical data presented in graphs.

    H. Draw upon the visual data presented in photographs, paintings, cartoons, and architectural drawings.

Standard 3. Historical Analysis and Interpretation

A. Formulate questions to focus their inquiry or analysis.

B. Compare and contrast differing sets of ideas, values, personalities, behaviors, and institutions.

C. Compare different stories about a historical figure, era, or event.

D. Analyze illustrations in historical stories.

E. Consider multiple perspectives.

F. Explain causes in analyzing historical actions.

G. Hypothesize influences of the past.

Standard 4. Historical Research Capabilities

A. Formulate historical questions.

B. Obtain historical data.

C. Integrate historical data.

D. Marshal needed knowledge of the time and place, and construct a story, explanation, or historical narrative.

Standard 5. Historical Issues—Analysis and Decision Making

A. Identify problems and dilemmas in the past.

B. Analyze the interests and values of the various people involved.

C. Identify causes of the problem or dilemma.

D. Propose alternative choices for addressing the problem.

E. Formulate a position or course of action on an issue.

F. Identify the solution chosen.

G. Evaluate the consequences of a decision.

STANDARDS IN HISTORY FOR GRADES K–4

Topic 1. Living and Working Together in Families and Communities, Now and Long Ago

- Standard 1. Family Life Now and in the Recent Past; Family Life in Various Places Long Ago
- Standard 2. The History of Students' Own Local Community and How Communities in North America Varied Long Ago

Topic 2. The History of Students' Own State or Region

- Standard 3. The People, Events, Problems, and Ideas that Created the History of Their State

Topic 3. The History of the United States. Democratic Principles and Values and the People From Many Cultures Who Contributed to Its Cultural, Economic, and Political Heritage

- Standard 4. How Democratic Values Came to Be, and How They Have Been Exemplified by People, Events, and Symbols
- Standard 5. The Causes and Nature of Various Movements of Large Groups of People Into and Within the United States, Now and Long Ago
- Standard 6. Regional Folklore and Culture Contributions That Helped To Form Our National Heritage

Topic 4. The History of Peoples of Many Cultures Around the World

- Standard 7. Selected Attributes and Historical Developments of Various Societies in Africa, the Americas, Asia, and Europe
- Standard 8. Major Discoveries in Science and Technology, Their Social and Economic Effects, and the Scientists and Inventors Responsible for Them

STANDARDS IN HISTORICAL THINKING FOR GRADES 5–12

Standard 1. Chronological Thinking

A. Distinguish between past, present, and future time.

B. Identify in historical narratives the temporal structure of a historical narrative or story.

C. Establish temporal order in constructing historical narratives of their own.

D. Measure and calculate calendar time.

E. Interpret data presented in time lines.

F. Reconstruct patterns of historical succession and duration.

G. Compare alternative models for periodization.

Standard 2. Historical Comprehension

A. Reconstruct the literal meaning of a historical passage.

B. Identify the central question(s) the historical narrative addresses.

   C. Read historical narratives imaginatively.

   D. Evidence historical perspectives.

   E. Draw upon data in historical maps.

   F. Utilize visual and mathematical data presented in charts, tables, pie and bar graphs, flow charts, Venn diagrams, and other graphic organizers.

   G. Draw upon visual, literary, and musical sources.

Standard 3. Historical Analysis and Interpretation

   A. Identify the author or source of the historical document or narrative.

   B. Compare and contrast differing sets of ideas, values, personalities, behaviors, and institutions.

   C. Differentiate between historical facts and historical interpretations.

   D. Consider multiple perspectives.

   E. Analyze cause-and-effect relationships and multiple causation, including the importance of the individual, the influence of ideas, and the role of chance.

   F. Challenge arguments of historical inevitability.

   G. Compare competing historical narratives.

   H. Hold interpretations of history as tentative.

   I. Evaluate major debates among historians.

   J. Hypothesize the influence of the past.

Standard 4. Historical Research Capabilities

   A. Formulate historical questions.

   B. Obtain historical data.

   C. Interrogate historical data.

   D. Identify the gaps in the available records, marshal contextual knowledge and perspectives of the time and place, and construct a sound historical interpretation.

Standard 5. Historical Issues—Analysis and Decision Making

   A. Identify issues and problems in the past.

   B. Marshal evidence of antecedent circumstances and contemporary factors contributing to problems and alternative courses of action.

   C. Identify relevant historical antecedents.

D. Evaluate alternative courses of action.

E. Formulate a position or course of action on an issue.

F. Evaluate the implementation of a decision.

UNITED STATES HISTORY
STANDARDS FOR HISTORY FOR GRADES 5–12

Era 1. Three Worlds Meet (Beginnings to 1620)

- Standard 1. Comparative characteristics of societies in the Americas, Western Europe, and Western Africa that increasingly interacted after 1450
- Standard 2. How early European exploration and colonization resulted in cultural and ecological interactions among previously unconnected peoples

Era 2. Colonization and Settlement (1585–1763)

- Standard 1. Why the Americas attracted Europeans, why they brought enslaved Africans to their colonies, and how Europeans struggled for control of North America and the Caribbean
- Standard 2. How political, religious, and social institutions emerged in the English colonies (http://www.sscnet.ucla.edu/nchs/standards/era2-5-12.html - C#C)
- Standard 3. How the values and institutions of European economic life took root in the colonies, and how slavery reshaped European and African life in the Americas

Era 3. Revolution and the New Nation (1754–1820s)

- Standard 1. The causes of the American Revolution, the ideas and interests involved in forging the revolutionary movement, and the reasons for the American victory
- Standard 2. The impact of the American Revolution on politics, economy, and society
- Standard 3. The institutions and practices of government created during the Revolution and how they were revised between 1787 and 1815 to create the foundation of the American political system based on the U.S. Constitution and the Bill of Rights

Era 4. Expansion and Reform (1801–1861)

- Standard 1. United States territorial expansion between 1801 and 1861, and how it affected relations with external powers and Native Americans
- Standard 2. How the industrial revolution, increasing immigration, the rapid expansion of slavery, and the westward movement changed the lives of Americans and led toward regional tensions
- Standard 3. The extension, restriction, and reorganization of political democracy after 1800
- Standard 4. The sources and character of cultural, religious, and social reform movements in the antebellum period

Era 5. Civil War and Reconstruction (1850–1877)

- Standard 1. The causes of the Civil War
- Standard 2. The course and character of the Civil War and its effects on the American people
- Standard 3. How various reconstruction plans succeeded or failed

Era 6. The Development of the Industrial United States (1870–1900)

- Standard 1. How the rise of corporations, heavy industry, and mechanized farming transformed the American people
- Standard 2. Massive immigration after 1870 and how new social patterns, conflicts, and ideas of national unity developed amid growing cultural diversity
- Standard 3. The rise of the American labor movement and how political issues reflected social and economic changes
- Standard 4. Federal Indian policy and United States foreign policy after the Civil War

Era 7. The Emergence of Modern America (1890–1930)

- Standard 1. How Progressives and others addressed problems of industrial capitalism, urbanization, and political corruption
- Standard 2. The changing role of the United States in world affairs through World War I
- Standard 3. How the United States changed from the end of World War I to the eve of the Great Depression

Era 8. The Great Depression and World War II (1929–1945)

- Standard 1. The causes of the Great Depression and how it affected American society
- Standard 2. How the New Deal addressed the Great Depression, transformed American federalism, and initiated the welfare state
- Standard 3. The causes and course of World War II, the character of the war at home and abroad, and its reshaping of the U.S. role in world affairs

Era 9. Postwar United States (1945–1970s)

- Standard 1. The economic boom and social transformation of postwar United States
- Standard 2. How the Cold War and conflicts in Korea and Vietnam influenced domestic and international politics
- Standard 3. Domestic policies after World War II
- Standard 4. The struggle for racial and gender equality and for the extension of civil liberties

Era 10. Contemporary United States (1968–present)

- Standard 1. Recent developments in foreign policy and domestic politics
- Standard 2. Economic, social, and cultural developments in contemporary United States

WORLD HISTORY STANDARDS FOR GRADES 5–12

Era 1. The Beginnings of Human Society

- Standard 1. The biological and cultural processes that gave rise to the earliest human communities
- Standard 2. The processes that led to the emergence of agricultural societies around the world

Era 2. Early Civilizations and the Emergence of Pastoral Peoples, 4000–1000 BCE

- Standard 1. The major characteristics of civilization and how civilizations emerged in Mesopotamia, Egypt, and the Indus valley
- Standard 2. How agrarian societies spread and new states emerged in the third and second millennia BCE
- Standard 3. The political, social, and cultural consequences of population movements and militarization in Eurasia in the second millennium BCE
- Standard 4. Major trends in Eurasia and Africa from 4000 to 1000 BCE

Era 3. Classical Traditions, Major Religions, and Giant Empires, 1000 BCE–300 CE

- Standard 1. Innovation and change from 1000–600 BCE: horses, ships, iron, and monotheistic faith
- Standard 2. The emergence of Aegean civilization and how interrelations developed among peoples of the eastern Mediterranean and Southwest Asia, 600–200 BCE
- Standard 3. How major religions and large-scale empires arose in the Mediterranean basin, China, and India, 500 BCE–300 CE
- Standard 4. The development of early agrarian civilizations in Mesoamerica
- Standard 5. Major global trends from 1000 BCE–300 CE

Era 4. Expanding Zones of Exchange and Encounter, 300–1000 CE

- Standard 1. Imperial crises and their aftermath, 300–700 CE
- Standard 2. Causes and consequences of the rise of Islamic civilization in the 7th – 10th centuries
- Standard 3. Major developments in East Asia and Southeast Asia in the era of the Tang dynasty, 600–900 CE
- Standard 4. The search for political, social, and cultural redefinition in Europe, 500–1000 CE
- Standard 5. The development of agricultural societies and new states in tropical Africa and Oceania
- Standard 6. The rise of centers of civilization in Mesoamerica and Andean South America in the first millennium CE
- Standard 7. Major global trends from 300–1000 CE

Era 5. Intensified Hemispheric Interactions, 1000–1500 CE

- Standard 1. The maturing of an interregional system of communication, trade, and cultural exchange in an era of Chinese economic power and Islamic expansion
- Standard 2. The redefining of European society and culture, 1000–1300 CE
- Standard 3. The rise of the Mongol empire and its consequences for Eurasian peoples, 1200–1350
- Standard 4. The growth of states, towns, and trade in Sub-Saharan Africa between the 11th and 15th centuries
- Standard 5. Patterns of crisis and recovery in Afro-Eurasia, 1300–1450
- Standard 6. The expansion of states and civilizations in the Americas, 1000–1500
- Standard 7. Major global trends from 1000–1500 CE

Era 6. The Emergence of the First Global Age, 1450–1770

- Standard 1. How the transoceanic interlinking of all major regions of the world from 1450 to 1600 led to global transformations
- Standard 2. How European society experienced political, economic, and cultural transformations in an age of global intercommunication, 1450–1750
- Standard 3. How large territorial empires dominated much of Eurasia between the 16th and 18th centuries
- Standard 4. Economic, political, and cultural interrelations among peoples of Africa, Europe, and the Americas, 1500–1750
- Standard 5. Transformations in Asian societies in the era of European expansion
- Standard 6. Major global trends from 1450 to 1770

Era 7. An Age of Revolutions, 1750–1914

- Standard 1. The causes and consequences of political revolutions in the late 18th and early 19th centuries
- Standard 2. The causes and consequences of the agricultural and industrial revolutions, 1700–1850
- Standard 3. The transformation of Eurasian societies in an era of global trade and rising European power, 1750–1870
- Standard 4. Patterns of nationalism, state-building, and social reform in Europe and the Americas, 1830–1914
- Standard 5. Patterns of global change in the era of Western military and economic domination, 1800–1914
- Standard 6. Major global trends from 1750–1914

Era 8. A Half-Century of Crisis and Achievement, 1900–1945

- Standard 1. Reform, revolution, and social change in the world economy of the early century
- Standard 2. The causes and global consequences of World War I
- Standard 3. The search for peace and stability in the 1920s and 1930s
- Standard 4. The causes and global consequences of World War II
- Standard 5. Major global trends from 1900 to the end of World War II

Era 9. The 20th Century Since 1945: Promises and Paradoxes

- Standard 1. How post–World War II reconstruction occurred, new international power relations took shape, and colonial empires broke up
- Standard 2. The search for community, stability, and peace in an interdependent world
- Standard 3. Major global trends since World War II

World History Across the Eras

- Standard 1. Long-term changes and recurring patterns in world history

II. Geography

NATIONAL GEOGRAPHY STANDARDS

The World in Spatial Terms

- Standard 1. How to use maps and other geographic representations, tools, and technologies to acquire, process, and report information
- Standard 2. How to use mental maps to organize information about people, places, and environments
- Standard 3. How to analyze the spatial organization of people, places, and environments on Earth's surface

Places and Regions

- Standard 4. The physical and human characteristics of places
- Standard 5. That people create regions to interpret Earth's complexity
- Standard 6. How culture and experience influence people's perception of places and regions

Physical Systems

- Standard 7. The physical processes that shape the patterns of Earth's surface
- Standard 8. The characteristics and spatial distribution of ecosystems on Earth's surface

Human Systems

- Standard 9. The characteristics, distribution, and migration of human populations on Earth's surface
- Standard 10. The characteristics, distributions, and complexity of Earth's cultural mosaics
- Standard 11. The patterns and networks of economic interdependence on Earth's surface
- Standard 12. The process, patterns, and functions of human settlement
- Standard 13. How forces of cooperation and conflict among people influence the division and control of Earth's surface

Environment and Society

- Standard 14. How human actions modify the physical environment
- Standard 15. How physical systems affect human systems
- Standard 16. The changes that occur in the meaning, use, distribution, and importance of resources

The Uses of Geography

- Standard 17. How to apply geography to interpret the past
- Standard 18. To apply geography to interpret the present and plan for the future

III. Civics and Government

CIVICS AND GOVERNMENT K–4 CONTENT STANDARDS

I. What is Government and What Should It Do?

A. What is government?

B. Where do people in government get the authority to make, apply, and enforce rules and laws and manage disputes about them?

C. Why is government necessary?

D. What are some of the most important things governments do?

E. What are the purposes of rules and laws?

F. How can you evaluate rules and laws?

G. What are the differences between limited and unlimited governments?

H. Why is it important to limit the power of government?

II. What are the Basic Values and Principles of American Democracy?

A. What are the most important values and principles of American democracy?

B. What are some important beliefs Americans have about themselves and their government?

C. Why is it important for Americans to share certain values, principles, and beliefs?

D. What are the benefits of diversity in the United States?

E. How should conflicts about diversity be prevented or managed?

F. How can people work together to promote the values and principles of American democracy?

III. How Does the Government Established by the Constitution Embody the Purposes, Values, and Principles of American Democracy?

    A. What is the United States Constitution and why is it important?

    B. What does the national government do and how does it protect individual rights and promote the common good?

    C. What are the major responsibilities of state governments?

    D. What are the major responsibilities of local governments?

    E. Who represents you in the legislative and executive branches of your local, state, and national governments?

IV. What is the Relationship of the United States to Other Nations and to World Affairs?

    A. How is the world divided into nations?

    B. How do nations interact with one another?

V. What are the Roles of the Citizen in American Democracy?

    A. What does it mean to be a citizen of the United States?

    B. How does a person become a citizen?

    C. What are important rights in the United States?

    D. What are important responsibilities of Americans?

    E. What dispositions or traits of character are important to the preservation and improvement of American democracy?

    F. How can Americans participate in their government?

    G. What is the importance of political leadership and public service?

    H. How should Americans select leaders?

CIVICS AND GOVERNMENT 5–8 CONTENT STANDARDS

I. What are Civic Life, Politics, and Government?

    A. What is civic life? What is politics? What is government? Why are government and politics necessary? What purposes should government serve?

    B. What are the essential characteristics of limited and unlimited government?

C. What are the nature and purposes of constitutions?

D. What are alternative ways of organizing constitutional governments?

II. What are the Foundations of the American Political System?

A. What is the American idea of constitutional government?

B. What are the distinctive characteristics of American society?

C. What is American political culture?

D. What values and principles are basic to American constitutional democracy?

III. How Does the Government Established by the Constitution Embody the Purposes, Values, and Principles of American Democracy?

A. How are power and responsibility distributed, shared, and limited in the government established by the United States Constitution?

B. What does the national government do?

C. How are state and local governments organized, and what do they do?

D. Who represents you in local, state, and national governments?

E. What is the place of law in the American constitutional system?

F. How does the American political system provide for choice and opportunities for participation?

IV. What is the Relationship of the United States to Other Nations and to World Affairs?

A. How is the world organized politically?

B. How has the United States influenced other nations and how have other nations influenced American politics and society?

V. What are the Roles of the Citizen in American Democracy?

A. What is citizenship?

B. What are the rights of citizens?

C. What are the responsibilities of citizens?

D. What dispositions or traits of character are important to the preservation and improvement of American constitutional democracy?

E. How can citizens take part in civic life?

IV. Economics

VOLUNTARY NATIONAL CONTENT STANDARDS IN ECONOMICS

- Standard 1. Productive resources are limited. Therefore, people cannot have all the goods and services they want; as a result, they must choose some things and give up others.
- Standard 2. Effective decision making requires comparing the additional costs of alternatives with the additional benefits. Most choices involve doing a little more or a little less of something; few choices are all-or-nothing decisions.
- Standard 3. Different methods can be used to allocate goods and services. People, acting individually or collectively through government, must choose which methods to use to allocate different kinds of goods and services.
- Standard 4. People respond predictably to positive and negative incentives.
- Standard 5. Voluntary exchange occurs only when all participating parties expect to gain. This is true for trade among individuals or organizations within a nation, and among individuals or organizations in different nations.
- Standard 6. When individuals, regions, and nations specialize in what they can produce at the lowest cost and then trade with others, both production and consumption increase.
- Standard 7. Markets exist when buyers and sellers interact. This interaction determines market prices and thereby allocates scarce goods and services.
- Standard 8. Prices send signals and provide incentives to buyers and sellers. When supply or demand changes, market prices adjust, affecting incentives.
- Standard 9. Competition among sellers lowers costs and prices, and encourages producers to produce more of what consumers are willing and able to buy. Competition among buyers increases prices and allocates goods and services to those people who are willing and able to pay the most for them.
- Standard 10. Institutions evolve in market economies to help individuals and groups accomplish their goals. Banks, labor unions, corporations, legal systems, and not-for-profit organizations are examples of important institutions. A different kind of institution, clearly defined and enforced property rights, is essential to a market economy.
- Standard 11. Money makes it easier to trade, borrow, save, invest, and compare the value of goods and services.
- Standard 12. Interest rates, adjusted for inflation, rise and fall to balance the amount saved with the amount borrowed, thus affecting the allocation of scarce resources between present and future uses.
- Standard 13. Income for most people is determined by the market value of the productive resources they sell. What workers earn depends, primarily, on the market value of what they produce and how productive they are.
- Standard 14. Entrepreneurs are people who take the risks of organizing productive resources to make goods and services. Profit is an important incentive that leads entrepreneurs to accept the risks of business failure.
- Standard 15. Investment in factories, machinery, new technology, and the health, education, and training of people can raise future standards of living.

- Standard 16. There is an economic role for government to play in a market economy whenever the benefits of a government policy outweigh its costs. Governments often provide for national defense, address environmental concerns, define and protect property rights, and attempt to make markets more competitive. Most government policies also redistribute income.
- Standard 17. Costs of government policies sometimes exceed benefits. This may occur because of incentives facing voters, government officials, and government employees, because of actions by special interest groups that can impose costs on the general public, or because social goals other than economic efficiency are being pursued.
- Standard 18. A nation's overall levels of income, employment, and prices are determined by the interaction of spending and production decisions made by all households, firms, government agencies, and others in the economy.
- Standard 19. Unemployment imposes costs on individuals and nations. Unexpected inflation imposes costs on many people and benefits some others because it arbitrarily redistributes purchasing power. By creating uncertainty about future prices, inflation can reduce the rate of growth of national living standards.
- Standard 20. Federal government budgetary policy and the Federal Reserve System's monetary policy influence the overall levels of employment, output, and prices.

APPENDIX B

Performance Expectations for
NCSS Thematic Subject Matter Standards

I. CULTURE

Social studies program should include experiences that provide for the study of culture and cultural diversity so that the learner can:

Early Grades	*Middle Grades*
a. explore and describe similarities and differences in the ways groups, societies, and cultures address similar human needs and concerns;	a. compare similarities and differences in the ways groups, societies, and cultures meet human needs and concerns;
b. give examples of how experiences may be interpreted differently by people from diverse cultural perspectives and frames of reference;	b. explain how information and experiences may be interpreted by people from diverse cultural perspectives and frames of reference;
c. describe ways in which language, stories, folktales, music, and artistic creations serve as expressions of culture and influence behavior of people living in a particular culture;	c. explain and give examples of how language, literature, the arts, architecture, other artifacts, traditions, beliefs, values, and behaviors contribute to the development and transmission of culture;
d. compare ways in which people from different cultures think about and deal with their physical environment and social conditions;	d. explain why individuals and groups respond differently to their physical and social environments and/or changes to them on the basis of shared assumptions, values, and beliefs;
e. give examples and describe the importance of cultural unity and diversity with and across groups.	e. articulate the implications of cultural diversity, as well as cohesion, within and across groups.

II. TIME, CONTINUITY, AND CHANGE

Social studies programs should include experiences that provide for the study of the ways human beings view themselves in and over time so that the learner can:

Early Grades	Middle Grades
a. demonstrate an understanding that different people may describe the same event or situation in diverse ways, citing reasons for the differences in views;	a. demonstrate an understanding that different scholars may describe the same event or situation in different ways but must provide reasons or evidence for their views;
b. demonstrate an ability to use correctly vocabulary associated with time such as past, present, future, and long ago; read and construct simple time lines; identify examples of change; and recognize examples of cause and effect relationships;	b. identify and use key concepts such as chronology, causality, change, conflict, and complexity to explain, analyze, and show connections among patterns of historical change and continuity;
c. compare and contrast different stories or accounts about past events, people, places, or situations, identifying how they contribute to our understanding of the past;	c. identify and describe selected historical periods and patterns of change within and across cultures, such as the rise of civilizations, the development of transportation systems, the growth and breakdown of colonial systems, and others;
d. identify and use various sources for reconstructing the past, such as documents, letters, diaries, maps, textbooks, photos, and others;	d. identify and use processes important to reconstructing and reinterpreting the past, such as using a variety of sources, providing, validating, and weighing evidence for claims, checking credibility of sources, and searching for causality;
e. demonstrate an understanding that people in different times and places view the world differently;	e. develop critical sensitivities such as empathy and skepticism regarding attitudes, values, and behaviors of people in different historical contexts;
f. use knowledge of facts and concepts drawn from history, along with elements of historical inquiry, to inform decision-making about and action-taking on public issues.	f. use knowledge of facts and concepts drawn from history, along with methods of historical inquiry, to inform decision-making about and action-taking on public issues.

III. PEOPLE, PLACES, AND ENVIRONMENTS

Social studies programs should include experiences that provide for the study of people, places, and environments so that the learner can:

Early Grades	*Middle Grades*
a. construct and use mental maps of locales, regions, and the world that demonstrate understanding of relative location, direction, size, and shape;	a. elaborate mental maps of locales, regions, and the world that demonstrate understanding of relative location, direction, size, and shape;
b. interpret, use, and distinguish various representations of the earth, such as maps, globes, and photographs;	b. create, interpret, use, and distinguish various representations of the earth, such as maps, globes, and photographs;
c. use appropriate resources, data sources, and geographic tools such as atlases, data bases, grid systems, charts, graphs, and maps to generate, manipulate, and interpret information;	c. use appropriate resources, data sources, and geographic tools such as aerial photographs, satellite images, geographic information systems (GIS), map projections, and cartography to generate, manipulate, and interpret information such as atlases, data bases, grid systems, charts, graphs, and maps;
d. estimate distance and calculate scale;	d. estimate distance, calculate scale, and distinguish other geographic relationships such as population density and spatial distribution patterns;
e. locate and distinguish among varying land forms and geographic features, such as mountains, plateaus, islands, and oceans;	e. locate and describe varying land forms and geographic features, such as mountains, plateaus, islands, rain forests, deserts, and oceans and explain their relationship within the ecosystem;
f. describe and speculate about physical system changes, such as seasons, climate and weather, and the water cycle;	f. describe physical system changes such as seasons, climate and weather, and the water cycle and identify geographic patterns associated with them;
g. describe how people create places that reflect ideas, personality, culture, and wants and needs as they design homes, playgrounds, classrooms, and the like.	g. describe how people create places that reflect cultural values and ideals as they build neighborhoods, parks, shopping centers, and the like.

IV. INDIVIDUAL DEVELOPMENT AND IDENTITY

Social studies programs should include experiences that provide for the study of interactions among individuals, groups, and institutions so that learners can:

Early Grades	Middle Grades
a. describe personal changes over time, such as those related to physical development and personal interests;	a. relate personal changes to social, cultural, and historical contexts;
b. describe personal connections to place—especially place as associated with immediate surroundings;	b. describe personal connections to place—as associated with community, nation, and world;
c. describe the unique features of one's nuclear and extended families;	c. describe the ways family, gender, ethnicity, nationality, and institutional affiliations contribute to personal identity;
d. show how learning and physical development affect behavior;	d. relate such factors as physical endowment and capabilities, learning, motivation, personality, perception, and behavior to individual development;
e. identify and describe ways family, groups, and community influence the individual's daily life and personal choices;	e. identify and describe ways regional, ethnic, and national cultures influence individuals' daily lives;
f. explore factors that contribute to one's personal identity such as interests, capabilities, and perceptions;	f. identify and describe the influence of perceptions, attitudes, values, and beliefs on personal identity;
g. analyze a particular event to identify reasons individuals might respond to it in different ways;	g. identify and interpret examples of stereotyping, conformity, and altruism;
h. work independently and cooperatively to accomplish goals.	h. work independently and cooperatively to accomplish goals.

V. INDIVIDUALS, GROUPS, AND INSTITUTIONS

Social studies programs should include experiences that provide for the study of interactions among individuals, groups, and institutions so that students can:

Early Grades	*Middle Grades*
a. identify roles as learned behavior patterns in group situations such as student, family member, peer play group member; or club member;	a. demonstrate an understanding of concepts such as role, status, and social class in describing the interactions of individuals and social groups;
b. give examples of and explain group and institutional influences such as religious beliefs, laws, and peer pressure, on people, events, and elements of culture;	b. analyze group and institutional influences on people, events, and elements of culture;
c. identify examples of institutions and describe the interactions of people with institutions;	c. describe the various forms institutions take and the interactions of people with institutions;
d. identify and describe examples of tensions between and among individuals, groups, or institutions, and how belonging to more than one group can cause internal conflicts;	d. identify and analyze examples of tensions between expressions of individuality and group or instructional efforts to promote social conformity;
e. identify and describe examples of tension between an individual's beliefs and government policies and laws;	e. identify and describe examples of tensions between beliefs systems and government policies and laws;
f. give examples of the role of institutions in furthering both continuity and change;	f. describe the role of institutions in furthering both continuity and change;
g. show how groups and institutions work to meet individual needs and promote the common good, and identify examples of where they fail to do so.	g. apply knowledge of how groups and institutions work to meet individual needs and promote the common good.

VI. POWER, AUTHORITY, AND GOVERNANCE

Social studies programs should include experiences that provide for the study of how people create and change structures of power, authority, and governance, so that the learner can:

Early Grades	*Middle Grades*
a. examine the rights and responsibilities of the individual in relation to his or her social group, such as family, peer group, and school class;	a. examine persistent issues involving the rights, roles, and status of the individual in relation to the general welfare;
b. explain the purpose of governance;	b. describe the purpose of the government and how its powers are acquired, used, and justified;
c. give examples of how government does or does not provide for needs and wants of people, establish order and security, and manage conflict;	c. analyze and explain ideas and governmental mechanisms to meet needs and wants of citizens, regulate territory, manage conflict, and establish order and security;
d. recognize how groups and organizations encourage unity and deal with diversity to maintain order and security;	d. describe the ways nations and organizations respond to forces of unity and diversity affecting order and security;
e. distinguish among local, state, and national government and identify representative leaders at these levels such as mayor, governor, and president;	e. identify and describe the basic features of the political systems in the United States, and identify representative leaders from various levels and branches of government;
f. identify and describe factors that contribute to cooperation and cause disputes within and among groups and nations;	f. explain conditions, actions, and motivations that contribute to conflict and cooperation within and among nations;
g. explore the role of technology in communications, transportation, information-processing, weapons development, or other areas as it contributes to or helps resolve conflicts;	g. describe and analyze the role of technology in communications, transportation, information-processing, weapons development, or other areas as it contributes to or helps resolve conflicts;
h. recognize and give examples of the tensions between the wants and needs of individuals and groups and concepts such as fairness, equity, and justice.	h. explain and apply concepts such as power, role, status, justice, and influence to the examination of persistent issues and social problems;
	i. give examples and explain how governments attempt to achieve their stated ideals at home and abroad.

VII. PRODUCTION, DISTRIBUTION, AND CONSUMPTION

Social studies programs should include experiences that provide for the study of how people organize for the production, distribution, and consumption of goods and services, so that the learner can:

Early Grades	Middle Grades
a. give examples that show how scarcity and choice govern our economic decisions;	a. give and explain examples of ways that economic systems structure choices about how goods and services are to be produced and distributed;
b. distinguish between needs and wants;	b. describe the role that supply and demand, prices, incentives, and profits play in determining what is produced and distributed in a competitive market system;
c. identify examples of private and public goods and services;	c. explain the difference between private and public goods and services;
d. give examples of the various institutions that make up economic systems such as families, workers, banks, labor unions, government agencies, small businesses, and large corporations;	d. describe a range of examples of the various institutions that make up economic systems such as households, business firms, banks, government agencies, labor unions, and corporations;
e. describe how we depend upon workers with specialized jobs and the ways in which they contribute to the production and exchange of goods and services;	e. describe the role of specialization and exchange in the economic process;
f. describe the influence of incentives, values, traditions, and habits on economic decisions;	f. explain and illustrate how values and beliefs influence different economic decisions;
g. explain and demonstrate the role of money in everyday life;	g. differentiate among various forms of exchange and money;
h. describe the relationship of price to supply and demand;	h. compare basic economic systems according to who determines what is produced, distributed, and consumed;
i. use economic concepts such as supply, demand, and price to help explain events in the community and nation;	i. use economic concepts to help explain historical and current developments and issues in local, national, or global contexts;
j. apply knowledge of economic concepts in developing a response to a current local economic issue, such as how to reduce the flow of trash into a rapidly filling landfill.	j. use economic reasoning to compare different proposals for dealing with a contemporary social issue such as unemployment, acid rain, or high quality education.

VIII. SCIENCE, TECHNOLOGY, AND SOCIETY

Social studies programs should include experiences that provide for the study of relationships among science, technology, and society so that the learner can:

Early Grades	*Middle Grades*
a. examine and describe examples in which science and technology have changed the lives of people, such as in homemaking, childcare, work, transportation, and communication;	a. examine and describe the influence of culture on scientific and technological choices and advancements, such as in transportation, medicine, and warfare;
b. identify and describe examples in which science and technology have lead to changes in the physical environment, such as the building of dams and levees, offshore oil drilling, medicine from rain forests, and loss of rain forests due to extraction of resources or alternative uses;	b. show through specific examples how science and technology have changed people's perception of the social and natural world, such as in their relationship to the land, animal life, family life, and economic needs, wants, and security;
c. describe instances in which change in values, beliefs, and attitudes have resulted from new scientific and technological knowledge, such as conservation of resources and awareness of chemicals harmful to life and the environment;	c. describe examples in which values, beliefs, and attitudes have been influenced by new scientific and technological knowledge, such as the invention of the printing press, conceptions of the universe, application of atomic energy, and genetic discoveries;
d. identify examples of laws and policies that govern scientific and technological applications, such as the Endangered Species Act and environmental protection policies;	d. explain the need for laws and policies to govern scientific and technological applications, such as in the safety and well-being of workers and consumers and the regulation of utilities, radio, and television;
e. suggest ways to monitor science and technology in order to protect the physical environment, individual rights, and the common good.	e. seek reasonable and ethical solutions to problems that arise when scientific advancements and social norms or values come into conflict.

IX. GLOBAL CONNECTIONS

Social studies programs should include experiences that provide for the study of global connections and interdependence, so that the learner can

Early Grades	Middle Grades
a. explore ways that language, art, music, belief systems, and other cultural elements may facilitate global understanding or lead to misunderstanding;	a. describe instances in which language, art, music, belief systems, and other cultural elements can facilitate global understanding or cause misunderstanding;
b. give examples of conflict, cooperation, and interdependence among individuals, groups, and nations;	b. analyze examples of conflict, cooperation, and interdependence among groups, societies, and nations;
c. examine the effects of changing technologies on the global community;	c. describe and analyze the effects of changing technologies on the global community;
d. explore causes, consequences, and possible solutions to persistent, contemporary, and emerging global issues, such as pollution and endangered species;	d. explore the causes, consequences, and possible solutions to persistent, contemporary, and emerging global issues, such as health, security, resource allocation, economic development, and environmental quality;
e. examine the relationships and tensions between personal wants and needs and various global concerns, such as use of imported oil, land use, and environmental protection;	e. describe and explain the relationship and tensions between national sovereignty and global interests in such matters as territory, natural resources, trade, use of technology, and welfare of people;
f. investigate concerns, issues, standards, and conflicts related to universal human rights, such as the treatment of children, religious groups, and effects of war.	f. demonstrate understanding of concerns, standards, issues, and conflicts related to universal rights;
	g. identify and describe the roles of international and multinational organizations.

X. CIVIC IDEALS AND PRACTICES

Social studies programs should include experiences that provide for the study of the ideals, principles, and practices of citizenship in a democratic republic, so that the learner can:

Early Grades	Middle Grades
a. identify key ideals of the United States' democratic republican form of government, such as individual human dignity, liberty, justice, equality, and the rule of law, and discuss their application in specific situations;	a. examine the origins and continuing influence of key ideals of the democratic republican form of government, such as individual human dignity, liberty, justice, equality, and the rule of law;
b. identify examples of rights and responsibilities of citizens;	b. identify and interpret sources and examples of the rights and responsibilities of citizens;
c. locate, access, organize, and apply information about an issue of public concern from multiple points of view;	c. locate, access, analyze, organize, and apply information about selected public issues—recognizing and explaining multiple points of view;
d. identify and practice selected forms of civic discussion and participation consistent with the ideals of citizens in a democratic republic;	d. practice forms of civic discussion and participation consistent with the ideals of citizens in a democratic republic;
e. explain actions citizens can take to influence public policy decisions;	e. explain and analyze various forms of citizen action that influence public policy decisions;
f. recognize that a variety of formal and informal actors influence and shape public policy;	f. identify and explain the roles of formal and informal political actors in influencing and shaping public policy and decision-making;
g. examine the influence of public opinion on personal decision-making and government policy on public issues;	g. analyze the influence of diverse forms of public opinion on the development of public policy and decision-making;
h. explain how public policies and citizen behaviors may or may not reflect the stated ideals of a democratic republican form of government;	h. analyze the effectiveness of selected public policies and citizen behaviors in realizing the stated ideals of a democratic republican form of government;
i. describe how public policies are used to address issues of public concern;	i. explain the relationship between policy statements and action plans used to address issues of public concern;
j. recognize and interpret how the "common good" can be strengthened through various forms of citizen action.	j. examine strategies designed to strengthen the "common good," which consider a range of options for citizen action.

APPENDIX C

NCSS Essential Skills for Social Studies

I. ESSENTIAL SKILLS FOR SOCIAL STUDIES: ACQUIRING INFORMATION

A. Reading Skills

1. Comprehension

- Read to get literal meaning
- Use chapter and section headings, topic sentences, and summary
- Differentiate main and subordinate ideas
- Select passages that are pertinent to the topic studied
- Interpret what is read by drawing inferences
- Detect cause and effect relationships
- Distinguish between the fact and opinion; recognize propaganda
- Recognize author bias
- Use picture clues and picture captions to aid comprehension
- Use literature to enrich meaning
- Read for a variety of purposes: critically, analytically, to predict outcomes, to answer a question, to form an opinion, to skim for facts
- Read various forms of printed material: books, magazines, newspapers, directories, schedules, journals

2. Vocabulary

- Use usual word attack skills: sight recognition, phonetic analysis, structural analysis
- Use context clues to gain meaning
- Use appropriate sources to gain meaning of essential terms and vocabulary: glossary, dictionary, text, word lists
- Recognize and understand an increasing number of social studies terms

3. Rate of reading

- Adjust speed of reading to suit purpose
- Adjust rate of reading to difficulty of the material

B. Study Skills

1. Find information

- Use various parts of a book (index, table of contents, etc.)
- Use key words, letters on volumes, index, and cross references to find information
- Evaluate sources of information—print, visual, electronic
- Use appropriate source of information
- Use the community as a resource

2. Arrange information in usable forms

- Make outline of topic
- Prepare summaries
- Make timelines
- Take notes
- Keep records
- Use italics, marginal notes, and footnotes
- Listen for information
- Follow directions
- Write reports and research papers
- Prepare a bibliography

C. Reference and Information-Search Skills

1. The library

- Use card catalog to locate books
- Use Reader's Guide to Periodical Literature and other indexes
- Use COMCATS (Computer Catalog Service)
- Use public library telephone information service

2. Special references

- Almanacs
- Encyclopedias
- Dictionary
- Indexes
- Government publications
- Microfiche
- Periodicals
- News sources: newspapers, news magazines, TV, radio, videotapes, artifacts

3. Maps, globes, and graphics

- Use map- and globe-reading skills
- Orient a map and note directions

- Locate places on map and globe
- Use scale and compute distances
- Interpret map symbols and visualize what they mean
- Compare maps and make inferences
- Express relative location
- Interpret graphs
- Detect bias in visual material
- Interpret social and political messages of cartoons

4. Community resources

- Use sources of information in the community
- Conduct interviews of individuals in the community
- Use community newspapers

D. Technical Skills Unique to Electronic Devices

1. Computer

- Operate a computer using prepared instructional or reference programs
- Operate a computer to enter and retrieve information gathered from a variety of sources

2. Telephone and television information networks

- Ability to access information through networks

II. ESSENTIAL SKILLS FOR SOCIAL STUDIES: ORGANIZING AND USING INFORMATION

A. Thinking Skills

1. Classify information

- Identify relevant factual material
- Sense relationship between items of factual information
- Group data in categories according to appropriate criteria
- Place in proper sequence
  - order of occurrence
  - order of importance
- Place data in tabular form: charts, graphs, illustrations

2. Interpret information

- State relationships between categories of information
- Note cause and effect relationships
- Draw inferences from factual material

- Predict likely outcomes based on factual information
- Recognize the value dimension of interpreting factual material
- Recognize instances in which more than one interpretation of factual material is valid

3. Analyze information

- Form a simple organization of key ideas related to a topic
- Separate a topic into major components according to appropriate criteria
- Examine critically relationships between and among elements of a topic
- Detect bias in data presented in various forms: graphics, tabular, visual, print
- Compare and contrast credibility of differing accounts of the same event

4. Summarize information

- Extract significant ideas from supporting illustrative details
- Combine critical concepts into a statement of conclusions based on information
- Restate major ideas of a complex topic in concise form
- Form opinion based on critical examination of relevant information
- State hypothesis for further study

5. Synthesize information

- Propose a new plan of operation, create a new system, or devise a futuristic scheme based on available information
- Reinterpret events in terms of what might have happened, and show the likely effects on subsequent events
- Present visually (chart, graph, diagram, model, etc.) information extracted from print
- Prepare a research paper that requires a creative solution to a problem
- Communicate orally and in writing

6. Evaluate information

- Determine whether or not the information is pertinent to the topic
- Estimate the adequacy of the information
- Test the validity of the information, using such criteria as source, objectivity, technical correctness, currency

B. Decision-Making Skills

- Identify a situation in which a decision is required
- Secure needed factual information relevant to making the decision
- Recognize the values implicit in the situation and the issues that flow from them
- Identify alternative courses of action and predict likely consequences of each
- Make decision based on the data obtained
- Take action to implement the decision

C. Metacognitive Skills

- Select an appropriate strategy to solve a problem
- Self-monitor one's thinking process

III. ESSENTIAL SKILLS FOR SOCIAL STUDIES: RELATIONSHIPS AND SOCIAL PARTICIPATION

A. Personal Skills

- Express personal convictions
- Communicate own beliefs, feelings, and convictions
- Adjust own behavior to fit the dynamics of various groups and situations
- Recognize the mutual relationship between human beings in satisfying one another's needs

B. Group Interaction Skills

- Contribute to the development of a supportive climate in groups
- Participate in making rules and guidelines for group life
- Serve as a leader or follower
- Assist in setting goals for the group
- Participate in delegating duties, organizing, planning, making decisions, and taking action in group setting
- Participate in persuading, compromising, debating, and negotiating in the resolution of conflicts and differences

C. Social and Political Participation Skills

- Keep informed on issues that affect society
- Identify situations in which social action is required
- Work individually or with others to decide on an appropriate course of action
- Work to influence those in positions of social power to strive for extensions of freedom, social justice, and human rights
- Accept and fulfill social responsibilities associated with citizenship in a free society

REFERENCES

Adams, M. J. (1989). Thinking skills curricula: Their promise and progress. *Educational Psychologist, 24,* 24–77.

Al-Khalili, J. (1997). *Black holes, wormholes, and time machines.* Bristol, England: Institute of Physics Publishing.

Allington, R. L. (1994). The schools we have. The schools we need. *The Reading Teacher, 48,* 14–29.

Allington, R. (2001). *What really matters for struggling readers: Designing research-based programs.* New York: Longman.

Alvermann, D. (1991). The discussion web: A graphic aid for learning across the curriculum. *The Reading Teacher, 45,* 92–98.

American Psychiatric Association. (2000). *DSM-IV-TR: Diagnostic and statistical manual of mental disorders.* Arlington, VA: Author.

Armour-Thomas, E., & Allen, B. (1993). How well do teachers teach for the promotion of student thinking and learning? *Educational Horizons, 71,* 203–208.

Armstrong, T. (1994). *Multiple intelligences in the classroom.* Alexandria, VA: ASCD

Avi. (1992). *The true confessions of Charlotte Doyle.* New York: HarperTrophy.

Backler, A. & Stoltman, J. (1986). *The nature of geographic literacy.* Bloomington, IN: ERIC Clearinghouse for Social Studies/Social Science Education. (ERIC Document Reproduction Service No. ED277601)

Banks, J. A. (1995). Multicultural education: Historical development, dimensions, and practice. In J. A. Banks & C. A. M. Banks (Eds.), *Handbook of research on multicultural education* (pp. 3–24). New York: Macmillan.

Banks, J. (1997). *Educating citizens in a multicultural society.* New York: Teachers College Press.

Benson, L. (1994). *This is our earth.* Watertown, MA: Charlesbridge.

Bereiter, C., & Scardamalia, M. (1992). Cognition in curriculum. In P. W. Jackson (Ed.), *Handbook on research on curriculum* (pp. 517–542). New York: American Educational Research Association.

Berenstain, S., & Berenstain, J. (1991). *The Berenstain bears don't pollute (anymore).* New York: Random House.

Bettelheim, B., & Zelan, K. (1982). *On learning to read.* New York: Vintage Books.

Bisland, A., Karnes, F. A., & Cobb, Y. B. (2004). Leadership education: Resources and web sites for teachers of gifted students. *Gifted Child Today, 27,* 50–56.

Block, C. C. (1997). *Teaching the language arts: Expanding thinking through student-centered instruction.* Needham, MA: Allyn and Bacon.

Bloom B. S. (1956). *Taxonomy of educational objectives, handbook I: The cognitive domain.* New York: David McKay.

Bolten, G. (1979). *Toward a theory of drama in education.* London: Longman.

Borba, M. (2001). *Building moral intelligence: The seven essential virtues that teach kids to do the right thing.* San Francisco, CA: Jossey-Bass.

Borich, G. D. (2004). *Effective teaching methods* (5th ed.). Upper Saddle River, NJ: Pearson.

Bowe, F. (2005). *Making inclusion work*. Upper Saddle River, NJ: Pearson.

Bransford, J., & Nye, N. (1989). A perspective on cognitive research and its implications for instruction. In L. B. Resnick & L. E. Klopfer (Eds.), *Toward the thinking curriculum* (pp. 88–102). Washington, DC: ASCD.

Bruener, J. (1977). *The process of education.* Cambridge, MA: Harvard University Press.

Burke, K. (1999). *The mindful school: How to assess authentic learning* (3rd ed.). Arlington Heights, IL: Skylight Professional Development.

Burnett, K. G. (2000). *Simon's hook: A story about teases and put-downs,* Felton, CA: GR Publishing.

Bussler, D. (2002). *Get service, get learning.* Unpublished manuscript.

Campbell, J. (1968). *The hero with a thousand faces* (2nd ed.). Princeton, NJ: Princeton University Press.

Campbell, J. (1988). *The power of myth.* New York: Doubleday.

Campbell, J., & Donahue, P. (1997). *Students selecting stories: The effects of choice in reading assessment.* Washington, DC: National Center for Education Statistics.

Cazden, C. B. (1998) . *Classroom discourse: The language of teaching and learning.* Portsmouth, NH: Heinemann Educational Books.

Chapman, E. (2003). *Assessing student engagement rates.* College Park, MD: ERIC Clearinghouse on Assessment and Evaluation College Park MD. (ERIC Document Reproduction Service No. ED482269)

Checkley, K. (1997). The first seven . . . and the eighth: A conversation with Howard Gardner. *Educational Leadership, 55,* 8–13.

Clark, C. M., & Dunn, S. (1991). Second-generation research on teachers' planning, intentions, and routines. In H. Waxman & H. Walberg (Eds.), *Effective teaching: Current research* (pp. 183–201). Berkeley, CA: McCutchan.

Clark, C. M., & Peterson, P. L. (1986). Teachers' thought process. In M. Wittrock (Ed.). *Handbook of research on teaching* (3rd ed.) (pp. 255–296). New York: Macmillan.

Cole, B. (1990). *The goats.* New York: Farrar Straus & Giroux.

Cooper, J. M. (1999). *Classroom teaching skills* (6th ed.). Boston: Houghton Mifflin.

Corporation for National and Community Service. (2004). *Students in service to America guidebook.* Retrieved November, 2004, from www.leaderschools.org/2002profiles/south.html

Cox, C. (1983). Forum: Informal classroom drama. *Language Arts, 60,* 370–372.

Craik, F., & Lockhart, R. (1972). Levels of processing: Framework for memory research. *Journal of Verbal Learning and Verbal Behavior, 11,* 671–684.

Csikszentmihalyi, M. (1990). *Flow: The psychology of optimal experience.* New York: HarperPerennial.

Cunningham, J. (1999). How can we achieve best practices in literacy instruction? In L. Gambrell, C. Morrow, S. Neuman, and M. Pressley (Eds.), *Best practices in literacy instruction* (pp. 24–28). New York: The Guilford Press.

Cunningham, P. M., Moore, S. A., Cunningham, J. W., & Moore, D. W. (1995). *Reading and writing in elementary classrooms: Skills and observations* (3rd ed.). White Plains, NY: Longman.

Danielson, K. E., & Dauer, S. C. (1990). Celebrate poetry through creative drama. *Reading Horizons, 31,* 138–147.

Deutsch, M. (1973). *The resolution of conflict.* New Haven, CT: Yale University Press.

Dickinson, P. (1990). *Eva.* New York: Delacorte Press.

Dole, J., Duffy, G. J., Duffy, G., Roehler, L., & Pearson, P. D. (1991). Moving from the old to the new: Research on reading comprehension instruction. *Review of Educational Research, 61,* 239–264.

Dossey, L. (1989). *Recovering the soul: A scientific and spiritual search.* New York: Dell.

Doty, K. A. (2004). *A long year of silence.* Edinborough Press.

Douglass, S. S. (2002). Teaching about religion. *Educational Leadership, 60,* 32–36.

Dye, G. A. (2000). Graphic organizers to the rescue! Helping students link—and remember—information. *Teaching Exceptional Children, 32,* 72–76.

Eagan, K. (1982). Teaching history to young people. *Phi Delta Kappan, 64,* 439–441.

Edelman, D., Liss, K., Coggins, C., & Rios, D. (1994). *Conflict resolution curriculum for middle and high school.* Asheville, NC: The Mediation Center.

Edmiston, B., Encisco, P., & King, M. L. (1987). Empowering readers and writers through drama: Narrative theater. *Language Arts, 64,* 219–228.

Edwards, L. C. (1997). *The creative arts: A process approach for teachers and children.* Upper Saddle River, NJ: Simon and Schuster.

Eggen, P., & Kauchak, D. (2001). *Strategies for teachers: Teaching content and thinking skills* (4th ed.). Needham Heights, MA: Allyn and Bacon.

Eisner, E. (1991). Art, music, and literature. In J. Shaver (Ed.), *Handbook of research on social studies teaching and learning.* New York: Macmillan.

Ellis, A. (2002). *Teaching and learning elementary social studies* (7th ed.). Needham Heights, MA: Allyn and Bacon.

Esslemont, J. E. (1980). *Bahaullah and the new era.* Wilmette, IL: Baha'i Publishing Trust.

Evans, N. J. (2000). Creating a positive learning environment for gay, lesbian, and bisexual students. *New Directions for Teaching and Learning, 82,* 81–87.

Feldman, D. H., Csikszentmihalyi, M., & Gardner, H. (1994). *Changing the world: A framework for the study of creativity.* Westport, CT: Praeger.

Freiberg, H. J., & Driscoll, A. (1992). *Universal teaching strategies.* Needham Heights, MA: Allyn and Bacon.

Gallagher, J. J., & Gallagher, S. A. (1994). *Teaching the gifted child* (4th ed.). Boston: Allyn and Bacon.

Gardner, H. (1983). *Frames of mind.* New York: HarperCollins.

Gardner, H. (1986). The waning of intelligence tests. In R. J. Sternberg & D. Detterman (Eds.), *What is intelligence?* (pp. 73–76). Hillsdale, NJ: Lawrence Erlbaum.

Gardner, H. (1995). Reflections on multiple intelligences: Myths and messages. *Phi Delta Kappan, 77,* 206–209.

Gardner, H. (1999a). *Intelligence reframed: Multiple intelligences for the 21st century.* New York: Basic Books.

Gardner, H. (1999b). *The disciplined mind.* New York: Penguin.

Gilligan, C. (1982). *In a different voice.* Cambridge, MA: Harvard University Press.

Gilligan, C. (1998). *Minding women: Reshaping the educational realm.* Cambridge, MA: Harvard University Press.

Girard, K., & Koch, S. (1996). *Conflict resolution in schools: A manual for educators.* San Francisco, CA: Jossey-Bass.

Glover, J. A., Ronning, R. R., & Bruning, R. H. (1990). *Cognitive psychology for teachers.* New York: MacMillan.

Goldstein, A., & Carr, P. (1996). *Can students benefit from process writing?* Washington, DC: U.S. Department of Education Office of Educational Research and Improvement.

Good, T., & Brophy, J. (1995). *Contemporary educational psychology* (5th ed.). White Plains, NY: Longman.

Gorski, P. (2000). The challenge of defining a single "multicultural education." Retrieved from www.mhhe.com/socscience/education/multi/define.html

Gorski, P., & Covert, B. (2000). *Multicultural pavilion.* www.edchange.org/multicultural/

Graves, D. (1983). *Writing: Teachers & children at work.* Portsmouth, NH: Heinemann.

Graves, M. (1986). Costs and benefits of different methods of vocabulary instruction. *Journal of Reading, 29,* 596–602.

Gunderson, L. (1996). Reading and language development. In V. Froese (Ed.), *Whole-language: Practice and theory.* Boston: Allyn and Bacon.

Guthrie, J., Van Meter, P., McCann, A., Wigfield, A., Bennet, L., Poundstone, C., et al. (1996). Growth of literacy engagement: Changes in motivations and skills during concept-oriented reading instruction. *Reading Research Quarterly, 31,* 306–332.

Harman, W. (1998). *Global mind change* (2nd ed). San Francisco, CA: Berrett-Koehler.

Hirsch, E. D. (1988). *A first dictionary of cultural literacy: What our children need to know.* New York: Houghton Mifflin.

Hodson, D. (1988). Toward a philosophically more valid science curriculum. *Science Education, 72,* 19–40.

Hoffman, H. (1993). Character education without turmoil. *Educational Leadership, 5,* 24–26.

Holt, J. (1983). *How children learn* (2nd ed.). New York: Delta.

Howard, J. (2001). *Michigan journal of community service learning.* Ann Arbor, MI: OCSL Press.

Human Rights Watch. (2001). Hatred in the hallways: Violence and discrimination against lesbian, gay, bisexual, and transgender students in U.S. schools. *American Journal of Health Education, 32,* 302–306.

Islamic Education Strategic Unit. (2004). *Singapore Islamic education system: A conceptual framework.* Retrieved May, 2005, from www.muis.gov.sg/English/Islamic_Education/others/SIES4web.pdf

Jacobs, D., & Jacobs-Spencer, J. (2001). *Teaching virtues: Building character across the curriculum.* Lanham, MD: Scarecrow.

Jensen, E. (2000). Moving with the brain in mind. *Educational Leadership, 58:* 34–37.

Johnson, A. (1996). Inference: A thinking skill to enhance learning and literacy. *Wisconsin State Reading Association Journal, 40,* 19–24.

Johnson, A. (1998). How to use creative dramatics in the classroom. *Childhood Education, 75,* 2–6.

Johnson, A. (1999). Effective lesson planning for effective skills instruction. *Journal of Reading Education, 24,* 15–19.

Johnson, A. (2000a). Creative dramatics: A perfect learning tool for gifted students. *Gifted Child Today, 23,* 30–33.

Johnson, A. (2000b). *Up and out: Using creative and critical thinking skills to enhance learning.* Boston: Allyn and Bacon.

Johnson, A. (2003a). *A short guide to academic and professional writing.* Lanham, MD: University Press of America.

Johnson, A. (2003b). Negative human potential. *Encounter: Education for Meaning and Social Justice, 16,* 6–12.

Johnson, A. (in press). *The inner curriculum: Activities to develop emotional intelligence in general education classrooms.* Unionville, NY: Royal Fireworks Press.

Johnson, A., & Graves, M. (1997). Scaffolding: A tool for enhancing the reading experiences of all students. *Journal of the Texas State Reading Association, 3,* 31–37.

Johnson, A. P. (2001). *A short guide to action research.* Needham, MA: Allyn and Bacon.

Johnson, D., & Johnson, F. (1999). *Joining together: Group theory and group skills* (7th ed.). Boston: Allyn and Bacon.

Johnson, D. W., & Johnson, R. T. (1991). *Teaching students to be peacemakers.* Edina, MN: Interaction.

Johnson, D. W., & Johnson, R. T. (1995). *Learning together and alone: Cooperation, competition, and individualization* (4th ed.). Needham Heights, MA: Allyn & Bacon.

Johnson, D. W., & Johnson, R. T. (2002). *Multicultural education.* Boston: Allyn and Bacon.

Johnson, D. W., Johnson, R. T., & Holubec, E. J. (1991). *Cooperation in the classroom.* Edina, MN: Interaction.

Johnson, D. W., Johnson, R. T., & Skon, L. (1979). The effect of cooperative, competitive, and individualistic conditions on student achievement on different types of tasks. *Contemporary Educational Psychology, 4,* 99–106.

Johnson, D. W., Johnson, R. T., & Smith, K. A. (1991). *Active learning: Cooperation in the college classroom.* Edina, MN: Interaction.

Johnson, D. W., Johnson, R. T., & Stanne, M. B. (2000). Cooperative learning methods: A meta-analysis. Retrieved October, 2004, from http://www.clcrc.com/pages/cl-methods.html

Johnson, D. W., Maruyama, G., Johnson, R. T., Nelson, D., & Skon, L. (1981). Effects of cooperative, competitive, and individualistic goal structures on achievement: A meta-analysis. *Psychological Bulletin, 89,* 47–62.

Jung, C. G. (1933). *Modern man in search of a soul.* New York: Harcourt Brace Jovanovich.

Kane, J. (2000). On education with meaning. *Encounter, 13,* 3–13.

Kapoun, J. (1998). Teaching undergrads WEB evaluation: A guide for library instruction [Electronic version]. *C&RL News,* 59(7), 522–523.

Kauchak, D., & Eggen, P. (1998). *Learning and teaching: Research-based methods* (3rd ed.). Needham Heights, MA: Allyn and Bacon.

Kelner, L. B. (1993). *The creative classroom: A guide for using creative drama in the classroom Pre K–6.* Portsmouth, NH: Heinemann.

Kelsey, M. (1997). *The other side of silence: Meditation for the twenty-first century.* Mahwah, NJ: Paulist Press.

Kohlberg, L. (1984). *Essays on moral development, Volume 2: The psychology of moral development.* New York: Harper & Row.

Krishnamurti, J. (1953). *Education and the significance of life.* San Francisco, CA: HarperCollins.

Lamme, L., L. & Lamme, L. A. (2002). Welcoming children from gay families into our schools. *Educational Leadership, 59*(4), 65–69.

L'Engle, M. (1962). *A wrinkle in time.* New York: Bantam Doubleday Dell Books.

Long Island Secular Humanists. (1999). Ten commandments for humanists. Retrieved May, 2005, from www.religioustolerance.org/chr_10c2.htm

Lukinsky, J., & Schachter, L. (1998). Questions in human and classroom discourse. Coalition for the advancement of Jewish education. Available from http://www.caje.org

MacGillivray, I. K. (2000). Educational equity for gay, lesbian, bisexual, transgendered, and queer/questioning students: The demands of democracy and social justice for America's schools. *Education and Urban Society, 32,* 303–323.

March, T. (1997). Working the web for education: Theory and practice on integrating the web for learning. Retrieved April, 2005, from www.ozline.com/learning/theory.html

Marks, H. M., & Louis, K. S. (1997). Does teacher empowerment affect the classroom? The implication of teacher empowerment for instruction, practice and student performance. *Educational Evaluation and Policy Analysis, 19,* 245–275.

Martorella, P. H., & Beal, C. (2002). *Social studies for elementary school children: Preparing children to be global citizens* (2nd ed.). Upper Saddle River, NJ: Prentice Hall.

Marzano, R. (1991). Tactics for thinking: A program for initiating the teaching of thinking. In A. Costa (Ed.), *Developing minds: Vol. 2* (pp. 65–68). Alexandria, VA: ASCD.

Marzano, R. J., Pickering, D. J., & Pollock, J. E. (2001). *Classroom instruction that works: Research-based strategies for increasing student achievement.* Alexandria, VA: ASCD.

Maslow, A. H. (1968). *Toward a psychology of being* (3rd ed.). New York: John Wiley and Sons.

Maslow, A. H. (1971). *The farther reaches of human nature.* New York: Viking Press.

Mastropieri, M. A., & Scruggs, T. E. (2004). *The inclusive classroom: Strategies for effective instruction* (2nd ed.). Upper Saddle River, NJ: Pearson.

Maxim, G. (2003). *Dynamic social studies for elementary classrooms* (7th ed.). Upper Saddle River, NJ: Prentice Hall.

Miller, G. M., & Mason, G. E. (1983). Dramatic improvisation: Risk-free role playing for improving reading performance. *The Reading Teacher, 37,* 128–131.

Miller, J. P. (1996). *The Holistic Curriculum.* Toronto: OISE Press.

Miller, J. P. (2000). *Education and the soul: Toward a spiritual curriculum.* Albany, NY: SUNY Press.

Milne, A. (1976). *Winnie the Pooh.* New York: Dutton.

Mullis, I. V., & Jenkins, L. B. (1990). *The reading report card. 1971–1988: Trends from the nation's report card.* Princeton, NJ: National Assessment of Educational Progress, Educational Testing Service.

National Center for Education Statistics (NCES). (2004). The nation's report card, NAEP data. www .nces.ed.gov/nationsreportcard/naepdata/search.asp

National Council for the Social Studies (NCSS). (1994). *Curriculum standards for social studies.* Silver Spring, MD: Author.

Narve, R. G. (2001). *Holistic education: Pedagogy of universal love.* Brandon, VT: Foundation for Educational Renewal.

Nelson, M. R. (1998). *Children and social studies: Creative teaching in the elementary classroom* (3rd ed.). Fort Worth, TX: Harcourt Brace.

Nhat Hanh, T. (1998). *The heart of the Buddha's teaching.* Berkeley, CA: Parallax Press.

Nhat Hanh, T. (1999). *Going home: Jesus and Buddha as brothers.* New York: Riverhead Books.

Nichol, L. (2003). *The essential David Bohm.* New York: Routledge.

Noddings, N. (1997). Thinking about standards. *Phi Delta Kappan, 79,* 184–189.

Park, J., Turnbull, A. P., & Turnbull, H. R. (2002). Impacts of poverty on quality of life in families of children with disabilities. *Exceptional Children, 68* (2), 151–170.

Parker, W. (2001). *Social studies in elementary education* (11th ed.). Upper Saddle River, NJ: Prentice Hall.

Paterson, K. (1977). *Bridge to Terabithia.* New York: HarperCollins.

Peterson, M., & Hittie, M. (2003). *Inclusive teaching: Creating effective schools for all learners.* Boston: Allyn and Bacon.

Perkins. D. N. (1986). Thinking frames. *Educational Leadership, 42,* 4–10.

Perry, M. L (2003). *Taneesah's treasures of the heart.* Pittsburgh, PA: Dorrance.

Piaget, J. (1983). Piaget's theory. In P. Mussen (Ed.), *Handbook of child psychology* (4th ed., Vol. 1). New York: Wiley.

Popham, W. J. (2001). *The truth about testing: An educator's call to action.* Alexandria, VA: ASCD.

Prawat, R. (1991). The value of ideas: The immersion approach to the development of thinking. *Educational Research, 20,* 3–10.

Pressley, M., Harris, K. R., & Marks, M. B. (1992). But good strategy users are constructivists! *Educational Psychology Review, 4,* 3–31.

Rabren, K., & Darch, C. (1996). The strategic comprehension behaviors of students with learning disabilities and general education students: Teachers' and students' perspectives. *Journal of Research and Development in Education, 29,* 172–180.

Reigeluth, C. M. (1997). Educational standards: To standardize or to customize learning? *Phi Delta Kappan, 79,* 202–206.

Renzulli, J. S., & Reis, S. M. (1997). The schoolwide enrichment model: New directions for developing high-end learning. In N. Colangelo & G.A. Davis (Eds.), *Handbook of gifted education* (2nd ed.) (pp. 136–154). Needham Heights, MA: Allyn and Bacon.

Reutzel, D. R., & Cooter, R. B. (1996). *Teaching children to read.* Englewood Cliffs, NJ: Merrill/ Prentice Hall.

Roberts, P. L., & Kellough, R. D. (2000). *A guide for developing interdisciplinary thematic units* (2nd ed.). Upper Saddle River, NJ: Merrill/Prentice-Hall.

Rogers, C. R. (1961). *On becoming a person.* Boston: Houghton Mifflin.

Rosenblatt, L. M. (1983). *Literature as exploration* (4th ed.). New York: Modern Language Association.

Rowling, J. K. (1998). *Harry Potter and the Sorcerer's Stone.* New York: Scholastic Press.

Ryan, R. (1999). *The strong eye of shamans.* Rochester, VT: Inner Traditions International.

Salend, S. (2004). *Creating inclusive classrooms* (5th ed.). Upper Saddle River, NJ: Pearson.

Santrock, J. (2004). *Educational psychology* (2nd ed). New York: McGraw-Hill.

Savage, T. V., & Armstrong, D. L. (1996). *Effective teaching in elementary social studies* (3rd ed.). Englewood Cliffs, NJ: Prentice Hall.

Scheider, M. E., & Owens, R. E. (2000). Concern for lesbian, gay, and bisexual kids: The benefits for all children. *Education and Urban Society, 32,* 349–367.

Silverman, L. K. (1993). Social development, leadership, and gender issues. In L. K. Silverman (Ed.), *Counseling the gifted and talented* (pp. 291–328). Denver, CO: Love.

Skeel, D. J. (1995). *Elementary social studies: Challenges for tomorrow's world.* Fort Worth, TX: Harcourt Brace.

Slavin, R. (1995). *Cooperative learning* (2nd ed.). Needham Heights, MA: Allyn and Bacon.

Snauwaert, D. T. (2001). Cosmopolitan democracy and holistic education. *Encounter: Education for Meaning and Social Justice, 14*(4), 2–4.

Society of Professional Journalists. (2004). Code of ethics. Retrieved April, 2005, from http://www .spj.org/ethics_code.asp

South Carolina Service Learning. (1994). *Service learning: K–8 manual.* Columbia, SC: South Carolina Department of Education.

Spinelli, J. (1990). *Maniac Magee.* New York: Little Brown.

Springer, L., Stanne, M., & Donovan, S. (1998). Effects of small-group learning on undergraduates in science, mathematics, engineering, and technology: A meta-analysis. *Journal of Educational Research, 69*(1), pp. 21–51.

Stanovich, K. (2003). *How to think straight about psychology* (7th ed.). Boston: Allyn & Bacon.

Starko, A. (1995). *Creativity in the classroom.* White Plains, NY: Longman.

Sternberg, R. (1990). *Metaphors of mind: Conceptions of the nature of intelligence.* New York: Press Syndicate of the University of Cambridge.

Sternberg, R. (1996). *Successful intelligence: How practical and creative intelligence determine success in life.* New York: Plume.

Sternberg, R. J. (2001). Why schools should teach for wisdom: The balance theory of wisdom in educational settings. *Educational Psychologist, 36,* 227–245.

Sternberg, R. J., & Williams, W. M. (2002). *Educational psychology.* Boston: Allyn and Bacon.

Strain, J. (1999). So what's world citizenship? [Electronic version]. *The Language Teacher, 23.* Retrieved from http://libwww.gijodai.ac.jp/newhomepage/kiy02000/10frank.pdf

Stringfield, S., & Teddlie, C. (1991). Schools as affecters of teacher effects. In H. Waxman & H. Walberg (Eds.), *Effective teaching: Current research* (pp. 161–179). Berkeley, CA: McCutchan.

Sweetland, S. R., & Hoy, W. K. (2002). School characteristics and educational outcomes: Toward an organizational model of student achievement in middle schools. *Educational Administration Quarterly, 36,* 703–729.

Talbot, M. (1991). *The holographic universe.* New York: HarperCollins.

Tolkien, J. R. R. (1954). *The fellowship of the ring.* Boston: Houghton Mifflin.

Tomlinson, C. (1995). *How to differentiate instruction in mixed-ability classrooms.* Alexandria, VA: ASCD.

Tomlinson, C. (1999). *The differentiated classroom: Responding to the needs of all learners.* Alexandria, VA: ASCD.

Tomlinson, C. A. (2001). *How to differentiate instruction in a mixed-ability classroom* (2nd ed.). Alexandria, VA: ASCD.

U.S. Census Bureau (2005). *United States Census 2000.* Available from www.census.gov

U.S. Department of Education. (1993). *National excellence: A case for developing America's talent.* Retrieved March, 2005, from www.ed.gov/pubs/DevTalent/toc.html

Vanzandt, C. E., & Hayslip, J. B. (1994). *Comprehensive school guidance and counseling program.* White Plains, NY: Longman.

Vaughn, S., Bos, C. S., & Schumm, J. S. (2003). *Teaching exceptional, diverse, and at-risk students in the general education classroom* (3rd ed.). Boston: Allyn and Bacon.

Verriour, P. (1990). Storying and storytelling in drama. *Language Arts, 67,* 144–149.

Wagner, B. J. (1988). Research currents: Does classroom drama affect the arts of language? *Language Arts, 65,* 46–55.

Walberg, J. J. (1991). Productive teaching and instruction: Assessing the knowledge base. In H. Waxman & H. Walberg (Eds.), *Effective teaching: Current research* (pp. 33–62). Berkeley, CA.

Walters, J. M., & Gardner, H. (1985). The development and education of intelligences. In F. Link (Ed.), *Essays on the intellect.* Alexandria, VA: ASCD.

Watts, S. (1995). Vocabulary instruction during reading lessons in six classrooms. *Journal of Reading Behavior, 27,* 399–424.

Watts, S., & Johnson, A. (1995). Toward reflection in teacher education: The role of dialogue journals. *Journal of Reading Education, 21,* 27–38.

Willis, S. (1993). Schools test new ways to resolve conflict. *Update: ASCD, 35*(10), 1–8.

Wittman, J., & Thompson, D. W. (2000). *Large group guidance activities: A k–12 sourcebook.* Minneapolis, MN: Educational Media Corporation.

Wood, J. (2000). *Adapting instruction to accommodate students in inclusive settings* (4th ed.). Upper Saddle River, NJ: Pearson.

Woody, D. (2001). A comprehensive school-based conflict-resolution model. *Children and Schools, 23,* 115–123.

Wolf, S. A. (1993). What's in a name? Labels and literacy in Readers Theatre. *The Reading Teacher, 46,* 540–545.

Woolfolk, A. (2005). *Educational psychology* (9th ed.). Boston: Allyn and Bacon.

Wraga, W. (1998). Implications of issues-centered education for the social studies curriculum. *International Journal of Social Education, 13,* 49–65.

Wraga, W. (1999). Organizing and developing issues-centered social studies curricula: Profiting from our predecessors. *The Social Studies, 90,* 209–217.

Yaffee, S. H. (1989). Drama as a teaching tool. *Educational Leadership, 46,* 29–32.

Yahoo! Inc. (2001). *Yahooligan's Teacher's Guide.* Available from http://yahooligans.yahoo.com/tg/

Yolen, J., & Harris, R. J. (2003). *Girl in a cage.* New York: Puffin Books.

Zarillo, J. (1991). Theory becomes practice: Aesthetic teaching with literature. *The New Advocate, 4,* 221–234.

Zemelman, S., Daniels, H., & Hyde, A. (1998). *Best practice: New standards for teaching and learning in America's schools* (2nd ed.). Portsmouth, NH: Heinemann.

INDEX

433

ABOUT THE AUTHOR

 **Dr. Andrew Johnson** is Professor of Holistic Education in the Department of Educational Studies, Special Populations, at Minnesota State University, Mankato, in Mankato, Minnesota. He specializes in holistic education, literacy instruction, strategies for the inclusive classroom, and gifted education. He earned his Ph.D. from the University of Minnesota. Before that he worked for nine years in the public schools as a 2nd grade teacher and as a gifted education coordinator before moving into higher education. His current areas of interest include spiritual intelligence, action research, thinking skills, and academic and creative writing. For comment or communication, visit his website at: www.teachergrowth.com